Fighting Years

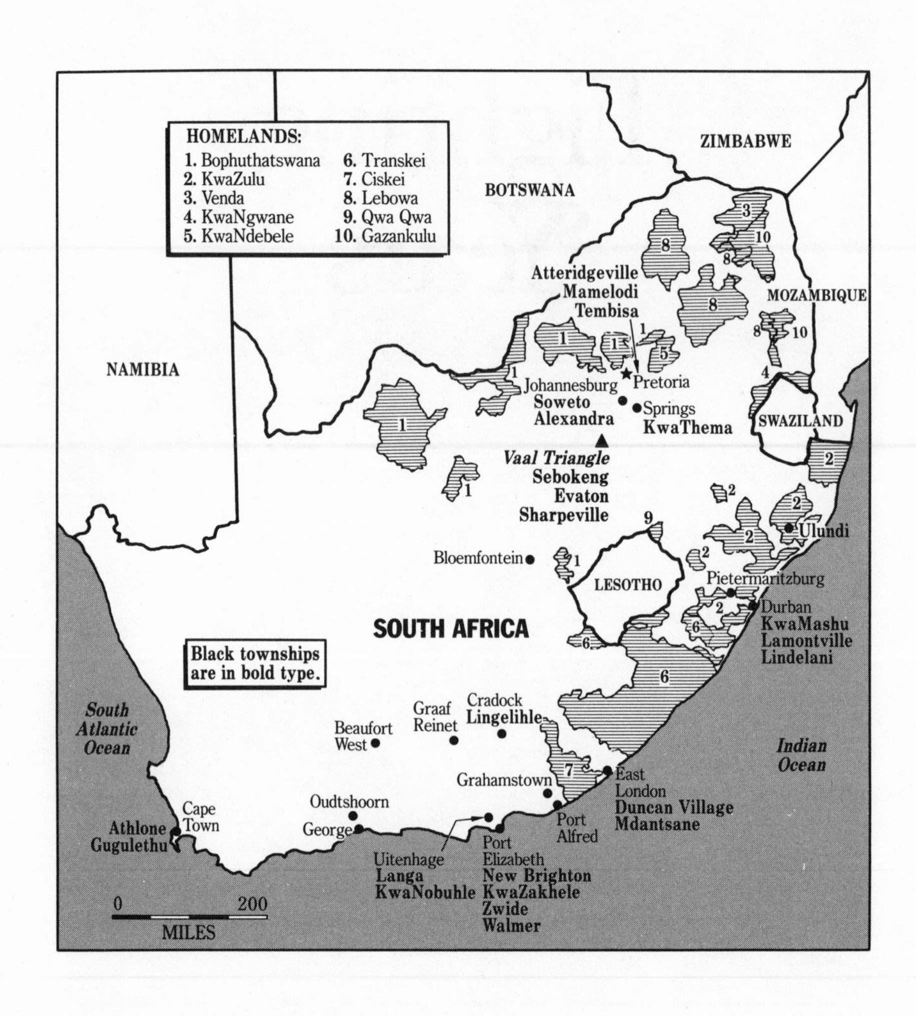
HOMELANDS:
1. Bophuthatswana
2. KwaZulu
3. Venda
4. KwaNgwane
5. KwaNdebele
6. Transkei
7. Ciskei
8. Lebowa
9. Qwa Qwa
10. Gazankulu
ZIMBABWE
BOTSWANA
MOZAMBIQUE
NAMIBIA
SWAZILAND
LESOTHO
SOUTH AFRICA
Black townships are in bold type.
South Atlantic Ocean
Indian Ocean
Atteridgeville
Mamelodi
Tembisa
Johannesburg
Soweto
Alexandra
Pretoria
Springs
KwaThema
Vaal Triangle
Sebokeng
Evaton
Sharpeville
Bloemfontein
Ulundi
Pietermaritzburg
Durban
KwaMashu
Lamontville
Lindelani
Beaufort West
Graaf Reinet
Cradock
Lingelihle
Grahamstown
East London
Duncan Village
Mdantsane
Port Alfred
Oudtshoorn
George
Cape Town
Athlone
Guguletu
Uitenhage
Langa
KwaNobuhle
Port Elizabeth
New Brighton
KwaZakhele
Zwide
Walmer
0
200
MILES

Fighting Years

Black Resistance and the Struggle for a New South Africa

Steven Mufson

BEACON PRESS • BOSTON

For my parents

Beacon Press
25 Beacon Street
Boston, Massachusetts 02108-2800

Beacon Press books
are published under the auspices of
the Unitarian Universalist Association of Congregations.

Printed in the United States of America

97 96 95 94 93 92 91 90   8 7 6 5 4 3 2 1

Text design by Mike Fender
Map by Brad Wye

Library of Congress Cataloging-in-Publication Data

Mufson, Steven.
Fighting years : Black resistance and the struggle for a new South Africa / Steven Mufson.
p. cm.
Includes bibliographical references and index.
ISBN 0-8070-0212-7 : $24.95
1. South Africa—Politics and government—1978– 2. Blacks—South Africa—Politics and government. 3. Government, Resistance to—South Africa—History—20th century. I. Title.
DT1967.M84 1990
968′.00496—dc20   90-52595
CIP

Contents

List of Illustrations

Preface

LIKE THE STAMP ACT CRISIS in America, the 1905 Revolution in Russia, and the 1980 Solidarity strikes in Poland, the black uprising from 1984 to 1986 in South Africa failed to topple a government but set a country on a course that made more radical change inevitable.

In 1989, the inauguration of a more conciliatory president, the pressing need to halt the decay of the economy, and the release of senior black political prisoners raised hopes that the beginning of the end of apartheid was near. Like spirits of a bygone era, Nelson Mandela, Walter Sisulu, and other leaders of the African National Congress in the late 1940s and 1950s emerged from a quarter century in prison, defying advanced age and legal restrictions to breathe new excitement into the movement to end apartheid.

Any talk of democracy or "talks about talks" to end apartheid were byproducts of the 1984–86 black uprising and the decade of struggle that preceded it. Although the ruling National Party survived those fighting years with its hands on the key levers of the state—the military, the Parliament and the civil service—its influence over other aspects of society was waning. Among whites, the party clung to a reduced electoral majority while the economy lagged. Among blacks, millions of people disregarded pass and residency restrictions while they built self-governing structures and informal associations that paralleled official government.

Blacks kept up no pretense of loyalty to the government. When the former ANC leader Walter Sisulu and his comrades were freed from jail in October 1989, blacks (and a few thousand whites) held a rally in a soccer stadium and openly few the flags of the outlawed organization. The size of the crowd rivaled that of the 1938 white gathering that galvanized Afrikaners and led to the first National Party government.

As a journalist I witnessed much of the 1984–1986 black uprising. As a staff reporter for *The Wall Street Journal*, I worked in South Africa in November 1984, April 1985, and from the first state of emergency in mid-1985 until the second state of emergency in mid-1986. I remained there for nearly another year as the correspondent for *Business Week* and a contributor to *The New Republic* and other publications. In May 1987, the government refused to renew my work permit and expelled me from the country.

This story, however, is not mine. I have tried to take the reader into the streets and homes of the black townships and to recount life-and-death confrontations in enough detail to reveal the strange mixture of planning and chance that makes history. The voices of this story are the voices of black South Africans themselves—mineworkers and students, parents and playwrights, shopkeepers and shop stewards, "comrades" and clergy—not just international celebrities like Archbishop Desmond Tutu and Winnie Mandela, but also the legions of people who worked in relative anonymity to turn a country upside down.

Acknowledgments

I CANNOT THANK all the people who shared their sofas, food, confidence, and friendship—from "shebeens" in Mdantsane to private white homes in Zeerust, from Salt River to Johannesburg's northern suburbs. Because many people are in delicate political positions, it is safer to omit their names and thank them personally.

I can name the institutions that helped me in the United States, especially the Council on Foreign Relations, the Ford Foundation, and the Alicia Patterson Foundation for journalists.

At the Council on Foreign Relations (where I wrote most of this manuscript), Michael Clough, senior fellow for Africa, shared many ideas, ran a South Africa study group, and first encouraged me to write this book. The director of studies, Nick Rizopoulos, encouraged me to finish it; William Gleysteen, his predecessor and now president of the Japan Society, agreed to give me the Maurice Templesman Fellowship, made possible by the generosity of the Ford Foundation and Maurice Templesman.

Financial support was the least of the Ford Foundation's contribution to this book. Bill Carmichael, former vice president of the foundation, was a source of encouragement, as he has been to many other people pursuing independent projects. John de St. Jorre gave me a rare and precious gift—his blunt view of early drafts.

The Alicia Patterson Foundation, administered by Margaret Engel, gave me a fellowship that enabled me to conduct research in the United States and to visit South Africa, England, and Lesotho in January 1988.

The Urban Foundation helped to fund research for the chapter on local negotiations.

Many individuals outside those institutions donated countless hours and valuable encouragement. My most devoted editors were friends who read several drafts of the entire manuscript: Laura Heberton, Linda Robinson, and Stephen Davis. Vincent Maphai, Aracelly Santana, and Jennifer Whittaker also read entire versions. James T. Campbell, Miriam Horn, Kathy Boraine, and David Lewis read portions.

The Council on Foreign Relations assembled a review group, whose members read and critiqued an early draft. The group included: Tom Karis, Karl Beck, Tom Lodge, Mark Quarterman, Gail Gerhart, Nomsa Daniels, Bill Carmichael, John de St. Jorre, and Mike Clough.

In addition to my own notes and experiences in South Africa, I have been able to draw on three unique archives. Tom Karis and Gail Gerhart shared the rich store of documentary material they are collecting for the forthcoming volumes of their authoritative South African history, *From Protest to Challenge*. Karl Beck shared his equally rich mental archive of anecdotes and his unique sense of the spirit of South Africa. The widow of Matthew Goniwe gave me permission to see her late husband's papers, which are stored at the Yale University library.

I also owe thanks to *The Wall Street Journal*, which first sent me to South Africa, to its managing editor, Norm Pearlstine, and especially to Lee Lescaze, now foreign editor.

For journalists in South Africa, nothing is as valuable or as fragile as their visas. In 1986, when I extended my stay in South Africa, Liz Weiner, Bob Dowling, and Keith Felcyn at *Business Week* cosponsored my visa along with *Elseviers*, a Dutch newsweekly. The dean of South African journalists, Allister Sparks, also lent his advice, encouragement, and friendship.

I'd like to thank Michael Kinsley, Jefferson Morley, and the editors of *The New Republic*.

Also thanks to Beacon Press and my editor Deb Chasman.

Finally, many friends and family members have contributed indirectly through their support and companionship. In South Africa: Helet and Chris Merkling, Mark Swilling, Mpho Mashinini, Siraj and Faeza Desai, Steve Shore, Jim Campbell, Andrea van Niekerk, Marcel Golding, Sue Albertyn, Cassim Saloojee, Max du Preez, Seth Mazibuko, Henry Fihla, the Maphai family, and the Fleischer family. In the United States my family and especially Heb, who never lost faith.

Introduction

THE FIRST FULL DAY I spent in South Africa, the blacks stayed home. They stayed home by the tens and hundreds of thousands. The bus stops were deserted, the trains empty. Factories in the country's industrial heartland came to a standstill and the streets of Johannesburg were eerily quiet, as though the city's inhabitants had fled an advancing army.

It was November 5, 1984, and I was on assignment for *The Wall Street Journal* to do an article about nuclear arms proliferation. That day, however, I filed a story about the work "stayaway" that I learned was the biggest general strike by blacks in a quarter century.

"Are they going to bring down the government?" a hard-boiled editor on the foreign desk growled over the phone.

"Well, no," I replied. "Some day, but not right away."

"So why do we want to run a story now?" he asked. I made a plea for my story, arguing that the strike was noteworthy in blacks' fight against the South African government policy of apartheid. The paper ran an abbreviated account the next day.

What I only dimly perceived during my first week in the country—and could not explain clearly then—was that the "liberation" of South Africa from white rule will not be an event. It will not come in a pitched battle or a decisive strike. It is possible that blacks will never storm the Parliament in Cape Town or the imposing Union Buildings that house government ministries in Pretoria.

What blacks call liberation is a process that has already begun in South Africa. It will not end when power is transferred from a white minority to a government that includes all South Africans, black and white. But just because liberation is a process does not mean it is any less revolutionary. Liberation means changing the way people work, govern, live, and think.

The black uprising that rocked the country from just before my first visit in 1984 until late 1986 was a vital part of that process, for two reasons. First, the uprising marked the end of blacks' submissiveness to white rule. Second, by rebelling against apartheid, South Africa's blacks were not only trying to destroy a repressive system, but attempting to create a new nation.

The gravity of this uprising was clear from the measures the government used to put it down. Tens of thousands of troops were called up. Twice the government declared a state of emergency. By the time the government suppressed the most public displays of protest, more than 2,500 people had been killed in political violence. More than 50,000 people passed through detention. The tenor and substance of South African politics—both black and white—had changed forever.

Evidence of a rebellious spirit was everywhere during these fighting years. This new attitude was the culmination of a revolution in the minds of ordinary black men and women, who once felt that struggling against white rule was futile. Since a student rebellion in 1976, blacks had been gaining confidence in their ability to effect change. "Listen to the way the postal worker sings, an ordinary worker who previously had no political feeling," Gabu Tugwana, a black journalist, said. "Now he realizes that the power is in his hands to change the workplace, and if so then the power is also in his hands to change his home, and if so then the power is in his hands to change his country."

Another black journalist, Aggrey Klaaste, deputy editor of *The Sowetan*, described the militant spirit of 1984–1986 this way: "When I was a youth, some twenty-five years ago, I had a younger brother who cried in fright when he saw a white face. Today I have sons, who when they see a white face go into a military pantomime, turn their little fists into pistols, cover their faces with a cloth. It is the age of the gun and tearsmoke."[1]

The uprising swept millions of blacks into political activity, participation on a scale never witnessed in South Africa. It drew on unskilled laborers and on the new class of professionals and entrepreneurs. It involved teachers and students. It infected townships such as the sprawling Soweto, with two million residents, and tiny "dorps" with a few thousand blacks. At its height, South Africa's black rebellion involved nearly every black South African in some form of protest: rent boycotts, consumer boycotts, school boycotts, general strikes, union activity, or street committees.

These campaigns were waged with an eye toward the new society that South Africans want to create. Again and again church, community, and labor leaders linked the birth of a new South Africa to the methods of struggle. A union leader urged miners to lay the seeds of a new society in the womb of the old. Anglican Archbishop and Nobel-Peace-Prize winner

Desmond Tutu urged mobs bent on execution to spare the lives of suspected police informers so that people could hold their heads high after liberation.

"In political struggle, the means must always be the same as the ends," wrote Patrick Lekota, a black leader who spent more than ten years in prison on various charges including treason. "How else can one expect a racialistic movement to imbue our society with a nonracial character on the dawn of our freedom day? A political movement cannot bequeath to society a characteristic it does not itself possess."[2]

A popular black school principal and political leader, Matthew Goniwe, wrote before his assassination that "if we are instruments of change, we must epitomise the society we want to bring about. People see in us the society we want to bring about. We want young men and women who are embodiments of the new South Africa."[3]

The vision of a new South Africa that emerged from the fighting years is fundamentally different from that of the old. With its vision of apartheid, the government stresses divisions among people. Apartheid suggests that there is no such thing as one South Africa, rather that there are several South African nations with the potential for tearing each other to shreds if they are not separated. The new vision attempts to redefine the South African nation as one that possesses an interdependent economy, a heterogeneous culture, a respect for human decency, and a common body politic.

To many observers, the uprising was a blur of petrol bombs and police batons. The political funeral of a black became the symbol of South Africa's fighting years. But this symbol was inappropriate, for during these years, a new South Africa was struggling to be born.

It is not a coincidence that publications launched during this period were given names like *New Era, Speak*, and *New Nation*. Nor did it seem presumptuous in January 1986, when the *New Nation's* maiden editorial, entitled "Time for a Change," said:

> In all periods of history, there comes a time when the autocratic has to give way to the democratic, when the unpopular has to give way to the popular, and when the old has to give way to the new.
>
> That moment has come for South Africa—and it cannot be stayed.
>
> Throughout the length and breadth of our land, the democratic voice of the majority has begun to assert itself, be it on the factory floor, in rural and urban communities, in the fields of learning and culture—in all aspects of our lives.
>
> This newspaper is born out of hope, and out of a firm belief and commitment to democratic ideals and values. . . .
>
> We stand for a society free of the prejudices of ethnicity, tribalism and sexism. Indeed, a society free of all the burden that have hitherto hindered our country and prevented it from making great strides towards the creation of a single, just and open society.

> We do not claim the birth of a new nation will be easy. What we do say is that its birth is inevitable. It is a tortuous path we have to travel—but we think it is well worth it. Come with us.[4]

The path would not be short. After reimposing a state of emergency in June 1986, the South African government hampered black resistance with the "iron fist and velvet glove." It detained thousands of activists while it addressed some of the social and economic grievances raised by black opposition groups. This dual campaign only confused the political issues of apartheid and black resistance in the 1980s and into the 1990s.

Apartheid in this state defied easy description, for the government learned it could shed the trappings of apartheid without giving up the essence of white power and privilege. Blacks already could eat at restaurants, see films at cinemas, and ride cars on trains that were recently reserved for whites. On a Saturday, "white" Johannesburg was a black city, full of black shoppers. Within certain boundaries, blacks long deprived of the right to own property could own houses. Jobs once reserved for whites opened up to all. Some blacks became millionaires.

The political battle lines blurred, too. White businessmen hailed a black man wearing the colors of the outlawed liberation movement as their ally. Blacks held a hero's funeral for a middle-aged white housewife who was their ally. A man of racially mixed background who spoke of black empowerment sat in the lily-white South African cabinet.

To an American, Pretoria's reform program could be confusing. In the United States the breakdown of segregation laws barring blacks from the front of buses, lunch counters, and state universities was followed by the Voting Rights Act, which guaranteed political franchise for all Americans. In South Africa, the end of petty apartheid may not lead to freedom for black South Africans. Economic liberalization need not mean democratization. The power of the state to stifle dissent grew ever wider, and Pretoria still didn't accept blacks as fellow citizens, much less as equals in governing the country.

It has been said that journalism is a first draft of history. If so, then this is a second draft. With the benefit of hindsight, I understand things I did not appreciate when I was in South Africa, and much that seemed incidental then appears significant now.

I have relied primarily on my own notes and experiences during the uprising, but also on documents and archives that were not available to me in South Africa. Where I have not provided footnotes, my sources are interviews and direct observation.

This book is not intended to be a comprehensive account of the events of South Africa's fighting years, but a selective look at events, personalities, and townships that will convey the spirit of black politics and society. I have sought to portray some of the leaders of the black uprising, to draw features on an otherwise faceless crowd. Most of these men and women are not familiar to foreigners; these people have not had the opportunity, money, or documents to travel abroad.

I have concentrated solely on black politics, because I believe that an attempt to deal as well with white politics would emphasize the contrasts between the two without doing justice to the complexity of either. Another reason is that I do not believe South Africa's liberation can be a gift of history, God, a revolutionary vanguard, or foreigners wielding economic sanctions. Black South Africans are the driving force for change within their own country.

This power tends to be overlooked by people on both sides of the debate over U. S. policy toward South Africa. In the 1980s, both the Reagan Administration's policy of "constructive engagement" and the anti-apartheid movement's advocacy of sanctions focused on white South Africans—one through friendly persuasion and the other through economic arm-twisting. I believe that the debate about apartheid—whether in Washington or in Pretoria—is controlled by the pace of events among black South Africans.

The book contains three parts. The first covers the end of black submissiveness and the rebirth of black political organization from 1976 through 1984. The second recounts and analyzes the 1984–1986 uprising. The third describes how black politics withstood the counteroffensive that the government launched in June 1986.

I have provided some information about the government, because it is not a passive observer of black politics. The government constantly confronts its foes with strategic problems. Its actions loom especially large in the final section of the book.

In the final chapters, the far-reaching consequences of South Africa's fighting years become manifest. South Africa under apartheid will never return to the time when blacks moved off the sidewalks and doffed their hats to white passersby. "Sure as the sun shall rise, another wave of black unrest will occur," a South African exile said. Only a negotiated political settlement could prevent it because South Africans know what the struggle is about to a greater degree than ever before. It isn't just about petty apartheid laws governing beaches and bathrooms, pass books and park benches—it's about human dignity, mutual respect and power.

Fast-Forward: *Banquets and Bullets*

ON SEPTEMBER 3, 1984, South African Prime Minister and Acting President Pieter W. Botha was the host of a lavish banquet at Cape Town's city hall. Sporting a tuxedo with a white bow tie, a gold medal around his neck, and ribbons on his chest pocket, Botha had cause to celebrate.

It had been a year of diplomatic triumphs. In February and March, Botha had secured non-aggression pacts with two of South Africa's Marxist neighbors, Angola and Mozambique. Earlier, both had given sanctuary to guerrillas fighting against South Africa, and South Africa had retaliated by fomenting dissident groups in each country and destroying vital power lines, bridges, and railways. In the first accord, Angola agreed to joint military patrols with South Africa to weed out anti-Pretoria guerrillas in southern Angola. In the second accord, signed before a thousand journalists and diplomats under an open-air pavilion on the banks of the Nkomati river, the Mozambican president swallowed his principles and agreed to expel the black South African exiles who were using Mozambique as a guerrilla base. As a result of the treaties, all was quiet on South Africa's western, northern, and eastern fronts.

The United States, Great Britain, and West Germany sent Botha telexes of congratulations. The accords gave Botha more international acceptance than any other South African leader had enjoyed since World War II. In May he embarked on an eight-nation tour of Western Europe, where he met with leading officials. He spent five hours with British Prime Minister

Margaret Thatcher at her country home, Chequers. In Italy, he had a two-hour meeting with the Italian prime minister and a half-hour audience with the Pope.

These diplomatic coups had eased foreign pressure against South Africa. Thatcher had made it clear that she opposed economic sanctions on moral grounds. In the United States, President Ronald Reagan, who opposed economic sanctions against South Africa, was coasting to reelection.

On his return to South Africa in June, Botha had completed the last details of a new constitution that created segregated houses of Parliament for "coloreds" (people of racially mixed background) and South Africans of Indian origin. In August, government opponents boycotted elections for the tricameral Parliament, but they could not prevent the selection of a full slate of representatives.

The new constitution took effect that very day, September third. The president under the old constitution, Marais Viljoen, retired. The banquet that night was held to bid him farewell. But the banquet also marked another notch in Botha's forty-six year political career. That night, Botha already knew that two days later he would be the sole nominee for the presidency, which the new constitution had transformed from a ceremonial post to the most powerful office in the country.

While the wine flowed at the banquet, a thousand miles away from Cape Town in the dusty black townships known as the Vaal Triangle, the first day of the new constitution was marked with a different kind of fanfare.

Three black townships—Sebokeng, Evaton, and Small Farms—form the heart of the Vaal Triangle, about an hour's drive along a flat road that runs from southwest Johannesburg across the high African plain, past fields of wheat, corn, and sunflowers.

Normally the township streets are quiet on work days. But on September 3, 1984, the streets were crowded, not in celebration but in protest. Angered by sharp rent increases and shut out of the new tricameral Parliament, residents of the Vaal Triangle held a general strike.

Instead of pomp and circumstance, September third in the Vaal Triangle was marked by murder and mayhem. Crowds roamed the streets and stoned symbols of power and privilege. Police moved in and fired tear gas and rubber bullets to disperse the crowds. New skirmishes broke out. Twenty-year-old Johannes Rantete, the son of a factory worker and a typical young black in Sebokeng, watched in wonder. Curious, he picked up a rubber bullet from the ground and held it to his nose. Suddenly he felt dizzy. His eyes teared and his skin burned, and he ran to a faucet. At the time, he thought the rubber pellet, not the white smoke, had caused his discomfort.[1] Such naïveté wouldn't last long.

Fire swept through businesses and fighting raged for three days. In one neighborhood of Sebokeng, Zone 11, people burned down the rent office, the post office, a liquor store, and a beer hall. They blocked off roads with stones, boxes, and anything else that could be carried. Three houses and several cars were burned. The gasoline station and the soft drink cash-and-carry store were attacked.

In other neighborhoods, the story was the same. Zone 14, the central business district, lay in ruins. Fire swept through a supermarket, three banks, a dry cleaner, a Kentucky Fried Chicken, a TV rental store, and a liquor store. Photographs in the papers the next day showed a man reaching in a window to loot a store while smoke billowed up from the other side of the building.

Before police could restore an uneasy calm, the Vaal uprising had claimed the lives of thirty-one people, including a thirteen-year-old schoolboy. More than fifty others were injured.

Among the dead were several black community councillors. A Sebokeng councillor was killed after shooting two youths in panic. On his corpse someone tossed a placard reading "Away with rentals! *Asinamali.*" Asinamali means "we have no money." Evaton's mayor fled after his house was burned down. An elderly woman donned his mayoral gown, danced down the streets, and pronounced herself the first legitimate mayor.

Johannes Rantete, the youth who learned the difference between rubber bullets and tear gas, later wrote about what he saw. Like others in the Vaal Triangle, he had little sympathy for the murdered community councillors who had helped bring on the protests by turning deaf ears to community complaints.

"No one should feel easy on the throne he has been nominated to occupy if he has not been freely elected by the public," Rantete wrote.

> This I say because if you keep on ruling defiant hearts, the time they revolt against you not one piece of your belongings together with your life will remain yours. If people are dissatisfied with you, it is better for you to resign before the terrible dark clouds overwhelm you in your wilderness; if you defy their needs, then you ask for a brutal retribution. . . . [T]he well-being of the community should not be ignored, or the response will be more horrible than the conflagration that destroyed Sodom and Gomorrah.[2]

Rantete's ominous words were meant for black community councillors representing the government. But it was a warning that P. W. Botha might have heeded. The Vaal uprising was the first wave of a rising tide of unrest that struck not only the industrial Transvaal, but also the isolated townships of the arid Karroo, the black townships of Port Elizabeth, the humid shantytowns of Durban, and the colored townships outside Cape Town. Every corner of black South Africa rose in protests ranging from boycotts to stone-throwing to shootouts. South Africa's most serious and prolonged black revolt had begun.

Lulled by the outward calm of the late 1970s and early 1980s, many whites were jolted by the Vaal uprising. But before the first shot was fired or stone cast, a revolution had begun in the minds of black men and women. The uprising was preceded by years of ferment in black politics and black thinking, dating to the Soweto student rebellion of 1976.

PART 1

Running Red Lights

At some point, a group of black youths started running through red traffic lights in Soweto. The signals, they said, had no legitimacy because no one had consulted the youngsters about the placement of the lights.

CHAPTER ONE

The Day That Never Ended

ON THE MORNING OF JUNE 16, 1976, Brigadier Ebenaezer van Niekerk reported to the Jabulani police station house in the western half of Soweto. To van Niekerk the sprawling black township seemed as quiet as usual, as orderly as its matchbox houses standing row on row. The coal dust from winter household fires had lifted and hundreds of thousands of black commuters had bundled into their trains and disappeared around the pale gold mine dumps to take up their places in the machinery of the "white" city of Johannesburg.

Brigadier van Niekerk sat down to a little paperwork. Work for a white Afrikaans-speaking policeman like van Niekerk was routine in those days. For seven years, he had driven alone without fear as he patrolled the township. Only once in his police career had the forty-year-old brigadier needed to shoot his gun. Indeed, he and a contingent of forty men were enough to keep the peace in half of Soweto, the largest black township in the country.

Within hours, all that would change. By noon, a black youth would lie dead and riots would begin sweeping across the township. By mid-afternoon, white troops would occupy Soweto to quell the unrest, but fighting would rage for three days. Fire and bloodshed would usher in a new era in South African politics.[1]

Beneath the surface in Soweto, resentment was simmering among black students. They were angered by a government rule that forced the use of the Afrikaans language in half the courses in the black school system, starting in 1975. "There was a need for blacks to learn Afrikaans for the labor market," says Andries Treurnicht, who was then the government minister responsible for black education. Though Afrikaners bristled at the memory of the early-twentieth-century British policy of forcing Afrikaners to study in English, Treurnicht saw no parallels with his own stance toward blacks. "This was not a policy of thrusting Afrikaans down the throats of people who didn't want it. It was a practical matter."

Black students didn't see it that way. Afrikaans is a language similar to Dutch that is used by Afrikaners, whites who make up just 8 percent of the country's population. To blacks, it was the language of police and employers, an instrument for giving orders. They believed that the imposition of Afrikaans was designed to train them for servitude.

Afrikaans was also, as one student put it, "a terrible academic pain." Already fluent in an African language (used through junior high school) as well as English (used in high school), most blacks were stumped by a third, unrelated language. "The kids were failing exams in thousands," recalls a black journalist. "So they saw Afrikaans as a means of suppression, you see, suppressing them from advancing educationally."[2] Lawrence Ntloaka, then a student, recalls that "For years, math, science and other subjects were taught in English. Then all of a sudden, they said this year they were turning around. It was horrible. When it came to technical terms, Afrikaans was ridiculous." The phrase for "specific gravity" became *soortlike gewig*, pronounced with a gutteral "g" not used in English. The word for "center of gravity" was completely different: *swaartepunt*.

The imposition of Afrikaans came at an explosive time, because the *swaartepunt* in black student politics had shifted dramatically in the mid-1970s. The emerging Black Consciousness philosophy was transforming the way young blacks thought, and infusing them with greater self-esteem. The introduction of Afrikaans frustrated those goals. The difficulty of coping with a foreign language in school causes "an inferiority complex," explained Stephen Biko, the most important black leader of the 1970s. The language problem "inculcates in many black students a sense of inadequacy. You tend to think that it is not just a matter of language. You tend to tie it up with intelligence."

At the end of May, student leaders in Soweto started traveling furtively from school to school to rally fellow pupils to protest against Afrikaans. The plotters were high-school students; most were teenagers, and none was over the age of twenty-five. They relied on a tight student network that included people like Seth Mazibuko, a tiny eighteen-year-old with thick-rimmed glasses, whose parents didn't know that he was vice president of an organization called the Soweto Students Representative Council. The Soweto leaders included most prefects, or head students, in the fifty-four high schools and junior secondary schools in the township. Others belonged to debating teams, church groups, or cultural societies.[3]

Teachers got wind of the student meetings. Some complained to Lekgan Mathabathe, the principal of the Morris Isaacson school, where key leaders were students. Mathabathe said he would discipline his students, but instead warned them to be more careful. "I knew what they were doing and I thought it was right," Mathabathe recalls.

Brigadier van Niekerk should have had an inkling that something was afoot when on June 9 he came across a group of black students at a junior high school. They had pelted his car with stones, smashing his windshield and hitting the brigadier once on the shoulder. He had thrown the car in reverse and avoided further confrontation. Even that, however, hadn't shaken the brigadier's feeling of security among blacks. He viewed the incident as an aberration. "I had no reason to fear these people," he recalls. "I had worked with them for thirty years."

On June 13, a black journalist named Harry Mashabela heard that black students were planning a march for June 16. Mashabela filed a story in advance of the march, but no newspaper editor dreamed that the plans of a bunch of black elementary and high-school students would amount to much. Mashabela's newspaper cut his article down to three paragraphs and buried it beneath other news of the day.

On the morning of June 16, 1976, Seth Mazibuko kissed his stepmother on the cheek and trotted off to school. Perhaps she thought the spring in his step was because it was Wednesday, sports day at Orlando West High School; she knew nothing of Seth's role in planning the events that were about to unfold.

That morning, Mashabela drove around to the handful of high schools in the township. At Thomas Mofolo Junior Secondary School and at Naledi High School in the Naledi section of Soweto, he found small crowds of children who started taking posters from underneath their clothing. At Morris Isaacson, students said their daily prayers as usual. A freckle-faced student, Tsietsi Mashinini, led two hymns, *Masibulele ku Jesu* (Let's pray Jesus; for He died for us") and *Nkosi Sikelel' i-Afrika*, the African national anthem. The students gave clenched-fist black-power salutes, pulled out "Away with Afrikaans" placards and streamed into the township streets. Mathabathe got there around 8 A.M., in time to see them leaving. A sign hung on the gate saying "No SBs [Security Branch police] allowed. Enter at your own risk."

From the east, west, and north corners of Soweto, students converged on Vilakazi Street, near the center of the township. Vilakazi Street was in Orlando West, one of the oldest parts of Soweto, and ran between Orlando West High School and the house of Winnie Mandela, the wife of the jailed black leader Nelson Mandela. As the crowd swelled, ululating girls danced in front of the crowd and students chanted "Power! Power!"

Brigadier van Niekerk wasn't overly concerned that morning when he saw black schoolchildren streaming across the open veld. Another officer went out to see what was going on. Around 10 A.M. his fellow officer urged van Niekerk to come stop the students. When Brigadier van Niekerk arrived, students—still dressed in their school uniforms of white shirts and dark pullover sweaters—were marching by the thousands and chanting slogans. Above their heads, the students held signs saying "To Hell with Afrikaans." With a handful of men and no riot equipment, Brigadier van Niekerk radioed to Johannesburg for tear gas and reinforcements.

The students had only vague notions of what they would do after the columns of protesters converged on Vilakazi Street. "There we would meet and decide the next step," recalls Seth Mazibuko. But there wasn't time to think about it. According to Mashabela, a policeman threw a stone at the students and students threw stones back. Moments later, the police opened fire, killing a thirteen-year-old black boy named Hector Pieterson.[4]

When police began shooting, the students stood dumbfounded for a few moments. "The students were so stunned, many didn't even run. They just stood there in the middle of the road," recalls Harry Mashabela. A youth scooped up Hector Pieterson's body and carried him to a car while Pieterson's sister ran alongside, crying. Students scattered and the fighting began. Blacks sacked delivery trucks, beat two white officials to death, and burned government offices and beer halls. Police dogs were stoned, knifed, and burned. Troops were called in to restore order and helicopters rescued white civil servants and teachers. Within forty-eight hours, sixty-five blacks were dead, sixty-two of them shot by police.[5]

June 16, 1976, was a watershed in black South African politics. In a sense, all black South Africans—no matter what age, no matter where they live—are children of Soweto. It shook older blacks out of their complacency. Aggrey Klaaste, a black journalist, wrote that "The first time I saw schoolgirls in their tunics marching on police armored vehicles, I could have wept. I could have wept to see this clean courage, this desperate venture to articulate that which was dangerously incomprehensible, from these children."

Nothing is as important as how that time is remembered by people who formed the core of revolt in the 1980s. Those memories would last long after many of the leading actors of 1976 had vanished from the scene, dead, exiled, or discouraged. For younger blacks, June 16 was a formative experience, a day that a generation would mark as the end of innocence and the birth of their political consciousness.

"Thats's when my life started turning upside down, when I really became involved," remembers Lawrence Ntloaka, later the head of a residents' association in Kagiso township near the white town of Krugersdorp. Regional president of Young Christian Students by the age of sixteen, Lawrence led a contingent of Kagiso students to the June 16 Soweto rally. There police turned them away with tear gas, which Lawrence tasted for the first time.

"We were at the school and heard lots of noise," recalls Fani, a neatly dressed willowy youth who ten years later became a community organizer in Soweto. "There were a lot of students chanting freedom songs. I had never heard anyone sing those songs before."

Tshidiso Mogale, who became a branch chairman of a Soweto youth group, was taking an exam when a group of students came up the road and disrupted the test. "It was a blessing in disguise," he laughs. "I couldn't understand the questions because they were in Afrikaans." At "Uncle Tom's" community hall in Orlando, they met a group running from the scene of the shooting. Mogale and others ran for cover, then decided to fight back. They waited on a road in the Dube section of Soweto, a common thoroughfare. When company cars and delivery trucks approached, a few youths called out and others came from backyards and stoned the vehicles. "They were easy targets," Mogale recalls.

Fezi Tshabalala, who ten years later became treasurer of a Soweto student group, was then a twelve-year-old pupil at a Catholic elementary school near the edge of the township. He remembers that Sister Mary dismissed students at 11 A.M. and ordered them to go home. Fezi walked across the street to the main bus depot and waited in vain for a bus. None of the buses were running. He saw smoke in the distance, but didn't know what was happening. So Fezi passed the time at the pinball machines. Each play cost ten cents and if he won he would win a rand. As the hours passed, he worried about the time, but didn't want to spoil his luck. He won almost fifteen rand, as much as a domestic worker earned in a week. Eventually someone took him to spend the night at the nearby house of a teacher. The next day, from the window of his teacher's house, Fezi watched youths burn and loot a delivery truck. He saw police fire tear gas and shoot some youths. His teacher told him to stay put until it seemed safe. Then he took a taxi home.

Twenty-year-old Mohlomola Ntoane, who a decade later was one of thousands of people active in street committees, was then a member of the Soweto Students Representative Council. On June 17, when unrest intensified, Ntoane collected a friend for a march to "town," meaning Johannesburg. But before the march began, his friend was shot by police near the Catholic church, Regina Mundi. "He died a funny death. He didn't collapse in a heap, but he fell like a pen. Perfectly straight. Later his mother asked me where he was. I didn't know what to say."

Some Soweto students dressed in the uniforms of laborers and used red ribbons on their arms. Taxis ferried them, and on trains workers tried to protect them. They carried rocks in the brown shopping bags that are common among people working in white Johannesburg. They were used to break windows in the city. "We called them 'African Bombs,'" recalls Ntoane, who later went to graduate school at the University of the Witwatersrand.

After the shootings in Soweto, unrest spread across the country. Ntoane traveled to black townships in the northern part of the country and told students about what was happening in Soweto. He taught them songs and slogans. The day after Ntoane visited one township, a beer hall was burned down. The day after he visited another township, an Afrikaans bookstore was burned down.[6]

With time, the turmoil subsided. The unrest had taken a heavy toll. Hundreds lay dead and the government still stood. At the second anniversary, Ntoane, who used an alias, was lying low while police looked for him. Lawrence, the boy from Kagiso, became the youngest person ever placed under house arrest, a restriction he broke often. The journalist Mashabela suffered a neck injury when he was beaten in detention; despite surgery, he would never be able to look to the side without moving his shoulders. Brigadier van Niekerk was transferred out of Soweto. He retired and became a part-time prosecutor at the Johannesburg magistrate's court, where I met him in a bare office. Instead of his old uniform, he wore a dark suit, somber as a *dominee*, or church minister. He didn't recognize the name Hector Pieterson, the first youth killed by police.

Mazibuko and two others were sentenced to jail on Robben Island, the prison off the coast of Cape Town. Mazibuko suffered from depression and hallucinations. The three would serve five years. Upon their release, they became active in politics again. These prison terms wouldn't be their last.

Thousands of students fled the country. Tsietsi Mashinini left and later had a nervous breakdown. After he recovered, he joined the outlawed African National Congress in exile. He spent some time in Moscow then moved to West Africa.

But the students of 1976 left behind a militant spirit. When asked later how change would come to South Africa, Fezi, the former pinball wizard, said "Bloodshed. We've got to fight." Fezi had come to expect violence as a matter of course. "If I am afraid forever, I will never be free," he said. "Dying is the highest part of the struggle. It is better to die on the battlefield than at home."

Student militancy was boosted when the government rescinded the rule that schools use Afrikaans for instruction. That schoolchildren had forced this retreat made an extraordinary impact on blacks. Three different government commissions formed in response to the student rebellion recommended reforms to defuse frustration in the townships. Though limited, these reforms enhanced blacks' ability to live in urban areas and to participate in collective bargaining through trade unions. In addition, damaged schools were repaired. Many were expanded and improved.

The lesson, according to Mazibuko, was that blacks must push the government. "Young people can turn a stone into a gun, bottles into bombs." Reforms by the government, Mazibuko believed, were the result of pressure from blacks. "When before 1976 did we hear the government say that apartheid is unworkable?"

The former principal of Morris Isaacson High School, Lekgau Mathabathe, later became the national marketing manager for Premier Milling

Co., but not before doing a stint in jail himself. Shortly after the explosion of student unrest, Mathabathe had joined the Committee of Ten, a group of black adults who tried to mediate between angry students and white authorities. But the government arrested the would-be mediators. Mathabathe spent four months in solitary confinement in late 1976 and another ten months in jail in late 1977 and 1978. There he and the other jailed members of the Committee of Ten persuaded the guards to allow political prisoners to hold a "prayer" meeting to commemorate the second anniversary of the student rebellion. When the prisoners chanted liberation songs and held their fists over their heads, the guards protested. "You said this would be a prayer meeting," the guards said. The black prisoners replied, "This is how we pray."

An Obedient Society

South Africa was once a law-abiding society. Blacks tipped their hats to whites, stepped out of the way on sidewalks, and made sure they went home before the curfews that were imposed on most black townships.

In the early twentieth century, black political leaders saw adherence to the law, however unjust, as proof that black South Africans were worthy of constitutional rights. In 1913, whites passed legislation summarily kicking tens of thousands of black sharecroppers off white farms to wander the roads half-starved. Yet Solomon T. Plaatje, a self-educated clerk, writer, and one of the founders of the forerunner of the African National Congress, "spared neither pains nor pence" to exhort blacks "to obey all the demands of the South African government . . . pending a peaceful intercession from the outside world." If the black peasants had broken the law and been "mown down," Plaatje said, "humanity would have been told that they were justly punished for disobedience to constitutional authority."[7]

In the 1950s, the black political leadership led a campaign of civil disobedience, but the average black still obeyed—and feared—authority. The black journalist Can Themba wrote a short story about a hulking black policeman nicknamed Ten-to-Ten because his night beat started when the first evening curfew bell sounded, giving blacks ten minutes to hurry home.

> By that hour every African, man, woman, and child, had to be indoors, preferably in bed; if the police caught you abroad without a 'special permit' you were hauled off to the battleship-grey little police station and clapped in jail. The following morning you found yourself trembling before a magistrate . . . It was strange how the first warning bell exercised a power of panic among us . . . there were ever women in their yards, peering over corrugated-iron fences and bedstead gates, calling in sing-song voices, 'Ten-to-ten!' as if the sound of the bell at the police station . . . was itself echoed, street after street, urging the belated on, homewards, bedwards, safe from the Law.[8]

When a young African draws a knife on Ten-to-Ten, the police officer grabs his attacker and flings him against a fence like a wet rag. Other township residents simply obey Ten-to-Ten, the way they obeyed any authority.

That was the way the architects of modern apartheid wanted it. Rather than creating a police state, the makers of modern apartheid wanted to create a self-policing state in which blacks knew their boundaries. When the government boasted that New York City had more police per capita than Soweto, it was boasting about the success of the psychology of repression, which had blacks so convinced of their impotence that actual repression became necessary only on occasion.

The government used two instruments—education and pass laws—to instill fear and subservience among blacks. In the 1950s, the government took over all private schools and universities for blacks and turned them into second-rate institutions. Funding was cut and teachers with political leanings were fired. Students were separated into tribal groups and mother-tongue instruction replaced English and Afrikaans at elementary schools. The curriculum was altered. Prime Minister Hendrik Verwoerd declared that education should not "create wrong expectations on the part of the Native" because there would be no place in white South Africa for Africans "above the level of certain forms of labor." Twenty years later, Treurnicht's view of the teaching of Afrikaans as a "practical" step in black education grew naturally from Verwoerd's teachings. A white newspaper declared in 1953 that the "academically educated non-European, with . . . his head full of book learning" could be "a social misfit and a political danger."[9]

The pass laws restricting blacks' freedom of movement also taught obedience. The laws required every black to carry a pass book that recorded his race and tribe. In theory, a black was a citizen of a country connected to his tribe, even though such mythical countries were nothing more than impoverished rural areas of South Africa. In white South Africa near urban centers, blacks were considered temporary sojourners. Without special pass book stamps, a black wasn't permitted to live in an urban area. Those stamps showed that a black had work and accomodation. Only after ten years of working for one employer and living in one place could a black become a legal resident of the area. During the life of the pass laws, police made more than eighteen million arrests for pass violations. In 1974–1975 alone, an average of 989 blacks were tried daily for pass violations.[10] Countless others were stopped and checked by police, who reinforced the idea of who was boss or "baas," in Afrikaans.

Frank Chikane, later chairman of the South African Council of Churches, received this message at age seventeen, when he was stopped by three white policemen who demanded to see his pass. Chikane rummaged through his jacket pockets where he thought he had left the pass. "I'm sure it's here, meneer," he said, using the Afrikaans word for sir. "What did you say?" one officer demanded. The diminutive Chikane, frightened and uncertain where he put his pass, searched his trousers. "Meneer, I had it when I left home. . . ." The policeman again asked if he heard Chikane correctly. Finally Chikane found the tattered pass, and held it out in both hands, careful that it should not tear. "Here, meneer, here it is." Ignoring the pass, the policeman struck Chikane in the chest, propelling him onto his back. Bewildered, Chikane held out the pass again and respectfully called the policeman "meneer" again. The second blow hit Chikane above the left eyebrow. Again and again the policeman hit him across the face. "Who's meneer now? You think you're my equal? Little kaffir, when you talk to me you say 'baas.'" Chikane lay on the ground. "You say 'baas' when you talk to me," the policeman said.[11]

In the minds of most blacks, the last gasp of African resistance to apartheid before 1976 only reinforced the futility of resistance. In 1960, black political groups mustered all their might against the white government and the pass laws. Events reached a climax in March 1960. Thousands of Africans marched on police stations and challenged police to arrest them for leaving their passes at home. In Sharpeville, a black township southwest of Johannesburg, panicky police shot and killed sixty-seven blacks and wounded 186 others. Across the country, black protests broke out in response to the shootings. People began burning their passes. A crowd of 30,000 marched into central Cape Town, not far from the steps of Parliament, and demanded a meeting with a government minister.

The government briefly wavered, and suspended the pass laws. But it quickly recovered its determination. It reneged on an agreement to meet with black leaders, declared a state of emergency, and outlawed the two leading protest groups, the African National Congress and the Pan Africanist Congress. Thousands of black leaders were arrested and hundreds of others fled into exile. The pass laws were reimposed.

The African masses failed to sustain their protests. Just weeks after black South Africans defiantly burned passes, thousands lined up for replacements. An ANC call for a general strike on April 19, 1960, fell flat.

In 1961, the remnants of the black political leadership launched a military campaign, relying on an underground network. For months it waged a sabotage campaign. But this too was smashed. In 1963, police uprooted the underground and jailed its leaders. So complete was the defeat that one dedicated underground leader escaped to London and became a writer about commercial law for a British law journal. The "wind of change" that in 1960 British Prime Minister Harold Macmillan predicted would sweep away colonial and white minority rule across the continent ran out of breath at the Zambezi River.

The psychological impact was as devastating as the organizational one. "The African's problems might always have been dependency, identity-confusion, fear, and a resigned apathy about the future, but at no time had these problems been more starkly apparent than in the 1960s, when all African initiatives and voices of dissent had been forcibly stilled," according to historian Gail M. Gerhart.[12] Can Themba, the black journalist and short-story writer whose columns in the 1950s had celebrated the vibrant life of a black Johannesburg neighborhood known as Sophiatown, moved to Swaziland. Sophiatown had been razed along with the spirit it embodied. Before his death in 1968, a disconsolate Themba wrote, "As I brood over these things, I, with my insouciant attitude to matters of weight, I feel a sickly despair which the most potent bottle of brandy cannot wash away."

Out of shame and futility, families that had been active in the 1950s hid their involvement from their children growing up in the 1960s. The son of a man who was working in exile with the PAC was told that his father was a migrant laborer in Benoni, a working-class town east of Johannesburg.

If students showed an interest in politics, many parents tried to dissuade them. Their admonitions went beyond parental protectiveness; parents believed protest was pointless. When in the 1970s Fani, the willowy student who in the 1980s had become a Soweto community organizer, told his parents about Black Consciousness meetings, they told him to stick to school. "They said the government was heavily armed," Fani recalls. "They thought that there was nothing you could do except survive."

When students marched and fought in Soweto on June 16, 1976, they defied the authority of both their parents and the government. Never again would young black South Africans be as obedient as they were before.

When troops came out, the youths stood and fought. Lacking the sense of mortality that comes with age, they challenged the might of the apartheid state with little more than petrol bombs and stones. A black actor later remembered attending a demonstration by black students in 1977 in downtown Johannesburg. With thousands of black youngsters mingling with the usual numbers of black office and factory workers, the white city was transformed. "Town was black, pitch black," the actor recalled. Police arrived and ordered the crowd to disperse in three minutes. But the black youths, confident that the police wouldn't endanger whites by firing tear gas or bullets in the center of Johannesburg, simply sat down in the middle of the street. Police issued more warnings through loudspeakers. The blacks answered by singing.

The police charged the demonstrators with batons, beating them around their heads and shoulders. The blacks hit back. "From a peaceful demonstration, it turned into something very ugly," the actor remembered. He and other blacks chased any white unlucky enough to be standing nearby. Several whites fled into a store, but slammed the door shut before a fifty-year-old man could get in. "He was trapped between the door and us, so six of us went at him and kicked him to pieces," the actor recalled. "I enjoyed that." The actor and some of his friends then spotted a young white couple drinking sodas and walking along the street as if nothing were happening. The black youths turned on them, too. Police reinforcements were arriving by then, so the actor ducked into Flamingo Dry Cleaners, borrowed a uniform from sympathetic black workers and escaped.

One of his friends piped up. Don't feel too sorry for the white couple, he said. "They're like the whole of white South Africa. Walking along, sipping their Cokes while the country is burning."

Tired of getting orders, black students wanted to dictate terms to the white government. "We are sick and tired of having terms dictated to us. The white man has got to learn that whichever way he goes, the direction is downhill—until he decides to turn away from his evil ways. The students do not want what is happening and what they do not want they will get rid of," the president of the Soweto Student Representative Council, Tsietsi Mashinini, told the editor of the black newspaper, *The World*.[13]

Black political leaders of the 1950s had demonstrated impatience and courage, but never the unadulterated rage that these youth possessed. The black leaders of earlier generations had worked hand in hand with white liberals and leftists, but the young blacks of 1976 showed little inclination to mix with whites. After Mashinini left South Africa, an American television interviewer asked him, "Do you hate white people?" Mashinini replied simply: "I hate white people." The interviewer then asked if that meant white South Africans must be killed. Mashinini replied, "Look . . . I would love to see a black and white South Africa where people can live happily ever after . . . but I don't see it. The people back at home are so bitter about the white people. Everybody feels like taking a gun and wiping the whole white population off the face of the earth in South Africa."[14]

In South Africa, many youths were eager to do just that. Mashinini's younger brother Mpho started ferrying youths to Swaziland for military training with the Pan Africanist Congress. "I was the money guy. If you wanted to escape, you came to me," he recalled. Thousands wanted just that. "South Africa was burning and we wanted to go out and get training and come back and fight and get it over with," Mpho said.

"New Fire"

Though thousands of young blacks flocked to the ANC and PAC for guns and training, the inspiration for the youngsters didn't come from the movements in exile. "We couldn't understand what [ANC president Oliver] Tambo was doing for twenty years," recalled one youth. "We heard he had a farm, that all those guys were taken over by the CIA." Mpho Mashinini, Tsietsi's younger brother who was sixteen at the time of the student revolt, recalled thinking, "We were the real struggle, the real heroes. People viewed the ANC as old and useless and saw themselves as the new fire."

That fire was started by Black Consciousness and its leading proponent, Stephen Biko. A former medical student, Biko had diagnosed why black South Africans were too weak to free themselves years after most of Africa had shaken off the colonial powers. That weakness had little to do with the force of arms, he said, and everything to do with the power of the mind. "Material want is bad enough, but coupled with spiritual poverty it kills," he wrote. "And this latter effect is probably the one that creates mountains of obstacles in the normal course of emancipation of the black people."

> The type of black man we have today has lost his manhood. . . . He looks with awe at the white power structure and accepts what he regards as the 'inevitable position' . . . In the privacy of his toilet his face twists in silent condemnation of white society but brightens up in sheepish obedience as he comes out hurrying in response to his master's impatient call. . . . Celebrated achievements by whites in the field of science—which he understands only hazily—serve to make him rather convinced of the futility of resistance and to throw away any hopes that change may ever come. All in all the black man has become a shell, a shadow of man, completely defeated, drowning in his own misery, a slave, an ox bearing the yoke of oppression with sheepish timidity.[15]

The 1976 riots drew white attention to Black Consciousness, but Biko had nurtured his views over the previous decade. His views arose out of a feeling that even within anti-government politics blacks took back seats to whites. In 1967, Biko went to a conference of students critical of the government. The group, the National Union of South African Students (NUSAS), was dominated by whites. Moreover the conference host, Rhodes University, refused to allow mixed-race accommodation or eating facilities. Afterwards, Biko stayed at the home of his friend Barney Pityana. For white students, "NUSAS was a nice friendly club, another game you played while at university. Then you grew out of it," Pityana recalled. For black students, NUSAS wasn't militant enough, Biko said. Other liberal organizations were not open to blacks. At a non-racial church conference, white participants discouraged blacks from defying restrictions of the Group Areas Act, which limited blacks to seventy-two hours in a white area. "Steve felt no common mind with these people about how students could act in a radical way. Blacks were isolated. We thought we had to be more willing to resist and violate the law," Pityana said.

The Black Consciousness Movement that Biko founded rejected the notion that whites could play a role in the liberation of blacks. "The main thing was to get black people to articulate their own struggle and reject the white liberal establishment from prescribing to people," said Pityana.

Underlying the organizational split with white liberals was an attempt by Biko and his colleagues to "recondition the mind of the oppressed."[16] Blacks needed to learn to speak for themselves, they felt.

The ideology of Black Consciousness was borrowed from foreign writers, such as the psychiatrist Frantz Fanon, whose banned book about the Algerian war against French settlers was widely read. To Fanon, the "native" had become psychologically incapacitated, no longer capable of action. The native detested white society, but was envious of it. Realizing that his own skin prevented him from ever attaining privilege, the native despised his own blackness. To liberate themselves, natives had to redefine their values, self-image, and entire outlook. Black Americans offered the idea of non-white unity, of closing ranks before entering white society. Americans contributed to the style and rhetoric of Black Consciousness. The very term "black" came from the United States and encompassed people previously known as

Africans, Indians, or coloreds. The phrase "non-white" defined blacks in negative terms. Black Consciousness coined its own slogans, such as "Black man, you're on your own" but echoed some American phrases like "relevance," "power structure," and "Black is beautiful."[17]

Both the rhetoric and the philosophy of Black Consciousness contradicted the fundamental principles of grand apartheid. Apartheid was designed not only to separate whites from blacks but to foster black parochialism by segregating blacks into tribal and linguistic groups. Black Consciousness asserted the common interests and background of those groups, and encouraged blacks to think of themselves as part of one nation.

In the early 1970s, Black Consciousness leaders launched an all-black student organization called the South African Students Organization (SASO) and the Black People's Convention, for adults. Through these groups, Black Consciousness became part of the shared frame of reference. Popo Molefe, a student active in church groups who later became general secretary of the United Democratic Front, said at his trial in 1987 that

> the philosophy behind the Black People's Convention was that they have to develop the attitude of mind that would enable Black people to overcome the attitude of feeling inferior to white people. They should strive to demonstrate that they had a dignity as any other human being and they were capable of doing anything that any other human being was able to do, anything that a white person was able to do.[18]

Biko canvassed for support in the churches, too. The Rev. Mcebisi Xundu, then based in a rural area of the Transkei, remembers Biko visiting the church leadership there. Biko pointed out to them, Xundo says, that

> the church at that time was full of Western values. Mary was white. Everything was from a white perspective. We had allowed ourselves to be vehicles of white domination. He didn't have any proposals, but he was trying to say, did we see that? And it was true. The church was colonial in every respect. It paid lip service to non-racialism.

The government paid perverse tribute to the power of ideas in the way it treated Black Consciousness leaders. In 1973 it restricted Biko to the remote area of King Williams Town. It later put nine Black Consciousness leaders on trial, but when Biko testified on their behalf, the trial turned into a Platonic dialogue on Black Consciousness philosophy. Biko became one of the most carefully watched people in the country, and was detained several times. Yet his ideas continued to seep down to high-school students through church, debating, and cultural societies outside state control.

On August 18, 1977, the government arrested Biko and kept him, naked, in solitary confinement. On September 7, he suffered a severe blow to the head during interrogation. Though he showed signs of brain injury, four days later police loaded him, helpless and naked, onto the floor of a van and transported him 750 miles to Pretoria. Biko died September 12 on a mat on the stone floor of a Pretoria jail. It was a brutal and undignified end for a man set on restoring human dignity to blacks. Upon the news of his death, riots broke out, until the government finally crushed all remnants of the Black Consciousness movement. On October 19, 1977, the government banned eighteen organizations associated with Black Consciousness, and the newspaper *The World*, whose editor, Percy Qoboza, symphatized with Black Consciousness. The day became known as Black Wednesday.

Biko's funeral was the first big political funeral in South Africa. As busloads of people neared the remote town, they passed black youths standing solemnly along the road with their fists raised. Prominent white liberals, such as the dogged parliamentarian Helen Suzman, attended. So did the black American diplomat Donald McHenry, who interrupted negotiations going on in Pretoria about the independence of Namibia from South African rule. At the funeral, 20,000 people marched and sang freedom songs. For five hours, speakers eulogized Biko. The Rev. Xundu, the Transkei Anglican priest, presided, appealing to God to take sides with the oppressed to overthrow the system.

CHAPTER TWO

Take Up the Black Man's Burden

People must not just give in to the hardship of life. . . .
—BIKO

It would take more than prayer to overthrow apartheid. In 1979, white South Africa began to recover from the student rebellion and international condemnation that followed the death of Biko. The government was again showing signs of economic, political, and military strength. The price of gold soared to new heights. Enough calm returned to the townships to enable Botha to pay a visit to Soweto, making him the first South African prime minister to set foot in the country's biggest metropolis. A U. S. surveillance satellite detected a distinctive double flash of light that suggested that the South African military had tested a nuclear bomb in the Indian Ocean.

In the black townships a different kind of fission was taking place. From 1979 through 1983 hundreds of black community organizations formed, local bursts of organizational energy that issued from the humdrum bread-and-butter concerns of blacks—housing, bus fares, and the forced removal of entire black communities.

Without directly challenging the authority of the state, these organizations mobilized black South Africans to stand up for themselves. Informal associations—including church, civic, and youth groups—reached beyond the student and intellectual circles where Black Consciousness had been strongest. Though seemingly disparate, these grassroots groups were linked by common economic complaints. The new groups appealed to a sense of unfairness shared by blacks who were residents of Soweto or migrants in the mine hostels, aspiring businesspeople or farm hands, pensioners or students. "Whites want to eat bread and butter while we eat dry bread," said a driver for a white-run newspaper company in Johannesburg. "They drink tea with milk while I must drink my tea black. Why? Because I'm a black man."

To people outside the townships, the years 1979 to 1983 were a period of calm between two spasms of black unrest. In fact, the events of 1976 never really ended. Instead, black resistance spread and gathered new strength. Organizations that formed during this period were the foundation for later resistance. By sticking to concrete issues and winning small concessions from the government, these organizations built a loyal following. Their origins explain the dynamics and durability of protest in the 1980s.

On October 10, 1979, eighteen days after the nuclear test, black community organization came to life in Port Elizabeth. Down the hill from the police station where Biko lay dying two years earlier and up the coast past the edge of the white part of town, six thousand blacks crowded into a hall in one of the townships and formed the Port Elizabeth Black Civic Organization (PEBCO). Four thousand more listened outside.

As chair, they elected the lanky, bearded Thozamile Botha, a Ford Motor Company trainee draftsman. Botha had attended the all-black Fort Hare University until the university was closed during the 1976 student rebellion. After classes resumed, Botha could not afford to pay tuition. He taught briefly at a black high school. He ran an association for students interested in science and technology, and was arrested for two months in late 1977 after he organized a benefit concert for jailed members of the association. In late 1978 he joined Ford.[1]

"Thoza was a very charismatic somebody," recalled Mono Badela, a black journalist and co-founder of PEBCO whose short stature, wide girth, and thick glasses made his appearance the opposite of Botha's. "He could present himself very well before the people. It was easy for the people to have faith in him. He was serious and looked educated about what he was doing."

PEBCO thrust itself into the midst of a housing crisis that was gripping Port Elizabeth's several black townships. Walmer township was located near the airport on the west end of the city. It provided maids and gardeners to Port Elizabeth's wealthiest white suburbs. Three other townships—New Brighton, KwaZakhele, and Zwide—lay, side by side, northeast of the city.

According to government figures, Port Elizabeth's townships had a housing shortage of 12,500 units. The Urban Foundation, a business-sponsored group, estimated the shortage to be far greater.[2] People were scrunched together in poor and overcrowded conditions. The average unit in the Port Elizabeth townships housed a main tenant family of six, plus a lodger family of four people.[3]

The housing shortage grew out of official ambivalence about the presence of blacks in urban areas. According to original apartheid policy, blacks were temporary sojourners in "white" South Africa, only visiting before returning to narrowly delineated tribal homelands. In the townships, the government owned all land and houses. Blacks were tenants; they possessed few amenities and had no incentive to undertake home improvements. As a consequence, black townships had a temporary look even though they had larger populations than the white cities they encircled.

The quality of houses varied widely. American automobile manufacturers were building their employees houses that would be suitable in a middle-class American suburb. But decent homes were exceptions.

In Red Location, a neighborhood of New Brighton, 900 families lived in former military huts that were made available for use by Africans in 1902 after the Boer War. The huts had no electricity or toilets. In other areas, tens of thousands of people didn't live in houses at all. In Zwide, where Thozamile Botha lived, there were 5,477 shacks. In KwaZakhele, families were living in quarters built for single male contract workers.[4] An entire new "township" of shacks had started to spring up along the southern edge of the black townships near the ocean. People called it "Little Soweto" or "Soweto-by-the-sea."

It took steps by the government to bring the housing crisis to a head and ignite community protest. In 1979, the government decided to knock down shacks and end rent subsidies, even though 45 percent of blacks couldn't pay full rent.

In early 1979, the Eastern Cape Administration Board destroyed Ford Village, where pensioners and the poor had lived in houses built in 1948 from large wooden packing crates provided by Ford. Some families moved to single men's quarters, on a "temporary" basis. At the hostels, two families stayed in each room. Other families were relocated to new houses in Zwide, but had trouble paying rent. The rents, charged on a sliding scale, ranged from two to four times the rates paid in Ford Village. Moreover, after three months, municipal officials installed water meters and started charging for water. Because of a storm drainage problem, the government also threatened to demolish a couple of hundred houses in KwaZakhele without making new quarters available.

In May 1979, the deputy minister for Cooperation and Development (the Orwellian name of the ministry for black affairs) declared that all 4,678 residents of Walmer Township would be forced to move to Zwide. Other black townships feared that the influx of blacks from Walmer would only worsen living conditions.

The reasons for the Walmer removal further angered blacks. The deputy minister said it was ordained by a 1961 decision to rezone the area for white occupation. Even without an expansion of white suburbs, the Group Areas Act required bigger buffer strips separating black residential areas like Walmer from the nearby white neighborhood, Walmer Estates. The government also wanted to "consolidate" black areas and promised better living conditions in Zwide. Finally, part of Walmer had to make way for a highway extension.

The government's actions turned housing into an ideal organizing tool. The housing crisis threatened every black constituency, class, and neighborhood—not just the poor, the indigent, and the migrants from the countryside.

On behalf of Zwide residents, Thozamile Botha haggled with government officials and won reductions in house rentals. Water charges were not implemented. People who had been evicted for failing to pay rent were helped by PEBCO to break down the locked doors of their former homes and move back in. Encouraged by this success, blacks from other townships flocked to PEBCO, which took up the defense of Walmer. After PEBCO threatened a black consumer boycott of white stores and the busses, the deputy minister for Cooperation and Development canceled plans to visit Walmer Township, and spared it from demolition.

Impressed by this success, Port Elizabeth residents soon brought other problems to PEBCO. The group won national attention when black workers at Ford went on a three-day wildcat strike to protest the dismissal of Thozamile Botha on the day PEBCO was launched. Two weeks after winning Botha's reinstatement, the Ford workers struck again. PEBCO co-founder Mono Badela recalled that the strike

> was something unheard of because Ford was regarded as *the* liberal employment institution in Port Elizabeth. It was the first multinational to accept the trade union, long before the government commission had recommended the recognition of trade unions. But Thoza was working at Ford, you see, and he exposed some of the fallacies. The working conditions were bad. There was discrimination in salaries and in job situation. Thoza was fighting such things. So he led the strike at the Ford Cortina plant.
>
> The strike, I think it lasted a week. Within the week there were strikes all over the place in Port Elizabeth in the automobile industries. Thoza was head of PEBCO and all the workers wanted PEBCO to participate. Hence we were asked to draft memorandums. From the factory floor workers would march in a *big group* to some church halls in the township where executive members of PEBCO would be to help them.
>
> I remember one night I was woken up by workers from General Tire. After the 10 o'clock shift they came straight to my house. They were going to start striking the following day, but they didn't know how to draft a petition to pinpoint their grievances.[5]

By January 1980, PEBCO claimed a card-carrying membership of 3,000 and was regularly drawing crowds of 10,000 to rallies held in soccer stadiums; no community hall was big enough. On January 10, Botha, Badela, and three others were detained. Botha and Badela were released on February 27, but banned from meetings and confined to their homes for much of the day.

The detentions caused disarray in PEBCO's ranks. Frustrated by house arrest after his release, Thozamile Botha left the country in May 1980. The acting president was forced out of office in August 1980 and for a while the organization went into eclipse. But later it would reemerge as a powerful community organization, credible because of the concessions and improvements it won for blacks' basic living conditions. "The challenge to the state is best if it rises from the bottom," Thozamile Botha said. "People didn't always understand what national political organizations stood for. Grassroots structures made people feel the structures were theirs."

Political activists quickly grasped the advantage of focusing on social and economic issues. Not only did such issues strike at the dearest concerns of township residents, but also many people were still nervous about political activity following the 1977 crackdown on Black Consciousness organizations. It would have been difficult to reconstruct black organizations that posed any direct threat to white rule.

One group to take up local economic grievances was an organization of Indians, whom Biko had urged to think of themselves as black. "We recognized a trough in the struggle and went to communities far removed from political rhetoric," said Jerry Coovadia, a physician and member of the Natal Indian Congress. Coovadia said the congress also recognized that it had become "an organization of activists." Its narrow membership was comprised of intellectuals and professionals; only eighty to ninety people attended annual meetings. The Natal Indian Congress needed a mass base.

In the late 1970s, members of the Natal Indian Congress formed the Durban Housing Action Committee (DHAC) to take up issues regarding education, housing availability, rents, and transportation. Their timing was just right. The white city council, which had previously comingled its finances with the finances of the Indian areas, had decided to make the Indian areas financially "independent." Because the biggest ratepayers, business and industry, were counted as part of white areas, the change meant higher taxes and fees for Indians. So DHAC rallied Indian women, who marched on city hall, a splendid colonial building in the center of Durban. DHAC also persuaded residents to protest the change in finances by lighting candles and turning off electric lights in the townships. The protests drew heavy turnouts.

In 1980, the Rev. Mcebisi Xundu arrived in Lamontville, a black township outside Durban, to minister to 118,000 migrant workers who stayed in single-sex hostels at the edge of the township. No clergy had ever ministered to the hostel dwellers, a group generally neglected by government and black community organizations alike. In the 1976 student rebellion, some students had clashed with people from the hostels.

Xundu, the Anglican who had presided at Biko's funeral, was the ideal minister for hostel dwellers. An earthy, oval-faced man with a slight speech impediment, Xundu had grown up in a small village, had worked in the Transkei, and knew the trials of wives and children left behind in rural homelands. His first name literally meant "advisor" or "counselor."

In 1982, Xundu was given a "dying parish" in Lamontville itself. The government was "phasing out" Lamontville and moving its residents to Umlazi, a nearby township that was technically in the KwaZulu homeland. The relocated Lamontville residents would lose the rights that permitted them to live and work in urban areas in white South Africa. The people would officially become citizens of another country, one recognized only by the South African government.

It was not the kind of parish that would help a minister climb the church hierarchy, but Xundu's stands within church institutions had never made him a favorite. When Xundu was studying to become a deacon, the principal of his theological college held a mass to pray for the soul of the white National Party president who had just died. Xundu refused communion. Later, to protest the law that barred blacks from marrying whites, Xundu refused to take out a license to perform marriages, a decision that sacrificed a minister's steadiest source of income. In 1962 he introduced a motion at a regional church meeting to equalize stipends for blacks and whites. Blacks, a majority of the clergy who earned half as much as whites, voted to overrule the church leaders and freeze white salaries. In the early 1960s, Xundu helped form Faith in Action, a group of Anglican clergy dissatisfied with the church's social and political postures. Xundu believed the church's role, in the words recited at his ordination, was to "publicly admonish, warn, and exhort people when they erroneously act against the mind of God." He said the church's failure to speak out was a sin of omission. In 1976, Xundu went to work full time for the Black People's Convention, a Black Consciousness outreach organization. But his work was cut short when the organization was banned. In October 1977, just after the Biko funeral, Xundu was detained and held for four months.[6]

In Lamontville, Xundu practiced his social gospel. Toward the end of 1982, the government-subsidized bus monopoly increased fares to Durban, where most blacks from Lamontville worked. Xundu treated the increase as a pastoral issue. "If this hike goes through it could mean that your child might go without a piece of bread or without a ballpoint [pen] for school," he told the elders of his parish. Xundu co-founded a committee that waged an eighteenth-month-boycott and provided alternate transportation for Lamontville residents. The committee arranged new timetables with fleets of minibuses driven mostly by township residents. Eventually the bus company rolled back its increase. At the beginning of 1983, the government hiked rents in Lamontville. The same coalition of leaders formed a group called the Joint Rent Action Committee (JORAC) to protest increases in rent and water rates.

Emboldened by the successful bus and rent protests, the JORAC coalition organized new protests until the government withdrew the proposed incorporation of Lamontville into the KwaZulu.

Meanwhile, black students were regrouping, too. While in detention in 1977, Murphy Morobe had been talking to a fellow student in the only meeting place then available: a toilet at the police station in Johannesburg. Morobe had been a student at Morris Isaacson in 1976 and had marched on June 16. He also served on the Soweto Student Representative Council and before long he would be convicted and sent to Robben Island for five years. While awaiting trial and sentencing, Morobe was planning for the future. His friend would be getting out of prison soon and Morobe was urging him to start a new student group. In 1979, with Morobe and others still in jail, the Congress of South African Students was formed.

Within months, 100,000 students went on strike in colored and African schools and on five black college campuses. Students demanded recognition for their own elected Student Representative Councils, a lifting of the age limits that kept many late starters and former class boycotters from completing their educations, and an improvement in the quality of teachers.

Between 1979 and 1983, COSAS built a network of branches in fifty urban areas. Demographic pressure pushed student organizations forward. In 1980, 55 percent of the African population was under the age of twenty. A baby boom boosted the school population from 577,000 in 1980 to more than one million in 1984. Sheer numbers thrust students to the center of black political protest. Classrooms provided natural meeting places even when meetings outside school were prohibited.

COSAS had a different outlook from the student organizations active in 1976. The 1976 rebellion convinced COSAS leaders that they needed to rally support outside the schools. "Outside school, there was the Black People's Convention, which had intellectuals as its base: professors, teachers, doctors, and so on. BPC had a low mass content. Ordinary mothers and fathers would not feel comfortable in such a structure because of the high-flown language," Morobe said.[7] Moreover, migrant workers from some Soweto hostels had fought against students when the students had tried to enforce a general strike. During the 1980 school boycotts tensions ran high between students and parents in many areas, especially in Port Elizabeth, where primary and secondary schools were forced to close.

So COSAS threw itself into community issues. During the 1980 school boycotts, COSAS raised strike funds and organized a boycott of red meat during a meat-workers' strike in Cape Town. In April 1981 COSAS led a march to protest increased rents in the Vaal area, and organized a national consumer boycott of Wilson-Roundtree candy in support of black trade-union members who had been dismissed for organizing the company's East London plant.[8]

In 1982, COSAS launched a network of youth congresses for young blacks who weren't in school. They included youths who had never returned to school after the 1976 rebellion, some who couldn't afford school fees, and others who had finished high school or college. Many were unemployed. About 250,000 young blacks were hitting the job market every year and only a minority could find jobs. Within a year, COSAS started twenty youth congresses for blacks below the age of thirty-eight.

In Soweto, COSAS leaders appointed a core group of five people to organize the crucial Soweto Youth Congress. The five quietly recruited young blacks in church groups, dance groups, and soccer clubs.

Rich Country, Poor Country

Poverty alone does not summon up a spirit of rebellion. If it did, black living conditions would have sparked a popular uprising long before the 1980s. A spirit of rebellion is based on the notion that poverty can be abolished, that it is the result of exploitation rather than scarcity.[9]

Although the South African government blames communists for stirring black discontent, the irony is that no propagandist could match the explosive message that apartheid sends to blacks. Black South Africans don't need to read Karl Marx; they learn the same lessons by seeing the way whites live next door. The opulence of whites' lives convinces blacks that they live in a rich country and that poverty isn't necessary.[10]

In the early 1980s, the gap between white and black appeared more pronounced than ever. Black living conditions had remained relatively stagnant, while the fortunes of whites had soared during the 1960s and 1970s. The problems of poor whites that had motivated the National Party in the 1930s had virtually vanished by the late 1970s, thanks to government patronage. White unemployment practically disappeared. Gold prices soared to a peak of $850 an ounce in 1980. Corporate profits climbed. White South Africans acquired televisions for the first time. They graduated from American sedans to BMWs and Mercedes. They build 375,000 swimming pools, one for every third white household.

Meanwhile three-fifths of black South Africans were living below the minimum subsistence level. When in 1978, social scientists measured inequality in fifty-seven countries, South Africa had the most lopsided distribution of wealth in the world.[11] Per capita income for whites was about ten times the per capita income for blacks. Unequal government spending skewed the balance of wealth further. Expenditure for white education and municipal services averaged seven times as much as spending for blacks on a per capita basis. And it showed.

In the black township of Alexandra, 180,000 people were crammed into one square mile of squalor. Deep gashes cut through the dirt streets. Shanties leaned like playing cards beside aging brick houses. In winter, the entire township was covered with a thick layer of soot from household coal and wood fires.

Among blacks, a sense of injustice smoldered. Every day thousands of workers walked from Alexandra across foot bridges over a four-lane highway to work as domestic servants in the white neighborhood of Sandton. There they saw private homes, public parks, and neatly paved streets.

Established at the northern edge of Johannesburg in 1969, Sandton was a tribute to the golden age of white South Africa. Whites spent hundreds of millions of dollars to convert it from farmland into one of the swankest suburbs in South Africa. Its winding streets were lined with rambling mansions and manicured lawns enclosed by high walls. Private tennis courts and swimming pools were as common as mailboxes.

Sandton possessed every convenience. At Sandton Center, a luxury highrise hotel and shopping mall, whites shopped at jewelry and clothing stores comparable to those found on Madison Avenue in New York. The center also had hair salons, art galleries, a cinema, restaurants, and a popular night club. Plush offices housed corporations escaping the inner city.

The contrast between Alexandra and Sandton was a monument to the injustice of apartheid, and it helped make Alexandra fertile ground for black trade unions and community organizations in the early 1980s. As in Port Elizabeth, housing grievances galvanized residents. In 1981, residents started a series of informal cultural, historical, and political discussion groups called *Ditshwantsho tsa Rona*. From these, three local committees were established. One consisted of residents who faced sharp rent increases for new houses. Another represented people living in temporary quarters awaiting promised new houses. The third committee spoke for people whose houses were zoned for demolition. From these, the Alexandra Residents' Association was formed, which was superseded by the Alexandra Action Committee, which would eventually rise up and seize control of the township.

The history of Alexandra shows how a reservoir of economic grievance, deeper than any rent or bus fare dispute, fed black political rebellion.

Newer black townships are placed tactfully behind mine dumps or hills, unseen and unnoticed by whites in their sheltered suburbs. Alexandra, however, was founded before the white Johannesburg suburbs fanned out to the north. Around the turn of the century the rectangular plot of land had been a farm on the outskirts of a tinier Johannesburg. When a widow tried to sell the farm, no whites wanted it. So in 1912 a land development company obtained special permission to sell the area to blacks, making Alexandra one of the few places in South Africa where blacks had the right to own property. As Johannesburg expanded, Alexandra became an "eyesore" and a threat to the insulated safety of white neighborhoods. So the government forced blacks to move further north to Tembisa or to distant sections of the South Western Townships, an area later known by its acronym, Soweto. In the late 1950s and early 1960s, 24,000 people were forced to move. Others lived under constant threat of removal. In 1963, the government abolished the freehold rights of 2,000 black property owners as prelude to relocating all families to other townships and converting Alexandra—"Alex" to its residents—into a dormitory township with 20,000 men and women housed in eight single-sex hostels. The first two hostels were opened in 1972. But blacks kept moving to Alexandra and many old-timers hung on. In 1982, Pretoria relented and allowed the rest of the township to stand.

Alexandra continued to suffer from neglect. In 1983 the township filled a small valley that fell away from a highway running from Johannesburg to Pretoria. Its boundaries were plain: on the west, the main road and a row of Indian-owned shops and fast-food joints; to the south, a white residential suburb; to the north, a handful of small factories with metal cages protecting the windows; to the east, a small creek with a graveyard on the far side. The gutted dirt streets were laid out in a grid. The avenues ran from first through twenty-second; seven streets named after prominent individuals (including Theodore Roosevelt) ran perpendicular to the avenues.

The most established members of the community, many of them former freeholders, lived in aging brick houses. Each plot held an average of fifteen families. Fewer than one in five families in the township had a house to itself. Hundreds of people lived in the five-story single-sex hostels. Blacks migrating from rural areas built cardboard and corrugated-metal shacks. Scores of people inhabited the shells of disused buses parked in a row along one street. Goats and cows roamed freely.

The life of the township took place in dirt yards and streets. Children ran barefoot playing with homemade toys made of twisted clothes hangers. They rolled old tires. Many adults drank at illegal bars known as shebeens. Others took in a different kind of opiate: church. On Sundays, a couple of thousand members of the Zion Christian Church gathered, dressed in distinctive caps and shoes, some in bright colored robes, and sang and stomped in unison.

Crime ran rampant. Alex had a history of tough criminal gangs. In the 1950s, two rival gangs called the Russians and the Americans had been powerful. Modern versions included the Skorpion gang, named for a Skorpion pistol, and the Amakabasa, one of whose members posed for a magazine while perched on top of a stolen BMW. One kingpin lived in a new apartment complex with records stacked to the ceiling next to his expensive stereo equipment. Half a dozen of his cohorts constantly hung around his door.

The discrepancy in living standards was built into the budget and machinery of apartheid. In the United States, taxes paid by business and industry help cover the cost of community services such as water, sewerage, electricity, road repair, and garbage collection. But since Alexandra was considered a separate municipality from Johannesburg and Sandton, even the factories one block north of the township were treated as part of a different tax base. Taxes paid by businesses and factories covered 55 percent of the cost of services in white areas such as Sandton. They contributed nothing to black areas.[12]

Though the adjacent communities could have been part of the same municipality, sharing services, Sandton had its own government that lavished privileges on whites while ignoring the needs of their black neighbors. Consider a handful of official statistics.[13]

Budget. The 1986–87 budget of Sandton totaled R70.3 million for a population of 65,000 whites and about 30,000 black domestic workers, who live in separate rooms in the whites' backyards. That comes to R740 per capita, counting the servants. The Alexandra budget totaled R20 million and about R111 per person.

Water. Sandton had 17,720 domestic water connections on June 30, 1985, and 800 fire hydrants. In Alexandra, virtually everybody shared communal water taps—about fifteen families per tap. With no drainage facilities, the ground around the taps turned into mud baths. There were no fire hydrants.

Sewers. Sandton maintained 550 miles of sewers and built 11.75 miles of new sewers. Everyone in Sandton enjoyed a flush toilet. In Alexandra, there were virtually no sewers and only 550 flush toilets. Residents disposed of feces in buckets, which often went uncollected. In those instances, residents dumped the buckets into open trenches that served as public sewers. I once saw a young child fall into such a trench during a rainstorm and nearly drown before being fished out by another child. These poor sanitary conditions were the cause of a 1986 outbreak of polio, a disease that has been eradicated in most of the developing world.

The outbreak of polio was the last thing needed to burden the South African health care system for blacks. On a typical Saturday night, the emergency room at Soweto's Baragwanath Hospital resembled Johannesburg's central bus station at rush hour. People milled around in the halls, waiting. Huddled on chairs, stretchers, and floors, a couple of dozen people had red labels with printed words "Urgent *Dringend*" pasted on their foreheads by triage nurses like stickers on express mail.

When I walked into the operating section of the emergency room, I came upon the bodies of five black men. Four were suffering from knife wounds inflicted in a fashion common among street brawlers: the attacker inserted his knife upward below the victim's shoulder blade, often puncturing the heart. The fifth man had been struck in the head by an ax. Two of the men lay unattended because there weren't enough doctors. One doctor held out stitching material and asked if I could finish suturing a patient so he could start on another.

Two of the men died. A nurse matter-of-factly attached a ticket with a number on each of the deceased: "Unknown African male." The bodies would lie in the morgue until claimed—*if* someone claimed them. If the men were migrant workers, their families in rural homelands might never find out what had become of them.

This was a quiet Saturday night at Baragwanath Hospital, the only hospital in Soweto. In addition to serving two million residents in Soweto, the 2,700-bed Baragwanath was the referral hospital for blacks throughout the Transvaal province. Tough cases were transferred there from an area the size of the entire midwestern United States. Notwithstanding its chaos, other black hospital staffs envied Baragwanath. In the Lebowa homeland, not a single doctor worked in four entire hospitals. Nurses alone cared for the patients.

White South Africans didn't share these poor services. Just a twenty-minute ride from Baragwanath Hospital stood the Johannesburg General Hospital, reserved for whites (and high security black political prisoners) until 1990 reforms. Like all major South African hospitals, it is a state hospital. But its patient load was light. With a 50-to-60 percent occupancy rate in the 1980s, the hospital closed several wards.

At Baragwanath, where the occupancy rate ran around 200 percent, many patients slept on the floors. Doctors and nurses at one point trucked donations of mattresses to the hospital in order to get patients off the floors. Some doctors brought their own toilet seats. Hospital administrators, angered by doctors who complained about conditions, declared defensively that there were never more than 500 patients without beds![14]

On the surface, living conditions in Soweto were respectable enough for the government to run tour buses to show foreigners the township. But behind the tidy gray exteriors, cramped quarters and poverty take a heavy toll.

Baragwanath and national health statistics tell the full story. Black infant mortality runs about 120 per 1,000 live births, ten times the rate for whites.[15] Black life expectancy is fifteen years less than for whites. Tuberculosis, virtually eradicated among whites, is epidemic among blacks. There are only 300 black doctors—one per 90,000 people. (The World Health Organization considers a ratio of one per 10,000 too low.) Though some white doctors worked in black hospitals, the ratio still falls well below the ratio for whites of one doctor for every 390 people.[16]

South African blacks had it better than other black Africans, whites often said. But nowhere else in Africa did people huddle together in such cramped conditions; a modest four-room structure housed an average of sixteen black South Africans. Health statistics suggested that black South Africans would have been better off elsewhere in Africa. A study by Operation Hunger, a famine relief organization feeding 1.3 million impoverished blacks in South Africa, showed that blacks in rural areas and in some urban areas fared worse than their counterparts in neighboring Lesotho, Zambia, Zimbabwe, Botswana, and Swaziland. According to World Bank figures, South Africa belongs in the category of "upper-middle income countries" with countries like Argentina, Brazil, Chile, Mexico, South Korea, Algeria, and Venezuela. Its per capita GNP puts it around the average of that group. But because of living conditions for blacks, South Africa ranked lowest in life expectancy, highest in crude death rate, and third highest in infant mortality rates.[17]

The Black Man's Burden

"I must ask you to give White South Africans credit," said South African Prime Minister D.F. Malan in 1953. "To them millions of semi-barbarous Blacks look for guidance, justice and the Christian way of life. . . . Half a century of intense development has brought about the upliftment of the Bantu far beyond that reached by him in any other country on the sub-continent."[18]

The myth that whites raised destitute blacks from poverty is a cornerstone of the white South African creed. That often-recited belief helps whites reconcile the gross inequality of the country with their sense of self-respect, their belief in their own moral rectitude.

Any South African black knows this myth is a lie. The economic history of blacks has been dispossession, not "upliftment," at the hands of whites. Blacks lived simply but comfortably before white settlement. Whites in South Africa systematically drove blacks from farms and grazing areas and herded them into rural slums, migrant labor camps, and black townships that became cesspools of discontent and despair.

Throughout the early 1800s blacks clashed with British colonists and Afrikaner pioneers in a series of "kaffir wars" over land and cattle. As they pushed north, Europeans subjugated traditional African kingdoms. In the Cape provinces, the influence of missionaries tempered white rule. Slavery was abolished in 1834 and qualified franchise was extended to certain Africans. But the Boer republics of the Orange Free State and the Transvaal refused to grant rights to Africans.

The discovery of diamonds in 1867 and gold in 1873, and the growth of sugar plantations in Natal, transformed the South African economy and the nature of racial conflict. Whites no longer hungered for land alone. They now needed cheap labor. But blacks were reluctant to work on mines, plantations, or railroad construction crews. The sugar barons of Natal began to import Indian laborers who worked on five-year contracts of indentured servitude.

Instead of importing cheap labor, mining companies and farmers compelled Africans into low-paying jobs by means of conquest and punitive taxation. In the Transvaal, subjects of the conquered Ndzundza chiefdom were indentured as farm laborers.[19] In another area, anti-squatting laws tore apart traditional African communities by prohibiting more than five "native families" from living together on private property. Africans who lacked the cash to pay taxes had their cattle seized, depriving them of their livelihood. In addition, whites meddled in tribal politics, helping rival chiefs usurp control of African polities in return for assistance with recruiting African labor.[20]

In 1905, the government instituted annual hut taxes that forced more African farmers and cattle grazers to sell their cattle and go to work in mines and on white farms. Bambata, a Zulu chief near Greytown, Natal, refused to provide census information for the hut tax. The government made plans to depose Bambata and install a more pliable chief. Bambata fled into the hills of Zululand, where he joined forces with a chief unwilling to provide laborers for the public works department. The two inspired the last major armed African resistance to white rule for more than half a century. But Bambata and his spear-carrying *impis* (warriors) were no match for white soldiers with guns. The rebels were cornered and mowed down in a gorge in the Nkandla forest. The conquerers cut off Bambata's head and displayed it to his followers. In all, about 4,000 Africans were killed in the "Bambata rebellion."

On June 16, 1913, the Union of South Africa government passed the Natives' Land Act. As one African writer put it, the law made the African a "pariah in the land of his birth."[21] The law barred Africans from owning or leasing property outside of narrowly delineated areas, which amounted to one eighteenth of the territory of South Africa. Even in that small area, land wasn't for sale. It was controlled by government-approved tribal authorities. (The African areas were later expanded to around 13 percent of South Africa.) The act not only prohibited land ownership, but also limited the ownership of cattle.

The Natives' Land Act wiped out an emerging class of African commercial farmers and sharecroppers. Nearly a million black South African sharecroppers, more than a fifth of the "native" population, rented land from white farmers and accumulated wealth in the form of livestock. With the passage of the law, it became a crime for a white to rent land to an African, punishable by fine or up to six months' imprisonment.

The intent of the act was hardly the "upliftment of the Bantu" that Malan referred to. Poor whites were jealous of the success of African landowners and sharecroppers, some of whom could outbid less-capable white tenant farmers. Wealthy whites weren't satisfied with high rents. They wanted to use Africans as cheap laborers. And white legislators stated plainly that they wanted to stop the gradually expanding ownership of private property by enterprising black farmers.[22]

The impact of the act rivaled the chaos of Stalin's collectivization of agriculture. White farmers extorted cattle and labor from Africans for pittances. If Africans refused their terms, white farmers evicted them. Unaware that the act applied to the entire country, thousands of Africans wandered, selling their cattle and other possessions in desperation as they traveled. Many starved by the roadside.

Sol T. Plaatje, an African journalist and political leader, crisscrossed the country interviewing dispossessed Africans. One family had grown an average of 800 bags of grain each season and sold wool from their livestock. Even after the white landowner received 50 percent of the proceeds as rent, the African family had earned £150 a year. After the passage of the Land Act, however, the white landowner wanted the family to turn over its livestock to him and work for £2 a month. Plaatje met another family whose infant died of hunger and exposure. With nowhere to bury the child in "white" South Africa, the homeless family buried it by the side of the road after nightfall. Plaatje wrote, "Even criminals dropping straight from the gallows have an undisputed claim to six feet of ground on which to rest their criminal remains, but under the cruel Natives' Land Act little children, whose only crime is that God did not make them white, are sometimes denied that right in their ancestral home."

The Natives' Land Act remains on the books, shaping South Africa's peculiar landscape. To this day, blacks cannot own property in 87 percent of the country. The number of black commercial farmers has never matched the modest numbers that existed at the turn of the century. The number of cattle that black farm laborers are permitted to own is usually limited to ten or fewer.

What of the 13 percent of the country that belongs to Africans? These chunks of land are scattered in segments in the midst of "white" South Africa. They are considered "independent" or "self-governing" states, recognized as separate, ethnically distinct nations only by the South African government. Pretoria hand picks tribal and regional leaders in these homelands, people noted for their loyalty to Pretoria rather than their competence or popularity. Moreover, the homelands are comprised of some of the worst land in the country, bereft of steady rainfall, mineral deposits, or harbors. The homelands are rural slums. Abandoned by men who become migrant workers, women, children, and the elderly are left behind. In a country that exports hundreds of millions of dollars of food a year, hunger is widespread in the homelands.

"Painful Memories"

Similar tales of dispossession to those Sol Plaatje recounted in 1916 are fresh in the memories of millions of black South Africans. Since the National Party took power in 1948, it has tried to strengthen the walls of apartheid and hold back the natural forces of urbanization and integration. While industrialization has drawn all races to the cities, the Group Areas Act and homeland policy has pushed blacks away. Sometimes, to keep the races apart, the Nationalist government has moved entire communities like pawns on a giant chess board.

Coloreds and Indians have fallen victim to the same treatment. By 1980, 115,000—one quarter—of all colored and Indian families had been compelled to move, "often losing their homes and businesses at derisory rates of compensation."[23]

As colored, Indian, and African families had to comply with the National Party designs in the 1950s and 1960s, resentment grew, making many people willing participants in organizations that formed from 1979 to 1983.

"This is a street with lovely and painful memories," said Xavier Stuart, a colored carpenter and vegetable vendor, as he strolled down Caroline Street, in the center of the white frontier town of Graaff Reinet. A cobblestone street with aging fruit trees and neatly scrubbed old plaster buildings, its warmth contrasted with the barren, forbidding landscape beyond the town. "My grandmother lived here," he said pointing to the left, "and we lived here. My father used to park his car under this palm tree." Stuart walked around the back of one building and scrambled part way up a lemon tree. "We used to climb this one. My initials are up there somewhere."

In 1964, the Stuart family was told to move to a new colored township, where in the early 1980s Xavier became a member of a community organization that protested high rents and poor living conditions. The old street was declared a white area. The old plaster houses, once slave quarters, were turned into an elegant hotel, the Drostdy. The houses were painted a sparkling white. The Stuart family house became rooms four through seven, each with double bed and bath. The community fruit garden was turned into a swimming pool. A cleaning woman was vacuuming the carpet in one of the rooms. We peered inside. "It makes a pain," Stuart said, pointing to his Adam's apple and biting his lip.

The Stuarts were paid R50 for their expropriated property. Many of the families forced to move from the cobblestone street were so strapped for cash that they sold their teak and yellowwood dining-room furniture for whatever they could get. Today much of that same furniture lends the hotel its old-world ambiance.

I went to the front of the hotel, where a stylish young white woman asked if she could help me. I asked what the buildings had been used for before they became a hotel. She said they hadn't been used at all since they were slave quarters. I asked how much the hotel charged for a room. Did I work for a company that had a discount rate? she asked. No, I replied. "Then you would pay the full rate," she said. For one night, the rate was fifty rand—the total amount paid for the Stuart's expropriated house—breakfast included.

The government also bulldozed dozens of African townships to make room for expanding white areas. In some instances, it displaced Africans who had freehold rights left over from turn-of-the-century British crown grants, exceptions to the Natives' Land Act. From the 1950s through the 1980s, township residents were loaded onto trucks and dumped in new places. From 1960 to the mid-1980s, three-and-a-half-million blacks were victims of forced removals.[24]

The most notorious case of forced removal was the destruction of Sophiatown, a raucous black area of Johannesburg that was the Mecca of black township culture in the 1950s.

> It was South Africa as it might have been. . . . Speak-easies vibrated with African jazz. Miriam Makeba's sweet sultry voice mingled with Hugh Masekela's husky-toned trumpet. Nelson Mandela, the leader of the African National Congress, stirred crowds with speeches in Freedom Square. As writer Nadine Gordimer recalls, white novelists jitterbugged with black poets at parties "that no one ever went home from."[25]

In 1955, seven years after the National Party came to power, Sophiatown was proclaimed a white area and government bulldozers rolled in.

Ramolao Makhene, who later acted in a dramatization of "Sophiatown," was eight years old when the township was demolished. His mother had run a Chinese numbers game and brewed beer from molded brown bread in a shebeen in Sophiatown. "I used to see war movies," Makhene recalled. "Suddenly the soldiers marched off the screen and were coming down Main Street." For fifteen years afterwards, he lived in garages in Soweto and Alexandra, earning himself the nickname "Valiant" because friends joked that he lived like a car.

When a white suburb was built on the rubble of Sophiatown, the government christened it Triomf, Afrikaans for triumph.

It was a hollow triumph. By transplanting black families, apartheid was laying the seeds for a resurgence of protest. Many children who were uprooted with their families grew up to become politically active.

One of the children trucked off to Soweto from Sophiatown was Popo Molefe, who would eventually go to jail for treason. "The family was extremely poor," Popo recalled. His father was a day laborer, his mother a domestic servant. Popo was the fourth of eight children. "We could not afford to maintain all those children."[26]

As a result, Popo was entrusted to his paternal aunt, who raised him with three of his sisters. In 1960, Popo's uncle died and his aunt went to work as a domestic servant. She moved to a backyard room in her white employer's yard and came home only once a month. Popo was eight years old.

Molefe occasionally visited his aunt. Because domestic servants weren't allowed to have visits from their families, Molefe hid in his aunt's room. Traveling through white suburbs, Molefe noticed the difference between white and black areas. "Even before you enter any white house you see these things. There are parks, there are nice hedge trees around some fences. There are lawns in the yards and on the pavements and so on. There are road signs at every important road intersection. These things are not there in the black townships."

Molefe felt uneasy in the white suburbs. Once he was traveling through the suburb of Westdene and a white boy his age started taunting him, calling him "kaffir" [the South African equivalent of nigger] and *"swart gat"* [black asshole]. Molefe tried to ignore him. "I was very scared. I was the only black boy in a sea of white people." But when the white boy slapped Molefe on the face, Molefe hit him back. A white woman walking the opposite direction scolded Molefe. "I could not understand why this woman should threaten me when she should have reprimanded this [white] boy; she was aware that he was the cause of the problem."

Popo started school when he was ten. Before then, his aunt couldn't afford the fees. But because he couldn't afford the required uniforms, Popo was unable to complete the year. He returned to school at age twelve, starting at the equivalent of kindergarten. His elder brother paid for two years of school. Popo's school fees stretched the family to the breaking point. His aunt was earning only R20 a month.

> Very often there was nothing at home. One had to go to school very hungry sometimes. I remember very specifically one day on my way to school, I think at that time I was in the Standard 3 [fifth grade] I was so hungry that morning that I became dizzy on the way and I had to stop and lean on the fence and finally I ended up having collapsed and fainted because I was very hungry.

In 1964, it snowed in Johannesburg, an unusual phenomenon. Popo had no shoes and owned only his school uniform: shorts, a shirt, and a sweater. He walked to school barefoot in the snow.

Teachers took pity on him. For four years, they paid his school fees. To obtain notebooks, Popo entered a competition run by Gold Cross, a company that sold tins of condensed milk. The school children who collected the most wrappers won notebooks. Later he received an academic scholarship. At the same time, however, Popo's family expected him to pull his own weight at home. He started working at age thirteen.

> I learned to fend for myself at a very young age. I had to do various things to earn a living . . . selling apples and peanuts at the football grounds, selling apples at the railway stations on weekends and late in the afternoons when workers were coming back from work. I also had to look for jobs as a caddy at golf courses on weekends. At a later stage, I began to work on Saturdays as a till packer [bagger] at supermarkets in order to earn a living.

Popo lived in the western part of Soweto, known as the "the wild west" because it was frequented by thugs and robbers. They posed a hazard to Popo and other youngsters who got up early to stand in line at the Johannesburg golf course for a turn to caddy. To get there first, Popo would wake up around three in the morning and catch the first train. Occasionally robbers chased children on their way to the trains. "There were occasions on which they actually got me and I had on those occasions to part with the little cents that I had."

The police provided little protection. Indeed, Popo grew to see them as another danger of life in the townships.

> During those days there were policemen called the Black Jacks. It seemed to have been a routine job of theirs to go at the wee hours of the morning (usually around 4 A.M.) into houses checking for permits, seeing if there were any illegals in the houses. This happened very often.
>
> When they came into the house they would knock on every door or sometimes knock on windows, lighting with the torches [flashlights] through the windows. Once they got in, they would get everyone out of bed. Sometimes when this happened other people had to get out of beds undressed or dressed in only night dresses and so on. It was very humiliating . . . in front of children, but that is how it happened very often and they would insult people, "get up," "do this," "who are you?" "where is your permit?"

Molefe was first arrested at around age twenty for not having his pass book. He was standing in front of his home and told the policeman that the permit was inside, but the policeman refused to let him fetch it. Instead the officer handcuffed Molefe and dragged him around the township before letting him go. Later Molefe failed to produce his pass at the Langlaagte railway station, where he had stopped to buy a ticket. He was locked in a cell until a friend went to Molefe's home and brought back his pass book.

At the age of twenty-four, Molefe finished high school. If the South African government had provided free compulsory education for blacks, he might have finished six years earlier in 1970, a peaceful year. As it was, Molefe graduated in 1976, the fateful year of the Soweto student uprising.

As a member of the South African Students Movement begun by Biko, and of the Naledi High School debating society, Molefe was close to many student leaders. In August 1976 he was detained for seven months. In 1979, he attended a meeting at a church in Soweto where blacks decided to form the Soweto Civic Association to articulate the bread-and-butter grievances of Soweto residents. In 1982, Molefe wrote a constitution for the Soweto Youth Congress. In December 1982, he was elected to the Committee of Ten, the executive committee of the Soweto Civic. The next two years would lift Molefe and black protest to new heights.

CHAPTER THREE

The Politics of Refusal

ON AUGUST 20, 1983, Popo Molefe was among a thousand delegates crammed into a community hall in Mitchells Plain, a vast middle-class colored township on the windy sand flats outside Cape Town. Reporters crushed against the stage, television lights glared, and supporters literally hung from the rafters to get a glimpse of the speakers, who feared the roof would collapse. Outside the hall, thousands of people gathered under a giant tent, while others sat in the open air, hardly noticing a light rain while they listened to speeches broadcast over loudspeakers.

The occasion was the public launching of the United Democratic Front, a nationwide anti-apartheid coalition made up of more than 575 of the youth and community groups that had sprung up over the previous four years. Though founded with the narrow purpose of promoting an election boycott, the alliance of Indians, coloreds, and Africans would grow beyond its original purpose and become the principle vehicle of protest in the 1980s, capturing the black imagination and challenging white rule. Even on the day of its birth, the front was the broadest coalition of groups opposing apartheid since the early 1950s. The people on the stage could have formed a hall of fame of South African resistance, with old warriors like the white Helen Joseph, who helped organize a women's march on the Union Buildings in Pretoria in 1956 and who was banned for many years; former ANC leader Archie Gumede; and the Western Cape leader Joe Marks. The younger generation included Molefe and the Rev. Frank Chikane, who had played active roles in 1970s student politics.

In the words of Rev. Chikane, whom years earlier had been beaten by police for addressing them "meneer" instead of "baas," the day would "go into the records of history as an important event bolstering the tide of the struggle, speeding up that day when the people shall say, 'We are free.' "

The crowd interrupted Chikane and other keynote speakers with applause, shouts of *amandla* (power), songs extolling jailed or exiled leaders of the outlawed ANC, and slogans such as "An injury to one is an injury to all." Mzwakhe Mbuli, a young political poet from Soweto, recited in his booming voice:

> Now is the time
> To review the burden of soil
> of nature ringed by the winds of time
> Now is the time . . .
> Now is the time
> to vomit back the remains of fascism to the bucket of imperialism
> Now is the time . . .
> Now is the time to give me roses
> keep them not for my grave to come
> give them to me while my heart beats
> give them to me whilst my heart yearns for jubilee
> Now is the time . . . [1]

The United Democratic Front printed a poster that became the UDF symbol. It depicted a mass of people against a field of red, shaped like a map of South Africa. The drawing was coarsely executed, perhaps suggesting that it was a poster of the people. In the front of the crowd, people were dressed like laborers, their faces radiating confidence and enthusiasm. With their backs straight and arms bent in firm right angles, they conveyed the idea of people standing upright for the first time in years, marching forward below a black banner with UDF written across it in large yellow letters. The river of idealized common folk flowed backwards in a perspective that gave the impression that an endless stream of humanity marched below the UDF banner. "UDF Unites—Apartheid divides," the slogan said across the top.

As the poster suggested, the UDF marked another step in the transformation of the psychology of blacks since June 16, 1976. Deeply influenced by Black Consciousness, the colored Dutch Reformed church minister Allan Boesak declared that the architects of apartheid expected their system to create "a people immobilized by the tranquilizing drugs of apathy and fear." Instead, Boesak proclaimed in a reference to the 1976 student rebellion, apartheid's defenders "faced a rising tide of political and human consciousness that swept away complacency and shook South Africa to its very foundations."

Boesak's speech marked the high point in a day of inspirational oratory. In his high-pitched voice, the short, neatly dressed Boesak named the worst pieces of apartheid legislation and insisted that the Front's members wanted equal rights in a undivided South Africa. "We want all our rights and we want them here and we want them now." Then he shifted to religious grounds, culminating, as Martin Luther King once did, with a line borrowed from the prophet Amos: "We shall not be satisfied until justice rolls down like a waterfall and righteousness like a mighty stream." He then discussed *Nkosi Sikelel' iAfrika, (God Bless Africa)* the church hymn that blacks regard as a national anthem. Building in intensity, Boesak said "I know that today we are singing that hymn with tears in our eyes. We are singing it while we are bowed down by the weight of oppression, and battered by the winds of injustice. . . . We are singing it now while . . . the blood of our children is calling to God from the streets of our nation."

But Boesak didn't want to leave the crowd on such a bitter note. He summoned up an image of a better South Africa, where they would sing their anthem "as free South Africans!" He said

> We shall sing it on that day when . . . no law will put asunder what God has joined together. We shall sing it on that day when in this rich land no child will die of hunger and no infant will die an untimely death; when our elderly will close their eyes in peace, and the wrinkled stomachs of our children will be filled with food. . . . With this faith we shall be able to give justice and peace their rightful place on the throne of our land. . . . With this faith we shall be able to speed the day when all South African children will embrace each other and sing with new meaning: *Nkosi Sikelel' iAfrika!*

The crowd broke into chants of "Boesak! Boesak!" until someone shouted "Amandla!" And the audience thundered "Awethu"—"is ours."

Space

The catalyst for the formation of the United Democratic Front was a series of government reforms proposed in 1982, which blacks saw as an "attempt to sugarcoat the bitter pill of apartheid."[2] A new constitution would create three segregated chambers of Parliament—for whites, Indians, and coloreds—and concentrate power in the office of the state president, a post to be filled by Prime Minister P. W. Botha. Parliamentary responsibilities were divided into "general" affairs and "own" affairs, safeguarding exclusive white residential areas, schools, and budgets and taxes. A President's Council controlled by white National Party members could overrule the Indian and colored chambers of Parliament. A white referendum was planned for November 1983 and elections were scheduled for August 1984. The colored Labor Party, formerly an opponent of the government, and the South African Indian Council announced their intentions to stand for election.

Africans, who made up 70 percent of the population, had no place in the "new dispensation." They would be represented only in the tribal homelands or by local black township councils, which had been reformed in 1982 by Piet Koornhof, a cabinet minister who had once told a press conference in Washington, D.C. that "Apartheid as you came to know it is dead."

P. W. Botha's slogan during the referendum campaign—"adapt or die"—convinced most whites that the National Party and Botha, a lifelong party apparatchik, possessed faint glimmerings of enlightened thought. The new constitution accepted that South Africa was a "multicultural society" (in Botha's words) and took some of the rough edges off the racist rhetoric of the early Nationalist rulers. Although the plan completely left Africans out of central government, the American and British governments cautiously welcomed the constitution as a step in the right direction, and it appeared that the Nationalist Party might end its international isolation and legitimize its rule at home.

The white referendum also was meant to ratify the government's official policy of gradual "reform" ("another perfectly good word ruined," one observer moaned) and effect change by evolution, not revolution.

In the November 2, 1983, referendum, white South Africans approved the new constitution by a two-to-one margin, a victory Botha said exceeded his "wildest expectations." But if Botha believed that the new constitution would be the crowning achievement of his half century of service to the National Party, he proved to be gravely mistaken.

In practice, the effects of the new constitution contradicted the intentions of its framers. While the authors of the constitution hoped to legitimize their power, co-opt greater portions of coloreds and Indians into a compact against Africans (or "broaden democracy," as officials put it), and win international acceptance, the new constitution did the opposite.

By holding a referendum on the new constitution, the government had to allow people to campaign openly against it. And by creating an opportunity for Indians and coloreds to participate—however marginally—the government also created an opportunity for them to protest by simply not participating. Local elections scheduled for November and December 1983 in the black townships gave the same opening to Africans. A low voter turnout would be interpreted as a rejection of the government.

The constitution thus created what black activists call "space," the narrow opportunities they have in which to dissent, conduct political activity, and demonstrate their displeasure with the government. That space begins within the mind of the individual. "No lie can live forever, and the fear of the gun is always overcome by the longing for freedom," Boesak said at Mitchells Plain.

"Even within a totalitarian system, especially one riddled with so many contradictions as South Africa, it is possible to find a crack in the structure, within which a seed may take root and grow, transforming the landscape in the process," wrote Mamphela Ramphele, Biko's former colleague and lover, a distinguished physician and social anthropologist. "This whole process of battling for space within which to operate is complementary to the wider political struggle for a fundamental redistribution of power. It should not be ignored or dismissed as irrelevant. It is a vital component of the new nation struggling to be born."[3]

"Space" isn't an idea unique to South African activists. Ruben Zamora, the Salvadoran leftist, says that finite "political spaces" with undefined boundaries are found in countries that are neither complete dictatorships nor true democracies. "There is a constitution and laws, but they aren't applied equally to all people," Zamora says. He compares opposition politics in such countries to being in a pitch-dark room full of furniture. You know the furniture is there, but you are not sure where. If you bump into a chair, it isn't so serious. You can move a chair. But if you bump into a piano, you might have to step back. Undefined size and shape are characteristics of political spaces. They can be discovered only by trial and error.

In part, these spaces open as a result of the government's quest for acceptance by Western democracies. But a more important element in creating space is the pressure blacks themselves apply on the government. The 1976 uprising forced the National Party to review apartheid, and spurred it, in the words of one academic, to "modernize racial domination."[4] In 1979, the government began to liberalize laws governing black trade unions, to improve black schools, and, in conjunction with the business-backed Urban Foundation, to improve township living conditions. These reforms provided opportunities as well as encouragement for political activity. Among blacks, the "reforms" were seen as "concessions." PEBCO's Thozamile Botha said, "People began to feel that the regime was not invincible. They only needed to increase pressure to bring changes."

A United Front

Plans for the United Democratic Front were conceived several months before the meeting in Mitchells Plain. At a January 1983 meeting held in the Transvaal to protest the South African Indian Council, Boesak called on government opponents to fight the new constitution and to boycott elections for the tricameral legislature if the referendum passed. He also called on Africans to boycott the black local elections scheduled for November and December 1983. "This is the politics of refusal, and it is the only dignified response that blacks can give in this situation," he said.

"In order to succeed," Boesak added,

> we need a united front. There is no reason why churches, civic associations, trade unions, student organizations, and sports bodies should not unite on this issue, pool our resources, inform the people of the fraud that is about to be perpetrated in its name and on the day of the election expose these plans for what they are.[5]

Boesak wasn't the first to call for a united front, but his speech was the spark.[6] That night, about thirty activists drew up a feasibility plan and picked a steering committee for what became the United Democratic Front. Though the sole purpose of the Front was to thwart the constitutional reforms, the preamble of the proposal for a united front was written with a grandeur of those embarking on a great enterprise:

> WHEREAS democracy is the means by which the free will of the people is expressed in electing their chosen representatives to govern, in the processes through which they rule and in the allocation of resources for the benefit of all the people;
>
> AND WHEREAS these truths are cherished by the whole of the civilised world and are goals for which women and men have given up their lives and are willing to die . . . [7]

The committee condemned the new constitution for being drawn up "without genuine consultation" and for entrenching "race and ethnicity [as] the only criteria for the right to take part in government."

Not all activists were convinced about the prudence of forging a national front. Patrick "Terror" Lekota, a former Black Consciousness leader who had just finished a six-year prison sentence, believed that the formation of a front was premature. Later, after becoming publicity secretary of the UDF, Lekota said he saw that "The flood [of opinion] was moving against me." He conceded that "A new spirit was abroad" in South Africa. Black politics was "full of debates and full of optimism. The government was talking about change and everybody was talking about change." It was an atmosphere "that invited free thought and free action taking," he said.[8]

The planning committee wanted to unite disparate grassroots organizations—like PEBCO, DHAC, JORAC, the youth congresses and COSAS—that had grown up between 1979 and 1983. In articulating a broader context, the UDF would rely on a very public style of protest: open meetings and appeals, and non-violent public protests. Before and after its official launch, the front kept meticulous minutes of its meetings. "There was nothing secretive or conspiratorial about it," Lekota said later. "Everything that I did I understood to be done publicly with public motives."[9]

The Calling

Whatever qualms people like Lekota had early in 1983, they were dispelled by the Mitchells Plain meeting. From its foundation, UDF had a tone of optimism. Its followers were propelled by the conviction that, as their slogans said, their "cause is just," the belief that apartheid was immoral and the messianic faith that "Victory is certain."

The sense of moral mission was reinforced by dynamic clergy in the UDF leadership such as Smangaliso Mkhatshwa, a Catholic priest from the Pretoria township of Shoshanguve; Frank Chikane, a young Soweto clergymen who ran the Institute of Contextual Theology, South Africa's center of liberation theology; and Rev. Mcebisi Xundu, the leader of community organizations in the Durban townships. Moslem leaders also backed the front.

These clerics had strained relations with the church establishment. The Catholic church was wary of Mkhatshwa's political activity, especially in light of the Pope's tepid attitude toward the Latin American liberation theologists. Chikane had been suspended by the Apostolic Faith Mission in 1980, the year he was ordained, because of his political involvement. In 1981 he had been suspended again by his conservative, evangelical church, and afterwards he was never posted to a congregation. Xundu had a history of friction with the Anglican church.

Each of them had bucked opinion within black politics as well as within their churches. In the early 1970s, most Blacks Consciousness followers spurned religion. While studying for a science degree at the University of the North in 1972, Chikane had attended church services on a nearby hill. Students had barred services from the campus. By 1974, however, Chikane and another member of the Student Christian Movement had moved into the mainstream student leadership.

The clergy in the UDF leadership broadened the front's appeal outside student circles. Seventy-eight percent of South Africans are Christians, and most of them attend church regularly.

The overarching voice of moral authority at the launch of the UDF was Allan Boesak. He excited black youths, to whom he could speak in the rhetoric of Black Consciousness. He had once declared that "When we speak about the affirmation of our Blackness, the affirmation of our creation as Black, it has nothing to do with *being resigned* to our Blackness. It is precisely what I indicated that it is: the affirmation of our Blackness, the affirmation of our creation as Black. *Black is beautiful.*" [10]

The irony was that Boesak himself said "I share much with Afrikaners culturally" and had once aspired to succeed by the standards of white Afrikanerdom. He had applied to the preeminent Afrikaans university, Stellenbosch, but had been rejected because he was colored. He finished his education in Europe. After the founding of the UDF, Boesak finally visited Stellenbosch, not as a student but as a guest speaker. Asked by a student what he would do if he were prime minister, Boesak joked that he would alter nothing in the statute books except to interchange the words "black" and "white." The brightest of Afrikanerdom didn't appreciate the jest. One student jumped up and pointed an accusing finger at Boesak. "I knew that's what you'd do," he exclaimed.

Boesak liked to tweak whites' moral complacency. Afrikaners liked to think of themselves as descendants of seventeenth-century Calvinist rebels who fled religious persecution in Europe. But the Dutch Reformed church, which was segregated into separate churches for Africans, coloreds, and whites, had provided the theological underpinnings for apartheid and given moral sanction to Afrikaners' supremacy. Boesak challenged apartheid theology in the language and idiom of Afrikaners themselves; every Sunday he preached in Afrikaans at a Dutch Reformed service, freely invoking John Calvin to buttress his own political views. Boesak said Afrikaners had distorted Calvin's theory of election by claiming that God had chosen the Afrikaner nation as a whole, rather than selected individuals. Thus purity of blood had become more important than spiritual calling.

In 1982, Boesak was elected president of the World Alliance of Reformed Churches, an international body, which made him nominally head of the white Afrikaans church. He would not however, be permitted to share a pew in that church. His church was situated in the colored township of Belhar, a relatively well-to-do colored township about halfway between Cape Town and Stellenbosch. "Speaking Afrikaans is not a divine sign," said Boesak, who speaks English at home with his children. "It is an accident of history. I use Afrikaans as a language of protest."

To undermine the legitimacy of National Party rule Boesak stood the theology of the Dutch Reformed Church on its head. In a 1979 open letter to the minister of justice, Boesak said that the Bible teaches that "where there is no justice, authority of the government is no longer derived from God, but it is in conflict with God. Resistance to such a government is both demanded and justified." Boesak added that Calvin himself "echoed this sentiment when he wrote to King Francis in the letter published as the prologue to his *Institutes:* 'For where the glory of God is not made the end of the government, it is not a legitimate sovereignty, but a usurpation.' . . . Calvin also stated clearly that 'wordly princes' lose all their power when they rise up against God. Christians should resist such a power, not obey it."[11]

For those coloreds, Indians, and Africans not inclined to rebel against authority, Boesak laid the charge of subversion against the government. Those that resisted the government were being loyal to a higher authority.

Boycott: The "Politics of Refusal"

To the government, the UDF was not answering a divine call, but the call of the ANC. The government later alleged that Boesak merely parroted ANC president Oliver Tambo, who had made passing reference to the need for a united front in a speech two weeks before Boesak made his first appeal.

But UDF publicity secretary Terror Lekota noted that Tambo and others had made such calls before without any effect. "If anybody is to be blamed for the formation of the UDF, it must be the government," Lekota said. "If the government did not introduce that [new] dispensation which was not satisfactory, we would not have had the ground to form the UDF." The government grossly miscalculated the impact of the new constitution. Instead of defusing tension and dividing non-whites, the constitution galvanized Africans, Indians, and coloreds in a way Tambo could never do.

Among Africans, the constitutional reforms were "seen as a clever way of denying the black people, African people, the right to participate in the government," said Popo Molefe, who was elected general secretary of the UDF.[12] "Every law that had been passed had always been decided for us by white people," Lekota added. Once again, "We had not been consulted."

According to a pamphlet distributed at the UDF's national launch, the government had given blacks "a third-class seat in their apartheid train" by setting up local black authorities and black councils under the Koornhof bills.[13] The local black authorities resembled an earlier scheme known officially as the Urban Bantu Councils (UBCs), but in the townships known as the Useless Boys Clubs. Molefe called the new local black councils poor "substitutes for a meaningful vote in the central government." To make matters worse, the new local authorities were born into bankruptcy. They were expected to be financially independent even though the normal sources of revenue for local government—property and sales taxes—weren't available. Sales taxes were paid to the central government, and by law the central government owned all the property in the townships. Moreover, the white cabinet minister for black affairs could veto any decision taken by the local black councils. The minister could dissolve any black council and dismiss its members. "It was really difficult to have a minister who is elected by a white constituency, who is accountable to the white constituency . . . meet the interests of the black people," Molefe said.[14]

Black leaders outside the UDF also condemned the local elections. Chief Mangosuthu Gatsha Buthelezi, chief minister of the KwaZulu homeland, called the black community councils "stage props for the political farce of the tricameral Parliament."[15]

The black local elections tested the UDF and its politics of refusal. In the November and December 1983 elections for black local authorities, African voter turnout slumped to 21 percent of registered voters, from 30 percent in 1978. The UDF contended that most Africans weren't registered and thus the true turnout ran only half that figure. In Soweto, voter turnout fell to 10.7 percent of registered voters, only 5.2 percent of eligible voters, according to the UDF.[16] Moreover, fewer blacks were willing to run for office. In more than a quarter of the wards, candidates ran uncontested.[17] Five entire councils were nominated and took office unopposed.

The UDF's call to "boycott the dummy elections" also appealed to Indians, who had their own peculiar history of oppression. South Africans of Indian origin descend mostly from workers imported between 1860 and 1911 by English sugar barons in the Natal province who couldn't entice Africans to work in the cane fields. The Indians worked as indentured servants, earning about one pound, ten shillings a month. Afterwards, most Indians chose to stay in Natal, then a British colony. As Indians grew successful running small businesses, whites became concerned about competition. In 1896 the first racially discriminatory law was passed against Indians, restricting their trading rights, job opportunities, and movement around the country.

The problems of indentured Indian laborers prompted the arrival of the young Mohandas K. Gandhi. Gandhi set up the Natal Indian Congress in 1894 and published a newspaper from a settlement called Phoenix on a small grassy hill fourteen miles from Durban. He also served as a stretcher carrier during the bloody Bambata rebellion. At the Phoenix settlement, Gandhi conceived his theory that *satyagraha*, a force of the soul, could topple empires. *Satyagraha* has been translated as passive resistance, though Gandhi preferred "firmness in the truth." It entailed civil disobedience, strikes, lying down on railway tracks, and facing police charges without running away or hitting back.

Three-quarters of a century after Gandhi returned to India, and forty years after the British withdrawal from India, South African Indians still couldn't vote, live where they wanted, or receive equal educations. Until June 1975, Indians needed permits to travel from one province of South Africa to another. Until 1986, Indians were forbidden from living in the Orange Free State.

Still the government believed it could woo Indian support by convincing increasingly prosperous Indians that they had a stake in the system and by fanning Indian fears of Zulu nationalism, which in 1949 had led to Zulu-Indian riots in Durban where most Indians lived.

Instead, the tricameral Parliament breathed life into Gandhi's principles. The Natal Indian Congress, revived in 1970, attracted new members, including Gandhi's granddaughter Ela Ramgobin. The Transvaal Indian Congress, dormant since the early 1960s, was revived in 1983. The Durban Housing Action Committee with its large Indian following joined the UDF. Ela Ramgobin and her husband Mewa joined the call for a boycott of the elections and their five children in 1984 aged fourteen to twenty-one, were all arrested at various protests.

The alienation of South African Indians revealed a flaw in government strategy. While its co-optive policies tried to divide people along class lines, its apartheid policies lumped different elements of each race together, building solidarity. The Durban Housing Action Committee was backed by both poor and rich Indians. The Natal Indian Congress commanded the loyalty of committed socialists, even though its president was a liberal who admired Gandhi and Winston Churchill. Though they differed on a new social order, they were united in opposition to apartheid.

When election day came in August 1984, just 20.29 percent of registered

Indian voters turned out, representing 16.2 percent of eligible voters.[18] Some new parliamentarians won election with as few as 100 votes, often representing fewer than than 5 percent of registered voters.

At first blush, coloreds should have made willing participants in the tricameral Parliament. Culturally close, coloreds and Afrikaners shared the same language, religion, and passion for rugby. (Africans favored soccer.) "A significant number of coloreds would consider themselves 'Afrikaans' in many ways," Boesak said. Many called themselves "brown Afrikaners" as opposed to "white Afrikaners."

For that very reason, though, coloreds were among the most embittered outsiders in the apartheid system. "They say 'Afrikanerdom' is a cultural concept, but it is a racist concept," Boesak concluded. The products of racially mixed marriages, coloreds were literally the children of Afrikanerdom, although spurned by their own flesh and blood.

The earliest apartheid legislation passed after the Nationalists' 1948 election victory—in particular, the Prohibition of Mixed Marriages Act and the clause in the Immorality Amendment Act prohibiting intercourse between whites and coloreds—was aimed directly at the colored. Mixed marriage and intercourse had long been banned for Africans.

The Nationalists also abolished the "entrenched clauses" of the constitution adopted by the Union of South Africa in 1910. Under these clauses, coloreds could qualify to vote on a common voters' roll with whites in the Cape Province. In some districts, they held swing votes. In 1956, the National Party packed the high court with Nationalist supporters after the court ruled that taking coloreds off the voter rolls violated the constitution.

Coloreds especially loathed the Group Areas Act of 1950, which forced hundreds of thousands of coloreds to move out of areas that the Nationalist government summarily declared "white." Many were moved to poor areas like Retreat; others were relocated to the monotonous middle-class colored township of Mitchells Plain. In 1983, the repeal of the act was coloreds' number-one priority. The refusal of the government to commit itself to erasing the Group Areas Act from the statute books convinced most coloreds that the government's commitment to sharing power wasn't even skin deep.

Yusuf Abrams was a schoolteacher in Retreat. One of his ancestors came from the Indonesian island of Java and worked for the Dutch East India Company as a chef. In return for his service, the company gave Abrams' ancestor land in the Newlands area of Cape Town. The land, and the large house on it, was within walking distance from stores and supermarkets and an easy bus ride to town. It was located near a park with a thick cool forest. His father, a sports fan, played cricket and rugby and held season tickets to the rugby matches at Newlands stadium. In 1950, however, the government passed the Group Areas Act barring blacks from living in areas declared "white." Abrams' father was paid R1,500 for the plot in 1963 and shuffled off to a colored township. After the expropriation of the house, the family grew bitter. The value of the Newlands property rose steadily (to close to R25,000 by 1984), while the Abrams family was forced to become tenants of the government.

After growing up feeling that they were close to white South African society, the Abrams family felt betrayed. "My auntie's husband fought in the second world war and never returned. And what did she get for it? We were conned into thinking we were fighting for democracy," Abrams said. After a time, Abrams' father stopped going to the rugby matches in compliance with a colored boycott of official government-sponsored sports events. Abrams' daughter became involved in student politics, winning a place on the unofficial students' representatives council in 1984 at the age of fourteen, a position that made her a potential target for detention. Abrams sympathized with his daughter. "My father told us not to protest or we'd be locked up. I don't say that to my daughter. I dare not. I'll have to stand by her. Perhaps she's doing what I should be doing." The entire family stayed home when election day came around.

Many of the people in Retreat came from District Six, in 1984 a vacant area that lay like a scar in the middle of Cape Town. District Six, walking distance from the center of Cape Town, was once a multiracial area with the stunning cliffs of Table Mountain as a backdrop and the sparkling ocean and harbor below. Under the Group Areas Act, the government declared District Six "white." In 1965, after a long dispute, the government bulldozed the area. P. W. Botha, then a deputy minister, signed the final order of execution. A newspaper ran a cartoon of a vengeful Botha in front of the bulldozers declaring with biblical irony, "Let there be white." The government leveled the stone-and-stucco houses in the crowded quarter, leaving only three boarded-up mosques in a grassy meadow as a memorial to the once-vibrant neighborhood. The Indians and coloreds who lived there were packed off to the barren sandy Cape Flats, where they lived in run-down housing projects ten miles from the center of town. "As poor as people were in District Six, life wasn't as harsh as it is on the sandy Cape Flats, away from everything," said Abdullah Mohammed Omar, an Indian advocate.

In the elections for the colored house of parliament, 30.9 percent of registered voters turned out at the polls despite unrest. The turnout varied from area to area. In the home district of the Labor Party leader Alan Hendrickse, 46.7 percent of registered voters cast their ballots, but in Retreat, only 11.1 percent of registered voters showed up. Many coloreds hadn't registered. The voter turnout represented 18.1 percent of eligible voters.[19]

A Somewhat United Front

Although the election boycotts were successful, the word "united" at times seemed a more wishful than accurate description of the United Democratic Front. By its nature, the UDF was a loose, somewhat chaotic body.

Though the unification of more than 575 organizations enabled the coalition to claim a membership of hundreds of thousands virtually overnight, it was a disparate grouping.

In early 1984, the UDF affiliates included:[20]

Region	Student Groups	Youth Groups	Trade Unions	Women	Civic	Religious	Political	Others
T'VAAL	12	16	8	8	30	11	9	16
NATAL	8	15	5	3	28	4	11	7
W. CAPE	23	271*	2	20	27	4	9	4
E. CAPE	3	13	3	2	2	2	4	4
ORANGE FREE STATE	1	1	—	—	—	—	—	—

* 235 of these youth organizations were affiliates of Inter-Church Youth.

The UDF did not make policy for its affiliates. The affiliates could take up UDF campaigns in ways they thought best suited to their constituencies. Some didn't respond at all. Soweto activists refused to collect signatures for one of the UDF's first campaigns—to get a million names on a petition against the new constitution—and the drive came up short of its goal.

Voting power within the front was not proportional to the size of the affiliates. Each affiliate had equal say, giving a lopsided voice to the plethora of student and youth groups around the country. Decisions were supposed to be reached by consensus. As a result, major decisions took excruciatingly long, often a couple of months, while the government could act swiftly and decisively.

While the UDF steadily gained public momentum, behind the scenes its founders quarreled over policy, tactics and strategy. One dispute focused on whether the front should endorse the ANC's Freedom Charter. The UDF initially took no stand in an effort to make the front as broad as possible and to draw in people who did not subscribe to the charter, but it still failed to attract the Azanian Peoples Organization (AZAPO) which regarded itself as the heir to the Black Consciousness movement.

Differences also emerged over the best way to use the space that had opened up as a result of the new constitution. At that time, the government was planning to hold separate referenda for Indians and coloreds after whites approved the new constitution. One UDF group favored contesting the planned referendum among Indians. "The Natal UDF was persuaded that it would be tactically good to contest the referendum. That's what our activists on the ground told us," said a leading member of the Natal Indian Congress. "We were confident that a majority of voters would say no and that that would be a more powerful statement than a boycott," the Indian Congress leader said later. Some leftists cited Lenin's endorsement of participation in the 1905 Duma as precedent.

Other factions disagreed. A position paper written after a fractious meeting in Port Elizabeth said that a referendum was risky because it could be rigged. "We are dealing here with a crook of a player in this game—South Africa is a stranger to fair play when it comes to things that threaten its very principles," the paper said. In addition, the UDF was unsure of its support. "The delegates from both the Western Cape and Transvaal have indicated that their communities may still vote 'yes'," the paper warned. Finally, the paper's authors worried that it would confuse UDF followers first to urge participation in a referendum and later a boycott of elections for the tricameral Parliament if the government's plan won. "We may be losers in the manipulated polls and find ourselves in an embarrassing situation of having to campaign for a boycott of the elections emanating from a referendum we have participated in."[21]

While the question of participation might seem a relatively minor tactical point, within black politics the critical fault lines were tactics, not ideology. So the dispute took on a special intensity, raging for more than two months without being resolved. The Natal UDF executive held firm, while the Cape leadership said that contesting the referendum was tantamount to participating in the new Parliament. The leadership from the Transvaal wavered. "Feelings were so strong that many felt it would destroy the UDF" in its infancy, one activist said later. At a stormy meeting in a church hall near Pretoria, the thirty members of the UDF national executive committee finally defeated the idea of contesting the referendum.

As it turned out, the government canceled the colored and Indian referenda and the issue became moot. Boycott became the front's tactic for all elections.

Hostility to anyone willing to participate in a government structure kept the UDF distant from Chief Mangosuthu Gatsha Buthelezi, chief minister of the KwaZulu homeland. Neither the chief nor his powerful Inkatha movement joined the UDF.

In order to placate all its factions, the UDF's policies were so vague and uncertain that its co-president Archie Gumede said at the founding conference that "It is not an organization. It is a front and it is composed of different organizations which do not agree necessarily in all respects with each other's point of view." It was impossible, Gumede said, to make a policy statement of any kind, except to say that the front was dedicated to the abolition of apartheid.

The strength of UDF affiliates at the grassroots level cemented the front during this disarray. The affiliates were gathering support by sticking close to the bread-and-butter concerns that had fed the growth of community organizations since 1979.

The mixture of political and daily concerns was reflected in the pages of the partisan press like *Grassroots,* a non-profit newspaper published by community activists in the Cape Town area. Though *Grassroots* was founded before the UDF, it quickly took up the UDF's cause. Written in Xhosa (a language spoken by most blacks in the Cape), Afrikaans, and English, its articles openly supported UDF campaigns and leaders. When the UDF launched the Million Signature Campaign to oppose the tricameral Parliament, the paper gave the campaign front-page coverage. In the first issue of 1984, *Grassroots* ran a photo of the UDF leadership looking on as Rev. Boesak made his signature the first on the petition. In March 1984, while the signature campaign was still lagging, *Grassroots* ran a headline that covered half the front page of the tabloid: "Thousands Sign For Freedom." At that point, according to a thermometer with the letters UDF in the bulb, only 10,000 people had signed in the Western Cape. The next month only 75,000 had signed nationwide, far behind the pace needed to reach a million signatures. While the campaign faltered, *Grassroots* played cheerleader. "The UDF is moving forward," it said optimistically.

At the same time, *Grassroots* paid close attention to the economic issues that underpinned the concerns of the UDF affiliates and the newspaper's original motivation. In its first issue in 1984, *Grassroots* ran a front-page story about a chemical workers' strike. Inside, it ran a two-page centerfold about the 12- to 15-hour days logged by dairy workers. The March issue ran a banner headline "Starvation Wages" about the Western Cape minimum wage, which ran well below the poverty line. The May issue featured a call for a R10-a-week raise for garment workers in Cape Town. The June centerfold explained the impact of an increase in the general sales tax. The journal's back pages were devoted to advice columns on everything from how to write a job application letter to who could qualify for a government maintenance grant, from the dangers of "hire purchase" (installment) plans to how to cook Greek lentil soup.

Blunders by the government kept these issues at the fore. Financially strapped by the recession that set in during the first quarter of 1982, the government increased the general sales tax (GST), cut bus and bread subsidies, raised township rents, and boosted water and electricity rates.

To many blacks, the new measures appeared to be connected to the new black councils. "Perhaps nobody knew quite how bitterly and how soon we would have to pay for this new system," Cassim Saloojee, a member of the UDF's Transvaal executive committee, said on the first anniversary of the UDF launch. Saloojee blamed hikes in rents, sales taxes, and bread prices on the government's need "to balance the books of these hopeless councils."[22]

In 1983, UDF leader Matthew Goniwe wrote that "a new approach to organization, mobilization, and education emerged after 1977—an approach which emphasized grassroots, democratic organizations *around issues which directly affected people.*" Unlike the African National Congress in the 1950s, everyday problems of housing, education, wages, and unemployment preceded more intellectual concepts like democracy.

However, the UDF was more than the sum of its parts. The founding of the UDF capped the rebirth of black organization and put hundreds of local community issues into a national political context. "Problems at local levels can be traced back to the lack of political rights and representation," Goniwe said.[23]

A Human Sciences Research Council survey conducted in 1984 revealed that small percentages of UDF followers said they like the UDF because it "represents all groups," "makes people aware of their rights," "helps people fight for their rights," or "will help blacks." Another 17.1 percent of UDF supporters said they supported the front because it "solves our problems." But twice as many, the largest single category of UDF supporters, backed the front because they believed it was "fighting for democracy."[24]

CHAPTER FOUR

The Forgotten Well

THE FOUNDERS OF THE UDF embraced and glorified the traditions of black resistance. By connecting the fledgling front to the past, the UDF tried to bestow dignity and legitimacy to its enterprise. In contrast to the 1976 leadership, the UDF founders treated the struggles of the past with pride, rather than shame.

To the extent that they knew black history, the students who rebelled in 1976 viewed the political organizations of the past, the African National Congress and the Pan Africanist Congress, as failures. They mistrusted the leadership that had bungled so badly. Other black students were oblivious to this history. Instead, as Mpho Mashinini recalled, students believed they were the new "fire" and that they would reinvent black resistance from scratch.

"Terror" Lekota, who had acquired his nickname because of his soccer prowess in school, was part of that generation. A leading figure in the Black Consciousness movement, Lekota was sentenced in December 1976 to six years in jail. In prison, Lekota underwent a transformation. Imprisoned with legends such as Mandela and Sisulu, Lekota had a "golden opportunity to learn the secret of the path my people had travelled . . . from the men who had given almost everything that they had for the cause of freedom." He found, he said, the "forgotten well of the history of my people" and emerged from prison in 1982 a history buff. He talked about the highlights as well as the failures of the past. When he became the UDF publicity secretary in 1983, he regaled people at rallies with stories from black resistance, stories omitted from the history books read in state schools.

Modern black resistance dates to the 1912 founding of the African National Congress, then known as the South African Natives National Congress.

The ANC was founded by the elite of African society: schoolteachers, literate clerks, chiefs, and professionals. They were for the most part modern Africans. They were Christians, moderate people educated by British and American missionaries. They cut across tribal lines.

In its first phase of protest, the ANC sent polite petitions to the British government. Its leaders believed they could reverse oppressive legislation and disenfranchisement by pricking the conscience of London, which, after all, had won the Boer War and made all of South Africa a British domain. "Place yourself in our shoes," Sol T. Plaatje wrote in *Native Life in South Africa,* the exposé of the effects of the Land Act that Plaatje published in England. "This appeal is not on behalf of the naked hordes of cannibals who are represented in the fantastic pictures displayed in the shop windows in Europe, most of them imaginary; it is on behalf of five million loyal British subjects." Plaatje reminded readers that it was the "the 200,000 subterranean heroes," Africans working in underground mines, who produced the gold "to maintain the credit of the Empire with a weekly output of £750,000 worth of raw gold."

But Plaatje's appeals failed to rouse the British. Faced with impending war in Europe and chastened by the cost of the Boer War, Britain had little inclination to intervene again in South Africa as long as it remained loyal to the empire.

During the second phase of protest, individual ANC notables took part in segregated government institutions, joining the powerless Natives Representative Council in 1936. Many ANC leaders hoped they could persuade the government to expand the Council's scope or use the Council to voice Africans' desires for full franchise. African and colored politicians outside the ANC, especially members of the All African Convention, believed the exercise was pointless and attacked the ANC for collaborating with the government. But the ANC allowed members to participate until the late 1940s, when they finally quit the Council in frustration, calling it a "toy telephone."

In 1949, a year after the National Party took power, the ANC adopted a "program of action," giving birth to the third phase of protest. The 1949 program transformed the ANC into a more vigorous vehicle of popular protest. It called for civil disobedience, strikes, boycotts, and stay-at-homes (general strikes). African nationalism was asserting itself. In pushing a more militant platform, the leaders of the ANC Youth League swept aside much of the ANC's old guard. "The old guard regarded the ANC as an exclusive club. They thought the ANC was an organization that belonged to them through their fathers," recalls Robert Matji, a Communist Party member and an ANC member who moved to the Eastern Cape to shake up its leadership. Within two years, he and other younger ANC members had captured the senior positions of the Eastern Cape.

In the Transvaal, militant African nationalists Nelson Mandela and Walter Sisulu were spearheading a similar overhaul. They toppled the authoritarian ANC president Xuma, who expected everybody to rise in respect when he entered at annual meetings.

After Xuma was ousted, Sisulu became ANC general secretary and Mandela the national organizer. Communist Party members Moses Kotane and J. B. Marks also joined the ANC executive. With a few exceptions like Matji, the ANC leadership remained elite. Mandela and Oliver Tambo were lawyers, the new ANC president Moroka a physician, and his successor, Lutuli, a chief. But the new leadership pushed a new agenda, sought to widen the ANC's base of support and to increase mass participation in ANC campaigns. In a circular, Matji bid "good riddance" to the "pleading, cowardly" and "tea-drinking leaders" of the past.[1]

In 1952 the ANC waged the Defiance Campaign, putting into practice the 1949 program of action. Africans crossed over to white lines at post offices and rest rooms, entered railway stations through "Europeans only" entrances, ignored curfews, and visited "native locations" without permits. Thousands were arrested. Small numbers of Indians and whites joined the protests. For the most part, they received light sentences or small fines. The daring of the campaign won new followers to the ANC. Paid ANC membership soared to about 100,000, but the ANC failed to halt new pieces of apartheid legislation.

In 1955, the ANC and its white, Indian, and colored allies convened a "congress of the people" on a private athletic field in Kliptown about fifteen miles from Johannesburg, where delegates adopted the "Freedom Charter," a statement of principles and policy that remains the movement's holy tablet today. Trouble followed, however. In 1956, the government arrested the top leaders of the ANC, charging them with treason. Also accused were leading Indian and white activists, including several members of the tiny South African Communist Party. The trial dragged on for more than four years until March 1961 when the court ruled that the prosecution had failed to prove that the ANC's policy was one of incitement to violence.

In 1959, the ANC split. A group committed to an exclusive African nationalism and opposed to the Congress Alliance with communists, whites, and Indians broke away to form the Pan Africanist Congress. Paraphrasing Abraham Lincoln, the PAC wanted government "of the Africans by the Africans for Africans" without guarantees for minority rights. PAC president Robert Sobukwe said "Because they benefit materially from the present set-up, [whites] cannot completely identify themselves with that cause."[2] There was no place for whites in the PAC struggle. The ANC's long record of failure, not a single victory in forty-seven years of protest, spurred these Africanists to look elsewhere for inspiration. The PAC flag showed a black map of Africa with a gold star shining forth from newly independent Ghana.[3]

Less than a year later, an anti-pass campaign initiated by the fledgling PAC precipitated the Sharpeville crisis. Police fired on demonstrators, killing sixty-seven people and wounding 186 others. Riots broke out. For a couple of weeks, the government reeled from the shock of riots and international condemnation. But soon it struck back. It detained thousands of Africans declared a state of emergency, and banned the ANC and PAC.

During the fourth phase of black resistance that preceded the docile 1960s, ANC and PAC followers turned to violence. Underground groups like Poqo, made up of PAC members, and Umkhonto we Sizwe, founded by the South African Communist Party and the ANC, launched bomb attacks over the next three years. In 1963, however, these groups were uprooted. PAC and ANC leaders either fled into exile or were captured and sentenced to long periods in jail on Robben Island, where Terror Lekota found them in 1976.

A Peculiar Alumni Association

Six miles past the luxury beachfront homes of Cape Town's Clifton Beach lies a tiny outcrop of limestone—a bleak, windswept island caught in the icy Benguela current that flows up from Antarctica. A Readers' Digest guide once listed Robben Island as "noted for its arum lillies" and "superb" view.

But Robben Island has been better known among blacks as home to more than 500 of South Africa's most important political prisoners, the rock where resistance has lived and grown. It has been a sort of graduate school for revolutionaries, where raw youths who have rallied school boycotts have discussed technique with elderly founders of the armed struggle who first masterminded bombing and sabotage campaigns aimed at overthrowing the South African state.

A South African hotel mogul wanted to buy the island and turn it into a gambling resort in the mid-1980s, but the government decided to preserve it as a prison, with scores of people tried every year for political crimes. The island's distance from the mainland across frigid waters makes it virtually impossible to escape.

In the late 1970s and early 1980s, many Robben Island prisoners began to return to the mainland after finishing their sentences. Such released prisoners formed a peculiar sort of alumni association, schooled in concrete cells and taught by a tenured faculty of lifetime maximum-security prisoners.

The government had hoped that half a lifetime behind bars would dampen the revolutionary fervor of two generations of political prisoners, one sentenced after the government crushed the military wings of the ANC and PAC in 1963 and the other imprisoned after the 1976 student uprising. Instead Robben Island alumni formed a network of activists who nurtured resistance.

"There is no rehabilitation in prison. Even an ordinary criminal is a more hardened criminal when he comes out," said Steve Tshwete, once a prisoner of Robben Island and the first UDF president of the Border Region straddling the Ciskei and Transkei homelands. Terror Lekota wrote to a friend that "Black communities have wallowed so long under the security of political rightlessness and economic deprivation that imprisonment only aggravates an existing condition. It is not something new."

As a result, political prisoners finish their sentences as determined to end apartheid as when they began. One man who left prison after nearly two decades told me during his first week on the mainland that his plans were uncertain because, "It isn't up to me. It is up to the organization and my comrades."

Robben Island alumni bolstered the leadership of the UDF and its affiliates in the early 1980s. Half the executive committee members of the Port Elizabeth Black Civic Organization were graduates of Robben Island, including Henry Fazzie, one of the first ANC members sent outside the country for military training in the early 1960s. Other former prisoners became organizers for black trade unions, and others have joined private educational programs such as the South African Council on Higher Education (SACHED).

When they return, most Island alumni possess a political maturity and a mystique that commands authority among more hot-headed radicals. Robben Island graduates, especially those sentenced in the early 1960s, form an important link between generations. Many of the ANC men who landed on the island for fifteen-year sentences in the early 1960s had joined the group during the late 1950s. They fondly remembered the peak of peaceful protest. (Long-term women prisoners were sent to various jails on the mainland.) However, although seasoned by years in jail, the men who first turned to violence against the government in 1961 also shared much with the angry youth of the 1970s and 1980s.

Robben Island veterans were usually patient and not easily discouraged. "Being on Robben Island taught me to listen to people. The old chaps there were a reservoir of knowledge," recalled Trevor Wentzel, a colored from the Cape Flats.

"There is no doubt about the significant contribution ex-political prisoners have and continue to make within the organization," wrote a University of the Witwatersrand student, Khehla Shubane, in a paper about the Soweto Youth Congress. Shubane, convicted in 1976 of helping young blacks cross the border to join the ANC, was himself a highly regarded product of the island. He said,

> These people enjoy a great deal of political trust within the organization. In an event of differences in opinion which threaten cooperation within the organization, people from prison have played a role of emphasizing the overriding importance of unity. Debate and differences of opinion within the organization, they argue, are crucial and should go on. This, however, should not threaten the unity which exists within the organization.

This maturity often grew on the island. Lekota recalls that, "Fighters with many years of struggle systematically passed onto us their accumulated experience." Through smuggled notes and discreet meetings, prisoners conducted courses in history, politics, and economics. They debated historical and current events in groups. Senior prisoners provided guidance and settled disputes between younger prisoners. Most older men were serving life sentences for roles in the ANC military wing, Umkhonto we Sizwe. Nelson Mandela and Walter Sisulu were the island's leading lights until 1982, when the government, realizing the political strength growing among inmates, transferred them to Pollsmoor Prison on the Cape peninsula.

Other senior activists took their place, including Govan Mbeki, a septuagenarian Communist Party member whose son, Thabo, is a leader of the ANC in exile. (Thabo used to write to his father but never received replies. He said that he assumed that his father never received his letters.) Author of a book on South African peasant revolts, the elder Mbeki was sentenced along with Mandela. Though his eyesight was weak and he tired easily, Mbeki ran classes on economics. A gentle man, he liked to bask in the sun and listen to other prisoners read the Sunday newspapers out loud while he commented on articles.

Harry Gwala became another influential teacher during his second sentence on the island. He taught about black trade unions and played a leading role in converting adherents of the Black Consciousness movement into members of the non-racial ANC tradition. "Tell me," Seth Mazibuko recalls Gwala saying to him once, "What is Black Consciousness?" Mazibuko responded with a variety of "Black is beautiful" slogans. "But are you a beautician or a politician?" Gwala pressed, urging Mazibuko to think more rigorously.

Conducting education in a maximum security prison is never easy. Inmates learned to cultivate allies on the prison staff and secretly pass notes during their recess periods. Some documents were smuggled inside books. The island was divided into several sections, isolating top political prisoners in single, seven-foot-square concrete cells. Although prisoners in communal cells had little contact with the leadership, clandestine communication continued.

Contact with prison guards gave prisoners insight into the thoughts of whites they would normally never come in contact with. People commonly known as the enemy became people. "Human beings, however lowly or less educated they may be, have their own value systems, intelligence and a conscience to go with," Lekota once said in a letter. "In their own humble ways they can discriminate between right and wrong when the two are contrasted. . . . That has been the discovery of many of us in the liberation struggle."

Lekota described the process of winning a warder's confidence.

> As they would have been harangued with the diatribe of us being enemies, we started by being always courteous to them:
>
> 'More meneer!' (good morning sir in Afrikaans.)
>
> 'What?' the chap wonders, 'A terrorist who speaks my language? Is courteous and friendly? But these people are supposed to be the onslaught.'
>
> Those questions led to doubts and soon enough genuine questions about what wrong we had done. Many of those who looked after us ended up with troubled consciences and very significant unanswered questions—not about us but about those who had assigned them to guard us and the system that they had to defend.

It is said that one of the guards committed suicide after he came to know his wards. Others are said to have passed correspondence courses with the help of inmates.

But Robben Island could not prepare prisoners completely for life on the mainland. There is a comfortable predictability about prison. Terror Lekota says, "Whereas in everyday life out of prison, Africans cannot tell the course their fate might or might not take, once sentenced to a prison term, they know with a certain confidence what tomorrow will bring. This is ordinarily missing in 'normal' life."

Many released prisoners returned to a world that only vaguely resembled the one they left. When Mbeki was released in 1987, he was taken by car back to the home he left a quarter century earlier. He needed help getting out of the car because he couldn't figure out how the unfamiliar car door handle worked.

One Island alumnus in East London said that when he waited at the bus stop, he would stare into people's faces, thinking he saw someone who looked familiar. Then he realized that after two decades it couldn't be the same person. "I don't recognize anyone," he said. Unmarried and in his mid-forties, he missed his friends on Robben Island.

Despite loneliness, the East London man possessed a distinctive attitude taught on the Island. As people clambered onto a bus one rainy day, a black woman behind him muttered that black people will never learn. "I couldn't let that pass," he recalled. So he turned and calmly explained why people forced into miserable living conditions might act that way. The woman stared and said, "You must not be from around here."

Past Is Present: Faces Behind the Front

Robben Island alumni were but a few of the thousand delegates at the UDF launch in August 1983, inconspicuously mingling with a vast cross section of black society. Like tributaries running into a stream, the major strains of black resistance merged into the UDF and shaped its course: the non-collaboration principles of the Unity Movement, the non-racialism of the ANC, and the self-assurance and militancy of Black Consciousness.

Every generation of African activism since World War II came together in the UDF: survivors of the ANC's Defiance Campaign of civil disobedience in the 1950s, former commanders in the ANC's 1961–1963 sabotage campaign, members of the Black Consciousness generation of 1976, founders of the Congress of South African Students in 1979, and a new 1980s generation of impatient teenagers.

From the ANC, the UDF borrowed the principle of "non-racialism" meaning that a person of any race—including white—would be welcomed into its fold. The first Western Cape executive committee included Andrew Boraine, a white University of Cape Town student leader whose father was a member of the white parliamentary opposition. The first Transvaal executive committee included Lloyd Vogelman, a white clinical psychology student at the University of the Witwatersrand. Helen Joseph was named a patron of the front. So was Denis Goldberg, a white civil engineer then serving a life sentence in prison for membership in the high command of the ANC's military wing in the early 1960s.

White intellectuals also worked behind the scenes to aid the front, writing position papers and mapping strategy. Jeremy Cronin, a white Cape Town academic, who served a prison sentence for ANC activity, was a voice in the Western Cape UDF. Indians and coloreds also held several key posts.

Though the UDF initially didn't endorse the ANC's Freedom Charter, the admission of whites to the front offended Black Consciousness proponents and Africanists, who felt that while whites might have a place in a post-apartheid society, blacks could liberate themselves only through their own efforts. In their view, whites had no role in the struggle for black freedom. Despite UDF overtures, the Azanian Peoples Organization (which saw itself as the heir to Black Consciousness organizations) and the National Forum stayed outside the UDF. "The word 'democratic' is code among charterists for 'including whites'," said Neville Alexander, leader of the National Forum, explaining why he wouldn't join the front.

However, many former Black Consciousness leaders like Chikane, Mkhatshwa, and Molefe joined. Curtis Nkondo, former president of AZAPO, defected to the UDF as did later Seth Mazibuko, one of the Soweto students who just finished his sentence on Robben Island. Half the AZAPO leadership crossed over to the UDF.

Their defections reflected an ideological sea change that had taken place in the late 1970s. Many former BC followers, the most prominent of whom was Lekota, adopted non-racialism after meeting ANC people in jail. Mpho Mashinini, arrested for alleged PAC activity, met an elder ANC operative, Joe Gqabi, who was simultaneously awaiting trial in Pretoria Central

Prison. "For the first time, I got a history of the movements. For the first time I understood the Defiance Campaign and why the PAC broke with the ANC," Mpho recalls. The prisoners argued at length "about fighting racism with racism." Many of the students were open to persuasion. In 1976, "Ideological differences were not that important," Mpho recalls. "All we wanted was to push the Boers to the sea." Gqabi, who was acquitted and later assassinated, had been a key figure in building an ANC following during the student rebellion. Another ANC man, Lawrence Ndzanga, had tutored about ANC history to "cells" of three students at a time, until he died in detention in 1977. By 1983, AZAPO was having trouble holding meetings on college campuses. At a meeting at the University of the Witwatersrand black dormitory in Soweto, supporters of non-racialism peppered AZAPO leaders with questions. Chikane and another leader made speeches opposing black exclusivism, and when they left the students were chanting and singing praises to Mandela and the ANC. So many BC followers switched allegiances that one analyst observed that BC became "a religion without a church;" while the BC philosophy remained strong, it had no strong organization to proselytize its cause.

At the UDF launch, Boesak, deeply influenced by Black Consciousness, said,

> We must remember that apartheid does not have the support of all whites. There are some who have struggled with us, who have gone to jail, who have been tortured and banned. There have been whites who died in the struggle for justice. We, therefore, must not allow our anger over apartheid to become the basis for blind hatred of all whites. . . . Let us, even now, seek to lay the foundations for reconciliation between whites and blacks in this country by working together, praying together, struggling together for justice.

Among students, many blacks had turned away from narrow black exclusivism when they formed the Congress of South African Students in 1979. Some pointed to Biko's collaboration with a white newspaper editor, Donald Woods. Others were impressed by a dynamic youth, Billy Masethla, who later joined the ANC in exile. "After the Black Consciousness organizations were banned in 1977, there was a review of strategies," recalled Lawrence Ntloaka, the Kagiso student who later became head of the UDF's main Kagiso affiliate. "If you are preaching racism in reverse, how are you going to transform society? How will you reverse yourself?"

With the turn toward a greater political ecumenism, blacks rediscovered ANC leaders in their midst. The 1983 UDF rally featured Frances Baard, then seventy-four, who in the 1950s had organized African unions and a potato boycott to protest brutal conditions for black farmers. Baard, who also co-founded the ANC's women's federation, opened the UDF meeting by saying the country was being run by a "clique of white lillies" and by calling on the government to "unlock the gates" of the prisons.

All three regional presidents of the UDF were members of the old guard, with strong ties to the ANC in the 1950s. Archie Gumede, a lawyer and chairman of the Release Mandela Campaign, was a defendant at the 1956 treason trial. Albertina Sisulu, a nurse, was the wife of Walter Sisulu, the ANC secretary general in the 1950s who with Mandela went to jail for life in 1964. Oscar Mpetha was a 1950s trade-union leader and Cape provincial ANC president in 1958. At seventy-four, Mpetha was sick and often in detention, but his co-presidents took active roles in the UDF.

Dressed in her blue nurse's uniform, Mrs. Sisulu worked in an airless space that was a combination of storage area, dispensary, records room, and examining room. In the back of the office, her employer Dr. Abu-Baker A. Asvat, an Indian general practitioner, sat in a space that doubled as office and examining room. He called Mrs. Sisulu "mama," a term of respect, for in many ways Mrs. Sisulu was mother of people in the struggle.

Since 1974, Asvat's office had been in a section of Soweto known as MacDonald's farm, a squatter camp on the south side of Soweto. While 177 white men governed amidst elaborate ceremony of Parliament in Cape Town, the most powerful woman in South Africa trudged to work across a field littered with broken bottles, discarded auto parts, and people huddled in shacks and abandoned buses. For journalists, among the few people to visit both settings, the degrading conditions surrounding the clinic highlighted Sisulu's dignity, while the grandeur of Parliament only underlined the ignoble character of government leadership.

Unlike many leaders of the UDF, Mrs. Sisulu was not a particularly gifted speaker. Unlike the internationally famous Winnie Mandela, Sisulu was neither beautiful nor telegenic. Stout and nearly seventy, she was a symbol of perseverance. "Albertina Sisulu is to South African politics what Penelope was to Odysseus," one acquaintance said.

Those who walked into Dr. Asvat's modest waiting room with its wooden benches and public-health posters, came to visit the nurse as much as the doctor. A Soweto activist walked in and greeted her. "Mama Sisulu!" "I'm here," she replied. "Compliments of the season," the activist replied. He greeted a patient he knew too. "Hello George! What are you doing here? Are you sick? I suppose illness does not discriminate."

Mrs. Sisulu peered through the wooden slats of the narrow window opening from her room into the waiting room. Her manner was polite but professional. She finished taking a patient's name, age, and medical history. After noting the blood pressure of the hefty man, she dropped some medication into a plastic sandwich bag and ordered him to "Lose weight! Please, lose weight."

"Black people should have high blood pressure," she said. "They have no place to work, no place to stay."

If anyone had reason to suffer high blood pressure, it was Mrs. Sisulu herself. In 1942, she met her husband Walter, a real estate agent. Since then, her life had been disrupted by political campaigns, imprisonments, and restrictions. Along with Mandela and other members of the ANC Youth

League, Walter Sisulu was one of the militants who pushed through the "program of action" in 1949 to make the ANC more forceful. After he became secretary general of the ANC, his wife was drawn further into activity with him. In 1958, she went to jail for leading protests against the extension of pass laws to African women. Mandela, then on trial for treason, helped prepare her defense. In 1963, she was arrested under the Suppression of Communism Act, even though Mrs. Sisulu harbors antipathy towards communism. She served ninety days in detention without trial with her oldest son Max, then seventeen. From 1964 to 1983, she was banned from political activity, including ten years of house arrest during which she could not leave her house from six in the evening until six in the morning. The threat of jail was so constant that she kept a packed suitcase at her house. She was in detention at the time of the UDF launch.

Because of restrictions on "Ma" Sisulu and Oscar Mpetha, the only co-president who could attend the UDF launch was Archie Gumede. I later met him in his law office in the center of Durban on a sweltering summer day. Despite the heat, he was the model of propriety. His tie was pulled tight around his neck and his starched white sleeves buttoned at the wrists. When he went to lunch, he donned his baggy brown suit jacket and took me to a modest coffee shop around the corner called Old Glory.

Gumede was the living embodiment of black resistance. Gumede was born in 1914, two years after his father, Josiah, co-founded the South African Natives National Congress. Josiah Gumede later became president of the movement, before conservatives forced him and his radical allies out of office. Archie Gumede joined the ANC in 1944 and played a role in the Defiance Campaign. In 1955, he was the senior Natal delegate to the Congress of the People that drew up the Freedom Charter. In 1956, Archie Gumede was among the 156 leaders charged in the marathon treason trial. In 1963, the government banned Gumede for five years. He spent the time studying law and opened a practice in 1970 at the age of fifty-six. In the late 1970s, he helped establish the Release Mandela Campaign, an affiliate of the UDF.

"Archie was a natural for several reasons," an Indian UDF leader from Natal explained. "First the question of a long track record was very important. Second, he is an African, and the liberation of Africans must be expressed by African leadership. Third, he is from Natal and we needed someone from Natal. He was most senior."

Sixty-nine years old when the UDF was founded, Gumede cherished the ANC history that had been forgotten by most black South Africans. "What was remarkable about the ANC in 1912 was that the founding fathers were able to come up with the idea that they should forget that they were Xhosas or Zulus or whatever. They had the idea of a *national* congress, of a nation formed by separate groups, not the recognition of each group as a nation." That the UDF was seeking a Zulu leader from Natal to balance its ethnic composition helped propel Gumede into the national leadership.

Gumede said his father also taught him not to let "the horizon of black people be set by the South African government." The early ANC leaders looked abroad for help. Months after the founding of the UDF, Gumede and other UDF leaders held a sit-in at the British consulate in Durban, asking for political asylum. The British refused and after several weeks the "Durban Six" walked out of the consulate and into the arms of the South African police. They were later released, but the sit-in won international publicity for the UDF.

The Natal lawyer's upbringing contrasted sharply with the bitter childhood of blacks in the 1970s. A typical young black who told me how he assaulted white pedestrians in a Johannesburg melee in 1976, explained that "Jesus tells us to turn the other cheek. Well, that would be okay if he gave us six cheeks." But Gumede was the product of a missionary education. Though those schools were taken over by the Nationalist government in 1953, Gumede retained his Christian principles. "I still go to church every Sunday," he told me. "Look at the leadership of the ANC. They were all products of missionary educations. For human relations, can you give me a better formula than love your neighbor as yourself? Or do unto others as you would do unto yourself?" He paused as though expecting an answer.

> You either have survival of the fittest, or mutual survival. If you talk of survival of the fittest you cannot acknowledge the existence of God. You should have no discipline other than the interests of self. And how as a human being with your weaknesses and vulnerability, do you not do what you want? Why should I not grab the next beautiful woman I see, the next piece of jewelry I see? Do we go back to the jungle?

Continually over the next few years, Gumede and Sisulu would return to the theme sounded at the UDF launch: that "discipline" was "absolutely essential." This discipline was not intended to stifle individualism, but to ensure that protest be conducted with decorum and united ranks.

Gumede employed Biblical references freely. At the August 20, 1983, UDF launch, he said "Moses led the children of Israel out of Egypt, there is simply no reason why the people of South Africa cannot move out of the apartheid state into a state in which all shall be free," he said.

In an era when young blacks liked to show their toughness and were reluctant to display emotion, Gumede wept openly at the political funerals of comrades killed in fratricidal violence.

Despite his Christian humility, Gumede was adamant in his demands for black dignity. "During the last world war," he recalled,

> how many farms were looked after by blacks while whites were away at war? Even during the Boer War that was so. Yet it seems to me that the white man enjoys a relationship with the black man like a man to his horse. But a human being is not a horse and can never be one. Therefore the time for riding comes to an end.

The UDF also drew on strains of black resistance that owed nothing to the ANC and saw people like Archie Gumede as bourgeois. From the Unity Movement, the UDF borrowed the principles of boycott and non-participation. These principles were preserved in their purest state by the portly, soft-spoken Richard Dudley, a retired colored schoolteacher who was president of the New Unity Movement in the mid-1980s. The Unity movement was founded in 1943 as a merger of groups that had refused the government's 1936 invitation of Africans to join the Natives Representative Council and other advisory groups. From the first, the Unity Movement considered the 1936 Natives Representative Council "a Jim Crow organization," Dudley said. The Unity Movement advocated a policy of "non-collaboration," which put it at odds with ANC as well as the South African Communist Party. Communists ran for (and won) seats in Parliament and on municipal councils. They held seats on the white Johannesburg municipal council up to the banning of the party in 1950.

"The ANC always looked upon special [segregated] systems of representation as means of fighting the system from within," said Dudley. "We said that any participation in alternatives that the ruling class set up would divide the people and strengthen the hand of the ruling class." The Unity Movement believed that only revolution could change South Africa.

The Unity Movement scorned the conservative, elitist elements of the ANC leadership. "It was necessary to break with the thinking of the ruling class and set up ideas of a new society," Dudley explained. Adherents of Marxist class politics, Unity Movement loyalists viewed capitalism as the enemy against which the entire working class (including whites) must eventually unite.

ANC partisans said that the Unity Movement had "Trotskyist leanings" and that their positions as intellectuals and teachers "made it impossible for them to participate in mass movements involving physical danger or imprisonment." ANC partisans said that "the only boycott practised [by the Unity Movement] was the boycott of the ANC."[4]

Disappointment with the Native Representative Council in the 1940s pushed the ANC strategy closer to Unity Movement principles. The Defiance Campaign put into practice principles of boycott and disobedience. But personal rivalries kept the two groups far apart. Efforts to resolve differences between the ANC and the Unity Movement repeatedly broke down between 1943 and 1946. Even today, Unity Movement loyalists view the ANC as soft on the issue of participation. Dudley notes that during the Defiance Campaign in the 1950s, the ANC sanctioned the participation by its members in township community councils. In the late 1970s, the ANC gave its blessing to the participation by Chief Buthelezi in the homeland government of KwaZulu.

The Unity Movement never won a large following, but its principles of non-collaboration had profound influence in the 1970s on BC leaders and in the 1980s on UDF leaders. During the UDF's early debates about how to oppose the new constitution, the arguments echoed those used by the Unity Movement in the 1940s. New Unity Movement pamphlets were widely circulated. Two Unity Movement pamphlets were among the papers found at the home of Matthew Goniwe, a key UDF activist in the remote black township of Cradock, after Goniwe was killed in 1985.

Though Dudley never joined forces with the UDF, many of his followers did. The prominant Indian advocate, Abdullah "Dullah" Mohammed Omar, an old Unity Movement sympathizer who turned down a position on the first UDF executive committee in the Western Cape, eventually became president of the UDF in the Western Cape.

From Black Consciousness, the UDF inherited legions of militants in their twenties, many of them veterans of confrontation with white authorities. Others were teenagers who had grown up in an atmosphere of sporadic violence, with memories of how in 1976 violence shook the government. These youths had few fears for their own safety and many were already acquainted with detention and torture. The UDF made a gesture to these youths by naming Martha Mahlangu as one of its patrons. Mahlangu was the mother of the executed ANC guerrilla Solomon Mahlangu, the first member of the 1976 generation to go into exile and return as a guerrilla.

Members of the old guard regarded the youngsters with a mixture of fear and wonder. "The youth today are hardened," said Robert Matji, the former member of the South African Communist Party who was regional secretary of the ANC in the Eastern Cape in the 1950s. The pepper headed Matji recalled that the militants of *his* generation "didn't have any idea about the brutality of the government. To be arrested on an allegation that you're engaged in political activity in the 1980s is something I wonder whether many of us would have been willing to participate in." Even when thousands of Africans were arrested in the Defiance Campaign, most only stayed in jail overnight; at most, they stayed two weeks, according to Matji. By the 1980s, however, it was clear that arrests could last indefinitely. Treatment changed in the early 1960s when police tortured suspected ANC and PAC guerrillas. In the 1970s, young rock throwers were treated more harshly than the most dangerous suspects of the early 1960s. Lawrence Ntloaka recalled that when he was arrested in 1977, he was forced to stand without sleep for seven days and nights. Whenever he dozed, police pricked him with pins. "By the fifth night, my feet were swollen. My calves were the same size as my thighs," he recalled. It took three days with his feet elevated for the swelling to go down. Then he was kept in solitary confinement for six months.

Lawrence wasn't alone. Mpho Mashinini, one of five people who launched the Soweto Youth Congress the same month as the UDF got off the ground, had also spent six months in solitary confinement. Gabu Tugwana, later deputy editor of a black weekly newspaper, had spent fourteen months in solitary confinement. Frank Chikane, on the first UDF executive committee and later head of the South African Council of Churches, had been hung upside down by his ankles. Khehla Shubane, a member of the Soweto Civic Association, was nearly suffocated with a wet canvas bag, then taken to an open window on the tenth floor of the Johannesburg police station so he could see where he might be pushed out. Monty Narsoo, later an analyst at the South African Institute of Race Relations, was given electric shocks on his genitals. Seth Mazibuko, later publicity secretary of the Release Mandela Campaign, was forced to crouch while police tied his genitals to brick, then made him try to stand up. The generation of blacks that came of age in the late 1970s and early 1980s had no illusions about the dangers ahead.

Yet they still risked confrontation. Shubane said that the youth of the 1970s were not prepared, like their parents, to "acquiesce in their own oppression." The obsequious behavior once regarded as a matter of survival had become an object of shame. Later Matji would say, "I saw a picture on television of a black youth confronted by a white policeman and sneering at the policeman as if to say, 'Come on and do your worst.' We would never have done that. In our day, when policemen kicked in the doors and kicked people around we all said 'baas, please baas.' Today the police might have to kill the boy before he said 'baas'."

Eight years had seen such defiance grow into an imposing array of black political organizations. Sentiments once displayed by rampaging students had been channeled into community groups, emerging black trade unions, and protest campaigns, culminating in the August 1984 election boycotts.

With different tendencies and generations loosely collected under the UDF umbrella, however, some UDF leaders were troubled by the absence of a clear ideological or philosophical line. On September 13, 1984, two weeks after the boycott of the Indian and colored Parliamentary elections, UDF general secretary Popo Molefe wrote a letter to one of the front's regional presidents.

> Since its formation, the United Democratic Front has been grappling with the problem of developing a common understanding of front politics, as well as a common approach at the level of tactics and strategy. Today, over twelve months later, this . . . remains unfulfilled. Experiences of the past eight months . . . indicate very clearly the seriousness of this problem and the urgent need to resolve it.[5]

By this time, however, more urgent issues were arising. Violence had erupted in townships southwest of Johannesburg and was trickling like lava around the country. South Africa's most serious black uprising had begun.

PART 2

The Fourth Front

CHAPTER FIVE

Violence

Enough! We are writing our history in blood.
—The Rand Daily Mail, March 23, 1985

Call it the violence of apartheid or the violence of revolt. All of us, like it or not, are trapped in this spiral of violence.
—Frederik Van Zyl Slabbert

OBLIVIOUS TO WHAT LAY BEFORE HIM, P. W. Botha confidently went ahead with his inauguration as president on September 14, 1984. He was sworn in by the white-haired chief justice under a faultless spring sky, with the chiefs of the navy, air force, army, combined defense forces, and the police looking on in full regalia. They would pass through the streets of the city where the buildings would be covered with bunting in the national colors—orange, blue, and white.

Meanwhile sporadic unrest persisted in the Vaal triangle, where thirty-one blacks had died in the first week of September. School boycotts swept the region; nationwide a quarter million black youths were staying away from classes. In mid-October, black youths on their way home from the funeral of a friend who had been killed by police stoned a car driven by a white woman. One rock struck and killed a three-week-old infant in the back seat.

In response, 7,000 South African troops sealed off Sebokeng on October 23. Soldiers were stationed around the edges of the townships and at intervals along the main roads. Police carried out house-to-house searches, checking permits, questioning children, and seizing banned literature. Nearly 400 people were arrested, summarily tried, and sentenced in special courts set up in the township. Few defendants received counsel. Those residents cleared of suspicion received indelible red marks on their hands, enabling them to pass through army road blocks and go to work.

The army had been used before in certain parts of the country, but not in more than sixty years in such an open display of force against the country's own citizenry. The army called it Operation Palmiet, an Afrikaans word for "bullrush."

The troop maneuver, like the turmoil on September 3, was only a prelude to things to come during the 1984–1986 uprising. Every week the elite special forces unit of the South African Defense Forces held intelligence sessions with four briefings on its operations: one about the western front near Angola, one about the eastern front near Mozambique, one about all other foreign operations, and one about operations *inside* South Africa's borders. At the beginning of 1984 the first two fronts dominated the weekly briefings. Gradually, however, the dominant topic became military and police operations inside the country, the fourth front, the front within.

Six months after the Vaal uprising, news of violence became as routine as the weather report. A typical police bulletin carried news of a dozen incidents of unrest, ranging from stone throwings to shootouts. Thousands of blacks took part in weekly rituals of angry confrontation, which often climaxed in deaths—which led to political funerals—which led to new confrontations.

The violence took many forms—pitting police against blacks, black rebels against black collaborators, black rivals against each other. Some incidents were planned, others were spontaneous.

In the case of the spontaneous Vaal uprising, bread-and-butter grievances inflamed the community months before violence began. The central government had cut grants and subsidies to the townships, essentially bankrupting the black municipalities as new black councillors took over. Lacking a tax base, in mid-1984 the black community councillors raised rents in the townships by R5.95 a month to an average of R39.50, excluding water and electricity. Services brought the average rent up to about R62. Though it didn't sound like much, it stretched the resources of people already living in poverty. The South African recession that began in 1982 had hit blacks hard, especially in the Vaal triangle, the most expensive place for blacks to live. A quarter of the people in the area had suffered real declines in their standards of living.[1] Between 1977 and 1984, rents for black residents of the Vaal Triangle had soared by 400 percent. Even *before* the 1984 rent increase, half the households were in arrears. The rent owed to the Lekoa Town Council, which was responsible for the area, already amounted to R2.2 million by June 1984.

Deprived of democratic channels of expression, township residents vented their anger about the rent hikes at informal meetings in the area called Small Farms. The usual contingent of militant youths played only a small role in the meetings, which were attended by a cross section of residents, especially pensioners. They turned to Rev. Lord McCamel, a community leader who ran a church founded by his father, known as the "lion of Africa," a term of respect. The church was a huge building by the standards of black townships, with Doric columns and a crown at the top of its seven-story clock tower. The hall had a balcony and a three-tiered platform in front, and was large enough to hold mass meetings.

As a result of the meetings, some residents sent letters to the councillors. The Vaal Civic Association made plans for the people to withhold the increase in rent but continue paying the old rates. Rev. McCamel, who also headed the Vaal Civic Association, was part of a delegation sent to negotiate with the township administrators.

The appeals fell on deaf ears. Local activists distributed pamphlets urging residents to stay home from work on Monday, September 3, in protest. The town councillors responded with pamphlets warning residents that if they didn't go to work they would lose their jobs and houses, and jeopardize the future of their children.[2] The stage was set for conflict.

Spontaneous violence over basic social and economic issues had broken out before. "Every so often the yoke becomes unendurable, something explodes, and for a while blind resentment takes control," Chief Albert John Lutuli wrote during the 1950s. Lutuli, who was president of the ANC, reflected that given the black burden in South Africa, it was a wonder that the average black didn't struggle more violently.

Lutuli doubted that explosions among blacks would lead to anything other than a cycle of "riot" and "counter-riot" because white South Africans saw the occasional bursts of black violence as evidence of blacks' violent nature. Before his death in 1967, Chief Lutuli said that white South Africans

> persuaded themselves against the evidence that they share South Africa with a barbaric and hostile black horde. It is as though they are perversely most afraid of us when we are friendly and disciplined and patient. The large, amiable dog in the yard is on a chain. You have been told that he is a snarling, dangerous cur. His amiability must therefore be a deception. You keep out of reach and jab repeatedly at him to rouse him to anger. If you succeed, that proves he is a wild and savage creature. Now and then you do succeed—the best-tempered animal gets sick of ill-willed pestering. Sometimes you do enrage him. Sometimes the chain made for him snaps. Then there is a riot. Whites see only the riot. Their reaction? Make a stronger chain.[3]

Lutuli won the Nobel Peace Prize in 1961. In October 1984, a month after the Vaal uprising, the Nobel Committee awarded the Nobel Peace Prize to a South African for the second time. The winner was Bishop Desmond Tutu, a fifty-three-year-old Anglican, who in 1978 had become the first black general secretary of the South African Council of Churches and turned the council into a force against apartheid.

The new Nobel laureate was a target of white hostility. To whites, "the black bishop" had committed the sin of expecting to live and be treated like a white man. That such a thing was possible first occurred to Tutu in the 1950s when the white priest Trevor Huddleston passed by on the street and tipped his hat to Tutu's mother. "I couldn't believe my eyes," Tutu said later.

"A white man who greeted a black working-class woman." The son of a teacher and a domestic servant, Tutu had become a teacher because he was too poor to go to medical school. When the government introduced Bantu Education, he joined the church. His new profession was good to him. He built himself a fine house in an area of Soweto known as Beverly Hills. His children had been educated at private schools in Swaziland and they dressed stylishly. Tutu had traveled extensively outside South Africa, notwithstanding the government's refusal to give him a passport from 1979 to 1981. He was indignant that his fame did not insulate him from "a whippersnapper of a policeman" who stopped him at a roadblock and asked him for identification. "Any policeman who says he does not know me does not deserve to be in the police force," Tutu said. On one occasion, Tutu's wife and daughters were strip-searched at a police station. "If they treat me [and my family] like that, what do they do to so-called ordinary people?" Tutu asked.

By the time Tutu gave his Nobel-Peace-Prize acceptance speech in December, the death toll in anti-apartheid protests since the Vaal uprising had risen to 150. Although Tutu did not endorse violent resistance to apartheid, it was clear to him, like Lutuli, that black South Africans had been patient, "peace-loving to a fault." In his Nobel speech, delivered three months after the Vaal uprising, Tutu said,

> We understand those who say they have had to adopt what is a last resort for them. Violence is not being introduced into the South African situation *de novo* from the outside by those who are called terrorists or freedom fighters, depending on whether you are oppressed or an oppressor. The South African situation is violent already, and the primary violence is that of apartheid, the violence of forced population removals, of inferior education, of detention without trial, of the migratory labor systems.

"A Most Unfortunate Incident"

The Vaal triangle carried a special significance among blacks. One of the Vaal townships was Sharpeville, where on March 21, 1960, white policemen opened fire on unarmed black demonstrators, killing sixty-seven people and wounding 186. The great majority of those killed were shot in the back. Press photos of the carnage appeared around the world, making Sharpeville synonomous with apartheid's brutality.

Twenty-five years later to the day, on March 21, 1985, Lieutenant Fouche and Warrant Officer Pentz reported to the police armory in the white town of Uitenhage and picked up enough weapons to star in the shootout scene of a wild west show: twelve twelve-bore shotguns and four R-1 rifles, the standard army rifle, 240 cartridges for the shotguns and eighty rounds of R-1 ammunition. Members of the patrol also packed their usual side arms: nine-millimeter automatic pistols.

Fouche and Pentz were heading for KwaNobuhle and Langa, black townships near Uitenhage. It was supposed to be a routine patrol, but when they returned later that morning, the two police teams had fired two R-1 rounds, forty-four shotgun cartridges, and at least four rounds of nine-millimeter ammo. Faced with about a thousand blacks walking up the main road of Langa, they had killed twenty blacks and wounded at least twenty-seven others in a brief shooting spree. Thirty-five of the victims were shot from behind, including an eleven-year-old girl who was fatally injured.[4]

It was, according to Law and Order Minister Louis le Grange, "a most unfortunate incident." But he stood by his police, who claimed they had prevented a mob armed with sticks, stones, and petrol bombs from attacking white homes in Uitenhage. Police said the mob had ignored a warning shot. The citizens of Langa said they were walking peacefully to a funeral. They said that the police had blocked the way and, without warning, opened fire.[5] Their lawyers later contended that police had intentionally provoked the confrontation and that police themselves had later scattered rocks on the road before taking pictures of the scene.

The shooting was the bloodiest incident in a quarter century and it remained the bloodiest single encounter of the entire black uprising. In this sense, the Langa massacre was unusual. In other respects, it was all too usual. About half the blacks killed in violence from 1984 through 1987 were shot dead by white police and troops.

Elements of calculation, coincidence, and confusion triggered the massacre. But it was an incident waiting to happen. The explosive emotions in Langa could have been found in any township. Frustrated police officers longed to prove their strength and determination, while weeks of clashes with police fueled a spirit of confrontation among blacks. With deep grievances, blacks felt entitled to exercise one of their last remaining rights, the right to mourn their dead.

On the surface, the town of Uitenhage looks an unlikely place for a bloody clash. It lies amid scrubland about a half-hour drive inland from the industrial city of Port Elizabeth. Modest-sized houses for whites line the road to the center of town, where a stone church sits near a sleepy traffic circle. Small stores line the central business district and a supermarket complex sits further along near two churches and a drab courthouse. In a couple of minutes you have traveled straight through to the far edge of town. On the right stand more homes belonging to whites.

The black township of Langa once stood just beyond those buildings, in sharp contrast to the tidy white part of town. Langa looked as if a bunch of scrap-metal and cardboard boxes had been stacked in a giant wastepaper basket then spilled across the landscape. "One of the things that struck me about Langa," recalled a white soldier who was patrolling the township around that time, "was the number of animals running around. Chickens, ducks, even a cow or two. I was appalled." One paved road, Maduna Road, wound from the white town through the township. Along the road were a handful of run-down shops and a Seventh Day Adventist Church. To the left lay an open field. Scattered up a small incline to the right were shacks and rickety houses along numbered avenues.

Whites found Langa uncomfortably close. The government was threatening to bulldoze the unsightly township and force the removal of residents to KwaNobuhle, a new township about six-and-a-half miles away behind a hill on the other side of Uitenhage. (KwaNobuhle literally means "at the place of the mother of beauty, or goodness," a name given by the government.) KwaNobuhle had better housing, and government said the move was good for the people. But Langa was walking distance from Uitenhage; from KwaNobuhle people needed to pay fares to ride buses to work. Moreover, there weren't enough houses for all the people in Langa. Many people simply moved to new shacks. Lifetime Langa residents saw the forced removal as a design to shove blacks out of sight. "I was born here thirty-six years ago. Why should I move?" asked a Langa resident at a meeting about the removal. "We used to play with white kids. You could shout Jannie and he could shout Sipho. We lived only a hundred yards apart. Now they want to push us and hide us behind the hill. We will not be hidden in the country of our birth. The police can come and shoot me dead. I'm not going."[6]

Meanwhile the expansion of housing for blacks in Langa ceased, despite the township's burgeoning needs. The aim: to encourage the move to KwaNobuhle and to discourage rural blacks from coming to the cities. But poor blacks who were kicked off drought-stricken farms flocked to Langa from other parts of the Eastern Cape anyway. Shanties sprang up. The shanties—"informal housing" as it was called by the big-business sponsored Urban Foundation—were tacked together with bits of wood, scrap metal, and packaging from automobile parts and insulated with newspapers.

By 1985, virtually no formal housing had been built since the township was established thirty years earlier. The government collected rents, but put little of that money back into the township. Half the people in Langa lived in shacks. There was no electricity. About 30,000 people shared twenty-eight communal water taps. Nearly 60 percent of working-age people were unemployed and the average income for a household of six was $90 a month.[7] The only thing Langa had in abundance was cause for grievance.[7]

"We would never live like this if the government cared about us," Michael Lunga told me as he sat rolling a spool of red yarn. Lunga, twenty-one, had worked for two years in Volkswagen's press shop and had earned $20 a week, a decent salary by black South African standards. But he was laid off during the slump in the auto industry and moved in with his sister in Langa. They shared a three-room shack, constructed of rusting pieces of corrugated metal and insulated with cardboard boxes. The cool autumn breeze blew through the cracks. The only furniture consisted of two small benches and a shelf with a few dishes. Lunga, his sister, and his two children shared a single bed. It looked like a squatter's place, but they still paid $8.50

a month to the town council. The four lived off a $22 monthly disability pension the sister received for a leg injury.

The political history of Langa mirrored that of other townships, from student revolt to socio-economic grievances to political protest. Its black students had joined the nationwide unrest in 1976 and 1977, attacking schools, shops, vehicles, and local government offices. Five local student leaders were sentenced to twelve-to-eighteen years in prison in 1978. In 1980, factory workers had staged walkouts and demanded a "living wage" of R2 an hour. Workers went on strike at the big employers, including a large construction company, a milling company, Goodyear, Volkswagen, and Bata, the Canadian shoe manufacturer. Union members and youths made up the two principle strains of activism in the area. A broad-based local civic organization was launched, but it petered out.[8]

In late 1983, the Uitenhage Youth Congress affiliated with the United Democratic Front to oppose the election of black community councillors. However, only sixteen candidates declared themselves for sixteen spots on the local council, so elections weren't held. People later said the councillors "elected themselves." Once in office, the councillors raised rents and service charges. Irate residents petitioned against the increases and the council backed down, but resentment lingered.

In 1984, students started boycotting classes. During the second half of 1984 and 1985 township mobs, led by militant youths who were boycotting school, launched attacks on symbols of authority and privilege, including buses, private cars, and buildings. By March 1985, black unrest was getting out of control. In the black townships of Port Elizabeth, Uitenhage, and Despatch together, blacks had destroyed or damaged 273 buildings and 604 vehicles, causing losses estimated at R2.77 million from September 1, 1984, through March 31, 1985.[9]

Rather than dampening unrest, white police fanned tensions in the townships. In South Africa police are usually vastly outnumbered. Usually forty or fewer patrolled a township of 40,000 people. These police, vulnerable and victims of their own propaganda about the black peril, were jumpy and unduly aggressive. They rode inside armored cars, typically with two in front and twelve in back with gunports and bullet-proof windows. In the hot weather, the top of the armored car could be opened and youths often tried to arch rocks inside.

The men who took police jobs usually were unskilled and inexperienced. Police could be teenagers. They needed only a tenth-grade education and started at salaries as low as $70 a week. After being taught they were superior to blacks, many of the young white police resented the handful of blacks who earned decent livings. One soldier who traveled with police recalled, "Every once in a while we would see a decent house or a Mercedes and one of the guys would say, 'Look, they're driving around in Mercedes! What are they complaining about?'"[10] Many of the police cultivated adolescent images of cowboys by spinning their tires in the dirt of the townships or by lounging outside the Uitenhage courthouse, where they would playfully toss their shotguns from hand to hand.

As the unrest increased, police and military action became increasingly random. One woman swore in an affidavit that one day her five-year-old son was playing with friends inside the yard in front of her house. "I heard the noise of the hippo [armored car] coming down our gravel road. I went outside to fetch the children. When I reached the front of the house I saw the hippo passing slowly. I saw two men on top of the hippo. The white man was still carrying his rifle. My child was cover in blood." A doctor removed bird shot from the child's legs, but the child still limped on a swollen right ankle.[11]

Steven Louw, a national serviceman then on patrol in the townships got an inside look at the actions of the police. Louw was sympathetic to the average cop or solider. Like most career soldiers and police, Louw came from a middle-class background. A native of Edenvale, near Johannesburg, he had never traveled to the Cape until he joined the army.

Shortly after finishing high school, Louw volunteered for the army's paratrooper battalion, with the ambition of becoming a career military officer. He became a driver after he injured a leg. "I was keen on the military life and I felt I would be doing good for my country," he recalled as he sat cross legged on the lawn behind his parents' house one night. He pulled out a photo album and flipped past a picture of himself in dark sunglasses and a brown army uniform, cradling a rifle and standing with his legs apart on top of an armored car.

When black unrest broke out in the Vaal, Louw volunteered for duty in the townships. In October 1984 he went to Tembisa, a township just north of Johannesburg near his parents' house. In early 1985 he volunteered again for two tours of township duty in the Eastern Cape. The Eastern Cape tours were markedly different from the one in Tembisa. In the Eastern Cape, the police and soldiers went on joint patrols. The police considered relatively minor actions "provocation," Louw recalled. "If we rode past someone who raised his fist, that would be considered provocation. The police didn't want us to arrest anyone though, because lawyers usually got them off. Instead we were told to administer our own justice." That justice was rough. The armored cars were designed with a box for food and other miscellaneous items. Soldiers and police often grabbed rebellious children and stuffed them inside the metal box. "Then we would drive around the veld and knock the kid around a bit. We called it 'scrambling.'" Once they seized a kid who raised a fist. Louw estimates the child was eight or ten years old. The soldiers dumped the young black in the armored car and left him there for quite a while. By the time they took him out, the kid was whimpering and bleeding. An officer ordered each man in the platoon to hit the youth once.

Even the white soldiers balked this time. The officer struck the child a few times and they dropped him on the side of the township furthest from where they picked him up.

Louw says his unit stopped and beat people at least once a shift. He says he began to feel that the police "really enjoyed it." Many of the troops were young and tried to prove their mettle by outdoing one another on duty. "We were young kids trying to outdo one another," recalled Louw. "Guys would come back bragging about what they had done that day in the townships the way they might have bragged about a girlfriend they had 'had' in the past."

Boredom set in, mixed with tension. Troops would plug the exhaust pipe of their armored cars with plastic containers from tear gas or ammunition. As they drove around the townships, the pressure would build up until the containers shot off like cannons. Toward the end of a sixteen-hour patrol, Louw's unit went to a "shebeen," an illegal black drinking establishment in someone's home. "The platoon leader said they must give us eight bottles of whiskey or we would turn them over to the police. The shebeen owner took him in the next room and bargained him down to six."

Sometimes police baited trouble. Louw says that once in a Port Elizabeth township, an army major stationed soldiers up and down a road, out of sight. "My job was to drive up and down the road and get someone to throw a stone," Louw recalls. The soldiers then planned to counterattack. That night no one came out and eventually the troops packed up and left.

On Louw's second tour in the Eastern Cape townships, he moved from Port Elizabeth to Uitenhage and Adelaide. Conditions had worsened. Blacks carried out short and quick attacks, then disappeared. In Adelaide, township residents piled up barrels as roadblocks to slow down the troops. Louw spent a couple of days just sleeping in the KwaNobuhle post office with his entire section. They parked their armored car in back and were ordered to protect the municipal garbage truck. "There they took away our tear gas and rubber bullets. We were given only live ammo. We were told that people were no longer respecting us because we were too soft."

Frustrated by their inability to snuff out unrest, many police officers longed for a tougher line. Though a later inquiry concluded that tear gas, rubber bullets, and bird shot had proved adequate for dispersing crowds and containing unrest, the police started using live ammunition. March had been a bloody month. From March 8 to 10, there were twenty-three incidents of arson and eighteen incidents of stone throwing in the Uitenhage and Despatch townships, causing damage estimated at R220,000. In quelling the unrest, police shot and killed six blacks.

Four days before the Langa massacre, a complaint was filed against Lieutenant Fouche alleging negligence and drinking on duty. White activist and Cape provincial council member Molly Blackburn had gone to the police station looking for a black youth whose parents said he had disappeared.

There she found the youth handcuffed to the leg of a table and being beaten by a black police officer with an orange plastic whip. The youth was bleeding from lacerations on the left side of his face and had traces of blood on his mouth. Blackburn argued with an officer and the youth was unshackled and taken away to the cells. But Lieutenant Fouche later shouted at Blackburn and told her to get out of the building. Blackburn said he was drunk, judging from his abnormally aggressive behavior and the strong smell of liquor on his breath.[12]

Unlike Fouche, some policemen tried to diffuse conflict. But in the fateful days before the massacre, even those honest efforts helped lead to disaster. Four blacks still had to be buried from the shootings in early March and Captain Goosen tried to push the funeral to a work day. He judiciously thought that would reduce the number of people who could attend and thus reduce the chances of violence. So he asked the local white magistrate to reschedule the funeral from Sunday, March 17. The magistrate obligingly ordered that the funerals be held in KwaNobuhle on March 21 and 22—unaware that March 21, the twenty-fifth anniversary of the Sharpeville shooting, would be celebrated with an emotional stayaway.

On the eve of the funerals, Captain Goosen realized his blunder and obtained another postponement. That night, police cars rode through the townships and announced through loudspeakers that the funerals had been postponed. The state radio stations also broadcast the announcement.

But the word didn't get around. The next morning a leading black journalist went to KwaNobuhle and was surprised to find nothing happening. Meanwhile, a modest crowd of people gathered in Langa's Maduna Square and waited for minibuses to take them to the funeral in KwaNobuhle. Just then, the first detail of police arrived in an armored car and told the people to get out of the vehicles. The Langa residents dutifully complied and started the long walk to KwaNobuhle along the usual route—which would take them along Maduna Road into downtown white Uitenhage itself, then across the Swartkops River (whose name literally means "black heads") and along a deserted stretch of road until they hit the new township.

Fouche had been in the township earlier. He had found everything quiet and had gone to KwaNobuhle. Now, radioed by Pentz, he returned. Pentz and Fouche formed an inverted V with their armored cars and waited for the crowd to approach. They testified later that the crowd was whipped into fury by a Rastafarian, who in their minds took on almost mythical characteristics of the figure whites fear most. With his long locks flowing, the Rastafarian leader wore a long coat. The officers later alleged that he wielded a petrol bomb in one hand, and a brick in the other. The crowd was singing a song in Xhosa. Neither police officer spoke Xhosa, though that was the first language of local blacks. A black police officer allegedly told Fouche that the words meant that the people were going to attack the white part of town.

Had Fouche taken a calm look, he might have realized that the group was simply confused about the postponed funeral arrangements. The kind of people in the crowd were unlikely to attack the white town. One woman carried an umbrella, commonly used to ward off the relentless South African sun. In the front of the group were children as young as ten and eleven. No song was sung about attacking white homes. The Rastafarian wasn't carrying a brick, but a notebook containing gibberish, some reggae verse, and a few words about Jamaican singer Bob Marley. Only one bottle could later be found as evidence of petrol bombs, but it remains unclear whether it contained gasoline or orange soda.

But Fouche noticed none of this as the crowd approached the armored cars. Some say the crowd closed to within twenty yards, some say twelve feet. Just then, a gangly fifteen-year-old boy named Kwanele Moses Bucwa appeared ahead of the crowd on a bicycle. He knew that there was supposed to be a work stayaway to commemorate the anniversary of the Sharpeville shootings, but he had decided to go to work anyway. Bucwa was going late, hoping that young "comrades" would have stopped looking for people breaking the general strike. As fate would have it, this unlikely hero rode straight into the crowd at this moment. He hesitated, then decided to cycle on the road right between the two armored cars. Fearful that the crowd would see that he was on his way to work, he first turned and raised his fist.

The cops, who said they assumed Bucwa was one of the radical youths provoking an all-out attack, opened fire. The police fired their shots so fast that many blacks in the crowd later said the police had used machine guns.

The black journalist Mono Badela arrived about forty-five minutes later. "To my amazement, as I approached a certain spot, there were the fire engines using hose pipes. I drove past. I went to a nearby shopping center and there were a lot of people assembled there. They knew me and called me. They said, 'See where they are washing, they are washing blood. People were killed there.' " Later soldiers ordered Badela to leave, and escorted him out of the township. On the way, Badela was taken once again past the fire engine, which was still hosing down the road.

It would be some consolation if the massacre had prompted introspection or reconciliation. But it didn't. It only made blacks and whites more resolute to fight each other. To justify the massacre, police placed stones on the road and took pictures to fan fears among whites that blacks would one day make the short walk to town and attack.

The official view was summed up by the South African Broadcasting Corp. The day after the massacre, the state radio avoided direct mention of the shooting. But the radio assured white listeners that the government's own decent reform efforts had led to unrest, saying "It is natural that change should evoke resistance." It warned that "radical extremes" wanted to "destabilize society" and "create the widespread impression that the government of the day is not in full control, that it is unable to carry out its first duty of maintaining law and order." The state radio cited "continuing outbreaks of obviously well-planned and organized demonstrations, riots and attacks on police and others who represent the authority of the state, even in situations where real grievances have already been dealt with to the satisfaction of the aggrieved." The conclusion? "It is more important than ever that the state should not only be capable of maintaining order, but must be seen to be doing so. To respond inadequately to that challenge would be playing into the hands of the revolutionaries."[13]

Among blacks, the Langa massacre also reinforced the notion that barriers of violence were being broken down—and that the liberation movement should respond in kind. The ANC's Radio Freedom condemned the "gestapo police" and "Le Grange, the killer" whose "trigger-happy boys—the police—have to open fire indiscriminately, mow down the mourners, for what it regards as defense." The broadcast asked, "How can we sit back and fold our hands, when the racist regime has declared war against us?"[14]

The question was rhetorical, but anyone who needed an answer got it the next day when unrest swept across the nation's townships. According to the March 22 daily unrest report, 17,000 students stayed away from classes in Uitenhage. Several police officer's homes were destroyed by petrol bombs. Police fired birdshot at stone throwers who damaged one of their vehicles. In other parts of the country, youths stoned police vehicles and police fought back with rubber bullets, tear gas, and whips. Two hand grenades were hurled at a municipal building in Soweto. In another township, youths hijacked a bus and smashed it into a government building. In at least eight other townships, officials' homes and cars came under attack.

"Black-on-Black Violence"

In a popular township musical in the mid-1970s, a black police officer threw down his cap, tore off his coat, and sang the finale with the rest of the cast. In a drama later staged by black workers, a conservative father saw the error of his ways and joined the revolution with his children. In another play, Jesus Christ landed at Jan Smuts airport.

But in reality, freedom rarely arrives in a burst of song and dance. In South Africa, it approaches with bloodshed, not only between whites and blacks but among blacks. The brutal fact is that black South Africans don't stand together hand in hand, much less sing the finale together. The power of the South African government has depended on that. The government relies on thousands of black police and informers. Their ranks outnumber the guerrillas in ANC training camps in exile. To recruit black police, the government plucks blacks from the ranks of the unemployed and bestows upon them fringe benefits in health and housing. To recruit informers, police use a combination of intimidation and solicitation. They threaten reluctant recruits by concocting charges against them and they pay those willing to help as little as R50 for a minor tip or as much as R1000 a month for a high ranking member of an anti-government organization.

The black collaborators were the first targets of popular violence during the fighting years. Not only were they vulnerable, but black collaborators' familiarity with the tight-knit townships made them most dangerous to black organizations. "There is a clear pattern to eliminate collaborators," Vincent Maphai, a mild-mannered philosophy lecturer at the University of Witwatersrand, observed in 1985. "However cruel that is, anti-apartheid groups see it as very important because without black collaborators apartheid wouldn't be possible. The pillars of apartheid aren't only the army and police, but the black collaborators."

Fighting between black activists and collaborators—lumped into a category of "black-on-black violence"—has been the subject of the endless shaking of heads. To South African whites, it confirms the latent barbarism of South African blacks. Whites can then justify their domination on the grounds that they are the only ones keeping blacks from the wholesale murder of one another. To foreigners, the fighting was a baffling sign that blacks couldn't unite to resist the government and that blacks still suffered from "tribal rivalries," a view encouraged by the government.

Underlying the puzzlement was the assumption that blacks are all the same, either all virtuous and oppressed or all dangerous and subversive. That assumption is a fallacy. Just as there are whites who have spoken out and gone to jail with blacks, there are blacks who have given their support to the government, whether out of fear, ambition, or a strange sense of loyalty. That political violence by blacks should hit at black authorities came as no surprise to people in the townships, who knew they had white allies—as well as black enemies.

There were examples of senseless "black-on-black violence": gangster thuggery, shebeen brawls, and rural clan fighting. But that was not what white South Africans pointed to when they talked of black-on-black violence. Instead they pointed to political battles, especially to the use of a weapon known as the "necklace."

The Necklace

Some called the killing of Tamsanqa Benjamin Kinikini justice, some called it revenge. Others called it plain savagery. When the angry mob was finished, all that was left of the KwaNobuhle councillor was a charred portion of his spinal cord. Two of his sons and two nephews also died that day, March 23.

Kinikini was the first black to wear a "necklace," which became the favored technique for killing black police, informers, and collaborators. In the "refined" version of necklace killing, a crowd forced an automobile tire doused with gasoline over the head and shoulders of a suspected collaborator and then set it alight. Trapped inside the tire, suspects could not lift their arms to free themselves. Sometimes extra gasoline was applied. Death came slowly and painfully to the unfortunate suspects, and entire townships learned to recognize the strange sweet odor of burning flesh and the acrid black smoke from the tires.

"The necklace . . ." the black journalist Mono Badela mused nearly three years later in a gravelly voice. Badela had witnessed the death of Kinikini. "Where it comes from? Nobody knows. Whose instructions? Nobody knows. All we know is that people were tired of being killed," Badela said. "People were angry. People had enough!"

Two hundred and two more blacks were killed at the hands of fellow blacks from September 1, 1984, through the end of 1985.[15] Most died by the necklace. But their impact never quite matched the shock that followed the killing of Kinikini.

The killing was far more personal than lobbing a petrol bomb at a house or pulling a trigger from several paces away. The mob had chased its prey, ignored their pleas, stabbed them, beat them, held them, crushed them and torn them limb from limb.[16] The attack was so savage that months later a court could not establish the precise cause of death of one of Kinikini's sons, Silumko. The medical examiner opined that the arms were amputated before the body was burned, that the head (95 percent of which was missing) suffered a massive assault, and that the burning explained the protrusion of the intestines through the abdomen and the missing genitals. The body was almost completely charred and the right thigh partially amputated. There were also multiple fractures of all the ribs.

The wrath of KwaNobuhle did not fall on Kinikini by chance. Kinikini earned peoples' enmity over time. A founding member of the community council for the township of KwaNobuhle in 1978, Kinikini faced rising hostility directed at blacks who held official positions sanctioned by the white government. In 1983, he was one of the sixteen councillors who "elected themselves" because no one else wanted to run for the sixteen spots on the council.

The council's decision in mid-1984 to raise rents to close its deficit also sparked hostility. The houses of several councillors were attacked with stones and petrol bombs. Their businesses were boycotted. In October the councillors called a public meeting to announce that they had backed down and canceled the rent increase. Mayor Ponana James Tini entered the crowded hall and announced the cancelation of the rent increase. But feelings were running too high. "There was a commotion, people from this end and the other end, saying he is a liar, no, there is going to be an increase. Then the people all just rose up and we saw we were going to be attacked, so we ran through a side door," Tini recalled later. "We were just pelted with stones." A month later students boycotting school blamed Kinikini for refusing to let them use the community hall to hold a meeting.

As the danger grew, the black councillors sought to protect themselves. Each carried a gun, Tini said later, and was protected by municipal police. South African Police also guarded Tini's property. To go to work, Tini was picked up by a municipal vehicle driven by a municipal police officer. He took to remaining indoors because he felt unsafe on the streets.

One by one, the councillors resigned. Tini quit when his son wouldn't go to school anymore because of the verbal abuse and mocking songs sung by his classmates. By February, Kinikini was the only holdout.

It wasn't any sense of public service that made Kinikini reluctant to resign. Kinikini had long stopped going to the monthly council meetings. Prestige, patronage, and pay kept Kinikini on the council. Kinikini had used that patronage to grant himself exclusive business licenses. His swanky house stuck out among the modest township homes. "This guy was a big businessman. He had a funeral parlor, and supermarkets. He had a huge house, you see. The house was one of the biggest in KwaNobuhle," said Mono Badela. The community started a boycott of Kinikini's businesses. It was entirely effective. Fearing that the funeral parlor would be attacked, Kinikini and his sons began sleeping at the funeral parlor to protect it.

Kinikini stood out even before his fellow officials abandoned him. "Not only was Kinikini the strongman of the town council of KwaNobuhle, but he was a leader of a vigilante group," according to Mono Badela. The group allegedly beat young black "comrades." Kinikini was suspected in the death of the brother of a Uitenhage black trade union leader. In another incident, Kinikini's son was allegedly among a group of seven men who had approached a young woman and her boyfriend on a street in KwaNobuhle. "Here, comrades" they said, motioning to the couple. They grabbed her and handcuffed her while her boyfriend fled. They took her to Kinikini's funeral parlor, raped her, stuck her in a coffin, and demanded that she identify the people who had stoned Kinikini's house. After they let her go, she reported them to police, but nothing came of it. She was bitter, but she wasn't surprised. She and others had lost all faith in institutions to carry out justice against the Kinikinis. Only "the people" were seen as capable of carrying out justice, and it would be swift and merciless.

Kinikini's close associate was his neighbor, Jimmy Claasens. Claasens had a number of shacks around the township that he used as retail stands. Casual laborers used to hang around his house looking for work. Resentful of the growing authority of young black activists, Claasens fought the "comrades" and worked with the police to round up youths suspected of attacking homes and businesses. He called his group the "Peacemakers." But the community saw him and Kinikini as vigilantes who kidnapped children. Young black "comrades" didn't even know Claasens' last name. They just called him "Jimmy the criminal."

Kinikini knew he was a target of community hostility, but he wasn't frightened until the Langa massacre. Then even Kinikini felt community anger reaching the breaking point. He sent word to a local UDF leader that he was ready to resign as soon as he straightened out some financial matters between him and the council. But the UDF leader told the go-between that it was too late; Kinikini's fate was sealed. The go-between never returned to Kinikini.

On the morning of March 23, hundreds of KwaNobuhle residents set out in search of four youths who had disappeared during the night. Suspecting that the youths had been locked up in the cold storage room at Kinikini's funeral parlor, a singing and dancing crowd of 3,000 gathered outside the funeral parlor at seven in the morning. Kinikini agreed to let two members of the crowd and two police (one white and one black) search the funeral parlor. They found no one. Later another police car came upon the crowd. An officer told the people that the youths were in police custody. He sent a member of the crowd to see for himself. This time, police shot tear gas to disperse the crowd.

The crowd's suspicions were well-founded, if erroneous. In fact, early that morning Claasens, Kinikini, Kinikini's two sons and two nephews, and a gang of Claasens's employees had seized three or four black teenagers, put them in the back of Claasens' pickup truck and delivered them to the police at a makeshift police base at the Uitenhage sports grounds. According to allegations by one of the youths, the teenagers were kept in the cold storage room for a little while, then taken to the bush at the edge of the township and beaten.

While the youths hung around the Uitenhage sports grounds, the crowd had attended the funeral that police had canceled on Sharpeville Day. Emotions were running high. Afterwards, a group of young "comrades" led people to question Claasens about "why he had assaulted and shot people." But Claasens wasn't home and the mob moved on. "The youth were in thousands, moving from one house to another house," recalled Badela, who was on the scene. "There was just destruction. Destruction. In broad daylight! By four o'clock there was not a single home of a policeman [left standing. They had been] new houses. They were all destroyed."

The crowd was angry, but it was not acting randomly. Tini, the former mayor of KwaNobuhle who had resigned eleven days earlier, said the crowd stopped near the gate of his house briefly without disturbing him.

Eventually the group returned to Kinikini's funeral parlor and attacked it with petrol bombs. The building caught fire while the mob danced outside. Many were armed with clubs, machetes, knives, and petrol bombs. Inside, Kinikini, his sons, and nephews barricaded the door and frantically tried to extinguish the flames. Kinikini must have suspected the end was near. Some say he shot his twelve-year-old son. The body was never found and no one is sure if it burned inside the funeral parlor of if the boy was killed elsewhere. The other son, the two nephews, and Kinikini decided to make a run for it when they realized they couldn't put out the fire. As they climbed out the window, the crowd shouted and ran after them. The remaining son let off three shots from his father's revolver.

None of the Kinikinis made it more than 200 meters. The son suspected of raping the girl was castrated while he was being beaten and burned. Kinikini tried to climb over a fence. People on the other side said they would help him, but they stabbed at his hands as he tried to climb the fence. He let go and ran, but was stabbed in the side of the neck. He fell to the ground and offered R5,000 for his own life. A youth told him that they didn't want his money, drew a knife, and stabbed him. Tires were thrown on the body and set alight. The body was almost entirely cremated by the flames. "This is a dog," people chanted over the smoldering remains.

"You could see the anger of the people [from] how they were killing," Badela recalled later. "It was a terrible thing. I never experienced that. I've never seen so, so much anger in my life."

A month after the death of Kinikini, I visited Langa and KwaNobuhle. I was guided by a sixteen-year-old from KwaNobuhle named Skwati Zamuxolo. Schools had been out for months. There was no local government. Black police had fled the townships. White soldiers and police intermittently passed through in armored cars and stared warily at people in the streets. "The government acts as an enemy to us," Skwati told me.

He took me to a cement church, where a mournful, longing chant went up as people slowly filed in. "Buya, buya," meaning "return, return," they sang in a song dedicated to Oliver Tambo, exiled president of the African National Congress. "Come to lead us." A community leader launched into a political speech as the ministers sat back. Another song began that was more upbeat. It meant, "My mother gives me a chance to take the AK-47/ Shoot, shoot."

Outside a dozen schoolchildren around eight or nine years old skipped up the street chanting as if they were singing hopscotch rhymes. Their verses were different, though. "Go to them guerrillas, come soldiers, Oliver is a leader, Mandela is a commander," they sang. Then they saw me looking at them, and burst into giggles.

Assassins, the Just, and the Just Assassins

The death of Kinikini highlighted the wrenching question of whether violence is necessary to overthrow apartheid and, if so, whether it should have limits.

Among South African blacks, the debate echoed Albert Camus' play "The Just Assassins," in which five Russian protagonists plotting the assassination of the Grand Duke disagree about whether to throw a bomb at his carriage if his children are riding with him. "There are no limits!" shouts Stepan, one of the conspirators. If revolution will create a new society, then it allows "the right to do anything and everything that might bring that great day nearer." But another conspirator, Kaliayev, answers, "I refuse to add to the living injustice all around me for the sake of a dead justice. Killing children is a crime against a man's honor." The hardened Stepan says: "Honor is a luxury reserved for people who have carriages-and-pairs." But Kaliayev says, "No. It's the one wealth left to a poor man."[17]

During the 1950s, black South African leaders condemned exceptions to the rule of non-violence. When scattered riots broke out in 1952 or when blacks in Cato Manor outside Durban killed nine cops during a police raid on illegal beer brewers in 1960, ANC president Lutuli described the deaths as "brutal." Lutuli called rioters "irresponsible" and viewed the incidents "with horror."[18] Non-violence was central to the ANC's campaign of civil disobedience, Lutuli argued.

> The challenge of non-violence . . . robbed them [white supremacists] of the initiative. On the other hand, violence by Africans would restore this initiative to them—they would then be able to bring out the guns and other techniques of intimidation and present themselves as restorers of order.[19]

Opinion shifted in 1960, after the Sharpeville shootings and the banning of the ANC and the PAC. "The time comes in the life of any nation when there remain only two choices: submit or fight. That time has now come to South Africa," said a stirring leaflet published for the launch of Umkhonto we Sizwe, which became the ANC's military wing.[20]

Even then, attitudes toward violence remained quaint by modern standards. The radical political theorist and psychiatrist Frantz Fanon, who was close to the Algerian rebels, had argued that "Violence is a cleansing force. It frees the native from his inferiority complex and from his despair and inaction; it makes him fearless and restores his self-respect."[21] By contrast, choosing a violent path weighed heavily on ANC leaders. Violence was a last resort to bring whites "to their senses," to use Mandela's phrase. The goal of ANC attacks, unlike that of the necklace, was to arouse whites, not blacks. The ANC leaders said they still hoped to avoid "the suffering and bitterness of civil war."

Umkhonto's leaders blamed the government as the aggressor for whatever violence they used. Apartheid itself was violence. It trampled human dignity and broke blacks' spirit. Like any aggressor, the South African government had given blacks a choice: forego your rights or your lives.

The government itself "set the scene for violence by relying exclusively on violence with which to answer our people and their demands," Mandela said in 1964. "Africans are turning to deliberate acts of violence and of force against the Government, in order to persuade the Government, in the only language which this government shows, by its own behavior, that it understands."

By taking violence to a new threshold, the necklace renewed the debate over the need for violence and limits on violence. Numbed morally and emotionally, many blacks felt there should be no limits. Raised in an era of conflict, harassment, and torture, young blacks were especially hardened; they thirsted for action and retaliation. In the weeks after the death of Kinikini, other suspected collaborators were necklaced. In Duduza, east of Johannesburg, a young woman was necklaced. A television crew captured the killing on film and it was broadcast in South Africa and around the world.

Initially, the UDF leadership responded ambiguously. Many sympathized with the angry mobs, believing they were provoked. Some believed any violence, even the necklace, would tarnish the international image of the government and prove the depth of the government's unpopularity.

Others believed that necklacing served a useful strategic purpose in safeguarding the organization from informers. Increasingly cut off, the police advertised in newspapers for informants and raised the price they paid for information. A UDF leader in Port Elizabeth privately acknowledged that he sanctioned the necklace killing of a notorious informer and gangster. In a speech at a funeral in Queenstown for youths killed in police shootings, the UDF's Eastern Cape publicity secretary Stone Sizane unambiguously endorsed violence and encouraged people to fight.

> When the youth die they do not die, but fall in the battle. We . . . must take over their spears, their AKs and go forward. When one nation subjugates another the first thing they do is disarm them. They disarm us and bring in their armed forces to kill and shoot us. They expect us to take it lying down. To wear black robes and mourn. To pray and ask God to liberate us. We say enough is enough. Now is the time to hit back. So that is why we say *amabutho* must ever be strengthened, must ever be organised. They must be mobilized to hit more and most effectively.[22]

Officially the front opposed violence; that never-wavering position distinguished it from the outlawed ANC. The UDF leadership realized that to endorse violence would only invite a swift crackdown on the front, which was designed to function openly and legally. To force a full-scale confrontation could only end in defeat for the UDF.

The front also was deeply concerned about losing control over popular protest. A document debated by the Transvaal UDF executive council said, "We have been unable to respond effectively to the spontaneous waves of militancy around the country."[23] But the leadership treaded carefully, not only to avoid a government crackdown, but for fear of losing influence with the militant youth they wanted to restrain. Better to avoid public debate and to influence quietly, many thought. As a result, in public there was a shameful shuffling of feet around the issue of the necklace.

I asked a friend who was typical of young activists how he felt about the necklace. He said he had strategic problems with the necklace, because it alienated people. But he didn't have any moral objections to the necklace. He once saw a suspected informer necklaced, and, though he was a youth leader, he did nothing to dissuade the executioners.

> The crowd found that this man had sold a number of people to the system. Some guys inside [prison] got together and it became clear who had sold them [to the police]. The man was twenty-six or twenty-seven. The crowd recounted a number of things he had done. He never denied it. He said he was forced by police to do these things. After admitting it, the people said it was too late for him to repent and too late for them to show mercy. They told him he had to be baptized by fire. They said you're going to face hellfires but you might as well face them here first. So they placed a tire around his shoulders. It was already doused with petrol. His hands were tied behind his back. There was nothing he could do. He was surrounded.

"I wouldn't go to the extent of necklacing someone, but I would never try to stop this," he said. "The necklace is too gruesome and brutal, but I must say it has helped reduce the number of informers and collaborators. It is 100 percent justified. How many people have died at the hands of the police? When I went into detention, two others had just died. They had been in the same row of cells as I was in. The police pushed one from the tenth floor. That is tantamount to necklacing. They break your ribs and scatter your brains."

Aligned against my friend, however, powerful forces within black society emerged to restrain the "just assassins." The first to speak out were black church leaders opposed to violence on moral grounds. Camus' Kaliayev saw behind a call for unbridled violence "the threat of another despotism which, if even it comes into power, will make of me a murderer—and what I want to be is a doer of justice, not a man of blood."[24] Like Kaliayev, church leaders saw an inextricable link between the tactics of liberation and the character of a post-liberation society and they were profoundly disturbed about the risk of ruining the new society before it was born.

Bishop Desmond Tutu was pivotal in the debate. In July 1985, Bishop Tutu and Rt. Rev. Simeon Nkoane were leaving a political funeral in Duduza when a portion of the crowd seized a suspected informer and began to force a tire around his shoulders. Bishop Tutu and Rev. Nkoane jumped into the middle of the mob and protected the suspected informer with their own bodies. They hustled him into a waiting car and the car sped off with the informer, leaving Tutu to confront the frenzied crowd. In a squatter camp outside George, Rev. Boesak did the same, risking his own life to prevent a suspected informer from meeting an agonizing death. On another instance Bishop Tutu lay down on the body of a suspected informer and told a mob that it would have to kill him first if it wanted to kill the informer.

A few days after the Duduza incident, Bishop Tutu addressed a hostile crowd at a political funeral in KwaThema, another destitute black township. "Our cause is just and noble. That is why we will prevail. You cannot use methods to attain the goal of liberation that are used by the 'system'. Why don't we use methods of which we will be proud in years to come?"

he implored. Thousands of youths there looked skeptical. In front of Bishop Tutu, just beyond a swarm of foreign journalists, lay the dark brown coffins of fourteen young blacks shot dead in clashes with police. No white leader had stepped between the trigger-happy police and the unarmed blacks to urge restraint. Even as Bishop Tutu spoke, white soldiers cruised around the soccer stadium and taunted the mourners by shouting, "This land belongs to us" in Afrikaans.

Sensing his audience's cool response, Bishop Tutu theatrically stretched his arms, as though offering himself in Christ-like sacrifice, and said

> I understand when people are angry or hurt and want to take it out on those we think are collaborators. But I abhor all forms of violence. I want to condemn in the strongest terms what happened in Duduza. Many of our supporters around the world said then "Oh, oh. If they do those things maybe they are not ready for freedom." Let us demonstrate the discipline of people who know that they are ready for freedom. At the end of the day, we must be able to walk with our heads high!

Many blacks lacked Bishop Tutu's moral fortitude, but shared his trepidation about the tactics of popular violence.

Many feared that the necklace would turn in against itself, brutalizing the executors as much as their victims. One commentator quoted Jung, who said that "the aspect of themselves which human beings sacrifice in the attainment of a given objective in their lives is reborn and returns, knife in hand, to sacrifice that which sacrificed it."[25] By sacrificing humanity in pursuit of freedom, freedom itself would later be endangered.

In an article in *Frontline* magazine, Soweto newspaper editor Aggrey Klaaste let out the anguished cry of a black parent worried about his children. One day Klaaste had driven past a group of boys and girls in attractive school uniforms squatting by a road in the Dobsonville section of Soweto. "The children looked decent, innocent, well behaved." He later learned that the group had killed someone with garden tools and set him on fire. "I was thunderstruck," wrote Klaaste. This was not the voice of a political strategist or moralist. His was the voice of a horrified parent, racked by guilt about his own failure to effect change.

> If there is one thing that South Africa will stand accused of in the future, it is turning these lovely kids into monsters. So why don't we stop them? Remember we turned them into heroes. We let them march on Casspirs and Hippos while we watched apprehensively. You might believe it is simply an aberration of these ugly times which is bound to disappear like a nightmare. Black parents cannot afford that luxury. We are responsible for this, we feel.[26]

Other blacks were frightened by the unpredictability of mob violence. A week after Kinikini's death, Johannesburg *Star* columnist Jon Qwelane was in Langa on a reporting trip and was mistaken one night by a mob of 200 men and youths, for a man they were hunting for, a local businessman who, they alleged, had amassed wealth by exploiting the poor. "To make sure there would be no travesty of justice and I would be given a fair trial, the mob had brought along the instruments of justice," Qwelane wrote wryly. "They carried axes, spades, pitchforks, stones and petrol." Qwelane protested and was saved by his hosts, several of them former detainees and former prisoners on Robben Island. But he said, "There is quite possibly no force more terrifying than a frenzied mob howling for 'justice'."[27]

Gradually people came to view necklaced suspects as victims rather than victimizers. Qwelane cited Maki Skosana, the Duduza woman who was stoned, kicked, trampled and finally set alight by a band of youths. They placed a heavy boulder on her chest as she lay whimpering for mercy, then they piled dry straw on her to speed her incineration. She protested her innocence to her last breath. "Shed a tear for Maki Skosana, for she is no more," Qwelane wrote. She "protested her innocence to the last, but it did not matter one whit to the mob. It did not matter, too, that the 'evidence' against her was flimsier than the latest negligee."[28]

Police and community members later said that Skosana had indeed been an informer, though only on petty criminal matters, not political activities. But in other townships there were cases of mistaken identities. In Alexandra township a woman police informer who had switched allegiances and was serving as a valuable double agent for local activists was set upon by a crowd and killed.

Another important force of restraint against necklace killings and mob violence was the ANC. Unlike Tutu, the ANC had no moral objections to using violence to end apartheid. However the ANC's view of violence fell within strictly defined boundaries. At the trial that sent him to jail for the rest of his life, Mandela told the court that "The ANC was prepared to depart from its fifty-year-old policy of non-violence to this extent: that it would no longer disapprove of *properly controlled violence*."[29] Mandela noted that the ANC shunned guerrilla warfare, terrorism, and open revolution and had opted for the most limited kind of violence—sabotage.

Mandela's notion of *controlled* violence was different from the chant by many young "comrades" on their way to do battle with soldiers or police: "Siyayinyova," meaning roughly "We are making chaos." These "comrades" camped out in packs, making petrol bombs and other rudimentary devices. Distinctions between combatants and non-combatants blurred.

Mandela's own colleagues in the ANC had been partly responsible for this development. They had called on blacks to make the townships ungovernable on the theory that the tumult in the townships would be an indictment of unjust laws and government rather than of the residents. And the unrest in the townships did demolish the notion that South African government's "reform" program was winning it support among blacks.

But the ANC unleashed a fury it had not intended. Quietly it started lobbying for restraint. It told people it was concerned about the emergence of a "Khmer Rouge element" of youths who were ruthless and uncontrollable. When Winnie Mandela, never as judicious as her husband, called on South Africans to topple the government with matchboxes and tires, the ANC was aghast. The South Africa Broadcasting System, sensing that Mrs. Mandela had damaged her own credibility, broadcast the speech. After seeing it on TV in Zambia, one of the ANC leaders called Mrs. Mandela and urged her not to give any speeches for a while.

Many militants had dismissed Tutu's position, saying, as my Soweto friend did, that "Tutu is an international figure. He has to be seen to be non-violent. But ordinary youths are not apologists for the dictates of the international community." Many blacks thought Tutu should consult political organizations instead of preaching to them. "Clerics want to come from above the struggle," one UDF leader complained. "They say 'don't do violence because we know what's best for you.'" Tutu also had blundered at the KwaThema funeral by impulsively threatening to "pack my bags" and leave the country if blacks did not restrain from using violence. "Go to where?" the UDF leader asked with disdain. "Does he think he is doing us a favor by being here?"

It was more difficult to dismiss the ANC. ANC leaders began to emphasize their traditional principles of discipline and consultation. They told militant blacks that they must work with others. Consultation became a buzz word for the movement, and with consultation, moderation. Adhere to military standards, youths were told. As the old ANC men on Robben Island used to tell the young political prisoners, consider yourselves prisoners of war. It you consider yourselves soldiers, be disciplined like soldiers.

In his essay "Reflections on Gandhi," George Orwell wondered whether the non-violent resistance Gandhi advocated would be possible in a totalitarian state. The premise of Gandhi's strategy was that non-violent resistance would "arouse the world" and prick its conscience. Yet Orwell noted that it is only possible to arouse the world if the world hears what you have to say. "It is difficult to see how Gandhi's methods could be applied in a country where opponents of the regime disappear in the middle of the night and are never heard of again," Orwell wrote.[30]

In early 1985, when black leaders in South Africa tried to control the extent and targets of violence, they were working under premises similar to Gandhi's. They enjoyed a certain amount of freedom of association, they could be quoted in the newspapers and could appeal to their fellow blacks as well as to their oppressors. But as political "spaces" narrowed and it became increasingly difficult to make protest heard, as the South African government wielded the implements of an Orwellian state, more and more blacks would wonder whether non-violent resistance was futile.

Individuals within black institutions—the church, the press, community groups, unions, and the ANC—would question the wisdom of restraint as they, too, fell under the government's repressive measures. Black unions resorted to defense committees. Some ANC leaders would urge the ANC to abandon its selective strategy of violence and wage war on the white population. And elements within the church establishment would push black clergy toward a more understanding attitude toward violence.

"The question of violence is not important to the people in the townships," said UDF leader Rev. Frank Chikane. "They are confronted every day by troops in the townships. There is not a 'violent option.' It is the necessity of the situation. You have to defend yourself. More people say that the ANC is not doing enough [violence]. It is a logical consequence of what the state is doing to the people." Chikane said that after he was released on bail in early 1985 during a treason trial, his house and family were attacked with petrol bombs. Members of the Soweto community organized volunteers to guard the Chikane home. At the time, he was preaching non-violence. "I was obliged to admit that I was only able to continue preaching non-violence because others were prepared to use violence to create this space for me."

Chikane headed the Institute of Contextual Theology, which had helped formulate a statement on the role of the church under apartheid. The statement, called the Kairos Document, urged churches to openly oppose the government and "participate in the struggle for liberation."

Kairos tackled the question of violence head on. "When Jesus says that we should turn the other cheek he is telling us that we must not take revenge; he is not saying that we should never defend ourselves or others," it said. The Kairos theologians criticized churches that pretended to be neutral and condemned all violence, a catch phrase that included guerrilla bomb attacks as well as the shootings and beatings by the government. The Kairos theologians said churches should not sidestep tough moral questions by issuing such blanket condemnations. "How can acts of oppression, injustice and domination be equated with acts of resistance and self-defense? Would it be legitimate to describe both the physical force used by a rapist and the physical force used by a woman trying to resist the rapist as violence?"[31]

As 1985 progressed, Bishop Tutu felt more and more pressured from all sides. As the highest-ranking black clergyman, Tutu was pressed to lead opposition to the government. Yet as he rose in the Anglican church hierarchy, becoming Bishop of Johannesburg in February 1985, he had to answer to more and more white members of his flock. As a Nobel-Peace-Prize winner, he also served as black South Africans' unofficial ambassador to the world at large.

The outside world and white South Africans had been repulsed, not aroused, by violence in South Africa. To which a weary Tutu said, "It's clearer and clearer to me that the West doesn't care about black people. All they spend time on is the violence of the ANC, yet [the government's] shooting [of] children is not violence. I'm tired, very tired of the hypocrisy. I'm sick and tired of trying to persuade white people that our people don't like violence."

That Tutu should sound so weary was natural. Even the chubby, gentle, jovial Luthuli—who had written that prison was an opportunity for reflection and that the racial diversity of the defendants at Treason Trial of the 1950s showed what a non-racial South Africa would look like—had his moments of despair. "Will the outstretched hand be taken?" he wrote on the concluding page of his autobiography. "I fear not, not by the devisers of apartheid. It is a black hand." As the outstretched hand was turned away, it clenched into a fist.

In 1984, the Nobel committee said that Tutu wielded "the weapons of the spirit and reason" and that he was "an exponent of the only form for conflict solving which is worthy of civilized nations." Yet Tutu believed that there were circumstances that justified violence. Behind his pleadings for the government to negotiate a solution to the conflict was the veiled threat that someday even Tutu might conclude that a violent war against apartheid might be just.

But in these fighting years, he kept trying to find a way between Umkhonto's stark "submit or fight" formulation of blacks' choices. He went to Lusaka, embraced ANC leaders, and urged negotiations. He went to the presidential residence in Cape Town, and urged Botha to enter into negotiations. The form of protest he favored was economic sanctions, hammering at the point that sanctions offered the last hope of avoiding a "holocaust." Thus he raised the specter of international isolation less than a year after President Botha's triumphant tour of Western Europe.

Even as Tutu pleaded his case, he doubted whether his message was getting through. The government's resolve was stiffening and young blacks were growing more militant. Tutu himself said that if he were a young black, he wouldn't follow a man named Bishop Tutu.

CHAPTER SIX

Dual Power

IN APRIL 1985, the chief of operations of the South African Defense Force, General Jan van Loggerenberg, received me at army headquarters in Pretoria. Amiable and erect, the graying air-force veteran said, "Responsible government cannot let things get out of hand."

Yet by the middle of 1985, the government had only a tenuous grasp on events in the townships. Black police had fled from their homes and black local government structures were rapidly disintegrating. In 1983 the government had set up thirty-four black local authorities, intending to have 104 functioning by 1985. But as unrest mounted, blacks were quitting the community councils like conscripts deserting a retreating army. In June 1985, a cabinet minister conceded that sixty blacks belonging to thirty-eight new local authorities had quit since the Vaal uprising. In addition, 197 blacks belonging to a total of 195 community councils, had resigned, including twenty-two mayors. The army called up 35,000 white soldiers to do one-month tours of duty in the townships, but the government was no longer able to impose its own order. By the end of the year, only four local authorities would be functioning.

The ANC egged on its compatriots. On April 25, 1985, the African National Congress issued a pamphlet bearing the slogans: "Make apartheid unworkable! Make the country ungovernable!" echoing a speech made by Tambo earlier that year. But the urgency of the ANC pamphlet was more an attempt to keep pace with, rather than inspire, events unfolding in the townships.

In the middle of 1985, however, a critical change in black strategy began to take place, arising principally from within the country rather than from the ANC in exile. Instead of making urban black townships ungovernable for the white-sanctioned administration, anti-apartheid leaders started tightening their own ability to orchestrate events in the black areas. Instead of simply thwarting government initiatives, black community organizations (generally affiliates of the UDF) tried to seize the initiative.

A confidential UDF discussion paper circulated in May 1985 argued that the new strategy would link the destruction of apartheid to the creation of a new society:

> Having established the illegitimacy of the S. African regime, it is necessary to project a popular alternative. . . . Where the apartheid puppets are no longer able to effectively function, a stage could be reached where the people's organisation assumed responsibility for organising the community to govern itself in a variety of ways from setting up health clinics to crime prevention.
>
> This will make people fully understand our vision of a future democratic South Africa. As long as utopian illusions aren't created amongst the people (leading to inevitable disillusionment), what these embryos of democracy will give birth to is a vision of a totally alternative society.[1]

The idea of controlling their own communities—and their own destiny—excited black South Africans and infused them with the romance of power often without appreciation of the responsibilities of power. Like the Paris Commune or the soviets of pre-Bolshevik Russia, the enthusiasm of ordinary citizens for a parallel government under their control confounded the expectations of the government and activists alike. Hannah Arendt's description of those earlier uprisings applies equally to South Africa's black townships in 1985: "What actually happened was a swift disintegration of the old power, the sudden loss of control over the means of violence, and, at the same time, the amazing formation of a new power structure which owed its existence to nothing but the organizational impulses of the people themselves."[2]

There was a strange duality to the nature of power during this period. Calm ruled the white South African cities and suburbs, where usually the only uniformed officers on the streets were traffic officers. Threats to white power seemed illusory. A popular song described an afternoon in the white areas this way:

> There's a smell of rotting peaches hanging thick on the ground
> And pink-bodied children making shrieking sounds
> And she's lying under leaves
> just waiting to be numbed
> By the smothering lull of suburbia hum.

Within the townships, however, Pretoria's power seemed illusory as UDF affiliates started to pose themselves as alternatives to the official government.

First in the small towns of the Eastern Cape, and later in big cities and other provinces, blacks answered to a new voice of authority.

Black Star over Port Alfred

The black township of Inkwenkwezi, whose name means "star" in Xhosa, is perched on a muddy hilltop overlooking the placid seaside resort of Port Alfred. For as long as whites in Port Alfred could remember, Inkwenkwezi had been a fixture in their firmament. Every morning the blacks walked down the hill, past the second-hand-furniture store, and across the narrow bridge over the lagoon into the "white" town. There they worked in stores, maintained roads, and tended lawns in the white neighborhoods. Blacks spent their money in the white-owned stores, then trudged back to Inkwenkwezi.

In June 1985, Inkwenkwezi veered from its orbit around the lives of whites in Port Alfred. The township's 14,000 blacks launched a boycott of all white stores, demanding improvements in living conditions in Inkwenkwezi. For two weeks, business in Port Alfred came to a near standstill. "Retailers suddenly discovered that about 70 percent of their business was black trade. Some guys along Wharf Street had about 95 percent black trade," says David Hansen, a local white businessman. "These people were wetting their pants," a township leader laughed. On June 19, a group of white business leaders went to negotiate with the black boycott leaders. I remember it was June 19 because it was my wife's birthday and she was cross that I was going off to talk to the blacks," Hansen recalls.

The meeting lasted three hours. Residents of Inkwenkwezi demanded that rent arrears be written off and that rent be reduced for pensioners. The blacks wanted to establish a municipal council that would do something about living conditions in the township, where people lived in houses made of mud and scrap metal and where the gutted dirt roads were virtually impassable by car.

Threatened with financial strangulation, the Port Alfred business community met the demands with unexpected alacrity. They persuaded police to withdraw from the township, obtained funds to create jobs in the area, persuaded the East Cape Development Board (nominally the landlord for the township) to give in to the rent demands, drew up plans for more equitable public works expenditure, and invited blacks to attend Port Alfred town council meetings. The boycott ended after fourteen days.

Port Alfred was a microcosm of South Africa's revolt, and its consumer boycott marked the beginning of the new era in black community politics. Until then, the UDF merely reacted to initiatives taken by the government, attempting to discredit them by showing people's disaffection through election boycotts, public rallies, and the million-signature petition. These strategies fell into what Boesak called the "politics of refusal."

But Port Alfred's black township had seized the initiative and set the agenda, forcing whites to respond. For the first time, a black community had wielded power, not just resisted it.

Within weeks, black consumer boycotts spread through the Eastern Cape, hammering white retailers in fifteen other towns. When blacks in the townships surrounding Port Elizabeth stopped buying from white stores, the impact was swift. The average white retailer in Port Elizabeth lost more than 30 percent of its business. Food, clothing, and furniture stores were hit hardest. One Main Street clothing store that catered to blacks had fewer than fifteen customers—none black—during the entire first two weeks of the boycott. B. A. Takeaways, a sandwich shop named after a character from the American television series "The A-Team," lost 70 percent of its customers. Furniture stores were hit twice: new sales plunged and many blacks stopped paying installments on furniture already bought. The furniture retailers didn't dare go into the townships to repossess the goods.

The Port Elizabeth Consumer Boycott Committee, which included representatives of various community groups, demanded an end to police misconduct, abolition of apartheid policies, the withdrawal of troops from the townships, improvements in black education, the unbanning of the ANC, and an explanation for the mysterious murder of regional leader Matthew Goniwe. To circumvent the corrupt and deadening bureaucracy that dealt with blacks, the boycott leaders wanted to use business leaders as a direct line to central government. The owners of Kolnick's, a fifty-four-year-old clothing store in the heart of the city, wrote a frantic letter to Botha urging that he meet black demands. Botha replied that he was "up to date with the circumstances . . . in your lovely city" and assured Kolnick's proprietors that the boycott was only due to "a minority group of people." It was scant assurance to Kolnick's, where blacks had accounted for eighty-five percent of sales.

"My phone has been ringing all the time with businessmen asking how they are going to survive," said Andrew Savage, an opposition member of the white house of Parliament. "Whites might delude themselves that they are independent and go about their business as if on another planet, but they're not. A flat-footed policeman can stand outside a shop, but can't get people to move inside. The boycott is the most sophisticated weapon with the best long-term opportunities."

Underlying the success of the consumer boycott was the extent to which South Africa had become an economically integrated country, despite the government's official policy of apartheid. Though kept in relative poverty, by virtue of their sheer demographic strength black consumers held 47 percent of South Africa's total buying power, compared to 40 percent for whites. Blacks trailed whites in just two major categories of purchases: liquor and cars.

"The [consumer] boycott is teaching white people that they can never be independent of us," said Tutu. Some blacks noted the irony of using a black boycott against a white government that officially advocated separate political and economic development for different races. That same government was alarmed when blacks actually threatened to stick to black stores in black townships. "Apartheid is being used to kill apartheid," said Port Elizabeth lawyer Silas Ntutuzelo Nkanunu.

Consumer boycotts also ushered in an era of black community organization that had more to do with governing than with ungovernability. The boycotts committed township leaders to a wide range of administrative responsibilities. Organizing a boycott was different from organizing a funeral rally or march. Blacks faced an array of strategic choices: when and what to boycott, what to demand, and when to negotiate. How would compliance be monitored and enforced?

The UDF affiliates also acquired powers of patronage during the consumer boycotts. In Uitenhage, the UDF local affiliate exempted a clothing store belonging to the Watson brothers, who years earlier quit white rugby to join a township rugby association, Within the townships, black entrepreneurs readily complied with UDF price guidelines because they were eager to reap the benefits UDF leaders dispensed by giving a store their blessings. "My sales have doubled," said Dan Qeqe, the owner of a sandwich shop and gasoline station at the entrance to the township New Brighton. He expanded his work force from six to ten.

The UDF affiliates had to settle a myriad of disputes. To ensure compliance with the boycott, groups of young "comrades" regularly inspected the parcels of blacks returning from white towns. In some instances, blacks found with purchases from white stores were summarily punished. "Comrades" beat them or emptied their purchases on the ground. Township residents called upon the UDF to control the young enforcers. Black hawkers appealed for special protection. To eke out a living, poor hawkers bought small amounts of goods from white wholesalers in town and sold them illegally along the township streets. Consumer boycott leaders wanted to protect legitimate hawkers without helping boycott cheaters. What was required were powers normally reserved for local government. In the vacuum left by the vanishing authority of the white administration boards and their proxies, the black community councillors, the UDF assumed such powers.

These powers were rooted in networks of street committees. Here again, Port Alfred and the Eastern Cape were at the forefront of experiments in self-government. "We are establishing a peoples' democracy," said Gugile Nkwinti, a thirty-six-year-old psychiatric nurse who was general secretary of a sort of self-styled peoples' republic of Port Alfred.

Nkwinti was a founder of that little republic. Originally from the townships outside Grahamstown, a college town about forty minutes' drive north of Port Alfred, Gugile Nkwinti moved to Inkwenkwezi in 1976 to work in a clinic. In late 1983 as political sentiments were rising to the surface of black townships around the country, Nkwinti tried to convene a general meeting of the township; only eight people showed up.

To overcome community apathy, Nwinti held a series of non-political activities. "You don't come to a township and say you're organizing politics," Nkwinti realized. "You need to get people to know you and trust you." Declaring 1984 the year of the aged, he organized a full day of entertainment for the elderly in the township. Then he started soccer clubs for the young blacks. He also advised people with illnesses. A year after the first attempt at a general meeting, Nkwinti felt confident enough to end meetings with the words, "Amandla. Viva Nelson Mandela, viva." And people responded.

Nkwinti had tapped a dormant volcano of civic energy. Within the township on the hill, blacks began to govern themselves for the first time. They held elections and policed themselves. They stopped paying rent to the government administration board in June 1985 and instead paid taxes of R0.20 a month to the Port Alfred Residents Civic Organization, the name of the black community group. Every member of the township belonged to an association of pensioners, workers, students, or youth.

The township was divided into streets and areas, each with representatives chosen by the residents. The township's central committee met every Tuesday, the twelve area committees (each with ten members) met every Wednesday, and the street committees met every Thursday. Said Nkwinti:

> We make decisions at the central committee on issues brought up by various organizations. When a decision goes out to the people, it goes out through the street and area committees. It's not one-way traffic, though. It's a two-way thing. Sometimes a street committee itself will decide on an issue and it will be taken to the central committee. It's very very beautiful. Marvelous.

New names signified a departure from the past. By using the name Port Alfred in the name of the civic instead of Inkwenkwezi, residents emphasized their belief that blacks and whites were part of one municipality. One area committee called itself a "soviet." The civic organization rechristened the township "Nelson Mandela Township" and sent a letter to Pollsmoor Prison inviting Mandela to attend a ceremony.

The civic organization also addressed issues of local concern. It raised money for a headstone at the old cemetery, where the graves were previously unmarked. The central committee occupied a building that was abandoned by the white-run administration board of the black township and turned the building into a day-care center. The street committees organized a boycott of a beer hall. After it went out of business, they proposed to turn it into a community center that students wanted to name after Oliver Tambo. Women from the township wanted to turn it into a self-help and handicraft center.

Street committees considered closing all shebeens at 8 P.M. Though the rule sounded harsh, Nkwinti noted that it represented a compromise. Some residents wanted the shebeens closed altogether. Prohibitionist feelings ran strong among many young comrades who saw rampant alcoholism as an obstacle to political mobilization. (This puritanical streak didn't extend to marijuana, however. Dagga, as it is called in South Africa, is popular among black youths.)

Later, even parts of the government came to recognize the civic as the real power in the township. When the Department of Education and Training wanted to appoint two new teachers to a school for the township, it solicited the opinion of the civic organization. It also sent architects to the civic to discuss plans to build a new junior primary school.

Ghosts of Cradock

The idea of street committee networks for the black townships germinated on the barren plains of the Great Karoo, where the sleepy white town of Cradock and the dusty black township of Lingelihle sit side by side as though huddled for protection against the arid expanse that surrounds them.

Cradock is the northern point of the Eastern Cape and was once a remote outpost of the British empire. Blacks in Cradock thus considered themselves part of the Eastern Cape's history of resistance to white rule. When Afrikaner pioneers and British colonists settled the province, they fought eight wars against the blacks, who proved unyielding to conquest or religious conversion. These battles, fought from 1780 until 1857, became known to whites as the "Kaffir Wars."

The stubborn resistance of the Eastern Cape blacks was recounted in a travelogue that was popular among whites in South Africa early in the twentieth century. Afrikaners settling the Cradock district in the 1830s cornered a group of "bushmen" in their ancestral cave. The Afrikaners' commander, Louw Pretorius, sent a fourteen-year-old boy to "offer terms of surrender." Korel, the chief, refused to surrender and sent the boy back. The Afrikaners, armed with guns, attacked. Fighting only with bows and arrows, Korel and his men killed seven of the Afrikaners before the well-armed whites battled their way into the cave and killed every man.[3]

Such stories became the stuff of white frontier folklore, but also lay the foundations of black protest. In the twentieth century, Cradock's township became a stronghold of the African National Congress. It produced many ANC leaders, including the general secretary in the 1940s, Rev. James Calata.

In 1983, more than two decades after the government tried to snuff out blacks' spirit of resistance by banning the ANC, Calata lay dying in his living room in the run-down Cradock township.

> Gertrude Calata recalls that her ailing father, the Rev. James Calata, convened a meeting of the ANC just as he had done many times as the organization's secretary general in the 1940s. But this time, he and his daughter were the only people in the room. "He was talking to ANC colleagues who were

> already dead," the daughter recalls. "He was telling them to plead with the people to shed the yoke of oppression."
>
> Two days later, Mr. Calata died, but the mystical spirit of the ANC he had conjured up survived; it spread from his house to inhabit the entire township. Residents say the funeral, held on the local soccer field, inspired a wave of political activism that made this rural community one of the most tumultuous places in the country. . . . [4]

At the time of Calata's death, a thirty-six-year-old schoolteacher named Matthew Goniwe was emerging as the natural heir to Cradock's history of resistance. Popular among militant students, Goniwe bridged the black generation gap and was a unifying force in Cradock's township.

The charismatic Goniwe led the UDF campaign against black community councillors. When they resigned en masse, Goniwe went with youths to take down the barbed-wire fences and wire-mesh window guards that surrounded the councillors' houses. It was a gesture of reconciliation, Goniwe said. Once the official had resigned from the dummy council he had no reason to fear his fellow township residents. "We have never fought the people in community councils," he wrote in his private notes, "We [have] fought the institutions from which they operated."[5] Goniwe filled the vacuum left by the council that quit. In August 1983, he founded the Cradock Residents' Association, which later ran a soup kitchen and helped people obtain pensions. He divided Lingelihle's 17,000 residents into seven zones. Forty activists were assigned to hold meetings where residents elected officials for each zone. The zones were sub-divided and representatives chosen for a network of street committees. The committees all fell under the residents' association, chaired by Goniwe. "He had the Lingelihle township outside Cradock in his hands," said black journalist Mono Badela.

A government proposal to transfer Goniwe to another teaching post in December 1983 and his subsequent dismissal sparked the most prolonged and widespread school boycotts ever in South Africa. In March 1984, Goniwe was held in solitary confinement for five months. For the rest of the year, 4,500 black pupils boycotted the township's seven schools. Students believed the government wanted to snuff out Goniwe's influence. From Pretoria to Port Elizabeth, students walked out of schools in sympathy. Within months, tens of thousands of students were boycotting classes. Aggravated by other issues as well, Cradock students stayed away from classes for a year and a half.

When fired from his job at the state secondary school in Cradock, Goniwe became a full-time UDF organizer, urging other townships around the Eastern Cape province to imitate the Cradock Residents Association. "After he had established Cradock, Goniwe went to the neighboring towns like Cookhouse and Somerset East to try to establish other civic bodies. The whole thing snowballed because of him," said Badela. "He was a born leader."

The government blamed Goniwe for fomenting rebellion and student boycotts. And Goniwe indeed referred to himself in his notes as a "revolutionary." "We should never be self-satisfied, because he who feels self-satisfied is not a revolutionary," he wrote.

Within the townships, however, blacks respected Goniwe because he brought stability to Lingelihle. He tried to instill in black youths a set of values that would be suitable in any Sunday school.

In notes Goniwe made in preparation for a speech to black youths, he wrote, "We want young men and women who are embodiments of the new SA." A young black must be "well-behaved" Goniwe wrote. He urged monogamous relationships rather than youths who "butterfly" with "so and so today and that one tomorrow." He admonished against drinking and drugs; "whilst comrades are not expected to be ascetics, we need hardly emphasize the benefits of cadres who are of sober habits." Despite the popularity of reggae music, Goniwe debunked Rastafarians as models for black youths. Goniwe said singers like Bob Marley and Peter Tosh had a positive side: they sang about oppression, urged people to "stand up and fight" and they "abhor[red] inequality." But Goniwe opposed the legalization of marijuana because it was a form of "dependence." He added that for activists, dagga use posed a "security risk." Goniwe disliked the slovenly appearance of Rastafarians. He said it was once fashionable to believe that to be a revolutionary one must have "unkempt hair" and a "dirty look." But Goniwe wrote that blacks could be "neat and still revolutionary" and "on the other hand, [could be] dirty [and] very reactionary." He noted that "A good personal appearance, a friendly smile and a hearty welcome help establish good relations."

He lectured youths, saying "If we are instruments of change, we MUST epitomise [the] society we want to bring about. [You] cannot over-drink and hope people will see you as representing a new society. [You] cannot be promiscuous [and] still tell people about [ending the] exploitation of women."

He wrote a nine-point "code of conduct" for activists that included much of this advice. The code also underlined the importance of honesty, warned that "comrades must avoid being haughty, bombastic or dominating," and advised that "one must trust people when one expects them to trust one."

Even at the height of his influence and popularity, Goniwe possessed humility and caution. "What does history prove?" he asked in his notes.

> That men have had power and have abused power. Even in revolutionary processes certain individuals acquire extraordinary power. . . . In this phase of the revolutionary process through which we are living, there are great dangers: the danger of vanity, the danger of conceit, the danger of deification, the habit of having authority, the habit of holding and exercising power.

On June 27, 1985, Goniwe left a meeting in Port Elizabeth and phoned his wife to say he was heading home. He never arrived. A couple of days later a search team found his charred and mutilated body in a clearing a couple of hundreds yards off the road where his car had stopped. Three of his colleagues who were traveling with him were found dead nearby.[6] Though no one ever proved who ordered the death of Goniwe, most blacks believed the government was responsible.

About 50,000 people from across the country crammed into the tiny township to pay their respects to the Lingelihle schoolteacher. Many arrived the night before and heard residents describe Lingelihle's street committees. As the crowd processed to the cemetery a group of youths unfurled a huge red flag with a hammer and sickle, and carried it aloft as black clergy walked below. Badela recalls that "People looked at it in disbelief. Nobody, at least in my period, had seen the red flag before. It was blazing red with priests under it. It was *huge*. Its appearance was hailed. There were shouts of amandla." Whether Goniwe himself was a communist was never made clear. But the red flag flew in the Cradock township and a scarlet velvet cloth was draped over Goniwe's coffin.

Emergency!

The night before the funeral, the South African government had declared a state of emergency in thirty-six magisterial districts, the first state of emergency since the Sharpeville shootings and pass burnings in 1960. Anticipating that thousands of activists would attend the Goniwe funeral, and hoping to trap them at roadblocks as they returned, the government waited until midday to announce the emergency over state radio.

"When at the funeral it was announced that Botha declared a state of emergency, you could see the leaders just vanish from the scene" to avoid capture, Badela recalls. Badela eluded the roadblocks, as did many others. Some spent the night hiding in the Lingelihle township. There they watched President Botha announce the emergency, *post facto*, on television. Botha characteristically wagged his finger for emphasis. "It felt like he was pointing right at us," one activist recalls. A busload of activists was detained in Johannesburg, leaving the bus floor littered with ANC pennants.

UDF Eastern Cape vice president Harry Fazzie evaded the dragnet for weeks. The police had pictures of Fazzie at every road block so the soldiers would recognize him. But Fazzie disguised himself. He dressed himself as a minister. Police searched Fazzie's own home and failed to recognize him, one story went. Fazzie even flew on the state-owned airline using a false name.

But within a few weeks, Fazzie was captured, as were thousands of others. By its own count, the government detained 7,996 people during the seven-and-a-half-month emergency. Monitoring groups put the figure much higher. To curtail demonstrations, the government also barred 102 organizations (most affiliates of the UDF) from holding indoor or outdoor meetings in eight districts. The Congress of South African Students was banned altogether.

A few weeks, later, Botha looked out the window of his wood paneled office with satisfaction. It was springtime and below the Union Buildings in Pretoria, purple jacaranda petals were floating to the ground. "We live in a world where there are forces that want to overthrow forces of stability. It's all over the globe," he told me. "I think we will be able to contain these agitators' attempts."

The belief that black unrest was stirred up by "agitators" guided the government strategy in 1985. If it removed the "agitators," the government believed it could restore a natural calm, like the atmosphere that prevailed in the white suburbs. In February 1985 the government arrested top UDF leaders and put them on trial for treason. The defendants included the biggest names in the UDF, ranging from Indian social worker Cassim Saloojee to black matriarch Albertina Sisulu, from the young Reverend Frank Chikane to the black patriarch Archie Gumede. According to the government's 588-page indictment in the case against sixteen of the UDF leaders, they were all part of a "revolutionary alliance" that included the ANC, the South African Communist Party, and the 1950s ANC trade union.

The "revolutionary alliance" had created, in the words of Deputy Minister of Law and Order Adriaan Vlok, a "pre-revolutionary situation" in an attempt to seize power from the Pretoria regime. The alliance fit into a communist-inspired onslaught spearheaded by the ANC. The red flag at Goniwe's funeral only confirmed that theory.

Rounding up the "ringleaders" of the black opposition was a tactic the government had used in the 1950s.[7] The aim wasn't so much to obtain convictions—since the charges of treason were flimsy—but to distract the leadership and cripple their organizations. The killing of Goniwe appeared to be a logical extension of the campaign against agitators.

The state of emergency also fit the pattern. By limiting the geographical scope of the emergency to thirty-six magisterial districts, the government was saying that black unrest was limited and that a few sharp raps at the troublesome points would push the lid on the situation.

The treason trials, the state of emergency, and the mass detentions only showed how gravely the government misunderstood the scope of the uprising that was just beginning in the black townships. That uprising was a popular insurrection on a scale never before witnessed in South Africa. "In the early 1960s, the resistance was inspired by the leadership," a defendant in one of the UDF treason trials said. "All the government had to do was arrest some leaders and exile others to bring the whole situation under control. Now there is so much anger in the atmosphere! Even in areas where you don't see concrete resistance, there is an anger that means things can explode in any part of the country."

And things did explode. On July 23, three days after the emergency was declared, more than 20,000 blacks rallied at a funeral in KwaThema, a township about forty miles outside Johannesburg. They danced, chanted, and vowed to continue resistance in a four-hour funeral service for fourteen blacks slain by police. "A ruler who doesn't rule according to God's law is an unjust ruler," Bishop Tutu told the crowd. "The system of apartheid is immoral. The system of this country is evil!" Though "furthering the aims of the ANC" was punishable by years of imprisonment, the throng in KwaThema sang and chanted the name of Oliver Tambo.

Notwithstanding heavy police and army patrols, the uprising continued in the townships. The toll from political violence rose to an average of three to four deaths per day. Each cycle of "riot and counter-riot" as Chief Lutuli had called clashes with police, culminated in a political funeral rally, a march, more violence, and counter-violence. At each funeral, ANC colors were draped on coffins and flown from flags and banners.

The ire of black students grew more intense in the wake of these battles. Groups of "comrades" roamed the townships, skirmishing with troops and watching for informers and collaborators. In Duncan Village outside East London, fierce unrest broke out in August. Students burned down twelve of thirteen schools and ripped up the few phone lines to the township. Nationwide, 294 African schools were damaged in unrest. Bishop Tutu warned that by detaining black leaders, the government had created a "leaderless mob."

Within weeks, however, lower-level leaders moved up to replace those on trial or in jail. They sustained boycotts and launched new protests. Consumer boycotts spread, first to the coastal city of East London, then elsewhere. Black mineworkers stopped buying from company stores in mine hostels. In Port Elizabeth, the emergency prolonged the boycott. When the boycott began, six days before the emergency, boycott leaders had secretly promised white businesspeople they would start negotiating after a week. However, when the appointed day arrived, the original boycott leaders were all in detention or on the run. Later residents lengthened their list of demands to include the release of emergency detainees, the end of the emergency, and the withdrawal of troops from the townships.

Student strikes widened. Soweto students started boycotting classes a week after the emergency was declared. At the peak of the boycotts, 674,275 African and about 360,000 colored pupils stayed away from classes, according to the Department of Education and Training. More than two-thirds of African secondary schools closed down.[8]

Pressure against community councillors mounted. In Mamelodi, a township outside Pretoria, three more councillors resigned. Joe Hlongwane, the president of the opposition Mamelodi Peoples' Party, quit after his business was boycotted. The mayor, Alex Kekane, resigned under pressure from his family. The remaining council members remained under tight police and army protection.[9]

"The fact is that the emergency failed to curtail resistance. It failed completely," says Badela. "Many people were detained, but we got new leaders coming up. It curtailed meetings and all that jazz and COSAS was banned, but the UDF remained strong. People came out in bigger numbers at funerals. That's how you could gauge."

The government tried in vain to quash the cycle of funeral rallies. On November 21, 1985, tens of thousands of residents from Mamelodi, led by mothers, marched to protest a ban on weekend funerals, the restriction against more than fifty mourners attending each funeral, high rents, and the presence of troops in the township. Mothers in particular had enlisted in the protest in order to preempt students, who they believed provoked police. But fighting broke out anyway when police tried to break up the march; thirteen people were killed and hundreds injured. The clash galvanized the township and united parents with the more militant students. The new militancy was symbolized by the appearance of portions of car axles propped up on street corners to look like cannons.

In the wake of the shooting, Mamelodi began to govern itself like the townships in the Eastern Cape. Street committees were formed. The government suspended garbage collection after a rent strike began, so the street committees launched "Operation Clean-up" and borrowed trucks from township businessmen. The campaign took aim at crime too. Youths built parks from scraps of wood, stones, and painted tires and named them after political symbols and leaders.[10]

The emergency made street committees more attractive than before. Emergency restrictions made it more difficult to hold open rallies and meetings, as the shootings in Mamelodi demonstrated. But street committees could withstand repression because they could meet inconspicuously. A street committee from East London's black townships met in downtown East London one day, casually munching sandwiches, leaning against a parking meter, and sitting on the curb as though on a normal work break.

The state of emergency did nothing to quell the black uprising. If anything, it swept hundreds of thousands of blacks into political action for the first time, from tiny dorps (small towns) to big townships. Protests erupted from sprawling Soweto to the tiny hamlet of Humansdorp in the Eastern Cape; from the sandy township of Athlone of coloreds to the sweltering Durban townships that had been relatively quiet for more than year.

"The emergency caught people unaware," said Mpho Mashinini, who was detained at the outset of the emergency for six months.

> The leadership was picked up and no one was outside to direct things. There was no UDF to tell people what action to take. It was left in peoples' own hands. As a result it changed the pattern of daily struggle. More people were mobilized and conscientized than ever before. It was amazing the stories we heard from those coming into prison for fourteen-day stretches.

The uprising included people never involved in politics before. Distinctions between ordinary people and activists blurred. In Graaff Reinet, a colored high-school secretary and her husband, Xavier Stuart, the carpenter whose childhood home had been expropriated, got involved in their community organization. In Hillbrow, a part of Johannesburg officially reserved for whites, a colored beautician took charge of a block committee meeting about how to protect the thousands of black and colored residents of the area. In Soweto, a black grocerystore owner joined his street committee. Philosophy lecturer Vincent Maphai's sixty-three-year-old mother, a devout Catholic who had once told her son to thank whites for his education and warned him to stay away from politics, was backing a rent boycott.

The extent of black involvement was due to heightened political awareness and the bluntness of the emergency as an instrument of repression. "The state of emergency affected everyone, unlike earlier repression when a specific paper or person or organization was banned," said Mpho Mashinini. Mpho, the younger brother of Tsietsi, who led the 1976 Soweto uprising, said, "The emergency did a great deal more organizing than the organizations ever dared to do. It affected the guy who sits at the shebeen, the guy who gets home from work at ten, later than the emergency curfew."

At the roadblocks set up to catch activists, every black was treated as a suspect. No black was too respectable to escape harassment. Eric Mafuna, a wealthy advertising consultant whose success was viewed with suspicion by black militants in the townships, was treated with equal suspicion and resentment by young working-class white police. One night on his way home, Mafuna was held at a road block. (He knew he was there more than an hour when the Voice of America news came onto his radio a second time.) Another time, on his way to dinner with the American ambassador, Mafuna and his wife were stopped at a road block. "There's my wife dressed to kill and me in my three-piece suit," Mafuna recalled later. "I'm told to get out of the car and 'spread them.' " Meanwhile teenage soldiers ordered his wife taken to a tent and strip-searched. She returned to the car in tears; Mafuna turned the car around and sped home. "I was so angry at that moment I could have done anything," Mafuna said later. "If one of those soldiers had been standing in front of the car I would have run him over."

In early 1986, the South African government faced a number of deadlines imposed by countries overseas. The Commonwealth had set a deadline for reform measures beyond which it would impose sanctions. International bankers were threatening to cripple the economy by refusing to reschedule the country's $22 billion debt if the state of emergency did not end. And in the United States a campaign to pass a sanctions bill was gathering momentum in Congress. Private companies were under pressure to pull out. At least twenty U. S. companies started winding down their South African operations in 1985. American university endowments, and city and state pension funds were selling off billions of dollars of stock in companies doing business in South Africa.

Eager to placate world opinion, the South African government lifted the state of emergency on March 7, 1986, and released the last 327 emergency detainees. Like detainees released earlier, they found that the black political landscape had changed. Mashinini said that "When we got out, we didn't stand out as activists anymore. Everybody was involved."

One of the last detainees to emerge was Kenneth Fihla, a leader of COSAS. Fihla had been kept in a cell with about thirty-six other prisoners. Police periodically hosed down the prisoners with water and left them to sleep in wet blankets, Fihla said.

When interrogated, Fihla was blindfolded, threatened, hourly given electric shocks to his fingers. Fihla, who was never charged, said his eight months in prison only hardened his resolve. "Detention can never stop me. It has only strengthened my commitment and involvement."

Comrades

By early 1986, the South African government's view of black agitators expanded to include "faceless so-called comrades" as well as the ANC and communists. Magazines and newspapers picked up on the young rebels who were in the front lines of battles with police. To many blacks as well as whites, the word "comrades" summoned up an image of unaccountable, reckless youths.

Who were the comrades? The phrase was popularized by ANC documents, Radio Freedom, and prisoners on Robben Island. But black youths were the ones brazen enough to call each other comrades in daily conversation and the word became their label. According to Badela,

> Usually the word 'comrades' applies to a group of youth, many of them members of the youth congresses. They formed themselves into groups and were those who were fighting the police and soldiers. At times they are called *amabutho,* which means a small battalion, or the Young Lions. They were the people who ensured that peoples' positions were carried out. They would help spread the word and protect the leaders. During stayaways, they would go to the station and ensure that people didn't go to work.

The comrades had bases all over the townships. They held their own meetings to plan action. The type of people who became comrades varied from juvenile delinquents who liked the thrill of fighting with police to idealistic youths, dedicated to ending apartheid. The former category had a special name of their own, "comtsotsis," a combination of the word comrade and the word "tsotsi," which means thug or criminal. Comtsotsis spoke little English, prefering a street patois called tsotsitaal (literally "thug language"; "taal" is the Afrikaans word for language).

The more idealistic youths often had been to high school or college. They insisted on educational and organizational meetings conducted in English, consistent with the idea that all blacks and whites should share a common nation and a common language. They elected general councils for the youth congresses, subdivided them into coordinating committees representing zones, which were subdivided again into branches. This way they hoped to make the youth congresses "accountable" to a large number of youths. The comtsotsis "did not like the idea of attending endless meetings and discussing issues which to them did not have a direct impact on what action the organization was to take," said a member of the Soweto Youth Congress. The comtsotsis also sneered at the people who spoke English; "To them such people are not tough enough for the kind of action they envisage."

An acquaintance introduced me to two young comrades. One was a languid-looking nineteen-year-old who was involved in unrest in the Vaal triangle in September 1984. The other, age sixteen, had been involved only three months when I met him in November 1985. He looked a bit more animated. Neither gave me his name; they were on the run from the police. Their English was weak; from time to time they relied on my acquaintance to translate.

The older one was acting as a coordinating chair of students in the Sebokeng area. Though COSAS was banned officially, he said it still functioned underground, thinly disguised by new names. "My own deskmate is in jail," he said impassively, "and I know the police are fucking him up."

The pair had become involved because of poor conditions at schools. The older one said that "when you go to the toilet [at the school] you would think a hog pissed there." Both found crowded classrooms. The older youth shared a classroom with about seventy-five students; the younger student had sixty-eight children in his classroom. The older one said he had to share a small plastic chair with another student.

Both urged fellow students to stay out of school until the government made significant concessions. They were aware that parents had doubts about the school boycotts. "Parents with no education want children to read and write for them," the older boy acknowledged. But he said the school boycott was the only form of protest open to students.

Neither youth had any qualms about the use of violence to bring people in line with boycotts. "There's a saying in Soweto. A whip from a tree branch is bent. You can't straighten it when it is dry; you have to do it while it is still supple," the older one said. He cited the expression as a reason for using physical persuasion against people who weren't supple. "You must warn them that they are hurting the struggle. If they don't listen, then they are disciplined in a physical way. Beaten up."

The two comrades weren't optimistic about the government's response to the boycott.

> We've talked so long with the government to bring repairs to [black] education. If the government doesn't give us those things, we won't be surprised. If not, then we'll consider other things, like taking the government from its seat by force. Blood for blood. The only thing is to leave education. You will get better education through the barrel of an AK.

Later the pair "skipped" the country and joined the ANC.

Other young comrades lived lives of conspiracy. "There are two types of petrol bombs," X explained to me. First there is the kind that has no fuse. You put sand inside the jar with petrol siphoned from a gasoline tank. When you throw the jar, the friction from the sand ignites the petrol. The more effective kind of petrol bomb you close with a rag, which you use as a fuse and light before you throw. This is more dangerous because it can explode in your hand, but it is more effective because it has more gasoline inside and you can be sure it will catch on fire.

One night X and three of his comrades attacked the funeral parlor of a community councillor. Two armed policemen were sleeping in the funeral parlor to guard it. The four youths were frightened and ran like hell after the attack. The two policemen were injured, but not badly. The funeral parlor was slightly damaged. "We are not professionals," X said later.

When I first saw him, W was lifting a heavy cardboard box out of the trunk of a car in the Salt River neighborhood of Cape Town. It was nearly dark and we could barely make out the outlines of the weathered mosques, the narrow streets, and the run-down one- and two-story houses with ornate columns. Some nights, this colored section of town near the coast was thick with salty mist from the Atlantic Ocean. Hugging the box to his chest, W turned to run into the house I had just left. "Don't bring that stuff in the house," my host hissed, suspecting that the box contained political pamphlets the government deemed subversive. "If I get in trouble, who's going to help get you out of jail."

A teenager, W was already a veteran of struggle. He remembered when he was a small child in 1976 going to a shopping center with his older sister. Police fired tear gas into the mall and shoppers screamed as they groped for handkerchiefs and fresh air. In later years, he had listened to his older brother's friends talk about revolution.

By the mid-1980s, W himself had pounded the pavements of the colored township of Athlone, stuffing pamphlets into peoples' hands and under their doors telling them about boycotts and strikes. He had boycotted school for a year. He had dashed through the cobblestone streets of Bokap, an old colored and Indian area overlooking downtown Cape Town, running from the police.

He had been lucky; he was never detained or hurt. He once had seen a friend hit by bird shot in the back, and watched helplessly as police dragged him off and beat him. He had longed desperately to have had "a bloody gun in my hand, not only so I could save my buddy but to hurt them and retaliate." But W had the wisdom of someone three time his age. "In politics, you can't be foolhardy," he said. "We want live heroes, not dead ones. We don't need martyrs. We've got enough of them."

The relationship between the comrades and the burgeoning township organizations was ambiguous. On the one hand, the comrades were the driving force behind township activity. They were foot soldiers in campaigns who stood on the front lines of battles with police and soldiers. On the other hand, the youths threatened to usurp the power of the township organizations and to ignore older activists. Veteran activists spent a great deal of time trying to influence the comrades. "Political commissars" were posted at the houses of UDF leaders in the Eastern Cape to discuss political issues with the young comrades any hour of the day.

Many parents favored township organizations in order to dilute the influence of the comrades and to integrate them into society as a whole. As the number of people involved in township organizations soared, "comrade" became an inclusive term, extended to anyone who joined the struggle against apartheid. Members of anti-apartheid organizations, whether young or old, would call themselves comrades, as casually as one might call someone "mister" or "old boy." Black trade union members called each other comrades. Even those seen as sympathizing with blacks could be called comrade. After I spent a weekend driving around the Port Elizabeth townships with local activist Mkhuseli Jack, blacks who had seen me greeted me on the streets of downtown Port Elizabeth as "comrade."

Mkhuseli Jack

In April 1986, Mkhuseli Jack, one of the leaders of the United Democratic Front and spokesman for the Consumer Boycott Committee, was in such demand among blacks and whites that he carried a beeper. In the city of Port Elizabeth, the twenty-eight-year-old Jack strode about as though he were mayor, carrying an attaché case to meetings with white businesspeople who were being strangled by the second black consumer boycott in less than a year. In the black townships, he was a hero. As he passed, black youths shouted, "Hey com!"—short for comrade.

At that time, the stature of the UDF rivaled that of the government. White businesspeople such as food wholesalers and bus company owners, long since despairing of police protection, negotiated with the UDF for safe passage for their vehicles. The Front fixed prices for staple commodities in black-owned stores to prevent price gouging during the boycott of white stores. The Front also issued licenses, with photographs attached, to street vendors. Though against government regulations, the hawkers operated under the authority of a permit stamped: M. Jack, Consumer Boycott Committee.

But Jack walked a curious line between political power and prison. Police would periodically arrest him or hunt him down for questioning. He had spent so much time in detention, he knew many of the local police by name. He had spent part or all of every year since 1976 in jail, including two six-month stints in solitary confinement. During the 1985 state of emergency, police handcuffed his hands to his ankles, hung him from a pole between two tables and took turns beating him. Because of the way victims of this treatment spin around during the beating, Jack called it "the helicopter." He was never charged with any offense.

Nonetheless, Jack displayed little malice or bitterness. Having come of age during the era of Black Consciousness, he possessed a self-confidence that seemed to emerge unscarred from repeated detention. Though he had ample reason to bear malice toward whites, he dealt with whites easily, whether they were activists like Molly Blackburn or adversaries like city officials and businesspeople.

Jack was a natural politician, more in the style of an American big city mayor than a leading light of revolution. He was pragmatic; questions of theory or ideology were secondary to action that would unify blacks and bend whites toward a non-racial society. Like Port Alfred's Nkwinti, Jack possessed an instinct for what ordinary people wanted and could take. When militant blacks asked him to press whites harder, Jack replied that "If we had pushed businessmen to the wall they would have said there is no sense talking to us." The first consumer boycott was called off in November 1985 after four months, much to the annoyance of some national black leaders who wanted to stage a "Black Christmas," a nationwide consumer boycott at the end of the year. Yet when businesspeople implored him to bring a second consumer boycott to an early end in April 1986, Jack replied, "We must talk, but not yet. It isn't the mood of the people."

One Saturday in April 1986, Jack started his weekend in Port Elizabeth in front of the UDF office listening to Indian businessman Rashid Abass, who wanted Jack to exempt Indian shops from the boycott. Abass had written a letter to Jack that pleaded, "When I get home and I see my sleeping innocent baby and the rest of my family, I just crack up wondering what I am going to do to provide for them. I don't see myself lasting another month unless I am given your blessings." Jack withheld his blessings. The Indian community "cannot benefit from the struggle without participating in it," he said. He agreed to discuss how Indians could be more active.

I gave Jack a lift to the black township of New Brighton, stopping at Qeqe's shop for a meat pie. Two black police officers were buying snacks at Qeqe's and Jack joked, "I see even the police are supporting the boycott." A bus full of black women had stopped for gasoline and the people on the bus pressed against the windows waving to Jack. A few blocks away, at the ramshackle house built of bricks, cardboard, and corrugated metal where Jack lived with his aunt and uncle, a group of giggling six-year-olds scampered over yelling his nickname, Khusta. "These are my best comrades," Jack said. "They tell me when the police have been around."

After chatting at his house, we headed for the funeral of two blacks shot by police. Along the way, he saw a group of black youths flag down a bus and turn it around toward the funeral. "The guerrillas never need transport," Jack laughed as the black youths hijacked the bus. As we neared the church hall where the funeral service was taking place, Jack turned suddenly into a narrow dirt road to avoid a police car he saw ahead. He shifted the car into neutral and waited a few moments. A woman from a house poked her head out of the yard and looked curiously at Jack. "I'm just running from the police, mama," he said. "Okay, that's good," she replied.

By the time we arrived at the funeral, the service was already in progress. Jack picked his way through the packed church hall. A couple of thousand people lined the pews, stood against the walls, and peered through the doorways. Two brown coffins rested on chairs on front. Around the stage, hundreds of youths were dressed in the khaki uniforms and black berets of the outlawed ANC. One girl had a photograph of a white woman, Molly Blackburn, pinned to her shirt and a photograph of Oliver Tambo on her beret. A priest smiled at Jack, winked, and gave the thumbs-up sign.

Jack climbed on stage. He joked with the crowd to relax the people, then exhorted them to stick with the consumer boycott."The loss of profits is no longer relevant to us. What is relevant is the loss of lives," he said pointing to the coffins below him. Then he pressed to the edge of the stage and recounted his recent detention by the police, or the "enemy" as he called them. At the police station ("filthy with the blood of our people") officers asked him to renounce statements urging civil disobedience. "They were not rude to me. I cannot lie," he said. They offered him tea. But he refused the tea and the officers' request for a renunciation of his own statements. Then in a full voice again, he shouted "I call on people now to defy every piece of apartheid law. These laws were made to keep us in slavery; how can you expect me to conform to them?"

By this time, the crowd was responding and sweat was pouring from Jack's brow as he shook off his navy blue blazer. "This is the moment of truth in our struggle," he declared.

Then he stepped again to the edge of the stage and spoke softly as though confiding in the crowd. He said that when he visited Europe he saw a South African comrade who left the country years earlier. Though Jack never said so, he implied that the exiled comrade belonged to the ANC and that Jack was bringing the gospel straight from the headquarters of the liberation movement. "If we want to value our freedom, that means we must work very hard so that we know how to use our freedom once we get it," Jack said. He quoted the title of Mandela's book ("There is no easy walk to freedom") and the title of Lutuli's autobiography ("Let my people go") and worked the crowd up to cheers of "Viva ANC," "Viva the leaders of the ANC," "Viva the leaders of the UDF," "Viva the poor people of our country," "Viva the struggle of our country."

At the cemetery, people lifted Jack on their shoulders and danced to chants of freedom songs. Thousands of people stamped their feet in the toyi-toyi, a warlike dance common at political funerals. "Hayi," they shouted, stomping twice; "hayi-hayi"; stomp, stomp, stomp. Someone thrust a plastic toy machine gun into Jack's hands and he waved it over his head to cheers.

As the crowd left the burial site, troops fired tear gas. We hurried to a house nearby and rinsed our faces and hands. Jack dabbed vaseline on his lips and nose, which he said would absorb some of the chemicals in the tear gas. Then we hurried to the car and he drove into the middle of a skirmish between stone-and-bottle-hurling black youths and soldiers firing tear gas. A grinning white soldier standing in the turret of an armored car aimed his gun at the windshield for a moment and Jack winced. Then the white soldier pointed it away. Jack surveyed the scene of dangerous brinkmanship and observed, "This happens every weekend."

As Jack drove past the armored car, he saw a lone black with a gun behind a house off to one side behind the armored car. Jack's eyes widened in amazement for the first time. Had the man turned the corner he could have gotten off a clean shot at the back of the white soldier. But the black with the gun lost his nerve and ran off between the houses.

As the sun set, flames from a burning house leapt up in the distance and Jack looked worried. At the funeral, a group of blacks had dug up two graves and pried open the stinking coffins of a sixty-eight-year-old woman and a forty-six-year-old man. People charged that the two had been killed by police and secretly buried by a township funeral parlor. The woman who ran the funeral parlor allegedly kept the burials secret in return for payments from the police. Jack had tried to ignore the exhumations and the main part of the crowd had stood with him some distance away. Minutes after the flames were visible, youths in the streets were whispering that a group had set alight the house and business of the funeral-parlor owner. "This is a tragedy," Jack said. "We didn't take this problem seriously enough."

The next day, Jack took me to the burned-out funeral parlor. Looters were carrying sinks and wood from coffins to make new houses or shanties. People crowded around the car and Jack asked what was going on. A woman nodded toward the smoldering funeral parlor and joked that people were even necklacing corpses. Jack shook his head. A young guerrilla reached into the car and snatched a pack of cigarettes from the shirt pocket of one of Jack's friends and passed them out. "My cigarettes have just been nationalized," the friend said. Jack laughed.

Jack drove away without admonishing the crowd. The funeral parlor and its owner were already "ruined" as Jack saw it. Indeed, three days later the woman died of her burns. The next time that such allegations of collaboration came up, the UDF would have to respond more vigorously to prevent another tragedy, he said.

Jack stopped at a crowd of older men in dusty dark suits and hats outside a community hall. Jack discovered that the men had unsuccessfully tried to hold a memorial service for the late Paramount Chief Sabata Dalindyebo, a Xhosa chief who went into exile because of his sympathies for the ANC. His rightful chieftainship was given away by the government to a more pliable chief. Jack saw the funeral as a chance to do something for rural people who weren't a solid part of the UDF constituency. So he volunteered to organize a funeral befitting the "Comrade King." The men were cheered and parted smiling. "I will use traditional Xhosa names, I will talk about the frontier wars [of the 1800s] and talk about my parents moving about the countryside and about my Tembu roots." The Tembu are a Xhosa tribe from the Eastern Cape, the tribe Mandela belongs to.

Jack's family name was probably given by a white farmer who didn't know or care about the family's African name. Jack's father was a farm laborer who died when Jack was young. After his death, the white farmer threw the family off the farm; without an adult male worker the Jacks were no longer useful. Eventually Jack's mother settled in a rural township and remarried.

In 1975 Jack went to Port Elizabeth for school, but was told he couldn't attend because he came from a farm and needed an urban permit. Jack organized other rural students locked out of school and led a protest. After three months, the school relented. During the 1976 student unrest, Jack was arrested for protesting the poor quality of black education. In the late 1970s Jack was instrumental in founding the Congress of South African Students.

Through all this, Jack's good nature was one of his greatest assets. In prison, he won over guards. When he managed to get transfered from prison to Livingstone Hospital for an eye infection, he quickly won over the hospital staff. He received special food, occasional visitors, and periodic use of a telephone.

In the early 1980s, Jack was elected to the executive of the Port Elizabeth Civic Organization. He was one of only two members of the PEBCO executive to survive six major upheavals in the PEBCO leadership.

On the Sunday afternoon when I visited him in April 1986, Jack attended the weekly meeting of the "Forum," a group of the more than forty heads of all the UDF affiliates in the Port Elizabeth townships. Jack went to argue against a UDF effort to force blacks in private schools to return to the government-run schools. The idea behind the initiative was to bring private-school students, mostly apolitical, under the influence of student organizations and make them part of school boycotts. Jack argued that the move would only divide the black community at a time unity was needed for the consumer boycott. He lost the debate.

In the evening, Jack moved on to a street-committee meeting. On the way, Jack said that the UDF was having trouble keeping up with the proliferation of street committees and had recently summoned street committee chairpeople. About 2,000 people had showed up. At this session, Jack asserted the need for eventual negotiations to end the consumer boycott. He said blacks must dangle carrots as well as sticks before whites in order to split them. He added that "Capitalists believe in every man for himself and God for us all. That's why we will divide them and that is why we must negotiate. If we just say we won't talk," he said mimicking a stubborn child, "they will be united against us." People at the meeting raised complaints. One person said that reading the boycott price list was like deciphering the horse racing charts in the newspaper. Jack took note. Another asked why fish oil wasn't on the price list. Jack explained that the price list included only staple foods "at very fair" prices while other items might cost more because they couldn't be purchased in bulk. An impatient youth in a black beret wanted to punish police informers and looked dejected when Jack reprimanded him. Street committees mustn't take the law into their own hands, Jack said.

As the meeting broke up, people said farewell to Jack, bidding him "Viva comrade."

Governing the Ungovernable

Street committees such as the one Jack visited had a historical antecedent thirty years earlier. In 1953, Nelson Mandela foresaw a sharp clash between Africans and the government, in which the people would "resist to the death the stinking policies of the gangsters that rule our country." Mandela saw danger in "the old methods of bringing about mass action through public meetings, press statements, and leaflets." In a detailed memorandum, Mandela set forth a plan to strengthen the ANC by organizing a cell system that could function without calling mass meetings, issuing press statements, or printing leaflets. The plan would enable the ANC to continue operating even if it were outlawed.

At the base of the pyramid of cells would be blocks of seven houses under unit stewards. The blocks would belong to a street with a cell steward. About seven streets would make up a zone, overseen by a chief steward. Four zones made up a ward, overseen by a prime steward. The prime steward and the ANC branch secretary constituted the branch secretariat.

Mandela's plan never got off the ground. Only a few ANC branches managed to implement the plan. ANC reports complained of "dissension, stagnation, and suspicion." Most Africans were reluctant to devote time to political organizing after long working days. And the ANC lacked financial resources to pay full-time organizers. Even among the ANC leadership, those outside the Transvaal feared that Mandela's plan was designed to centralize power with the Johannesburg-based ANC executive. Moreover, ANC activity was still open and legal, and many leaders saw no urgency in making preparations for more repressive times.[11]

Though the idea of a cell system was not entirely original, the "M-Plan"—as Mandela's proposal became known—acquired a notoriety that lasted into the 1980s. To blacks, similarity between street committees and the M-Plan connected the fight of the 1980s with a tradition of African resistance. To the government, linking street committees to the M-Plan provided further evidence of a "revolutionary alliance."

Not all the reasons for the appeal of the street committees were revolutionary; many township residents favored them for conservative reasons. The street committees could break up bands of youths and make them work with cross sections of black society. Thus street committees could forge a more representative and moderate consensus. The street committees could also reimpose law and order in the townships and fill the vacuum left by the government as white administrators fled and black community councillors resigned. In Alexandra township, for instance, the town council resigned en masse after the mayor, Sam Buti, visited Mandela in jail and was convinced to throw in his lot with anti-government forces. Moses Mayekiso, a trade unionist who took a lead in organizing street committees, said he merely stepped into the vacuum. "People were sick and tired of the whole system. People wanted street committees and I was responding to peoples' demands."

To young militants, though, the street committees also represented tools for mobilizing and tightening control of the black community, especially when it came to informers and those too apathetic to comply with consumer boycotts. As the members of the community with the most energy and time on their hands, youths were powerful forces in the street committees, which quickly spread from the Eastern Cape throughout the country.

On February 5, 1986, residents of Alexandra gathered at a clearing that had been rechristened Freedom Park to discuss how to copy the street committee networks of the Eastern Cape townships. According to minutes of the meeting:

> The purpose of introducing street or avenue committees in Alex is to unite the people of Alexandra and to look at peoples' problems in order that they be solved. The struggle in Alex is backward, & therefore the street Co. is a step towards concientising & building unity amongst residents, to fight their problems. Further it is to encourage discipline in our society concientising people of their struggle, to ensure mass control of the struggle and proper democracy.[12]

By the time the state of emergency was lifted, a pyramid of self-government was taking shape. At the base of the pyramid were yard committees, based on plots shared by about fifteen families each. "The people of the yard should come together, forget about their tribal differences, classes, and their education and form a yard committee," the minutes said. Two representatives from each yard committee attended meetings of block committees, the next step in the pyramid. Each block committee elected a chair, secretary, and treasurer. Each block committee in turn elected four representatives to attend street committee meetings, organized along the twenty-two numbered avenues running across the township. Each of the street committees elected two representatives to "the Supreme Body," a forty-four person executive committee known as the Alexandra Action Committee, headed by Moses Mayekiso, general secretary of the Metal and Allied Workers Union.

The activists of Alexandra set high standards and strict guidelines for committee members. A memo of the Alexandra Action Committee detailed that "(1) a rep must be well disciplined, devoted and loyal to the people whom he/she represents. (2) He must be in a position to listen to what the people want and must share ideas with them. (3) A rep has no chance to dictate since he is elected by the people."[13]

The documents of the Alexandra Action Committee reflect the community's pressing concerns, which the government hadn't addressed at any level: unemployment, police harassment, informers, high taxi and bus fares, low wages, high rents, poor education, poor housing, the demolition of shacks by police, the presence of troops in the township, and the "bucket system" of sewerage. Mayekiso talked about starting cooperatives for the unemployed and bulk-buying schemes to reduce prices. "We want people to help each other," he said.

The action committee heard complaints against businesses and drew up a selective list of stores to boycott. On April 21, consumer boycotts went into effect against fifteen different establishments, ranging from a large retail chain, Jazz Stores, to community councillors' businesses, to two shebeens in the township.

The action committee also changed street names. Instead of names like Roosevelt and Hofmeyer, they used names like MK (short for Umkonto we Sizwe), Steve Biko, Soviet, Mandela, ANC, Slovo (after South African Communist Party chief Joe Slovo), Sobukwe (after the late leader of the Pan Africanist Congress), Bazooka, and Oliver (after ANC president Tambo).

Before long, police detained Mayekiso and interrogated him about the street committees. "They are feeling that this is Mandela's M-Plan," Mayekiso said after his release. "Their attitude was that we were doing the work of the ANC." Though Mayekiso may not have been acting at the behest of the ANC or the imprisoned Mandela, he wasn't ignorant of the history of the M-Plan. Privately Mayekiso conceded that "There's no difference" between the M-Plan and the Alexandra Action Committee network.

The most controversial aspect of the local street committees was when they functioned as peoples' courts. Mayekiso explained that "people were tired of taking problems to the police." Their lack of faith in the police and courts were reflected by a popular joke. It was said that once a Zambian and a South African were talking. Though Zambia is landlocked, the Zambian boasted about his country's minister of naval affairs. The South African asked, "But you have no navy, no access to the sea. How then can you have a minister of naval affairs?" The Zambian replied, "Well, in South Africa you have a minister of justice, don't you?"

By April, the action committee was dealing with four to five cases a day, he said, ranging from settling marital problems to prosecuting rapists and "*tsotsis.*" "The committee can mete out punishment and judgment" Mayekiso said, but he was fuzzy about the punishments meted out. "We are against harsh punishments of other townships where people are burned. We don't want to be like the police. We want to create unity."

Alexandra's activists were so confident that they had created a liberated zone that they kept detailed records of street committee cases, records later presented as evidence in a treason trial against Mayekiso and others. In one month, the Seventh Avenue street committee met under a tree in a fenced-in yard, and heard at least twenty-six cases, including four charges of assault, four domestic disputes, a complaint about the retrenchment of employees, three charges of theft, three of attempted murder, one housebreaking, one of "bewitching" and practicing witchcraft, one of "supporting tribalism and being bossy," and several others. In two months, the street committee at Nineteenth Avenue heard at least 169 cases, including twenty-one cases of theft, twenty-seven cases of assault, and thirty domestic disputes ranging from a husband leaving the house for another woman to problems disciplining children to a disagreement over lobola, the bride price. The committee also heard more explicitly political cases. One young woman was accused of running away from her boyfriend and "bad talk about the comrades." One person was charged with "not cooperating with a stayaway." Two were accused of "working with the system," one of "being a sellout," and another of "selling out to the police." But there were also indications that the committees could be used to curb the comrades. One case was brought over a "threat of burning."

The authority of the courts dramatized how far community organizations had gone toward taking over the normal functions of government. Later, when the government arrested and charged Mayekiso and four others with treason, subversion, and sedition, the government alleged that

> during the period 1985 to June 1986. . . . the accused unlawfully and with hostile intent [attempted] to coerce and/or overthrow and/or usurp and/or endanger the authority of the state . . . [and] . . . to seize control of the residential area of Alexandra . . . by establishing so-called organs of people's power and/or of self-government.

Dual Power

Thomas Jefferson said that the "the vigor given to our [American] revolution in its commencement" was due to the "little republics" based on individual American townships that had "thrown the whole nation into energetic action." Through local action, "there was not an individual in their States whose body was not thrown with all its momentum into action."[14]

So, too, in South Africa by the middle of 1986 there was hardly a black in the country who was not caught up in some form of action and organization. South African blacks had become what Jefferson called "participators in government" within their own "little republics."

However, the community organizations that flowered during the first emergency often fell short of Jefferson's democratic ideals. In its first flush, the romance of power ran away from its responsibilities, leading to abuses.

A woman caught breaking the boycott in Port Elizabeth was forced to drink detergent she had purchased in town. Comrades in Langa township took a woman who had bought goods in Uitenhage, tore up her new shoes, tore her clothes, and painted her. A news photographer reported that youths enforced a general strike in Soweto by chasing adults away from train stations with *sjamboks,* the whips used by police. At times, comrades raising money from black businesspeople to benefit the UDF resembled an extortion racket; behind their solicitation was the implicit threat that stingy blacks would feel repercussions. One Soweto businessman began a fund to make sure donations went to the UDF—and so that the fund could issue a sticker he could show the next comrade who asked him for money.

The danger also loomed that street committees would no longer be vehicles for the open exchange of ideas. Instead, like the Jacobin clubs during Robespierre's reign of terror, street committees could become instruments of control by spying on people and denouncing dissidents.

Some UDF affiliates insisted that people bow to their authority. Port Elizabeth lawyer Fikile Bam wrote that "the almost complete control that the UDF established over certain townships . . . made it intolerant even of passive opposition or dissent." In part, this was a matter of necessity, Bam noted.

> The success of its most important programs, such as the setting up of alternative structures, implied mass conformity. Deviations or exemptions on the part of a few would not only undermine morale and solidarity, but promote opposing groups. A people's court needed to have complete jurisdiction within its allocated area to be seen to have authority.

The court could not permit persons indicted to escape jurisdiction by pleading allegiance to another organization, like AZAPO. "Accordingly, an element of coercion became part of the persuasive process from the beginning and fell into the hands of the younger comrades," Bam said.

This coercion naturally alienated some township residents. The popular musical playwright Gibson Kente wrote two shows critical of UDF tactics and strategy. In *Bad Times,* Kente questioned the wisdom of sanctions, poked fun at overbearing comrades, and bemoaned violence. In one skit, the ANC was spoofed as the CNA, the name of a magazine and stationery chain store. The plot was simple. A struggling theater troupe needs money to produce a play. Despite the admonitions of his wife, who wishes he would get a decent job, the troupe's manager turns to a Zulu money lender. But the play is canceled when kill-joy comrades declare a "Black Christmas" and ban entertainment during the holiday season. Meanwhile the economy deteriorates; the troupe manager's wife loses her job, and a walk-on character sticks his head in a trash can and gnaws on some garbage.

"It was a statement," Kente said. "Political organizations are merely using people for their own ends. Necklaces, petrol bombs, and school boycotts; how do they benefit us?"

Humorous portions of the show assuaged the sensibilities of some township residents—but not all. After the first act of a performance in Sebokeng township, five youths stopped the show. The young comrades objected to a scene that mocked Desmond Tutu (dubbed Bishop Nobele) for his support of sanctions. Kente jumped onto the stage and urged them to judge the show after the entire performance. Swayed by his plea, the audience shouted down the youths, and the show went on. "To me that was a moment of glory," said Kente.

Kente's next work, *Sekunjalo* [*That's What We Expected*] portrayed a grim, post-revolutionary South Africa in which Communist Party leaders dressed in red togas win the first elections and impose a one-party state. Blacks, unskilled after years of school boycotts, have trouble getting jobs and the police detain an opponent of the new regime much as they detained people in 1985.

Both white and black politics in South Africa possessed strong authoritarian traditions, from Zulu chiefs to the National Party. For all their faults, however, the street committees and various UDF affiliates came close to instilling a respect for democratic procedure. They raised the common person to an equal level in the conduct of public affairs. The strength of community organizations with independent-minded leaders and members may be the best safeguard against future dictatorship.

Street committees generally did *not* resemble cells during the Jacobin Reign of Terror. On the contrary, they helped forge a moderate consensus that would have been lacking were South Africa's fighting years led only by the new teenage generation of comrades.

"It is of absolute importance that we don't confuse coercion, the use of force *against* the community, with people's power, the collective strength of the community," said Zwelakhe Sisulu at the National Education Crisis Committee conference called at the end of March 1986 to urge students to end school boycotts. "When bands of youth set up so-called 'kangaroo courts' and give out punishments under the control of no one with no democratic mandate from the community, this is *not* people's power." Sisulu warned that where organization was weak, young people "have tended to apply force instead of political education to persuade the community to support" consumer boycotts or general strikes. "This has had the effect of alienating some people from the struggle."

Sisulu's address was essentially a state of the union message for blacks. Sisulu, the son of Walter and Albertina Sisulu, was editor of the *New Nation,* a black weekly newspaper that practiced advocacy journalism. He told the youths that before staging a boycott or general strike they must discuss the tactic with all sectors of black society. Street committees and people's courts must be seen as "acting on a mandate from the community and under the democratic control of the community."

From a small room in ANC headquarters in Lusaka, ANC national executive committee member Mac Maharaj viewed the emergence of black township organizations with excitment. "These are remarkable developments," Maharaj said, because at times "black people control their own lives." While the influence of the informal township government remained tenuous because of police and the financial muscle of the white regime, Maharaj said, the black townships still achieved "moments of dual power" with official governing bodies.[15]

The phrase "dual power" was a loaded one. Maharaj borrowed it from Lenin, who argued in *Pravda* on April 9, 1917 that revolution against the Provisional Government of Kerensky was possible. Lenin said a "second government" already existed. In many areas committees, or *soviets* made up of armed workers and peasants, had replaced the police, the army, and the official bureaucracy. The soviets constituted a form of "direct rule" that Lenin compared to the Paris Commune of 1871. He said the Soviets of Workers' and Soldiers' Deputies could lead to a revolutionary dictatorship "based on the direct initiative of the people from below, and not on a law enacted by a centralized state power."[16]

There was a crucial difference: the South African government wasn't tottering as did the Czarist and provisional governments of Russia. Though sanctions, inflation, a debt crisis, and international isolation weighed heavily on the South African government, these crises fell far short of the trauma that World War I had had on Russia. Moreover, uncertainty in Pretoria didn't match the vacillating weakness of Kerensky.

Government stability led to disappointments for Africans fighting apartheid. In April 1986, Nkwinti was having trouble putting his finger on what the township had acheived. Of the eighteen job-creation projects that came out of negotiations with businesspeople, only one took place in the township. When the white town council sent bulldozers to repair the roads in Inkwenkwezi, the East Cape Administration Board ordered them to stay off the board's property. Living conditions in the township remained dismal. Moreover Nkwinti felt threatened by right-wing whites and police, who he feared were "polishing their rifles" to kill him.

"I want to strike a note of caution," Zwelakhe Sisulu said at the NECC conference.

> If we overplay the regime's weaknesses and ignore their strengths we shall be fooling ourselves. . . . It is important that we don't misrecognise the moment or understand it to be something which it is not. We are not poised for the immediate transfer of power to the people. The belief that this is so could lead to serious errors and defeats."
>
> We are, however, poised to enter a phase which can lead to a transfer of power. What we are seeking to do is to decisively shift the balance of forces in our favor.

Short of overthrowing the government, black South Africans could begin to establish democratic organizations. It was possible "to move towards realising people's power now, in the process of struggle, before actual liberation," Sisulu said. "In some townships and schools people are beginning to govern themselves, despite being under racist rule," in "semi-liberated zones." Sisulu added, "People are beginning to exert control over their own lives."

CHAPTER SEVEN

Black Mamba Rising:
Black Trade Unions

We
have dared to fight back
even from the bottom of the earth
where we pull wagons-full of gold
through our blood

We have come from the sparkling kitchens
of our bosses

We have arrived from the exhausting
tumult of factory machines

—FROM A POEM BY TWO WORKERS,
HLATSHWAYO AND QABULA[1]

WHILE BLACK COMMUNITY POLITICS had been gathering force since the Soweto student rebellion, the black trade-union movement had been traveling a parallel course, reaching a climax during the uprising. The union's strength, said a rubber company driver who wrote poetry, was like that of a black mamba, a venomous African snake that grows to a length of twelve feet.

The black trade-union movement had begun at 3 A.M., January 9, 1973, when a group of disgruntled black migrant workers at the men's hostel of the Coronation Brick and Tile Works in Durban awoke their colleagues and urged them to meet at the local soccer stadium instead of reporting to work. Some men went to the nearby plant and exhorted workers on the night shift to join the rally. Two thousand strong, the workers marched in two columns to the stadium, defying heavy traffic and a government ban on unauthorized marches. As they entered the stadium, the workers chanted a Zulu phrase "Filumuntu ufesadikiza," meaning "Man is dead but his spirit lives."[2]

Two days later, the Coronation workers reluctantly returned to work with a modest raise after urgings from their traditional leader, Zulu King Goodwill Zwelithini. They had demanded a threefold increase in wages to a minimum of R30 a week, but settled for a R2 increase for a new minimum of R11.50.

Though modest, the gains by the Coronation workers inspired employees at other plants in the Durban area. On January 25, 6,000 textile workers from the Frame Group went on strike. Suffering from near-starvation wages of R5 to R9 a week, Frame workers wanted a minimum of R20 a week. The strikes spread from factory to factory and within days 30,000 workers throughout Durban were on strike, affecting twenty-nine firms and the municipality. Garbage went uncollected and gravediggers refused to work. To save perishable food, white volunteers loaded meat and vegetables. Skirmishes with police broke out on several occasions.

The spontaneous Durban strikes marked a watershed in labor relations in the same way that the 1976 riots altered student and community politics. Prior to the Durban strikes, black workers—and blacks in general—had little faith in their ability to alter the society they lived in. Labor laws, pass laws, and security legislation were used to stamp out strikes. Through the 1970s, South African legislation included the "Masters and Servants Laws" which made it a crime for any African to "desert" his white employer. Strikers could be considered deserters and a clause of the Riotous Assemblies Act forbade strikes.[3] The Industrial Conciliation Act passed in 1924 omitted all Africans from its definition of "employee."

The Durban strikes aroused black workers across the nation and showed the power of collective action. Although most workers eventually settled for raises of about R2 a week—far short of their original goals—that modest pay hike was more than twice the total of all the raises paid by Frame, for one, over the previous six years.[4]

Though black unions had been smashed along with the ANC and PAC in the early 1960s, the Coronation workers demonstrated that a militant spirit still stirred within the rank and file. By the end of the year, 90,000 workers had gone on strike, costing employers 229,000 lost shifts, more than seven times the number lost in the previous eight years.[5]

What made it possible for black labor to flex its muscle was a profound shift in the position of blacks in the economy. For a decade the South African economy enjoyed a spectacular growth rate of six to eight percent a year. White South Africans had advanced to an unparalleled level of wealth; swimming pools proliferated and overseas travel became commonplace. A greater variety of automobiles were built in South Africa than anywhere else in the world. But blacks had been left behind. Real black wages remained the same or declined during the decade, fanning resentment among black laborers.

At the same time, blacks had moved into semi-skilled jobs. The speed and magnitude of the South African economic boom pushed whites into white-collar jobs and created a demand for skilled black workers. This trend continued through the 1980s. "Only a decade ago, it was news when a few black bricklayers were grudgingly permitted to work on Durban building sites provided they used garden trowels instead of bricklayers' tools," a foreign diplomat commented in 1985. "Now blacks are building-crane operators, shop managers, accountants, long-haul truck drivers, traffic cops, architects, physicians, reporters, bank clerks—without incident." In 1973, in anticipation of greater semi-skilled labor needs, big companies had already started to negotiate with white unions to loosen job restrictions so that blacks could fill vacant positions previously reserved for whites. It took up to three weeks to train blacks to do many jobs by the end of the 1970s. As blacks moved into these slots, they became more vital to their employers. "The costs of exchanging the labor force became substantial," says a leading labor-relations manager. By becoming less expendable, semi-skilled black workers vastly increased the leverage of blacks in the workplace.

When black workers used that leverage in Durban, they shook up the white business community. White factory managers and business executives were forced to confront crowds of workers, pleading with and threatening them through bullhorns to go back to work. Since black unions were illegal, there were no union leaders to negotiate with.

The experience transformed the attitudes of employers toward black trade unions. The giant Anglo American Corporation conglomerate hired two progressive labor-relations representatives, Alex Boraine (later a Progressive Federalist Party member of Parliament) and Bobby Godsell, a recent university graduate who had witnessed the Durban strikes in 1973. They began pushing for a reevaluation of the liberal position toward black trade unions, suggesting that unions were attributes of an industrializing country. Over the next five years, businesspeople gave volumes of evidence to a government commission that opened the way for the formation of recognized black trade unions in 1979.

The government and business plans for black trade unions were limited and self-serving. Both wanted mechanisms to channel black labor unrest. "The unique task that faces us is the resolution of conflicting interests and competing demands that are inevitable in our society. The management of conflict in all spheres of our lives will be essential for peace and prosperity," said Nic Wiehahn, a white former railway worker and academic, who designed guidelines for black trade unions.

Under Wiehahn's rules, unions would be compelled to use formal negotiating processes and abide by industrial court decisions. Strikes could only be held after lengthy mediation and then only a month after declaring an impasse. Both business and government wanted to make labor relations a bureaucratic process whose agreements would be enforced upon black workers by union leaders instead of managers. They saw unions as tools to make agreements stick—and to avoid loss of working days through strikes.

The new labor regulations took a number of steps to encourage unions to play by the new rules. Wiehahn's proposals restricted political activity, stiffened penalties for illegal strikes, and increased government oversight of labor relations. Only those unions that registered with the government would be recognized as the legal representatives in their factories. Only registered unions could collect membership dues through "stop orders," automatic deductions from the worker's paychecks.

In the eyes of many in business, the extension of trade-union rights to blacks was something generously bestowed by business and government. It was evidence of the government reform program, they said. But Anglo's Godsell had a different view. He said the 1979 labor legislation simply recognized inexorable change. "Trade union rights were given by skills, not by legislation. Workers in Durban had no union rights in 1973, but they struck anyway. No one has granted anybody rights. We have simply acknowledged changes in the power base of black workers."

Blacks viewed the new trade-union rights as a result of "struggle." In that process, the unions followed a pattern parallel to black community organizations. A spontaneous burst of protest (accompanied by violence) was followed by a self-serving government reform program. The government reforms had unforeseen consequences. Blacks approached the reforms with skepticism, but used the space created to build organizations. The organizations won followers by tending to their bread-and-butter concerns. Later the organizations would openly voice the political aspirations of blacks.

It didn't take long for the unions to overstep the circumscribed limits within which they were intended to operate. Even before the Wiehahn reforms were unveiled, black trade unions were winning recognition agreements with companies, especially with subsidiaries of foreign companies such as Ford. Many of the new unions refused to register with the government and saw use of the government labor-relations bureaucracy as collaboration. Nonetheless, these unregistered unions were able to force companies to negotiate with them.

Impressed by initial gains, black workers rapidly joined the emerging unions. Despite black unemployment of 25 to 30 percent, and the worst economic slump in South Africa since the Great Depression, unions flourished through the 1980s—and their members were ready to strike. In 1979, the western Cape was hit by a wave of strikes involving stevedores, meat and cold-storage workers, construction workers, textile mill hands, fishermen, and engineering workers. In 1979 and 1980, strikes hit auto factories in the eastern Cape. In 1982, an average of a thousand black workers a day went on strike. By 1986, the two million members of trade unions held 1,150 strikes costing South African industry 6.6 million work days of labor.[6]

Cast Boy

I work here in Boksburg but my spirit is in Mahlabathini. My spirit is there because I come from the countryside. . . . But for twenty years now I have worked in the factories on the East Rand. My land is too small for me and my

> family to live on. So for the sake of my family I was forced to leave my home. I left when I was a young man to work in the factories far away. The bus drives through the night from Mahlabathini to Boksburg. It is a very long journey.

So begins the history of Mandlenkosi Makhoba, a former foundry worker whose story was dramatized in a worker play and published by his trade-union federation under the title *The Sun Shall Rise for the Workers.*[7] His journey from rural KwaZulu to become an urban factory worker and trade-union member traces the physical and psychological journey made by migrant laborers across South Africa in the 1970s and 1980s.

Makhoba worked as a "cast boy" at a foundry. He sorted and cut scrap metal from dumps and fed it into a furnace. Mokhoba then carried the molten metal in heavy pots and poured them into molds. After a number of times, the "cooled metal becomes stuck to the pot like porridge when it is left to become hard" and Makhoba would have to chip and scrape the pots clean. Because they weren't given proper safety boots, gloves, or overalls, the workers often burned themselves when bits of the white hot metal spilled. "I have been burned so many times I can't count," Makhoba wrote. Salaries were so low that the R10-a-month rent he paid for a shared room without electricity or heat or water was a financial burden. New machinery in the late 1970s meant the workers poured three times as much molten metal as before, but they received no raises.

In theory, the workers were supposed to be able to complain to management through black *indunas*—or head men. But the indunas only enforced the company rules and made sure the workers didn't slack. Eager to please the white bosses, the indunas came up with the idea that laborers should change clothes before clocking in to save the company money.

One Saturday in 1979, a worker whose brother-in-law worked at another factory persuaded some of his co-workers to come to a union office in Benoni. His co-workers suspected that this union was like some of the fly-by-night companies that came around the worker hostels collecting "insurance" money or payments on an installment plan. Those companies inevitably went out of business and disappeared with the workers' money.

Even after an organizer at the office of the Metal and Allied Workers Union (MAWU) convinced the workers that the union was different, many were cautious. The risk of losing their jobs worried them. The employers, Makhoba said,

> knew that as soon as they expelled us we would lose a place of residence, because we would not be able to pay the hostel fees without the money we earned. Then the pass office would be indifferent and instruct us to go back where we came from. . . . If they send you back home, and back home there's a drought, and you can't get any new job, it's a death sentence.

But the workers were angry about the dangerous conditions and low pay. So Makhoba and others organized the foundry in a series of meetings. "At these meetings everybody had a chance to speak. Some people wanted to move quickly, while others were more cautious." In twos and threes they started joining, until all fifty-five black foundry workers signed up for the union.

The company refused to recognize MAWU; instead it wanted to talk to a liaison committee consisting of workers and indunas chosen by management. When workers failed to heed efforts to form the liaison committee, the company proposed its own constitution to the union. Talks reached an impasse and the company promised it wouldn't fire anyone as long as everyone kept working. Perhaps the shadow of Durban hung over the company.

Confusion broke out, however, when a worker was fired. Other workers lay down tools and the company called police to arrest them. The police assaulted the strikers at prison and the company fired them in June 1979. A court ruled later that the workers had struck illegally and fined them.

"We learned many things in the foundry. But we also made mistakes," Makhoba wrote in the booklet distributed by FOSATU's educational unit. "I tell you of our actions and of our mistakes so that you will not make them. We have been defeated . . . but we have not been crushed."

MAWU stood by the strikers. After two years, the union lawyers won cash compensation for the assault by the police. Many of the strikers found work elsewhere; others were rehired by the foundry. "The bosses needed our skills. They need our strength. Even today they cry for our experience," Makhoba boasted.

Their strike was the first of a wave of strikes. Despite setbacks such as Makhoba's, the union's militant stance and attention to its members attracted more and more members. By the end of 1980, MAWU had 12,000 members. By the end of 1981, it had 23,000 members in sixty factories. Many others sympathized with the union and honored its strike calls.

The story of Makhoba's personal awakening was published in 1984 and spurred union growth. On shop floors around the country, other black workers were also standing up to the bosses. The explosions in political consciousness in black communities and the workplace reinforced each other and swelled nationwide union membership to more than half a million by 1985.

COSATU

On November 30, 1985, the nation's biggest black trade unions merged to form the Congress of South African Trade Unions, the culmination of four years of negotiations. Overnight the federation became the most potent force in black politics and the most imposing black organization ever launched, with 450,000 dues-paying members. At birth, COSATU had four times as many members as the big ANC union in the 1950s; within two years COSATU would double that number.

The worker-poet Qabula celebrated the occasion in verse.

> Here it is: COSATU
> The tornado snake of change
> We lathed its teeth on our machines
> The day this head raises
> Beware of the day these teeth shall bite.

COSATU called for equal pay for equal work, for wider union rights, and for the introduction of a national minimum wage. It also placed heavy emphasis on political goals. COSATU backed the principle of one person, one vote, disinvestment by foreign companies, nationalization of the mines, the withdrawal of troops from the townships and the unbanning of the Congress of South African Students. The president of the new labor federation was Elijah Barayi, a fifty-three-year-old personnel assistant at a gold mine near Carletonville, in the western Transvaal. In the 1950s, Barayi belonged to the ANC Youth League and participated in the Defiance Campaign. Now he called for the resignation of P. W. Botha and for the installation of jailed ANC leader Nelson Mandela as president. Barayi issued an ultimatum, threatening that COSATU would call on workers to burn their passes if the pass laws were not abolished within six months. "We will instruct everyone to burn their passes and ignore policemen who order blacks to produce their passes," Barayi told 10,000 union representatives at the meeting at a stadium in Durban. "COSATU will not just fold its hands. . . . COSATU is part and parcel of the liberation struggle."

At a press conference afterwards, the new COSATU general secretary Jay Naidoo reaffirmed Barayi's stand. "Workers will attack those issues that affect them directly, for when they leave the factory floor and return to the townships, they are faced with housing, transport, rent, and other community problems." Days later, Naidoo flew to Lusaka to consult with the ANC and SACTU, the outlawed union from the 1950s that was affiliated with the ANC.

COSATU united the most powerful forces and personalities in the black trade-union movement. The first and most established of these were the unions that were previously part of the Federation of South African Trade Unions (FOSATU). These unions grew up in the wake of the 1973 Durban strikes and organized workers by industry. FOSATU unions stressed solid organizations in factories. They devoted attention to recruiting, securing recognition agreements from employers (modeled on American recognition agreements), training shop stewards, and winning concessions so they could point to concrete victories. FOSATU also took a flexible approach to registration with the government's Department of Manpower. If registration was advantageous, then the unions often registered.

FOSATU unions avoided overt political affiliation, lest it split its own members, who had a range of political leanings. Moreover, many union organizers feared that popular political organizations like the UDF would abandon the interests of organized labor for some other political agenda.

The second and most politically outspoken strain of COSATU came from the unions that were affiliated with the United Democratic Front: the General and Allied Workers Union, the South African Allied Workers Union, and the National Federation of Workers. These unions had sprung up after the labor reforms of 1979 and had grown extremely fast in the early 1980s. Saawu at one time claimed 100,000 members. Often they signed up members at mass township meetings. As a result, membership tended to be regional, rather than organized across a certain industry. The UDF general unions often lacked enough members in a company or a plant to negotiate on behalf of its members. They failed to obtain recognition agreements and refused to register with the government, as a matter of principle. Factory floor networks remained weak and the UDF unions had trouble keeping their members.[8]

The third force within the new federation was the National Union of Mineworkers (NUM), the union representing workers in the nation's most vital industries—gold and coal mines. The NUM was started by the Council of Unions of South Africa (CUSA), a group rooted in Black Consciousness that rejected any role for whites as union organizers. When CUSA refused to join COSATU, the NUM broke ranks and joined COSATU. (CUSA remained an independent alternative for black workers. Together, CUSA and another union group loyal to Black Consciousness claimed nearly half as many members as COSATU.)

No union possessed more potential strength than the National Union of Mineworkers, of which Barayi also was a vice president. Half a million laborers worked in the mines that built South Africa into a modern industrial country. In 1986, they hauled 108 million tons of ore to the surface, yielding 606 tons of gold. They accounted for 42.3 percent of the country's foreign exchange earnings. South Africa produces more than a third of the total world gold supplies.

COSATU also welded two philosophical strains within black politics. The "populists" in the UDF unions favored broad political action and alliances with black community groups. The "workerists" in FOSATU favored a more cautious approach to politics and a greater focus on workplace issues.

A debate seesawed between the two factions. One issue of *Isizwe,* the journal of the UDF, featured an article on "the errors of populism" shortly after the launch of the trade-union federation. The tract criticized populists for failing to take into account class differences. The journal added that "populism often relies heavily on emotional mobilization. It often downplays the task of solid organizing."[9] Six months later, *Isizwe* published another article, "The Errors of Workerism." Workerists, the article said, romanticized unions as a progressive vanguard. The article argued that the trade-union movement could not be equated with the working class. Many working-class people were unemployed or not members of unions. Moreover, *Isizwe* added, "Nowhere in the world has the working class achieved victory without large numbers of allies among other groups." The critique also deplored the "economism" of workerists who believed that the economy was the key to liberation and who "see apartheid oppression as simply a mask behind which capitalist exploitation is hidden."[10]

These tensions over strategy mirrored deeper philosophical differences within black politics. Some activists emphasized the racists aspects of apartheid, while others focused on class and economic inequality. On the one hand, UDF co-president Albertina Sisulu told a foreign diplomat that "We have never objected to the idea of a ruling class. We just want a government which has the interest of all South Africans at heart." On the other hand, a young friend of mine from Athlone who also was active in various UDF affiliates, told me "Racialism is the paint on the wall." The real problems, he said, were "capitalism and international imperialism."

To gain a united front among the unions, the new federation papered over differences on politics and strategy. FOSATU and NUM made important concessions to the UDF unions, giving the smaller political unions lopsided representation in the COSATU executive committee. But the bigger, better organized FOSATU and NUM won a commitment to organize one union for each industry. Eventually, such union mergers would reduce the clout of the UDF-affiliated general worker unions.

At the opening conference, keynote speaker Cyril Ramaphosa, the general secretary of the mineworkers' union, walked a fine line between the two philosophies, making overtures to both.

> As trade unions we have always thought that our main area of activity was on the shop floor—the struggle against the bosses. [But] workers have long realized when they are paid lower wages that it is a political issue. What is difficult is how to make the link between economic and political issues. . . . When we do plunge into political activity, we must make sure that the unions under COSATU have a strong shop-floor base not only to take on the employers but the state as well. Our role in the political struggle will depend on our organizational strength.

Tensions between "workerists" and "populists" were exaggerated by people who hoped the federation would disintegrate. Opponents of the federation must have been cheered by the backstage bickering about Barayi's inflammatory speech at COSATU's opening conference. Workerist union leaders were taken aback by Barayi's blunt ultimatum about pass laws to

Botha and by an unbridled attack he made on KwaZulu homeland leader Chief Mangosuthu Gatsha Buthelezi, who had chosen to work within apartheid's structures. Many unionists believed Barayi was foolishly courting retribution from the government and risking the alienation of tens of thousands of COSATU members who also belonged to Buthelezi's organization, Inkatha.

As time went on, however, the differences between the two union camps grew smaller. Political unions learned from the workerists and paid greater attention to workplace issues, shop-steward training, and organization. Those that failed to do so lost members and influence to the workerist unions.

The workerists changed too. The 1985 state of emergency made political involvement unavoidable. Overlapping concerns were embodied by Chris Dlamini, the former president of FOSATU and first vice president of the new federation. FOSATU and Dlamini had been known for solid workplace organization and focus. They had won the respect of major employers. Dlamini's power was apparent at the Kellogg plant in Springs, about forty miles east of Johannesburg. Though Dlamini was an employee, he was treated with deference due an executive. He had his own office and telephone extension. Whenever he needed to tend to union business, he took time off, usually still dressed in his white work apron.

Dlamini was associated with the workerist wing of COSATU, but he had lobbied with local companies to make improvements in living conditions and schools in KwaThema, the nearby black township. FOSATU also had endorsed one person, one vote and lent selective support to UDF campaigns, most notably the massive general strike in November 1984 to protest shootings after the Vaal uprising, demand the withdrawal of troops from Sebokeng, and support African students boycotting schools. Alliances forged in the heat of that general strike swept away theoretical discussions and ultimately led to the formation of COSATU. Moreover Dlamini's teenage daughter was active in the student organization, COSAS. When police raided the Dlamini household at the beginning of the 1985 emergency, it wasn't clear whether they were looking for Chris or his daughter. He eventually returned home, but his daughter remained in hiding. At the time COSATU was founded, Dlamini hadn't seen his fugitive daughter for about two months. "There is no way the unions can divorce themselves from what is happening in South Africa," Dlamini said.

Barayi, after a stern admonition from other COSATU leaders, was soon sounding a more moderate line that took into account all the COSATU constituencies. In an interview just after the foundation of COSATU, Barayi said, "COSATU was formed to concentrate on the broader political issues. Of course, I do believe this should start with the workers on the factory floor. COSATU should not neglect issues such as wages or working conditions, because that is where our strength comes from."[11]

Mineworkers

Every morning at 4 A.M. groups of forty miners shuffle into a metal cage the size of an elevator. The cage plummets toward the center of the earth slightly faster than a subway train. Those inside are thrown into darkness, except for the beams of light that shine from their work helmets. They swallow to make their ears pop as they adjust to a change in altitude that's like dropping three times the height of the World Trade Center in a little more than a minute.

After the cage eases to a stop, the miners walk out into a warm, dank cave. They don black slickers and trudge to a giant metal door. It swings open and they walk inside. The door swings shut behind them with a crash and for a moment they are sealed inside a dark room. At the far end another door swings open into the heart of South Africa's wealth: the gold mines.

It is slightly cooler on the other side, thanks to giant refrigeration units that pump cool air underground, but its still warm. Sweat runs down the workers' faces and chests in steady streams. The miners march to that day's work-face in a tunnel about the height of a normal room. Water drips down the walls and into gulleys dug along floors. The tunnels can be confusing. So it is valuable to know that the water in the gulleys always runs toward the cage.

At the gold seam, miners hunch on a rock shelf about thirty inches high to chisel the gold. A miner in front sits on the wet rock with a jack hammer. The noise is deafening. Ore dust fills the shelf. Miners carry the ore to a large metal buckets that are wheeled on small rail tracks to a central collection depot. Other members of the team are wedging horizontal pieces of timber at right angles to form a pile that holds up the roof of the mine, a roof that is sagging under the weight of anywhere from one to three miles of earth. As they work, the shelf is closing behind the work face. In days, the opening can vanish.

The shelf extends for thirty to fifty meters, and sometimes it runs at an angle of thirty degrees or so. For eight hours a day the miners scrunch inside the shelf. If you lean on your left elbow, your right shoulder touches the roof of the mine.

About 600 miners die every year in the mines, but there are few tips that miners can give newcomers. Some people say the rock "talks." But when working, the only sounds you hear all day long are the jackhammer and the pounding on the timber props. If you hear the rock "talk," it's too late to do much but wait for the roof to fall in.

To James Motlatsi, the first noise sounded like a drum. The second sounded like thunder. When the rock above his head collapsed and buried him in a gold mine several thousand feet below the surface, there must have been a third noise, but Motlatsi never heard it. When he awoke later in a hospital, Motlatsi learned that it took other miners an hour and twenty minutes to dig him out and bring him to the surface. Three weeks later, he was back at the same job. "When you work in the mining industry, you will end it like a soldier. If someone is trapped and killed you just take him out and continue with the same job."

Motlatsi has been a soldier in the mining industry since 1970, when as a nineteen-year-old he left his home village, Mohale's Hoek, in the mountains of Lesotho, an independent country surrounded by South African territory. Scarce in industry and natural resources, Lesotho relies on miners' remittances for virtually its entire gross national product.

Like his father and grandfather, Motlatsi left Lesotho to find work in South Africa's mines. Today he is president of the National Union of Mineworkers. His journey from village to Johannesburg, from underground drain cleaner to union leader traces the growth of black trade unionism in the mines. Motlatsi may not be as savvy as the union's lawyer and general secretary, Cyril Ramaphosa, but Motlatsi is a working man's working man, hardened by experience. Ramaphosa speaks Soweto English; Motlatsi speaks the language of the mines. While Motlatsi is disarmingly modest in private, he is a firebrand on the stump, the embodiment of the growing assertiveness of black miners.

Motlatsi's village is more than six miles from the nearest road. Over the mountains, it is a three- or four-hour trip by foot or Land Rover. "I wouldn't even say it is undeveloped. It never even tried to be developed," Motlatsi says. His father was rarely home because he worked at Crown Mines, the gold mines near Johannesburg, then at diamond mines in Kimberley. Like all migrant workers, Motlatsi's father was too far away to come home on his day off, even if his meager wage had enabled him to afford the trip. He received two weeks vacation a year; for the other fifty weeks his children were fatherless.

The younger Motlatsi left home to earn more money for the family, which had three children. He joined his father, who was working at the Welkom gold mines. Motlatsi worked his way up the ladder of mining jobs. He started as a "lasher" cleaning drains underground. For a ten-hour-and-forty-nine-minute shift (including a one hour round-trip commute from the surface to the gold seam) Motlatsi earned forty cents. After a couple of months, Motlatsi was promoted to "box attendant," hauling waste rock away from the work-face. Nine months later, he was promoted to store attendant.

In those days, black miners were treated "like dogs," Motlatsi recalls. Shortly after going to work at Welkom he was assaulted by a white shift overseer. "He assaulted me because I was the new worker in the gang and for no other reason," Motlatsi says. When Motlatsi tried to lodge a complaint, the mine manager called him into his office.

"Do you have cattle at home?" he asked.

"Yes," Motlatsi replied.

"Do you ever plough?" the manager asked.

"Yes," Motlatsi said.

"What do you do when one of the cattle doesn't do what you want?" the manager said.

Motlatsi said he would kick it.

"That is why the shift overseer kicked you," the manager said, and hitting Motlatsi he told him to get of the office before he hit Motlatsi again.

Pressed by his sisters to earn more money, Motlatsi soon managed to win a job as "timber boy" building the packs of wood, brick, and cement that support the ceiling of the mine. This series of promotions brought his salary up to seventy-one cents a shift. Later Motlatsi earned eighty-two cents a shift as a machine operator drilling rock. He was a winch driver and a team leader by December 1973.

At that time, Motlatsi tried to get a better job in construction. He joined a company that was building dams near Vereeninging. Because the law doesn't allow blacks to stay in white towns, the construction workers slept out in the open veld for three months, even in the rain. "The company didn't know or care to know. All it wanted was for us to show up in the morning," Motlatsi recalls.

During this shadowy part of his career, Motlatsi became a commander in the Lesotho Liberation Army, a unit trained by the ANC. The Lesotho Liberation Army was formed to unseat the Lesotho Prime Minister Jonathan, who long had been unpopular among the Basutho. Jonathan had been elected in 1965, thanks in part to the South African government, which prevented miners from casting absentee ballots. In 1970, miners came home from South Africa in droves to vote, but Jonathan declared a state of emergency and nullified the results. The ANC-trained Lesotho Liberation Army began to form in 1972 and 1973. But the nascent rebellion in the mountain kingdom was crushed by the South African military to prevent an unfriendly force from gaining power across the border. Thousands of sympathizers fled Lesotho and took refuge as workers in the South African gold mines, where ironically they became more troublesome politically than they would have been if left alone in Lesotho.

In April 1974, Motlatsi went back to the mines. On April 22, 1975, he survived a rock burst. He advanced to team leader again, then was promoted to the personnel department in September 1975. "It was a corrupt situation in the personnel department," Motlatsi says. Many personnel officers extorted money from blacks seeking jobs. Although it was clean, safe, above-ground work, Motlatsi says it was the mining job he hated most.

In 1982, Motlatsi read in the newspapers about attempts to start a mineworkers' union. One of his fellow workers who was hitchhiking to Soweto got a lift from Cyril Ramaphosa, a young black lawyer who wanted to start the union. Motlatsi called Ramaphosa right away. At the time, Motlatsi was on vacation selling goods such as trousers and blankets. With the time he had left, Motlatsi and Ramaphosa recruited a seven-person planning committee to begin signing up members. Many miners were skeptical. Because the union was asking for dues, many miners were suspicious that the union was just another scam. To put their minds at ease, the union used workers from the mines rather than outside organizers. "That helped avoid questions about where you were from," Motlatsi recalls. Within weeks, they recruited 18,000 members. Just three months after Motlatsi and Ramaphosa met, a congress of 1,800 workers elected Motlatsi the first president of the National Union of Mineworkers and Ramaphosa secretary general.

Today Motlatsi and Ramaphosa are the heads of a huge organization. The NUM has a coterie of lawyers, a multimillion-dollar-a-year budget, and offices constantly crowded with miners. Motlatsi and Ramaphosa have become world travelers, rallying support from abroad. Motlatsi can knowledgeably discuss British and Zambian miners, compare western and socialist countries, and with healthy skepticism. "Show me a country—capitalist or socialist—where the workers' demands have all been met. No way. It doesn't exist."

At home, the NUM has trained hundreds of shop stewards and developed a sturdy network of officials in the shafts and on the hostels. Nearly 300,000 workers pay dues to the union; another one- or two-hundred thousand miners back the union and are likely to sign up. The only thing holding back faster growth is the limited capacity of the union itself to service so many members. Its fame extends well beyond its organizational limits. At one mine he visited for the first time, Ramaphosa was greeted by workers who lined up like an honor guard receiving a visiting head of state. In a crossword contest run by the predominantly black-read *City Press,* the only question every respondent answered correctly was the one asking them to identify the NUM general secretary, Ramaphosa.

One morning in 1986 around 2 A.M. Marcel Golding's telephone rang. The manager of a gold mine had fired five workers. Ten thousand other miners stopped working. Now the manager was phoning because he wanted the twenty-seven-year-old Golding, an official of the National Union of Mineworkers, to tell the miners to go back to work. Golding told the manager to speak to the shop stewards, then he rolled over and went back to sleep.

An hour later, the shop stewards telephoned and said Golding would have to come and settle the dispute. At five in the morning Golding arrived at the mine and the wildcat strike was still in progress. The workers wouldn't budge. A metal barrel was found for Golding, who stands around five-and-a-half feet tall. He climbed up and shouted a couple of slogans. The miners roared back their approval. Talks between shop stewards and management followed. By the end of the morning, the five fired workers were reinstated pending a hearing and the rest of the miners went back to work.

Even though the NUM had spread the fame of leaders like Ramaphosa and Motlatsi, the driving force behind the union remained the combativeness of the ordinary workers. By 1985 and 1986, one-day wildcat strikes were commonplace. Much of the union leadership's efforts went into restraining the rank and file, which was heady with its newly discovered power and eager to strike.

To Golding, who became assistant secretary general of the NUM, that militancy was no surprise.

> The life of a miner is terrible. You wake up around two in the morning to prepare yourself to go on a shift at 4 A.M. You must be at the rock face at four and it can take about two hours to get dressed and get down the shaft. You work for eight hours in an eighty-two-centimeter hole in a crouched position with rock above your head that can cave in at any minute. Around you is heat at an unbearable temperature and noise like the sound of a drill. You work under a white miner who shouts abuse, calling you "kaffir." At the end of the day, you don't go back to your wife like white miners. You go back to a hostel that you share with twenty guys. At the more backward places, you still have cement bunks. In the summer, the hostel is bloody hot and in the winter it is bloody cold.

For decades miners had endured such conditions. In places like Lesotho, working on the mines was a way to show one's manhood. It also provided an escape from the hopelessness of rural slums. Once men went to the mines, the companies did everything to ensure that the miners remained obedient. Forcing miners to live in single-sex hostels and cutting them off from their wives and families was another way of degrading and dehumanizing them.

The union radically altered labor relations simply by suggesting that miners no longer act as willing participants in their own exploitation. Like Black Consciousness among students, trade unionism fomented a revolution in the minds of workers.

One way the miners tested their muscle was by inviting women—wives and girlfriends—into the single-sex worker hostels, in direct violation of company and government regulations. Lucas Mnyehbezi, age thirty-one, was one of those who violated the rules. He had worked at a coal mine near Witbank, east of Johannesburg, in a single room shared with four other workers, each with a tiny locker and a foam mattress on a bunk bed. Mnyehbezi earned about $100 a month and sent half of that home to his family. He banked about $25 a month and the rest went for beer at the company bar. "After working, I was feeling bad. I used to just get to the bar. Sometimes I used to go outside the hostel and sit on the lawn and think about home." Once a year he visited his wife and five children in KwaZulu several hundred miles away. Lonely, he took a girlfriend, who moved into the hostel with him in 1987. Dozens of other workers on the coal mines followed suit. The government and company stood by without taking action. "I would bring my wife and children if there were proper accommodation," said Mnyehbezi, who paid six head of cattle for his bride. Later that year, the company began to talk openly of building housing to accommodate miners' families.

The miners' assertive mood was bursting forth at the NUM's fifth congress on February 25, 1987. The union bused shop stewards from all over the country to a rented hall near Soweto. The workers arrived in groups from different mines and sang freedom songs. The huge banner hung from the ceiling with the words "Socialism means freedom," while another said, "Organize or starve." The union proclaimed Nelson Mandela, who briefly worked as a mine security officer, as the honorary life president of the union. Motlatsi spoke in Sotho and English, and his speech was translated simultaneously into Zulu. A fugitive leader of the UDF invoked "Comrade Lenin" and conflated "racist oppression and capitalist exploitation." Outside the hall, union officials were doing brisk business selling T-shirts. On the front of the shirts, a black mineworker stood against a red background with his fist raised in front of a gold mine. On the back, the T-shirt declared: "1987 Mineworkers Take Control."

Power and Dignity

"When people gain economic power, it must be exercised in order for it to be recognized," asserts Anglo's Bobby Godsell. In a three-week walkout in 1987, the 300,000 members of the country's biggest black trade union, the mineworkers, struck with the full force of their economic power, clashing with the country's largest mining and industrial conglomerate, Anglo American.

It was the biggest strike in the country's history and it badly bruised both the mining companies and the union. In the process, the strike revealed much about the astonishing extent of the union's power—as well as its limits. And it demonstrated the effectiveness of union organization: operating with tremendous handicaps, the union could still command the loyalty of a workforce that was no longer afraid to voice its demands.[12]

The strike was presaged by months of negotiations. The union demanded wage increases averaging 55 percent, enough to make up for the 16-to-17 percent inflation rate and to close part of the gap between the wages of black and white workers. As the deadline for talks neared, the union cut its demands to 40 percent, then to 30 percent. The companies, represented by the Chamber of Mines, stood firm on an offer of increases between 16 and 23 percent, depending on the job category. The companies warned that the glory days of gold mining were over. Rising capital costs, declining quality of South African ore, and competition from overseas posed long-term threats to the companies and the number of jobs available. The unions pointed to the industry's record profits, a real increase of 44 percent between 1975 and 1986. The union also alleged that 85 percent of the black mineworkers earned wages close to the poverty line.

In previous years, the NUM and Anglo American pulled back from the edge of confrontation. Anglo American, the most liberal mining house, whose workers made up 70 percent of the NUM membership, split from the other mining houses and offered more money. In 1987, though, several factors discouraged Anglo from breaking ranks to achieve an early settlement. Godsell later said,

> We thought that this was not only a strike about this year's wage but a strike about future bargaining patterns. We had lived for a couple of years with what I would call bargaining by brinkmanship. We thought we had to go through a strike experience at least once in order to indicate that the threat of a strike was not always going to move us where NUM wanted us to be.[13]

Moreover, the NUM said it wouldn't accept a "split offer" in which conservative mining houses failed to match the Anglo terms. The NUM appeared eager to test the resolve of its members; it had followed the lengthy bargaining process and was entitled to stage a legal strike.

Neither side expected the protracted battle that ensued. For three weeks, the black mineworkers stayed out on strike, displaying a combativeness exceeding the wildest expectations of NUM leaders. "We never thought that the strike would last more than one week," said Motlatsi later. The simple task of communicating with membership was awesome. There were strikers at forty-five different mines, most without telephones, located hours away from Johannesburg. The head office had only a handful of full-time employees; the rest were ordinary workers.

For the NUM leadership, the August walkout posed immediate strategic choices. At first the union leaders wanted the miners to go back to the homelands where they wouldn't risk face-to-face clashes with police. But branch chairs of the NUM rejected the idea, refusing to pass the message to the miners.[14] The branch chairs said if striking workers stayed together on the mine compounds, it would be more difficult for the mining companies to force anyone underground. Besides it was too expensive for workers to go home. And if strikers returned to the homelands, it also would make it easier for the companies to dismiss them and hire replacements.

The NUM leadership relented, mindful also of how difficult it would be to find its members in the homelands or in foreign countries. So the miners stayed in the hostels. The companies threatened to cut off food supplies to the hostels (which were on company property) and they barred union officials from entering the hostels to talk to workers. The miners took control of ten of Anglo American's twenty-eight hostels. They controlled access to the area and ran the kitchens and washing areas. "This worried us," said

Godsell, who said that a couple of boilers blew up because workers didn't know how to run them. "This was Paris-Commune-type activity."

Employers were angered by the union's fiery rhetoric. Motlatsi gave an interview to British television vowing that the NUM would close down the mines and bring down apartheid. Godsell said, "I believe he should be free to express his views—asinine or otherwise—but it affects peoples' attitudes. You can't expect employers to enthusiastically participate in their own demise."

Police action inflamed the conflict. The NUM charged mine security with intimidating strikers. The companies charged the NUM with intimidating miners who wanted to work. (The NUM represented about 55 percent of the workers on the mines.) After a clash between police and workers outside a store near the President Steyn mine, the NUM walked out of the talks.

In the second week of the strike, miners on some mines where the NUM wasn't yet recognized were advised to return to work. At Landau colliery, workers went back to work after management threatened to shut down the mine. Most of the rest of the industry, however, remained crippled.

As the strike entered the third week, both sides wanted a settlement. The companies began to fear extensive damage to the unserviced mines as alarming technical reports began to come in. So management issued ultimatums, threatening to dismiss 22,000 workers if they didn't return to the mines by August 28. More workers would be dismissed every day. The NUM was risking its entire painstakingly constructed organization.

In public, both sides remained adamant. They almost seemed paralyzed. The NUM couldn't give in without some concession and the mining houses didn't want to budge under pressure. Indeed the mining houses didn't even want to approach the NUM to resume talks. "We were at a stage in the conflict where face was an important issue," Godsell said. "The chamber [of mines] wanted the NUM to approach them."

Godsell, his stringy hair hanging over his gaunt face, broke the deadlock August 24 by offering to reopen talks unconditionally in reply to a question at a press conference, a roundabout approach that angered other members of the Chamber of Mines. The NUM responded and the two sides agreed to boosts in holiday and death benefits equal to a 1.7 percent increase in the overall package.

One final twist of NUM politics remained, however. To the shock of the Chamber of Mines, the NUM executive committee rejected the settlement on Wednesday, August 26, and vowed to continue the strike. Godsell suspected that Ramaphosa hadn't backed the contract. Ramaphosa insisted the rank and file wasn't satisfied. An NUM source said that Ramaphosa, who had brought a mattress into the office so he could take naps while staffing the office around the clock, was racked by uncharacteristic exhaustion, doubt, and indecision. Thursday morning Anglo fired 45,000 workers—

including Motlatsi. Other companies fired another 15,000 miners. On Friday the NUM reversed its position and accepted an offer virtually identical to the one it had rejected two days earlier. The mining houses called it a "victory for collective bargaining." "Many members wanted to keep striking even then," said Motlatsi. "But in the end, we made a tactical retreat. It was better than starting from scratch."

The strike's toll on both sides was heavy. To keep open, many gold mine ceilings need constant reinforcement. During the strike, the pressure of the earth simply packed about 10,000 props into the walls of the openings, closing off Anglo mine stopes, or excavations. To reopen the mines required costly blasting and new props. Moreover, the cost of replacing the fired workers was high. Months after the contract settlement, Anglo finally agreed to rehire most of the dismissed workers. Nearly half had been rehired anyway.

For the union, the cost was high, too. Eight miners died in clashes with police and mine security officials, 500 were injured, and 400 arrested. In addition, the NUM spent months repairing the damage to its own organization. Although only 20 percent of its members were fired, Motlatsi said, 70 percent of the shop stewards were fired. Motlatsi felt the companies were trying to weed out the best union people and weaken the NUM. Those shop stewards who were rehired said that mine management would only recognize them as miners' spokesmen if the stewards were reelected.

Five months after the strike ended, Motlatsi was still touring mine hostels to discuss the lesson of the walkout. As he pulled into a coal mine hostel, workers crowded around him. He entered a brick meeting hall where workers were already assembled. The formalities began with the singing of *Nkosi Sikelel' iAfrika,* the black national anthem. The workers sang with reverence and with their fists held above their heads. The regional union organizer jumped onto a table and exhorted the miners to get to their feet. Groups of them started dancing the toyi-toyi, and singing freedom songs. "Hold it you guys/Hold it you strong guys/The guns of these guys remind me of Oliver Tambo." Motlatsi flashed his infectious smile and moved his hips a little, but looked awkward. A man in orange work clothes led the miners in cheers of "Viva Tambo Viva," then "Viva Ramaphosa Viva," and "Viva Motlatsi Viva," each time followed by a deep throated chorus of "Viva." More vivas followed for the Freedom Charter, the ANC and COSATU.

Motlatsi climbed up on the table. He started modestly and quietly, making a point about the retiring president of chamber of mines. He rebutted accusations that the NUM had become a political organization and he urged the miners to talk to young toughs allegedly recruited from Zululand to disrupt the union and to convert them into dedicated union members. "Because they are coming with a fighting spirit, put them in the workers' defense committees. Put them up front," he said to laughter. He urged the miners to avoid fighting between ethnic groups.

Whites try to divide us according to our language. But whites speak Portuguese, English, and Afrikaans and call themselves white. They are united! Why do we agree to be divided?" The room was suddenly silent. He also discussed the strike.

> The enemy must be disappointed now. He thought that by dismissals and arrests they would destroy our organization. They thought that when they stopped the leadership from talking to workers. But they found the workers were more militant! We will never retreat. We will all reach our destiny!

Miners began crying "Viva Motlatsi" in approval. "We will all be liberated. I wonder whether people understand what is liberation. You have a home, nothing is disturbing you. When you get a job, you get proper accommodation and no police come knocking. There aren't separate schools for blacks and whites. There will be peoples' education." The workers were relaxed as Motlatsi finished. He led a cheer of "Amandla awethu" meaning "Power is ours." After another song, the workers crowded out of the meeting hall. Outside, the miners lay dishes of pap and meat, the staple hostel meal, in an arc on the ground before Motlatsi. He crouched and they shared the food, eating with their fingers.

When Cyril Ramaphosa announced that the NUM accepted the contract that settled the three-week 1987 miners' strike, he ominously called the strike a "dress rehearsal" for a greater showdown. Indeed, despite the union's failure to achieve a better settlement, the strike was an impressive show of force by the black union. The NUM had been severely handicapped in its confrontation with the companies. The protracted bargaining process required by law before a strike can be called had given companies time to stockpile coal and gold and make contingency plans. At the same time, the union wasn't permitted to accumulate a strike fund. Assistance from sympathizers overseas was disrupted by government efforts to curtail foreign funding.

Yet the union commanded the loyalty of black miners. "The NUM showed it can take guys out for a long time," Godsell said. Just before the strike, Zulu migrants were bused to the Landau colliery to be housed separately from strikers and to work as scabs. However the Zulu scabs were impressed by the NUM's campaign to bring miners' wives and girlfriends to the hostels. They joined the union soon after the strike began. Despite the failure of the NUM to win its wage demands, miners were impressed by its strength. Motlatsi said that during the strike, the union received applications from 50,000 miners wanting to join the union, about the same number as those dismissed from the jobs.

The most amazing aspect of the strike was that the government did not intervene. The first time a mineworkers' union went on strike, the union members were bombed by the South African air force, softened up with some heavy artillery, and charged by bayonet-wielding infantry. That was in 1922 and the strikers were white miners protesting changes in the color bar that prohibited Africans from taking certain jobs from whites. The interference by the government in 1987 was mild by comparison, even though the strike cut off the main source of South Africa's foreign exchange. Police harassed some workers and those migrants dismissed were deported to their homelands to Lesotho. But these actions couldn't weaken the strike.

Though the government later proposed drastic amendments to labor legislation that would hinder strikes, it clearly wanted to let this strike run its course. Perhaps the government wanted, in part, to leave the country's premiere avowedly liberal, white, English-speaking institution, Anglo American, in the lurch and force Anglo itself to take measures against the NUM, which it did. But some government officials also wanted to preserve the collective bargaining process. Some company officials did too, especially the more far-sighted ones like Godsell.

To Godsell, the strike and its resolution went to the heart of South Africa's future.

> Democratic society doesn't drop from the sky. It is painstakingly shaped by conflict in society. The strike was marked by anger and the NUM often says things I don't like. But we can *deal* with them. We have a grudging personal respect. That respect is the lifeblood of a future democracy.
>
> Labor relations are a little patch of post-apartheid South Africa, because it is where blacks have some real power. We don't deal with unions because we pity them. In other areas whites often act because they are guilt-ridden about blacks. Our relationships with unions are based on an acceptance of common dignity, because we recognize the black worker's *power.*

Following the mineworkers' strike, many union officials suffered a letdown. The T-shirts declaring 1987 as the year mineworkers would "take control" suddenly had bitter irony. "Life is so bleak in the mines that workers will grasp at anything, however imperfect. But you can't organize 400,000 workers in four year," one NUM organizer said. Problems typical of big unions emerged. A regional NUM organizer suspected of stealing R50,000 was beaten up by miners. They stripped him of his pants, pulled his genitals and went for their knives. He escaped out a window—without his pants. The organizer accused the regional chair of the theft, but the investigation stalled. The regional chair was an important power on the national executive of the union. "I suppose this is how the teamsters started," one troubled organizer said. I tried to rouse one discouraged organizer by asking him if the previous years amounted to nothing but a hill of beans. "A large hill maybe, but beans is definitely the currency," he replied.

Other COSATU organizers were worried that COSATU and its major affiliates had simply grown too quickly. "At first we had a slogan: 'Every factory a fortress.' It was true then. But now unions are bigger and less organized. We lose representation at factories all the time. We're still growing because you just say 'COSATU' and people join. But we now accept a certain attrition rate too." COSATU's newsletter complained that central executive and regional executive committee members were ignoring calls from the head office. "In the first executive meeting after the Second National Congress, we barely made a quorum," the COSATU *News* griped. Other "delegates from affiliates arrive and leave at times they choose."

But the black trade union movement placed a strong emphasis on democracy and strived to achieve that ideal. The idea of a "mandate" began with the trade unions and spilled over into other organizations. Community organizations imitated the unions, borrowing from FOSATU the maxim and practice of holding leadership accountable—and recallable. In some townships, union shop stewards played roles in civic organizations. In Langa, Volkswagon stewards wielded influence. Metalworker leader Moses Mayekiso presided over Alexandra.

To some, the commitment to worker control seemed all show. But to the rank and file it was real. Union leaders ignored it at their own peril. The old FOSATU unions and the NUM maintained aggressive worker-education programs for the rank and file. The president of every union was required to be a full-time worker. NUM's full-time professionals, such as Ramaphosa and Golding, earned the same amount of money as top mineworkers: $500 to $700 a month.

Union leaders avidly read about the international union movement. The NUM studied the collapse of the British coal miners' strike of 1985 and accusations that British coal miners' president waged the strike without a ballot by the membership. Motlatsi had visited Zambian and Zimbabwean miners and come away unimpressed. Motlatsi was also busy reading *Perestroika,* Mikhail Gorbachev's book on reform in the Soviet Union.

Ordinary workers remained militant and eager to fight the bosses. They remained the driving force behind the labor movement even when organizers were discouraged. The relationship between ordinary blacks and their political leaders had reversed. During the 1970s, organizers had to coax workers into joining unions. In the 1980s, workers displayed boundless enthusiasm and expectations. If lack of discipline and realism were problems, at least the defeatism of the 1960s was not. "The battle in the factories has not only strengthened the movement for change, but has also given birth to a type of politics which has been rarely seen among the powerless here: a grassroots politics which stresses the ability of ordinary men and women, rather than 'great leaders', to act to change their world," wrote Steven Friedman, a veteran commentator on labor politics.

Learning to Dance

In 1988, a delegation of black union leaders went to a meeting at the Anglo American Corp. headquarters, a stone monolith designed to be a cross between a bank and a cathedral. The only room spacious enough for the unexpectedly large, twenty-seven-person trade-union delegation and employer representatives was the board room.

It would have been an odd scene to Anglo American's founders, whose portraits hung on the board room walls. Beneath their gaze their well-heeled successors sat face to face with miners who had cleaned ditches 3,000 feet below the earth, workers who had spent months in detention, whose homes ranged from impoverished villages to township matchbox houses. For five hours, one employer representative recalls, "The union delegation heaped moral abuse on employers" giving them an elementary lesson in Marxist analysis. For one hour after that, the two groups held a pragmatic discussion of why it was in their mutual interest to oppose new labor legislation limiting the rights of black trade unions. It was a rare instance of labor and management together discussing ways of opposing the government.

That such a meeting should take place at all, let alone end in a tense recognition of the two sides' mutual interest, marks nothing less than a revolution in South African politics. For the first time, blacks possess real power and the confidence to use it. Once treated as a passive, faceless workforce—"boys" in the eyes of management—the black workers have bargained terms of employment with the mightiest and richest corporate officers in South Africa.

How the black trade unions used that power said a lot about the character of black politics. Once in possession of power, blacks would aggressively use it to redress long-standing grievances. Their rhetoric would be militant, but their actions, and those of the black leadership, could still be pragmatic. They recognized the limits of their own power and understood the usefulness of compromise and patience. "In university, if you criticized Stalin, you were automatically a Trotskyite. If you criticized Trotsky, you were automatically a Stalinist," said Marcel Golding. "We didn't know what power was all about. I've become less ideological and more pragmatic. I wish my friends from university could sit at the bargaining table and see what raw power is."

Black workers succeeded in wielding power because they had forged national trade unions across corporate, tribal, and regional lines. As the trade-union movement has gathered force, the workers have struck a blow against the old system of "baasskap," which had robbed blacks of their dignity. Through the trade unions, blacks forged a new identity. On T-shirts, in slogans and song, and in industrial action, black workers were asserting themselves.

"Comrades," said a union leader at a meeting of the National Union of Mineworkers,

> We wish to control our lives on every front. To start this process is to lay the foundations of a new democratic order. It is a task we cannot postpone. Because of the kind of society we want to build, we must build today and not tomorrow or on liberation day. As one great teacher of struggle put it: "The birth of a new society must be laid in the womb of the old."

One night, a tall, dark-haired American who had worked for an advertising firm in South Africa for several years sat in an easy chair in his plush office. Resting his feet on a glass top, steel frame coffee table, the American, Steve Shore, recalled an unusual advertising seminar he had given for members of COSATU and other progressive organizations.

> They recognized the need for more effective communication so they came to me. I played it as I would to a regular client. I talked about strategy, target markets, and making their message palpable to the audiences. I said that red banners and the hammer and sickle might give them a warm feeling in the pit of their stomachs, but it frightens industrialists, who are supposed to sit down and deal with the unions. That kind of advertising does more to alienate the target market than it does to build communication bridges.
>
> I said you must put yourself in the consumer's mind and sell the idea of a more equitable society. If you're talking about safety in the mines, don't talk about exploitation of mineworkers. Rather say that a safer workplace is a more productive workplace.

Shore sketched an advertisement as an illustration. It showed a domestic worker on her hands and knees scrubbing the floor and a dog watching her. The slogan: "Who leads a dog's life anyway?" Since there had just been a series of mine disasters that cost scores of lives and suspended operations in several mines, Shore proposed an ad with the slogan: "Investing in mine safety makes cents."

"I wasn't getting a helluva lot of feedback during the presentation," Shore recalled. The low point came when he used examples of British social-issue advertising campaigns. The approach was too subtle and too closely tailored to British television audiences. "It went totally over their heads. There was no response at all," Shore said.

Then a union representative made an observation that transformed Shore's feelings about the frustrating day. Indeed, it transformed his entire view of the black struggle in South Africa.

> There was one guy in particular who hadn't said a word and who I thought understood nothing. It turned out he was quiet because he understood everything, better than I did. He said I was dealing with a sophisticated approach. But he said there isn't room at this stage in the union's development as a worker organization to put itself in the minds of the [white] audience. The goals of the workers were, at this stage, first and foremost to forge an identity among themselves, not to build bridges. The symbols and phrases and banners and colors were the exact things they needed to build unity among the workforce.
>
> Then I realized that the entire presentation had been wrong. It had been like by saying "You know, fellas, that toyi-toyi is a great little number, but if you could just learn a ballroom waltz." It is clear that what appears to be crude by Olgilvie and Mather standards is spot on target in their evolution at this stage. COSATU is giving birth to a new nation. Other kind of subtleties don't have a lot to do with what's going on. They are using a whole new type of

vocabulary that makes all kinds of alarm bells ring [for whites]. But it is very important because it is *their* vocabulary and not the vocabulary of the boss man. That vocabulary will probably refine itself, but it is a new society. Possibly I should start to understand their concepts and attitudes. Maybe I should learn the toyi-toyi first, before they learn the waltz."

CHAPTER EIGHT

A Culture of Revolt

STRIKES, DEMONSTRATIONS, and the stamping of feet were only surface signs of a more profound and long-lasting change in the way blacks saw themselves and their place within society. That change mattered more than any particular organization or protest and it found expression in a culture of revolt that flourished during South Africa's years of rebellion.

An exuberance and optimism permeates South Africa's culture of revolt, the opposite of the "dark fury" or alienation of revolt in the western tradition that ranged from Buchner's Woyzeck to Camus' stranger, from Wright's native son to punk rockers. Black South Africans *assert* God, culture, community, and family against a state trying to emasculate these elements of black society. Black South Africans aren't rebelling against the idea of institutions, but against a specific set of institutions. Their revolt therefore doesn't produce visions of an existential rebel alone in a hostile world, because blacks never regarded as theirs apartheid's institutions and conventions. Neither are South Africans alienated from mainstream society, like many outsiders, underdogs, or minorities who rebel against dominant cultures. Black South Africans form a majority and they remain firmly rooted in black society, tradition, and community. Their revolt is an act not of negation but of assertion and celebration of the coming of an alternative culture—and a new society.

As with political organization, the renaissance of black culture can be traced to the early 1970s and the ideas of the Black Consciousness movement. Steve Biko diagnosed the problem of oppression in South Africa as a problem of culture. Because whites described African culture in derogatory terms, black South Africans were ashamed of their history, their "primitive" religion and art.

Indeed blacks were ashamed of their skin. "There were these wigs you would find with the ladies, some of them with long European hair in order to hide their African hair," recalled Terror Lekota. "The African women would use all these creams, skin lightening creams. They tried to be white."[1]

African women's notions of beauty were seen by Biko and his associates as evidence that blacks felt it was somehow wrong to be black. In an essay entitled "We Blacks," written under the pseudonym Frank Talk, Biko said that whites had not been "satisfied merely with holding a people in their grip." Biko said that "with an unnerving totality" whites had

> turned to the past of the oppressed people and distorted, disfigured and destroyed it. . . . No longer was reference made to African culture; it became barbarism. Africa was the 'dark continent.' Religious practices and customs were referred to as superstition. The history of African Society was reduced to tribal battles and internecine wars.[2]

This relentless denigration of black African culture had created a sense of inferiority that rendered black South Africans incapable of action and, above all, incapable of revolt. To black South Africans, revolt seemed futile.

Biko realized that political revolution would have to be preceded by a revolution in how blacks saw their past and culture—their very blackness. Blacks would have to proclaim their pride in being African, for without a sense of self-respect and self-worth, blacks could never demand that whites respect them.

In Biko's eyes, culture not only reflected black thinking but also shaped it. Culture could have a political function in breaking the psychology of oppression and restoring black dignity. At a student rally, he introduced traditional drummers and poets, stimulating an entire generation of activists and artists. "That was the first time poetry made sense," recalled Duma Ndlovu, who later worked in theater. Traditional verses and songs sounded surprisingly fresh. "We recited a Venda poem whose words meant 'We will conquer them and kill them,' " Ndlovu recalled. When police asked the students what the poem was about, the students said innocently it was about the Vendas and the Zulus.

The New Praise Poets

Biko's call for a reinterpretation of African tradition came none too soon. Like topsoil washed from the banks of the Tugela river, black South Africans' largely oral traditions had been eroding for decades. By the 1970s, many were preserved only partially in the writings of white missionaries and historians, or recollected only dimly by older members of rural black communities.

One of the lost African arts seized upon by students was the praise poem, a recitative performed (often with dance) during the eighteenth and nineteenth centuries at important tribal occasions. The praise poem was once the most grand and perfect expression of how African society saw itself and its leaders. The praise poets, or *imbongi,* held important political positions. Despite the autocratic structure of African tribal society, they were free to criticize chiefs. As praisers and counsellors to kings, they served as intermediaries between rulers and subjects. While paying homage to their patrons, praise poets were not obsequious. A drunken king defeated and imprisoned by white settlers was said to walk a path "littered with broken bottles."[3] The poets recounted history, characterized African leadership and reflected popular opinion. In a description that reflected more awe than admiration, the warlike King Mzilikazi was called

Thou tiger of kings, standing erect,
Defeater of monarchs, standing alone;
Eater of nations, consumer of men.[4]

African kings took to heart the advice of the *imbongi.* For instance, Mzilikazi heeded his praise poets' anxiety about impending battles with rival tribes. During the performance of one praise poem, visiting white missionaries noted that the king was a "pensive listener."[5]

Unlike modern blacks, the *imbongi* suffered no crises of identity or place. They summoned familiar images from the surrounding landscape: wildlife, trees, rivers, and mountains. When describing the savage wars waged by Shaka, who united the Natal tribes into a vast kingdom, the praise poets portrayed his military genius and power through nature.

The old women were left in the abandoned sites,
The old men were left along the tracks,
The roots of the trees looked up at the sky.[6]

As white missionaries won converts, praise poems acquired biblical rhythms and Christian messages, while retaining an indigenous sound and power. In a style reminiscent of the Old Testament's use of parallelism and repetition, the praise poet and convert Ntsikana composed a hymn that began

He is the Great God, who is in heaven;
Thou art Thou, Shield of truth.
Thou art Thou, Stronghold of truth.
Thou art Thou, Thicket of truth.[7]

The mysterious and unknowable "thicket" was a rich metaphor for Ntsikana's Xhosa listeners, who believed that the spirits of deceased ancestors buried in sacred places in the forest could send sickness and misfortune if their memory or customs were neglected. The thicket is also where the

Xhosas took refuge to wage guerrilla war against white settlers. By using the image of the thicket, Ntsikana bridged the gap from one set of beliefs to a new faith.

Praise poems fell into obscurity with the disintegration of traditional tribal society at the turn of the century. The migrant-labor system siphoned off the strongest workers to newly discovered gold mines. Industrialization and urbanization threw blacks into dehumanizing township melting pots. Kings and chiefs suffered humiliating military defeats at the hands of the white settlers. The majesty of praise poems no longer seemed appropriate.

I had heard that Western Kunene was part of a generation of township poets inspired to resuscitate the tradition of praise poetry a century later. But the thirty-one-year-old Western Kunene looked like a gangly schoolboy. Our meeting had been arranged by mutual acquaintances, and we met at the home of a white woman in Port Elizabeth. In this strange setting he was at first subdued and exceedingly polite. When he began to recite, however, Kunene was transformed. His voice became full and his diction was backed by the force of conviction.

Born in Cradock in 1956, Kunene came from a line of poets. When Kunene was growing up, his father composed a poem for him and recited it often. The more he recited the poem, he told Western, the stronger Western would become. Western's father composed poems for every child in the family and even one for the dog. His father had his own poem, handed down by Western's grandfather and great-grandfather, each of whom had been traditional poets. "He is a terror to his equals, he is a blessing to the girls," his father's poem went.

The younger Kunene left the arid Karroo as a boy and migrated to the bustling townships of Port Elizabeth. He drifted from work to school and back to work. He attended a black college called Vista, where students had formed poetry-writing groups. Later he worked in a Goodyear plant and did some union organizing, took classes at the predominantly white University of Port Elizabeth, and worked as an unskilled laborer for the state railway.

Like his father, Western Kunene had a knack for poetry. At a young age, he won a competition sponsored by *Drum* magazine, a popular publication aimed at blacks. But unlike his father, who recited verses as talismans for the family, Western Kunene wrote a political poem called "How Long Will We Suffer?" The poem said Africa needed authentic leaders and attacked the corrupt governments of Nigeria and Lesotho.

During the uprising, political funerals in Port Elizabeth's black townships provided a platform for Kunene and other poets. Kunene's poems struck chords across age and class lines. Like the old praise poets, he mirrored popular opinion. He spoke about events in the townships, such as the necklace.

I have seen their smoke
Billowing from our dusty shacks
trailing towards heaven with painful cries
that pierce God's secret chambers.
And I, with eagle eyes, have watched
As they choked and chilled God's warm endurance
Til they invaded the angel's sacred serenity.
Then a loud voice in a bowl of fire
cried "alas" to the makers of this dry discrimination
for the Lord will cast a trail of troubles
upon these stubborn stones.[8]

Instead of the rustic imagery of the nineteenth-century praise poets, Kunene substituted images familiar to township residents: billowing smoke, dusty shacks, painful cries, and tear gas, the "air that chokes."

Kunene described his poetry as a self-conscious political exercise. "The Verwoerdian era will be blasted to pieces by my vowels and syllables," he said. Kunene's own philosophy was a peculiar mixture of Baptist Christianity and revolt. Kunene's father was a pastor in the Apostolic Faith Mission Church and Kunene the younger believed that he could foresee the future. "I act as a prophet in my church. I usually dream of any unpleasant thing that is about to happen and the church elders will make all the necessary things that will stop the occurrence of that event," he said. He believed poetry was his destiny. But his jumble of Christianity and African tradition appealed to people dreaming of better things to come, who believed they had a destiny to run their country.

Africa the land of my origin
The land where my ancestors dwell
Where my blood and my soul originated
Where my joys and my sorrows end

You are my eternal right, Africa
You are my sole pride on earth
And no man on earth
Can ever deny my right to possess you, Africa.

Your mountains are standing still
And marvelling at the fate of your children
You rivers are rushing with rage
And protesting this inhumanity

At night the moon saunters
And meditates over this humiliation
All night the stars flicker
And inform *Him* of this dehumanization

Your darkest hour is long
That's why we grieve in despair
The tears of your children have moved
The Heavens above to sympathy

Listen all children of Africa
Don't give up though the pace seems slow
For the day's around the corner
For I have seen Him put on His robe
And stride down to solve Africa's problems.

This poem shows how Biko's generation masterfully used praise poetry. At the outset, Kunene specifically invokes African tradition. By calling South Africa "my origin" and "my right," he is reclaiming South Africa as a black land. While remaining within Christianity, Kunene draws on animist traditions that inspirit mountains and rivers, moon and stars. Finally, Kunene asserts in religious imagery that political victory is certain.

Throughout the poem, the language itself evokes an era when blacks were closer to the land, before they were shuffled off to degrading townships. In contrast to the poverty and violence that surround his audience, the grandeur of rivers and mountains seems constant and immutable.

Though he dressed in ordinary street clothes and didn't do traditional dances, performance was central to Kunene's readings, as it was to the old praise poets. Between political speeches by community leaders, Kunene serenaded the crowds with his lilting sing-song delivery, elongating the vowels and hammering the consonants.

Though political funerals revived publicly performed poetry, modern township poets differ from earlier praise poets. The old ritual of reciting the geneaology of chiefs is irrelevant to the township meltingpots, where people belong to different tribes or to none at all. Instead the township poets praise heroes fallen in skirmishes with the government. These new objects of praise are common people distinguished by sacrifice rather than royal lineage. In praising them, the township poets are propagating a new history of black resistance that is not taught in state schools.

Township poets still play a role criticizing South Africa's rulers. Unlike the praise poets who were privileged speakers in authoritarian societies, today's township poets enjoy none of those protections. In both the Transkei and the Ciskei, black homeland governments have placed restrictions on praise poets. Only outside the establishment do the township poets have the ears of people's leaders. As a result, the tenor of township poetry differs from earlier praise poetry. Township poets are protest poets. The purpose of their rhetoric is to endow the voiceless with voice and to arouse their listeners to action.

No one embodied the angry voice of protest better than the twenty-eight-year-old unemployed Soweto-based poet Mzwakhe Mbuli, who first read aloud when he was chosen to play the voice of God in a church youth group skit about Job. The son of a truck driver and a domestic servant, Mzwakhe became famous for his powerful verse. Tall and lean, his voice pounded words like a drum.

> Admire me, I am the beats
> From the conga drums of Thabazimbi
> I convey royal messages to the people
> Listen to the rhythm
> Listen to the beat
> From Congo river to the great ocean
> I am like a telex of culture. . . .
>
> I am the drum beats of change in Africa
> Deafening the ears like the winds of change
> Get it from me.[9]

A commercially made tape called *Change Is Pain* became a township hit and spread his reputation as the poet of the struggle. "What do the people think? What do they feel? Just listen to Mzwakhe," said Albertina Sisulu.[10] Often his verse contained angry messages for whites. In one poem, he says, "God has given life unto man, and man has taken life from man. . . . God forgives—I don't, for the heart of Africa is bleeding." In another, he issues a call to action.

> Africa, do something for the spear has fallen
> Pick it up and fall to battle,
> Pick it up and fight side by side for these freedoms,
> Pick it up, fight side by side for a democratic South Africa
> For the spear has fallen.[11]

Show Business

Like township poetry, theater has played a powerful political role in South Africa, transforming blacks' view of themselves and calling them to action. On stage, black South Africans have expressed sentiments in the name of art that they dare not do in the name of politics. The immediacy of the stage and the interplay between actors and audiences have stirred people from apathy.

"For too long we have been silent, with no ways to express ourselves," said a theater review in a black community newspaper, *Grassroots*. "We can use drama to express the hopes, suffering and joy of our people."[12]

Inspired by Black Consciousness, the explosion in black political theater began in the early 1970s. Activists formed a company called the People's Experimental Theatre (PET), whose constitution stated that the company's work would be "a means of assisting Blacks to reassert their pride, human dignity, group identity, and solidarity." In 1973, PET produced *Shanti,* a play about an illicit relationship between an Indian woman and an African man that takes place against the backdrop of a mounting guerrilla campaign for independence. The leading characters break down the wall between actors and audience and preach radical ideology directly to their listeners. The play was written by Mthuli Shezi, a Black Consciousness leader. Two years later, Shezi was killed after being pushed under a train in a fracas with a railway official. Other PET actors were arrested and the company dissolved.

By that time, other black theater groups were putting politics on the stage. A company called Workshop 71 produced a series of political plays. In *Survival,* Workshop 71 portrayed prison life and suggested that for blacks the entire country was a prison.[13]

The company folded when most of its members sought asylum in the United States while on tour with *Survival.* But some of its style was sustained by Ramolao Makhene, a university library worker the troupe had recruited after spotting his expressive face in a theater audience. In 1976, Makhene joined Junction Avenue Theater company. He starred in a play called *Security* about a black man who applies for a job as a security guard only to discover the job is for a dog. The employer decides the black man will do and trains him to be a dog.

Many of the new political plays instantly galvanized township audiences. On one occasion, Makhene recalls, a black township audience demanded an encore after a performance by Workshop 71 and the company repeated the entire play.

To some theater-goers, the plays inspired by Black Consciousness seemed tedious reenactments of real life. But the BC generation of playwrights *wanted* to portray a reality they felt had been denied by whites and blacks, no matter how stark. Their goal was political conversion, not entertainment.

The Black Consciousness movement spawned polemical theater, such as the 1984 production of *Gangsters. Gangsters* open with a white security police officer named Major Whitebeard and a black police officer named Jonathan standing on opposite sides of a large red cross that is leaning against a platform. Draped on the cross lies the body of the poet laureate of Soweto, dressed in black and with a hood over his head. The black poet is dead. The two police officers circle round and round the cross wondering how they will conceal the evidence of torture on his body and explain the poet's death. Upon hearing that the poet has been lying like that for a week, Major Whitebeard says, "So, so!" He pauses. "So this is serious!"

After the opening scene, the play flashes back to scenes where Major Whitebeard warns the poet to abandon his "inflammatory" public poetry readings. "Your poetry is responsible for the creation of a violent frame of mind," he says. Major Whitebeard urges the poet to pay less attention to "the negative aspects of life" and "cheer [people] up by talking about the good things that surround them—by telling them of the natural beauty that surrounds them." He then recites a poem in Afrikaans about flowers and nature.

"What kind of flowers will ever grow in Crossroads?" the black poet replies. "If that poet of yours lived in Alexandra, he would write about stagnant pools of water and the smell of shit filtering through the streets at night because there is no drainage system."

The author of *Gangsters* was typical of the generation of new playwrights. Born in 1951, Maishe Maponya was the son of a painter. When he was eleven years old, government authorities forced his family to move from Alexandra township and resettle in the Diepkloof, a new section of Soweto. Later Maponya became an insurance clerk in a large corporation and began writing in his spare time. He then founded the Bahumutsi Drama Group of Soweto and won a British Council award which enabled him to go to the Edinburgh Festival in Scotland. He saw a production of *The Measures Taken* by Bertolt Brecht, which he said influenced a play he later wrote called *The Hungry Earth,* a "lecture-demonstration" about the conditions of black working-class life. Maponya called his work the "theater of the dispossessed."[14]

Before the emergence of the Black Consciousness theater, township drama was dominated by the work of Gibson Kente, still the most successful theater producer in South Africa. Unlike the early Black Consciousness playwrights, Kente entertains first, and preaches second. He follows the dictum that if he can pry open the audience's mind with humor, then he can hammer in the nails of reason. With twenty-two smash hit musicals in twenty-seven years, he is the Andrew Lloyd Webber of the townships. "Gibson Kente is *show business,*" says Mannie Manim, director of the internationally acclaimed Market Theater in Johannesburg.

Yet Kente's plays seldom appear at the Market. Few white South Africans have ever heard of him. But his itinerant shows play to packed community halls in the black townships across the country.

A typical Kente venue I visited early one winter was in the dreary township of Tembisa. Thick coal dust hung in the air. The streets were dark, obscuring the rows of identical brick four-room houses built in the mid-1950's. An armored car with white soldiers guarded the entrance to the township. Deep within the township, though, the community hall was buzzing with anticipation. When Kente's show began, people watched in rapt attention, occasionally shouting their approval or disapproval and hissing for quiet when the din and poor acoustics made it difficult to hear.

Kente's shows welded the peculiarly American art form of the musical with the poverty and rootlessness of life in the townships. Kente describes his typical setting as "slum and untidy." The place: a typical black township. The grist for his shows: "the adventures, humor, hazards and frustrations of the township that seem unacceptable even to its residents."[15]

Kente treats this dehumanizing setting differently from the polemical young playwrights of the 1970s. Like classic American musicals, Kente's shows possess an air of innocence. His plots are simple; his endings usually happy or uplifting. He ennobles the downtrodden common person while poking fun at everyone from comrades and gangsters to philandering priests and dreamers of better lives. Kente makes all this entertaining with the help of moving melodies and rousing dance scenes. Kente says, "I try to accommodate the two extremes: something for the intellectuals and some township jargon so that even the *tsotsis* can enjoy them."

The dialogue and melodies reflect the unique black township amalgamation of pop and traditional culture, ranging from the hymns of the Seventh Day Adventist Church to migrant worker dances to American musicals and blues. The singers are backed up by a small band including an electric bass and guitar, drums, and a couple of horns. Kente says his favorite American musicals are *Fiddler on the Roof, Annie,* and *West Side Story.*

Gibson Kente lives in the Dube section of Soweto, where he received me late one morning. A crew was pointing sets in the driveway. The son of a laborer, Kente started writing songs for choral groups and quartets in high school, and later became a talent scout for a record company. The first musical he saw was *King Kong,* a South African stage production about a local heavyweight boxer. The play was staged at Dorkay House, a racially mixed arts center in the late 1950s and early 1960s. Soon Kente produced his first musical called *Manana the Jazz Prophet* about a priest who feels that church services could be livened up by introducing American gospel tunes instead of somber Anglican hymns.

He has been churning out shows ever since. In 1967, Kente formed his own company. Kente writes the scripts and scores himself, and designs the mobile sets, which can be dismantled in five-to-seven minutes. The shows cost about $5,000 each to produce. On a good night, ticket receipts top $2,000. The best turnouts often come in small, remote townships where the arrival of a Kente show might be the biggest—perhaps the only—event of the month. His financial success made him the first truly independent black artist, free from government patronage, corporate subsidies, or white pressure.

Virtually every black director, writer, or performer has started with Kente, including most of the BC generation of actors and actresses. Manim says, "Gibson Kente has been the training school for black actors."

In the early 1970s, even Kente felt the political transformation taking place. His 1974 musical *How Long?* conveyed a growing impatience among blacks. The show portrays a strict police officer enforcing the country's pass laws. The play depicts the officer as heartless or ridiculous, but in the end he, too, is a victim. The policeman is forced to act against his own son, who has lost the birth certificate needed to prove his urban residency rights. Finally the police officer throws down his cap and jacket and sings the title song with the cast.

The sequel, *Too Late,* was also about a black police officer harassing township residents. The sympathetic victims are a drunken doctor, three pickpockets and thugs (disguised as Zion Church members in the opening scene), a woman selling beer illegally, and a hobo. The young hero, Saduva, is arrested for not having his pass. Prison changes him from a frightened innocent to a foul-mouthed, hardened young man, who buys a knife and comes within a breath of stabbing the policeman in the closing scene. A crowd forces the two apart, but it is a bitter standoff. "What's changed him?" one of the characters asks about Saduva. "What's put hatred in him? . . . Tomorrow the poor young boy will be labelled dangerous and against the laws of the country. Forgetting that politics were forced on him. It's like being thrown into the rain and expected not to get wet."

Black students felt the two plays captured the anger of the mid-'70s. So did the police. After riots broke out in Soweto on June 16, 1976, Kente was detained for five months. Notwithstanding his stint in jail, Kente became unpopular for his political views, which have become conservative by the 1980s standards of the townships. When P. W. Botha's title was changed to State President, Kente sent him a note of congratulations. He said that President Botha "sometimes says beautiful things, but doesn't know how to say them." Kente also appeared on state television, which is boycotted by most black artists and activists. In 1979, black activists ran Kente and his troupe out of the politically charged city of Port Elizabeth. Kente said he received threatening letters warning him against returning.

Black theater has reflected wider changes in black politics. As non-racialism gained currency, some actors began to work with whites at the Market Theater or with the Junction Avenue Theater Company in Johannesburg. Though Kente has become unfashionable in political circles, black playwrights have learned lessons from his success. "BC had become an elitist group. People would flock [to the theater] from all strata of life, but [the actors] would talk this A1 English with no translation. They lost the masses then," said actor Ramolao Makhene.[16] A1 English is the proper English required for high school graduation.

In the mid-1980s, two veterans of Kente's troupe, Mbongeni Ngema and Percy Mtwa, merged the politics of the Black Consciousness movement with Kente's entertainment flair. So while the two wrote overtly political plays, they also leavened the plays with humor and farce. Both Ngema and Mtwa drew on musical backgrounds. In addition to playing in Kente musicals, Ngema had learned guitar at age eight from his father. As a youth, he listened to traditional Zulu music and the Beatles, who were as popular in South Africa as they were elsewhere.

Using minimal sets and small casts, the actors evoked different scenes by using few props besides a chair or a box. A pink plastic nose transformed a black actor into a white police officer, politician or employer. Ngema and Mtwa's plays had scanty plot lines and often resembled a collection of skits, loosely tied to a theme.

Their first hit, *Woza Albert,* speculated about what would happen if Jesus (or "Morena") came back to earth in South Africa. After several slapstick scenes, the government decides to imprison Morena, calling him a "cheap communist magician." He dies in detention, but comes back to life in the last scene. He walks across Table Bay from Robben Island prison, zaps the spectacular Table Mountain into nothing, and raises black political heroes from the dead.

Ngema and Mtwa worked separately after that, but their plays remained similar. Ngema adapted *Asinamali (We Have No Money)* from a play produced during the 1983 rent strike in Lamontville township, outside Durban. Most of the characters were ordinary laborers, sucked into politics by daily issues.

Some of the most provocative pieces of political theater have emerged from the Junction Avenue Theater Company, founded as an all-white troupe in 1976 but later composed mostly of blacks. The company has specialized in revising official versions of South African history.

Two weeks before the Soweto student uprising began in June 1976, the company made its debut with a play called *The Fantastical History of a Useless Man.* In it, the actors reenact South African history in irreverent vaudevillian style. The play dubbed the 1652 landing of Dutch settlers an "invasion." It depicted the Anglo-Boer War as a boxing match. The Useless Man, a white everyman who was the protagonist, was portrayed as a spectator to this history. At one point he is offered a machine gun, but he can't bring himself to take it.

For whites, the play had a discouraging message. "The most we can do," the white Useless Man says, "is be the least obstruction." But for blacks, the play ended on a more provocative note, when the Useless Man says, "The third act is in the streets."[17]

Junction Avenue also performed *Randlords and Rotgut,* a dramatization of a University of the Witwatersrand academic's history of the use of liquor by mining houses as a means of social control in the gold mines at the turn of the century. A version of *The Bacchae* was done with African song and myth.

In 1986, Junction Avenue staged *Sophiatown,* a play based on a true tale about two black journalists who place an ad in the newspaper for a white woman to come live in Sophiatown. A young Jewish woman shows up and the play explores two estranged worlds. The black sportswriter and the white woman fall in love, but are forced to part when government bulldozers come to tear down the township and truck its residents to the remote Meadowlands section of Soweto.

The play was based on the recollections of people interviewed by the cast. In the process, the cast members themselves were transformed. The lines between art and reality blurred.

In the play, a cautious "shebeen queen" tries to dampen her daughter's rebellion against second-rate schooling. But in the end, she is so angered by the destruction of Sophiatown that she shouts in rage and refuses to get off the truck in Soweto. The part was played by a former domestic worker who was recruited to join Junction Avenue when its white director overheard her singing in his friend's kitchen. Like the shebeen queen, she has been transformed. "I always felt small, self-pitying. Now I know I can do anything."[18]

The rebellious daughter in the story was played by a young woman who herself rebelled in June 1976 and was detained for twelve days. The lines she said in character were the same as those she said in real life a decade earlier: "I don't want this Bantu education, Mamma. It's for the gutter."[19]

Ramolao Makhene, who played Mr. Fahfee, a Sophiatown numbers runner, grew up near Sophiatown in a shebeen where his mother ran a numbers game.

These similarities between art and life lent power to the drama, even though the action had taken place thirty years in the past. And the play had an immediacy for black audiences when it ended with the sound of an iron bar hammering against a metal telegraph pole. "Wake up," Makhene shouted in the voice of Mr. Fahfee. "They can't stop us forever."

Popular History

"What is history?" asks Jakes, the black reporter in *Sophiatown*. "It's only history if you steal something really large—like a country."

"Ja, well," says Mr. Fahfee, "We're going to steal it back."

How people view history says much about how they view themselves. Revising history was an important part of the culture of revolt. "A people without a positive history is like a vehicle without an engine," Biko wrote. "They always live in the shadow of a more successful society."[20]

During the first World War, when blacks felt inferior to whites, a black South African studying medicine in Scotland wrote a book called *The Bantu Past and Present*, which historian Leonard Thompson describes as "scarcely distinguishable from the accounts of his white contemporaries." The black physician called blacks "an indolent, lethargic, and dreamy race of men, and their history one dull, dreary, featureless scene of barbarism and incompetence."[21]

Texts used in South African state schools have put across the view that blacks have stood outside the mainstream of civilization. General history texts start with Egypt, Greece, and Rome and end with the Reformation and Counter-Reformation. Texts on South African history recount white settlement and expansion from 1652 through the 1830s from the white point of view.[22]

Biko said that "part of the approach envisaged in bringing about 'black consciousness' has to be directed to the past, to seek to rewrite the history of the black man and to produce in it the heroes who form the core of the African background."

This task was taken up in the 1980s by people composing a political mythology to sustain black resistance and to discredit the government. In 1986, the *New Nation* newspaper sought to popularize an alternative view of black history and to construct a pantheon of black heroes. Every issue had a special pullout section called the Learning Nation, featuring history lessons written in a simple style. Instead of starting with ancient Egypt or Greece, the Learning Nation began its history lessons with an article entitled "Slavery—the Facts." The article contradicted myths about white settlement of Africa by saying that whites exploited rather than civilized the continent.

Slavery, it said,

> was a system whereby Africa was forced to export its most valuable product—labour power—in exchange for goods that did not help to produce anything in Africa. Goods such as guns, cloth beads and metal pots were used up quickly. They did not enrich Africa. On the other hand, the slaves who went to America were forced to produce silver, cotton, sugar and tobacco. These products fed the fast-growing European factories. . . .[23]

In keeping with the philosophy of non-racialism, an inset box highlighted the contributions of a white and a black abolitionist: British liberal Granville Sharp, "who succeeded in arousing the conscience of the British people," and Pierre Dominique Toussaint L'Ouverture, a slave leader who, inspired by the French Revolution, led a slave revolt in the former French sugar colony of Haiti.

In its second issue, the *Learning Nation* introduced a series about working-class leaders. The first profiled Frances Baard, a woman living in Mabopane near Pretoria, who had spoken at the UDF launch at Mitchells Plain in 1983. The article described Baard's work as an organizer for the Food and Canning Workers' Union in the 1940s.

> She remembers those days: "The hours we worked were long and the wages and working conditions were terrible. Often we were locked inside the factory and not allowed to leave until we finished the days' quota for canning. That meant leaving the factory late at night and most of us were women, she said.[24]

Such tales stressed the humble origins of black leaders, thus suggesting that ordinary readers could rise above their own circumstances. And each had a moral for the present. "It was the unity of the workers, she notes, that finally led to improved working conditions at the factory," the article on Baard said.

At the office of the *New Nation*, acting editor Gabu Tugwana seemed more preoccupied with the present than with the past. His desk was littered with empty Coke bottles, page dummies, and notes on the latest-breaking news. News broadcasts played softly from a radio on the shelf. But Tugwana saw the mission of the history supplements as identical to that of news stories: to stimulate action by making people more aware. Tugwana recalled that his schoolbook

> said [that Dutch settler] Jan van Riebeck discovered this country in 1652. As they walked inland they found these blacks—nomads—from somewhere

around the equator. All the Dutch had when they arrived was biltong [beef jerky]. Later they had thousands of cows. There is a gap between what they had when they came and what they had ten years later when they start talking about blacks stealing cattle. Where did those cows come from?

The government wants the people to forget their history. The less you know about your background the less you care about the future. If you know that you had something and you had it taken away from you, then you strive to get it back.

The new history material, though often produced by white liberal and radical academics, is popular among blacks. A book called *Right to Learn* sold 18,000 copies in the mid-1980s. Each copy was circulated several times. "Good books have legs," an academic said. The University of the Western Cape "people's history" workshop produced two black history booklets called *Let Us Speak of Freedom*. The *New Nation* received hundreds of requests for reprints of the Learning Nation.

A magazine called *Learn and Teach* also featured articles about blacks' past. In a 1987 issue, the cover story was an obituary of Gert Sibande, who had organized farm workers in the eastern Transvaal for the ANC in the 1950s. The article told how Sibande founded an ANC branch in Bethal and evaded police to attend the Congress of the People in 1955. He was a defendant in the Treason Trial, and the last Transvaal provincial president of the ANC before the organization was banned. The rousing article said, "He was called the Lion of the East because like a lion, he was a fighter until the very end."

Autobiographies by blacks were also popular. Petrus Tom, a union organizer from the Vaal triangle, published *My Life Struggle,* recounting events from his childhood, through the Sharpeville massacre, and up to the Vaal uprising. "My message to the working class is that nobody will liberate you except yourselves," he concluded.

The National Education Crisis Committee, chaired by *New Nation* editor Zwelakhe Sisulu, and Skotaville Press published a book entitled *What Is History?* It encouraged people to write their own histories and advised them about how to search through documents and do interviews. "Our old people are our libraries," it said.

History as a subject, is not just a collection of dead facts about the past. It is the story of how the world of today came to exist. . . . If we do not understand the past, it is more difficult to change the present or look ahead to the future.[25]

"Hath Not a Kaffir Eyes?"

Shifts in black politics have changed the way black writers and artists approach their audience.

In 1890, an African Jubilee Choir toured Britain to raise money for an industrial school for Africans. They performed the first half of their program in the vernacular, decked out in native dress, and the second half in

English, in sober Victorian attire, in order to demonstrate to Europeans the native's potential to become civilized.[26]

In the early 1900s, Solomon T. Plaatje used literature to impress blacks' common humanity upon the people Plaatje believed could do something to relieve blacks' suffering: whites in South Africa, world powers, and especially the British, who had won the Boer War and nominally ruled South Africa at the time.

Plaatje was a sort of Renaissance man: journalist, novelist, pamphleteer, and politician. In 1912, he was elected first secretary general of the South African Native National Congress (later the African National Congress). Though he never went past fifth grade in school, his writings were extensive: a historical diary about the Boer War; a fifteen-page pamphlet about white-black sexual relationships that sold 18,000 copies when published in New York; translations of five of Shakespeare's plays into Sechuana; a moving exposé of farm conditions caused by the 1913 Land Act; and a book of Sechuana proverbs.

Thanks in part to Plaatje's translations of Shakespeare, many black South Africans have read *A Comedy of Errors, The Merchant of Venice, Othello, Much Ado about Nothing,* and *Julius Caesar.*[27] At a meeting in the 1980s, a black trade union leader paraphrased Antony's funeral speech in *Julius Caesar.* He said, "I'm here to bury Botha, not to praise him." The line evoked hearty laughter.

Plaatje also wrote the first novel written in English by a black south African, thus making the thoughts of blacks accessible to whites. The novel, *Mhudi,* is a tale of love lost and reunited. Two children are separated by wartime calamity, lost in magical forests of ferocious lions and kind strangers, and then joyfully reunited. Their style of addressing each other is modest, polite, and poetic, reflecting Plaatje's reading of Shakespeare. "From henceforth," the leading man says to his beloved Mhudi in the closing lines of the book, "I shall have no ears for the call of war or the chase; my ears shall be open to one call only—the call of your voice."[28]

After the Land Act of 1913, Plaatje turned his pen to describe the plight of the thousands of African sharecroppers kicked off white farms and left to starve by the roadsides. Plaatje's 1916 exposé, *Native Life in South Africa,* made an eloquent plea for compassion. Like *Mhudi,* it was written in a language and style that Plaatje hoped would appeal to white South African and foreign audiences. The chapters of *Native Life* begin with epigraphs from sources as varied and familiar to his intended readers as the Bible, an Afrikaans prophet, English, German, and French poets, and an American World-War-I correspondent. At the start of one chapter, he takes liberties with *The Merchant of Venice* by replacing the word "Jew" with "kaffir."

> Hath not a Kaffir eyes? Hath not a Kaffir hands, organs, dimensions, senses, affections, passions? Is he not fed with the same food, hurt with the same weapons, subject to the same diseases, healed by the same means, warmed and cooled by the same summer and winter as a white Afrikander?[29]

Plaatje was keenly aware of the power of culture, but while he used culture to appeal to whites in their own language, recent black culture reflects the populist politics of the 1970s and 1980s. Most blacks now believe that change will be wrung from reluctant whites only when masses of blacks stage a popular uprising.

With the death of the politics of petition, it is no longer necessary for black culture to appeal to, or be understood by, whites. Much of modern black culture is written entirely or partially in the vernacular, regardless of the author's fluency in English. Even when writing in English, like Mzwakhe, black poets and playwrights are addressing blacks. The physical appearance of today's black cultural figures emphasizes this change. The Congress leaders at the turn of the century, conscious of their roles as the elite intermediaries between European and African societies, maintained dress and demeanor that would have looked appropriate in the white Parliament. Today's political leaders often wear T-shirts with political symbols and colors easily identified by the ordinary black.

Nothing demonstrates the shift in audience better than the flowering of worker theater and poetry. After the legalization of black trade unions in 1979, dozens of black trade unions began to organize workers and raise money by performing poetry or plays in the black townships and single-sex hostels. The poems and skits especially appealed to apolitical migrant workers, many of whom come from rural areas. Almost every factory has performed a play about working conditions and the benefits of trade unions.

"Culture has an important role to play in the struggle we're fighting on a day-to-day basis," said labor leader Jay Naidoo. As a result, Naidoo said, "We aren't interested in radical chic theater. We want culture to relate to people on the ground." To people like Alfred Qabula.

Alfred Temba Qabula drove a forklift at the Dunlop tire and rubber factory in Durban. Cut off from conversation by the persistent noise of the factory and his forklift, Qabula passed hours alone with his thoughts.

In the early 1980s, he started writing plays and poems in his head while working. Soon he emerged as a praise poet, praising the union instead of traditional kings. Speaking in Zulu, he called his trade-union federation a "moving forest of Africa," echoing the "thicket of truth" the convert praise poet Ntsikana saw in God in the late nineteenth century.

Qabula grew up in the rural Pondoland area of Transkei. His father was a miner and sugarcane worker; his grandfather was a migrant transport worker. Seventy percent of the men from the area where Qabula grew up still subsist by migrant labor. As a teenager, Qabula joined the African National Congress Youth League. In the late 1950s, when soldiers put down a revolt in Pondoland, Qabula escaped in the night, hid in the forests, and "lived with the animals for a year."

In 1964, he resurfaced and joined a construction gang in Carletonville gold mining area. He worked as a laborer and later as a plumber. He quarreled about wages (whites were earning R70 a week versus his R24 a week) and joined Dunlop. When the Metal and Allied Workers Union recruited members at Dunlop in 1980, Qabula was the first to join. In 1982 the union won a majority of the plant, but Dunlop refused to negotiate with workers in the steering committee.

In 1983, the union launched a boycott of Dunlop products. To spread the word about plant conditions and to rally support for the boycott, Qabula and some other workers produced a play called the *Dunlop Workers' Play*. The play described working conditions at the plant. It also recounted highlights of South African workers' struggles, such as the potato boycott of the 1950s that protested farm labor conditions. The play took some flights of fancy. A Dunlop worker talks to American astronaut Neil Armstrong and asks how things are on the moon. Armstrong says there isn't any water, but there is plenty of land. The worker asks if Armstrong can take him there. Then the worker pauses and asks if Dunlop can take its factory there. Armstrong says yes, it's possible, and the worker grows worried. If so, he says, then Botha can make workers carry identity documents and there could be jails too. In the wake of the play and boycott, Dunlop agreed to negotiate with the union.

Qabula began to recite poetry at meetings of the Dunlop local of the metal workers' union. "I was the only man on a forklift truck," Qabula explained. "It gave me freedom in my head, where I composed all these things. Most of the poems were composed around midnight on the night shift. The noise always gives me ideas."

> We see the railway tracks
> the highways, the buildings and factories . . .
> we hear
> the trains
> the motor cars and machinery
> the bombs going off
> the sound of gunshot
> and you refuse to ask them why they are conducting themselves like that
> You don't complain
> when they are making so much NOISE![30]

Like the township poets, Qabula saw his poems as offshoots of traditional African oral poetry and at first he performed in the traditional costume of an *imbongi*. "I had heard poems at home in the rural areas so I knew a lot about praise poems," he said, sitting in a union office in Durban. "They were soft poems. They talked about love or chiefs. In the rural areas, some traditional people composed them to praise chiefs, especially on Christmas and other holidays."

By contrast, Qabula's first major poem praised FOSATU, his trade-union federation.[31] Qabula decided to "talk about hard things, about the struggle. I thought I'd praise the people who are turning the wheels in industries. It's time for us to write about ourselves. We hold the hot iron. We know about the hardships of being a worker." The poem melded industrial conflict and the rural landscapes familiar to many migrant workers. After calling FOSATU a "moving forest of Africa," Qabula tells workers:

> Escape into that forest,
> The black forest that the employers saw and ran to for safety.
> The workers saw it too
> "It belongs to us," they said,
> "Let us take refuge in it to be safe from our hunters."
> Deep into the forest they hid themselves
> And when they came out they were free from fear.
> You are the hen with wide wings
> That protects its chickens.
> Protect us too with those sacred wings of yours
> That don't choose the colors of the people.[32]

Qabula also wrote a parable comparing the trade union movement to a beautiful fruit tree growing in a trash dump. Farmers chop it down, burn it, then bury the remains under broken glass, the rubble of bricks, and old irons. But soon a man living in an old scrapped Toyota sees the tree growing again and bearing fruit."Maybe I am dreaming," the man wonders.

> Maybe I am mad.
> No, I am well.
> What I see is a real thing.
> The fruit tree is grown up again
> It's producing in tens, hundreds, and millions
> It is producing first grade fruits.
> Everybody is going to the dumping place
> Even the animals.

Qabula recites the poem with vigor, his hands motioning over his shoulder, then twisting forward with enthusiasm. "The dumping place is the working class," he explained. "The employers don't think anything can happen in the dumping place, where there is a heap of filth."

Since the *Dunlop Workers' Play,* workers at dozens of other factories have produced plays. Mannie Manim of the Market Theater in Johannesburg said,

> There must be a play per factory. The workers are expressing themselves through these dramatic pieces. They are showing their lives, their situation, their factories—maybe even showing what they'd like these things to be. They use lots of song and abrasive laughter in order to laugh at bad things. The plays aren't as polished as what we usually produce, but after all the actors are working for a living. And when the plays perform to union audiences, it's a wonderful theater happening, full of excitement.

The plays have helped inspire a broad political awakening among laborers and spurred organizational advances. Rapidly growing black trade unions, in turn, have reinforced the workers' new-found artistic confidence.

When British Tire and Rubber workers went out on strike, they traveled across the country with a play called *The Long March*, a burlesque about their hardship and the intransigence of the BTR management. The play portrayed scabs as rats and white management as villains in ill-fitting suits and fleshy clown noses. While the strike dragged on, *The Long March* raised money for a strike fund and sustained worker morale. At the end of each performance, the worker-actors stepped forward, one by one, stating their names and saying, "Still on strike."

The artistic awakening among workers spread beyond theater. FOSATU (later merged with COSATU) sponsored workers' choirs. Though their quality was uneven, the choirs spread the militant spirit of the trade unions. Workers from the Clover dairy product plant sang words which meant:

> Black nation came in blackness
> We don't have a spokesman in Parliament
> We'll die battling.
> But now we have a spokesperson
> Which is FOSATU
> And here is the spokesperson which is FOSATU.

Employees of Simba Quix sang,

> Wake up, wake up, wake up Africa
> All workers let them help each other
> Let them work
> Build the nation with your work
> Let's stand, FOSATU, with your work.

Qabula aroused other workers like Mi S'dumo Hlatshwayo, a van driver at Dunlop. Hlatshwayo had grown up in the townships and listened to poems in Black Consciousness groups, but he wasn't inspired until he heard Qabula. He then wrote "Black Mamba Rising," a poem that compared the trade unions to the venomous African snakes. "Our poetry boosts the pride of other workers and uplifts the dignity of the black workers," said Hlatshwayo, who went to work full time for COSATU.

Hlatshwayo also was influenced by poetry he heard at the St. John's Apostolic Church, an independent African church which he joined after he was healed of a serious illness. The lay preachers' messianic sermons integrated the traditions of praise poetry, comparing Christ to a furious black buffalo who cut through shrubs to proclaim his victory on earth.[33] Qabula wrote a poem comparing Mandela to a black buffalo. "When it was on the island of Patima / It roared and danced / and its calves heard it from different directions."

For Hlatshwayo, the adaptation of the traditional praise poem form is a self-conscious effort to follow Biko's injunction to reach into the past to create a new present. "We must not take a single tradition and incarcerate it," Hlatshwayo says.

> We have taken the African praise poem presentation and changed the content to fit the times. Many people come from the country where praise poetry is still done. They find it easy to relate to patterns that they know and understand. The praise poet presentation is very powerful. It excites the people. It excites the very person delivering the poem and majestically links him with the past and present.

Once listeners are drawn in by the presentation, Hlatshwayo hopes they will get the message. "We [poets] talk about longing for a better world. We forge a new world, a new culture that comes out of our poetry."

The vibrant poetry coming from the trade unions was largely unnoticed by the white audiences that Sol Plaatje once tried to touch. Performed at union rallies in townships or hostels, worker culture wasn't seen by whites. Had it been, it couldn't be understood. When translated on paper, the plays and poems were bereft of the sound and force of performance.

When an article in a white newspaper gave a lukewarm review to translated worker poems, Qabula reacted angrily. "My poems weren't dedicated to university people. I didn't go to university. Maybe I'm from a hostel or a compound or a shack. But I was talking to other laborers. If it doesn't come across to you, you mustn't worry. It belongs to the working class. It doesn't belong to you."

National Anthems

Like the fictional Major Whitebeard in *Gangsters,* South Africa's ruling National Party knows the power of culture. The party itself made use of culture in its own climb to power in the late 1930s and the 1940s.

In 1938, right-wing Afrikaners campaigning under the National Party banner reenacted the Great Trek Afrikaner pioneers had made a century earlier. The long march, made with ox wagons and in nineteenth-century costume, culminated in a rally with theater, folk dancing, and song. The distinguished Afrikaans poet N. P. Van Wyk Louw was commissioned to write a play for the occasion, a 'patriotic' foundation myth to extol the heroism of the Afrikaans founders and discover in their suffering the source of Afrikaner nationalism. After every sermon and speech, the crowds sang a new Afrikaans anthem *Die Stem van Suid Afrika,* [*The Voice of South Africa*] which eventually replaced *God Save the King* as the country's national anthem after the National Party took power in 1948. "We shall live, we shall die, we for thee South Africa" said the new song.

One of the speakers at the 1938 rally was Hendrik Verwoerd, later prime minister and architect of modern apartheid. In the name of nationhood, Verwoerd called upon white South Africans—Afrikaners in particular—to defend everything dear to *die volk* (literally "the people" in Afrikaans). Nary a folk dance or hymn or poem was recited in Afrikaans without a sense of militant determination to guard Afrikaner identity, and by implication the National Party and apartheid.

In power, the National Party has been equally attuned to the political dimensions of culture. The government tolerates a certain amount of black culture with political content, but also silences many artists. The level of government sensitivity varies depending on the performer and the venue. For instance, the government allowed the play *Survival* to play to white audiences in Johannesburg. It knew that the small white audiences weren't going to be incited to protest in the streets; besides, allowing the play to be performed assured white critics that they lived in a liberal society. But the show was shut down by police in Soweto, where there were no pretensions to liberalism.

An incident in early 1986 revealed much about the government's sensitivity. Swept up by enthusiasm at a black political rally, a white South African woman working for the British Broadcasting Corporation raised her fist and, along with the rest of the audience, sang the words to a hymn, *Nkosi Sikelel' i Afrika,* the Xhosa words for *God Bless Africa.* The Pretoria government was enraged when it learned of her act from its police informers, and an embarrassed BBC dismissed the woman.

Anti-apartheid groups rushed to her defense, arguing that *Nkosi Sikelel' i Afrika* was just an old church hymn. Composed in the early 1890s by a member of an independent African church in Johannesburg, *Nkosi Sikelel' i Afrika* later became a standard hymn in the Ethiopian and African Methodist Episcopal churches.

However, like virtually every aspect of culture, *Nkosi Sikelel' i Afrika* had acquired political overtones. The lyrics were written in powerfully idiomatic Xhosa. "God Bless Africa," it began. "Raise high her horn."[34] Because of the emotional power of the hymn, African nationalists adopted it as an anthem. It is the national anthem of several African countries. It is sung by black South Africans at virtually every major black political rally or funeral. Blacks routinely call *Nkosi Sikelel' i Afrika* their national anthem.

Thus the BBC and the government maintained that singing the hymn was a political statement and violated the correspondent's reportorial objectivity. Although on the surface the hymn's words are no more partisan than those of *Die Stem,* the National Party government has long understood the use of cultural symbols for the acquisition of political power. The government was guided by a political, not critical, judgment of culture as a statement of belief and identification.

The government has taken a two-pronged approach to culture. Knowing that culture can rally people to a cause, the government has made certain forms of expression difficult. Opposition newspapers have been threatened, praise poets like Mzwakhe detained, plays prohibited in the townships, and books banned. At the same time, aware that culture can be insidious, the government has tolerated or nurtured forms of culture such as television and night clubs that might make blacks forget about politics.

Dr. Huxtable, I Presume

One day in Soweto, a political committee meeting was dragging on late. The committee leader glanced at his watch and saw that is was almost time for "The Cosby Show" to begin. He felt a little guilty about adjourning the meeting just so he could catch a television show, but he figured the group could use a break. Still, he strolled out to his car a little sheepishly. As he turned the ignition, several other committee members piled inside. Was he going home? they asked. Perhaps they could come and watch "The Cosby Show" on his television.

Television is one form of culture the South African government permits. Just as the government hoped to make blacks forget the past by giving them sanitized history texts, perhaps it hoped to make blacks forget the present by turning their attention away from revolt to a world of make-believe.

American television shows flood the airwaves, even in the homes of black activists. One night I sat in a run-down Johannesburg apartment over the E'Loise escort agency where two political leaders were hiding. One of them, Seth Mazibuko, sat with his wife Lindi at his knee. In the background, "M*A*S*H*" came on the air. Hawkeye smiled, Radar bumbled. American helicopters and people in U.S. army uniforms ran around the Hollywood scrub that passed for Korea. Lindi watched attentively while Seth glanced back and forth from time to time while talking about political strategy.

Another time I visited an activist in a private home in Mdantsane township. The house was large enough to belong in any nouveau riche American suburb; the appliances towered over pieces of furniture. A large television set was the centerpiece of the living room. On the screen, Bill Cosby, dressed in one of his beautiful sweaters, was teaching one of his daughters to ride a bicycle while sternly admonishing the older daughter about her boyfriend. His son dragged his feet upstairs to do school work. Three of the leaders of the Mdantsane Residents' Association sat transfixed. The discussion of consumer boycotts wandered while the show played.

I couldn't help wondering what Biko, who dropped out of medical school to pursue politics, would have thought about the popularity of Dr. Cliff Huxtable, Cosby's character. Biko had attacked America's "selfish desire to maintain an imperialistic stranglehold" on South Africa. And Biko had spoken often about the unique qualities of African culture and the pernicious influence of western culture. "'Black consciousness,'" he wrote,

> seeks to show the black people the value of their own standards and outlook. It urges black people to judge themselves according to these standards and not to be fooled by white society who have white-washed themselves and made white standards the yardstick by which even black people judge each other.

Did the Cosby show suggest a different yardstick? Biko never saw the Cosby show. The show didn't exist and besides South Africa had only had television a few months when Biko was beaten to death in detention in 1977.

Only a decade later, television sets could be found in the homes of 93.7 percent of whites, 22.1 percent of blacks, 92.6 percent of Indians, and 61 percent of coloreds.[35] There are four principal stations, all owned by the government. The first private network was licensed in 1986 on the condition that it not show any news. Each of the government stations was designed for a different audience. TV1, which includes many programs in Afrikaans, is directed at whites, coloreds, and Indians. TV2 and TV3 are directed at black audiences and include shows in various tribal languages. TV4, initiated in March 1985, is a broader entertainment channel that runs "The Cosby Show." Commercials often show both blacks and whites, but not in the same scenes.

But just as the segregation of blacks and whites in neighborhoods, transportation, and the workplace has proved impractical, apartheid in television hasn't worked out as planned. In 1986, about a quarter of TV1 viewers were black, while TV4 appealed to people of all races. Hein Kern, general manager of TV2, TV3, and TV4, insisted that politics played no role in programming. "I'm not politically minded. I'm going for a mass audience and that's that."

Thus "The Cosby Show" transcends barriers of race, creed, or color. Rather than spread "white" standards as Biko feared, "The Cosby Show" has deracialized standards, prompting people like Carl Coetzer, the white general manager of a bus company, to come up with a plan to settle the racial conflict in South Africa. He called it "the Cosby plan."

"Bill Cosby is the personification of civilized man. And civilized man should run my country," he said. Coetzer, an Afrikaner, advocated qualified franchise with multiple votes based on "the three pillars of civilization:" education, work, and ownership. In each category, a South African could receive up to three votes, plus one for leadership within the community, for a maximum of ten votes. The plan was designed to give people who were like Cosby the biggest say in how to run the country. "The Cosbys of this world, irrespective of color, will vote for the Cosbys of this world. Then we won't have the rabble voting for some dictatorship like the rest of Africa," said Coetzer.

It was one of the many ironies of South Africa, where whites claimed to want political power to preserve white culture, values, and way of life, that the black American comedian embodied those values. "The Cosby Show" was the most popular show on South African television—among whites as well as blacks. (Trailing it in the ratings were: "Dallas," "Golden Girls," "Dynasty," "Murder, She Wrote," "Winds of War" and "The A-Team.") Coetzer said: "You'd be surprised what that man has meant to the Afrikaner. The Afrikaner doesn't mix with black men. The television brings the black man's quality right into his living room. And his kids see him, too."

Not all whites were pleased about Cosby's popularity. Andries Treurnicht, parliamentary leader of the white official opposition Conservative Party, said, "I'm not too keen on that Cosby show." He believed the government was using television to "condition people for certain ideas." Liberal ideas, that is. "We are treated to it to condition us to have multiracialism, to promote socializing and familiarizing across the color bar. It may even lead to a sort of mixed community," he said in horror, adding, "We as white people don't want that."

Indeed, "The Cosby show" did not dull blacks' desire for change any more than the state of emergency had. If anything, the show raised blacks' expectations. Black South Africans envied Cosby/Huxtable. One of Cosby's fans is Henry Fihla, a grocery store owner in Soweto, who promised to buy a second television so his wife could watch "Dynasty" while he and the children watched Cosby. "If successful in America," he observed, "you can really go places, never mind the color of your skin." The Cosby show "has shown me something, something that can be attained. Cosby is a big doctor, he is consulted, he has authority, and he receives full respect due to him. This is the kind of thing we blacks want here in South Africa."

Nor was "The Cosby show" likely to take up enough time to distract activists from political goals. The political activist Mazibuko said he was a fan of the Cosby show. "I especially like his beautiful jerseys," the activist said with a wry smile. But Mazibuko, who was in hiding at the time, said he didn't get to watch it very often. "Really," he said, "there are more important things to do than watch the Bill Cosby show."

As she swayed on the dance floor of "5 to 7," a club in a colored township, Laura Wilkenson's mind couldn't have been further from the grandeur of praise poems, Black Consciousness, or street battles with police vehicles. Lights throbbed from the floor and a small globe of mirrors rotated overhead, casting multicolored reflections around the walls of the club and across peoples' faces. Laura Wilkenson, daughter of the club's colored owner, stepped closer to me; our hips bumped together. Her dreadlocks tumbled around her shoulders. The disc jockey played one American hit after another, then made a smooth segue from a song with a driving beat to a slow dance number.

Why this club was called "5 to 7" was beyond my comprehension, because it seemed to operate from 7 P.M. to 5 A.M. By the time a group of us closed the place, the sun was rising over the dusty township. We squinted as our eyes adjusted to the morning light. It was as though we had been dreaming of a glamorous New York lifestyle or as though we had snoozed on an overnight airplane flight and awakened on another continent.

The dream-like effect was intentional. As surely as township poems and drama was about remembering the struggles of blacks, the night club was about forgetting, which may be why the South African government licensed black night clubs for the first time in the 1980s.

Inside the box-shaped club, there was no window onto the outside world and everyone seemed to unwind and forget and dance the night away. All evening, rolls of green-and-brown ten- and twenty-rand banknotes flashed at the bar; one round of drinks followed another. A young woman passing by our table ran her fingers through my hair and said hello in an offhand manner. (A friend, Ben Minaar, jumped up and made a drunken defense against what he thought had been the start of an assault on my honor.) People mixed easily and shuttled back and forth from bar to dance floor in an inebriated haze. Packed night after night, the club could have been in New York. In fact, the dance floor, lights and mirrored walls were copied from New York clubs and much of the equipment was imported after owner Teddy Wilkenson visited the United States. "I love New York. There is so much happening there. If we had any brains, South Africa would be like that," said Wilkenson. He was certainly doing his bit, and was eager to do more to spread American pop culture. "If B. B. King, Gladys Knight and the Pips, or the OJs came, we would make money like water," he said.

Mr. Wilkenson wasn't doing badly. 5 to 7 was one of a number of extremely successful clubs explicitly designed to imitate American discoteques. And black South Africans, temporarily oblivious to the insurrection around them, flocked to the clubs. In 1982 Wilkenson spent 750,000 rand (then equal to more than three-quarters of a million dollars) to fix up the club after he returned from the United States. In three years, he said, he made nearly all that money back.

"I think there should be an exception to the cultural boycott so that Frank Sinatra can come sing in South Africa," said a black man named Boyce as he cradled a beer in a dimly lit shebeen in the black township of Mdantsane. The other men around the coffee table groaned.

It was Friday night and the small, split-level, four-room house had been turned into a smoky drinking lounge. Some people were dancing in the next room. Sitting on the arm of my chair was a lean, young comrade nicknamed Star Black, who said little but kept smiling. A union organizer, Mike, had taken me to the party. Another man slumped in a chair, a white cap pulled down over his forehead. A clean-cut, dapper-looking man turned out to be a former inmate from Robben Island. His name sounded like the Arabic "Fahd," though I later learned his true nickname was Fudd, derived from the comic strip character Elmer Fudd. A hulk of a man named Majaj anchored the gathering. He had served eight years on Robben Island for ANC involvement. There he seemed to have acquired a wisdom and maturity to which the others deferred. He also had a good job as a personnel manager at the grocery store chain, Pick 'N' Pay, though that laid him open to playful jabs from Mike, who kidded him about abandoning the masses and betraying the working class.

"Sinatra is a criminal!" Majaj replied. He reeled off a partial list of allegations linking Sinatra with organized crime in the United States. To heap crime upon crime, another man said, Sinatra had broken the cultural boycott of South Africa by playing at Sun City, a miniature Las Vegas constructed on a scrubby patch of a black homeland, Boputhatswana, that only the South African government and a handful of American booking agents recognized as "independent," and thus exempt from the cultural boycott. (One wag quipped that the homeland was the only television station with its own parliament.)

"Who's a criminal?" Boyce said philosophically. There was a thoughtful pause as the sounds of Ella Fitzgerald floated in from the next room. He looked at me. "We're both criminals. You're an American in South Africa and I'm a South African who's been to America. Besides Sinatra isn't really a criminal. Crime is only his second nature."

Majaj shot back. "Second nature is a man's driving force. It's like people who claim to be socialists, when capitalism and competition is man's driving force." He looked at Mike.

One of Sinatra's detractors stirred the waters by suggesting that the really criminal thing about Sinatra was the way he sings. The room erupted, with most of the men roaring their approval while Boyce led a small chorus of good-natured outrage. More beers were ordered, and Star Black brought some more bottles. Everyone was getting soused. Mike was leaning heavily against my shoulder. The man with the white cap slumped deeper into his chair. Fudd maintained a sense of equilibrium.

Near Majaj sat a short man who, with a look of great concentration, lowered his glass and spoke. "I want to state my philosophy," he started, and began talking about politics and non-racialism and future presidents of South Africa. One faction of the shebeen began to shout him down, but Boyce intervened and said "No, man, say your piece." The room fell into a polite but restless silence. "I wouldn't mind if Slabbert (referring to a white Afrikaans progressive politician) became president if there were elections. If there were free elections with one man, one vote there might not be a black president." Somehow he saw this issue as connected to the presence of me, a white person, and to the discussion of Sinatra. How it was connected, though, none of us could tell. "Man, you're on a higher plane," Majaj said. "We weren't talking on such a high plane." In a way, however, we were all on the same plane. Like the popularity of the Cosby show, the easy comaraderie of the night club and the shebeen gave hints of what a non-racial society could be like.

Conversation about Sinatra slowly got rolling again. Boyce was telling me eagerly about his visit to the United States a few years earlier. He had visited Harlem, Philadelphia, and New Jersey. "What is the most famous restaurant in New Jersey?" he asked. I didn't know. "Well, we went there."

Songs of Freedom

When the official South African tourist board proposed a trip for American arts journalists in 1987, the only black arts the trip featured were tribal dances at a safari ranch, cave paintings in the Drakensberg mountains, a tribal crafts shop in Cape Town, and potters, wood-carvers, and basket makers in the backward Venda homeland.

At the Heia Safari ranch, tourists wandered among the huts of an "authentic Zulu village." One journalist wrote,

> As the show begins, a wild-eyed *sangoma,* a witch doctor, enacts a ritual sacrifice of a swooning young maiden. The audience titters at his buffoonery, his strutting and leering and stumbling. At intermission, the wizened old Zulu king steps into the audience to sell tapes and records, and tourists pose for pictures alongside elaborately costumed natives.[36]

The South African government has become the staunchest defender of "pure native" culture. Because whites define such culture as primitive, its preservation (albeit in an emasculated form of bloodless sacrifices) sustains an ideology that deems blacks separate and inferior. The rebel Afrikaans poet Breyten Breytenbach lamented that the white view of African culture is limited to Ndebele huts, Xhosa pots, and Zulu beads. To whites, colored culture meant the Cape Coon Carnival in January, a festival rooted in nineteenth century American minstrel shows in which actors with black face parodied blacks.

The erosion of "pure native" culture threatens the premise of apartheid. In style as well as content, the recent explosion in black South African culture flies in the face of state dogma and its concept of separate nations. The riot of influence in black township culture—from American jazz to Zulu folk guitar, from rock and roll to European hymns, from Shakespeare to Sechuana proverbs, from Bertolt Brecht to tribal praise poets—undermines Verwoerd's vision of separate nations with separate cultures.[37]

Music in particular has floated above racial barriers, blaring its heterogeneity. A popular black pianist known as Dollar Brand (who later changed his name to Abdullah Ibrahim and went into exile in New York) took Dutch Reformed Church hymns and turned them into dreamy jazz tunes with seductive saxophone solos. Mbaquanga music, which had roots in Zulu and Sotho culture, also incorporated strains of white colonial missionaries' music, black American gospel music, Motown rhythm and blues, and metallic rock and roll. Once spurned by black artists as unsophisticated, mbaquanga music has become popular.

In 1970, a fifteen-year-old white boy named Johnny Clegg learned traditional Zulu-style guitar picking and migrant-worker dances at black hostels in Johannesburg. When word of Clegg's talent reached Sipho Mchunu, a rural Zulu who was working as a gardener in the Johannesburg suburbs, Mchunu became indignant. He found Clegg and challenged him to a competition to prove he could outplay the white teenager. The two became a duo, playing informally at shebeens, black hostels, and rooftops of apartment buildings where black laborers live. Clegg was frequently fined for not having a permit to visit black townships. "Long ago," they later sang,

> There was a sound in the night
> A Kwela man
> Singing under the street light
> With a cheap guitar
> He gave his sorrow a smile
> And he sowed his songs
> In the alleyways mile upon mile.

In 1976, they recorded their first hit, a traditional Zulu song. But the government banned the group from state Radio Bantu because Clegg was "polluting" African culture. Later Clegg and Mchunu formed a group called Juluka, a six-piece band with three whites and three blacks. Juluka recorded both in English and Zulu. Their songs blended western folk, rock, and traditional African music, showing a generation of new musicians that African music could be modern, have a dance beat—and stay distinctly African.

When the group burst onto the white pop charts, it became South Africa's first "crossover" band, popular with black and white audiences. Their fans ranged from rich white suburban teenagers to migrant workers who didn't speak English. Johnny Clegg became a lecturer in social anthropology at the University of the Witwatersrand, the country's leading English-speaking university, while keeping up his activity with the group. Clegg spoke migrant Zulu slang, and he and Sipho delighted audiences with high-kicking migrant-worker dances. Johannesburg clubs clamored to book Juluka, and the group won its demands that segregated clubs admit both black and white patrons.

The government still kept Juluka off the radio, though the group's music was never more political than the relatively mild song "Mana Lapho," or "Stand Your Ground," whose Zulu and English lyrics meant:

> Voices in the air of those gone before sing
> "Mana lapho"
> There's nowhere to hide which side you stand on
> "Mana lapho"
> The time is drawing near, can you hear
> "Mana lapho"
>
> Can you hear a long-sung song of freedom
> They tell lies, oh man, for they say our song of freedom is dead
> Mana lapho mana la

Mana lapho
Stand your ground for here is a matter
and it speaks of freedom.

What South African music's clear-throated sounds have in common with township poetry, township theater, and all forms of black culture of revolt is self-assurance and assertiveness. By breaking the bonds of tradition, township music's melodies and rhythms defy the subservience expected of black South Africans. It is joyful and expectant.

Thus its attraction for Paul Simon, who made his album *Graceland* in South Africa in the mid-1980s. Singing "black" music became the fashion among South Africans such as P. J. Powers, a white female vocalist backed by a black band called Hotline. P. J. Powers was an unlikely candidate for a singer in a largely black band. Born Penelope Dunlop, the daughter of a wealthy businessman, she had a mop of blond hair and a raspy voice similar to Rod Stewart, the British pop star. But she was raised in Natal, spoke some Zulu and sang music that both blacks and whites liked. Her repertoire included cheerful songs such as "Township Jive" and "I'll See You in Soweto."

A lively black band called Stimela also became popular. It recorded *Look, Listen and Decide*, a smash hit of the mid-1980s. Though released in the middle of a government crackdown, the tape was exuberant. Some of the group's songs were humorous, such as one about a man who has paid *lobola* (a bride price) for his wife, but is worried even after he has taken her home because he didn't get a receipt. The favorite cut from the tape was "Whispers in the Deep," a song that captured the mood of the township uprising and was known by its Zulu name "Phinda Mzala," meaning "Say it, cousin." The government clinched the tune's popularity by banning it from the state-owned radio station. So while the government was trying to dampen the fires of rebellion, Stimela's song could be heard everywhere, on cassette players, in shebeens, and in homes. The song begins with upbeat, syncopated chords and the lead band member Ray Phiri laughing and laughing in the background. When he starts to sing in Zulu and English, the words are simple: "Say it again cousin, don't be afraid, speak up your mind, don't hide yourself."

CHAPTER NINE

Black, Green, and Gold: *The African National Congress*

ON MARCH 5, 1986, WINNIE MANDELA entered the stadium in the black township of Alexandra like a nervous bride, a train of admirers behind her. She emerged from beneath a black, green, and gold canopy of flowers—ANC colors—bunched like a map of Africa. The crowd, gathered for the largest political funeral in South African history, chanted slogans and waved ANC flags. An honor guard and family members of the people killed in clashes with police surrounded a row of fresh coffins. Dust rose as youths stamped their feet in the warlike *toyi-toyi*, brandishing wooden guns carved in the shape of Soviet-made AK-47s. Photocopied pamphlets from the ANC urging black police to join the fight against the white government were handed out: "They have to put you in uniform because they are few and we are many. Brother Soldier, policeman! Now is the time to choose! Stop killing your own people!"

After speeches and songs, the throng spilled out of the stadium, down the gutted streets, down Mandela Avenue, down Tambo Avenue, down Slovo, Sisulu, and ANC avenues. It surges past the burned-out shells of cars serving as makeshift roadblocks against armored cars. By the thousands, people crossed the creek at the bottom of Alex and climb up the bank to the cemetery.

Behind them, the streets of the township overflowed with residents. While army sharpshooters stood at the edges of the township and watched through rifle sights and binoculars, about 75,000 people jammed the dusty streets;

their brightly colored shirts and dresses turned the gray township into a carnival of protest.

Ten fighting years had propelled the ANC to the forefront of black politics. Though its name was taboo in the mid-1970s, during the mid-1980s the ANC flag flew openly at funerals and its slogans were shouted at rallies. The names of Tambo, Mandela, Sisulu, and other ANC leaders were spray-painted across walls, billboards, and bus stops.

In the face of police action and a mudslide of unfavorable propaganda, the mere survival of the ANC would have been something of a triumph. But the ANC had done more than survive. Its unwavering insistence on one person, one vote had set the black agenda for South Africa's future. The ANC had become the ghost at any bargaining table the South African government arranged. Its influence could be measured not only in the townships but in Parliament, where the government wasted its breath trying to malign it. When the Bureau of Information printed a pamphlet designed to discredit the ANC, the material was snatched up in the townships because it contained the first legally printed photograph of Nelson Mandela. Earlier, newspapers were obliged by law to blacken out his eyes.

Originally led by the elite of African society, the ANC's membership peaked at 100,000 during the 1950s. After the ANC was outlawed in 1960, the organization went into eclipse. ANC guerrillas demonstrated an uncanny knack for walking into police ambushes, while others were captured and turned state's evidence. In the 1970s, the Black Consciousness movement, which rejected any role for whites in the struggle against apartheid, gained preeminence, due in part to leaders such as Biko. During this time the ANC liberation technocrats toiled in relative obscurity in cramped, unmarked offices in London, and behind rusty gates in an alleyway parallel to the main thoroughfare in Lusaka, Zambia.

Events since the end of the seventies have changed all of that. "The ANC is the premier black political organization," said Desmond Tutu. It has become a broad church of resistance with room in its pews for capitalists and communists, white and black, young and old. "In 1981, the Congress of South African Students had a long debate about whether to make its colors black, green, and gold. Now it goes without saying," said a student leader. The country's biggest black trade unions and anti-apartheïd organizations adopted the ANC's Freedom Charter as their credo. In polls, more than 30 percent of blacks openly admitted their support for the ANC and more than half openly backed Nelson Mandela, despite the danger of being accused of "furthering the aims" of the ANC, a crime then punishable by fine and imprisonment. In one poll, Mandela had almost three times as much support as Chief Mangosuthu Gatsha Buthelezi, the more conservative Zulu leader. In private, blacks indicated even broader support for the ANC.

The explosion of student unrest and the crackdown by the government in 1976 drove thousands of students into exile. For those who remained, the October 19, 1977, banning of all Black Consciousness organizations forced them to seek new direction. The ANC seized the opportunity to recruit the generation of 1976. This was possible in part because older members of the Black Consciousness movement had ties to the ANC. Rev. Mcebisi Xundu, for example, who presided at Biko's funeral, first became aware of politics at age twelve, when he met the ANC leader Rev. Calata. "It began to go into my veins even then," Xundu says. "By the time I met Biko I was already steeped in non-racialism." Barney Pityana, one of Biko's top lieutenants, belonged to an eight-member "ANC cell" as a high-school student in the early 1960s. The group held regular political discussions. Even at the height of his Black Consciousness activity, he received copies of *African Communist* and the ANC monthly magazine *Sechaba*, from London through the regular overseas mail. "BC was never intended to become an alternative liberation movement," Pityana said later. In 1978, Pityana fled the country and pledged his support to the ANC.

Younger members of the Soweto generation were attracted to the ANC because of its unapologetic use of violence to force an end to apartheid. "We are not dealing with the British colonial government," said Mac Maharaj, a lean Indian with a graying goatee who co-founded Umkhonto we Sizwe and served twelve years in jail. Maharaj said that, "When we went on a hunger strike [on Robben Island], the wardens came and laughed at us and said. 'Well, you suffer, not us.' The armed struggle makes people sit up."

Mararaj himself had paid a heavy price for his commitment to the armed struggle. He joked with one visitor to Lusaka that when he couldn't withstand beatings and interrogation after his capture in the early 1960s, he would insult and swear at an ill-tempered police officer so that the officer would let loose a heavy blow and knock Maharaj unconscious. In 1987 he suffered from kidney ailments that might have been related to his treatment in detention.

The ANC was better prepared than the rival PAC to receive and give military training to the angry youths, even though the PAC was ideologically closer to Black Consciousness. Many PAC recruits were stranded in Lesotho, unable to reach bases. Internal bickering hindered PAC organization. One recruiter captured by police remains convinced that he was betrayed by a PAC commander after a quarrel over the PAC's inability to transfer recruits from Lesotho to PAC bases.

The ANC, by contrast, brought youths to bases in Zambia and Tanzania, where top ANC officials met them. "What enhanced its image was when the children of 1976 left in droves and wrote back," a high-ranking UDF member recalled. The youths reported that they met Tambo and were given honorable receptions. "It gave new confidence in the ANC," the UDF official said. Tutu adds, "The fact that many of its members have paid a very heavy price has enhanced its prestige and credibility." In the townships, children sing

> Where is Tambo?
> He is in the bush
> He is teaching the soldiers the art of guns
> That they should be one, that they will come.

The ANC likes to say that it took raw youths and gave them political education. The ANC taught the youths about the virtues of non-racialism, as opposed to the racial exclusivism of the Black Consciousness movement. Thousands of youths who came in search of guns were channeled into schools at the ANC base in Tanzania.

But the strong-willed youths taught the old exiles a few things, too. The ANC exiles could expect no deference from the new recruits. "I was at Dar es Salaam when the first group arrived," recalled ANC executive committee member Johnny Makatini, shaking his head in disbelief, ten years later. "It took me hours to sell them on the Freedom Charter. Even then, I don't think they bought it. Their slogan was simply, 'Those not with us are against us.'" Tambo gave a speech and the students said they didn't agree with some of the things he said. "We were never like that," Makatini said. "We benefitted from older leadership."

Pallo Jordan, who left South Africa in 1962, compared members of the 1976 generation with his own contemporaries.

> Most of us came from units inside with assignments given by the organization at home, which we had to fulfill. Not so in '76. People came out on their own.
>
> In our day, organizations were legal and we held open meetings. We were accustomed to distributing leaflets openly at bus stops. We would saturate neighborhoods by sticking pamphlets under doors and in letter boxes. The worst that would happen is you get busted for littering.
>
> Now the illusions about legality have been all blown away. We had to unlearn attitudes toward legal institutions. These are people who grew up in an atmosphere of terrible repression. They come with many of skills and attitudes that are attuned to underground work."

The transformation of the ANC by the generation of 1976 is as important as the transformation of the youths by the ANC. Not until 1988 did the first members of the 1976 generation win positions on the ANC national executive committee. But from the moment of their arrival, the youths gave the ANC a hardheadedness about a harsher era of repression and a new sense of urgency.

The youths also revived the ANC's ailing military wing, Umkhonto we Sizwe, literally "Spear of the Nation," often called MK. "This new generation is a model for MK," said Umkhonto chief of staff Chris Hani. "It has transformed MK. Eighty percent of MK comes from the post-1976 generation. They are much more motivated."[1] One of the youths who fled in 1976 and joined Umkhonto was Richard "Barney" Molokwane, who took part in three of the most daring Umkhonto attacks: those against the Pretoria military headquarters, the Sasol coal-to-oil plant, and the nuclear-power installation. He died in a shootout with police.[2]

Spear of the Nation

It seemed odd when South African police captured a guerrilla from the African National Congress carrying a book whose cover read *The Renaissance*.

Inside, however, the title page turned out to be from a novel from the Penguin Crime Series, "Murder without Icing." Further inside, the police discovered, pages 10 through 112 were missing. Instead, the rebound book included "An Elementary Handbook on Explosives" put out by Umkhonto we Sizwe. There were chapters with titles such as "How to Make Napalm" and "The Self-Igniting Molotov." There were helpful tips on fuses and detonators: "Under no circumstances must you test these when they are connected to the explosive. It could be the last thing you ever do."[3]

A rising number of ANC attacks during the mid-1980s showed how well ANC agents could apply these meticulous instructions. At the end of 1985, ANC executive committee member Thabo Mbeki told me that "If white South Africa has a hazy notion today of how great the crisis is in the country, twelve months ahead it won't be so hazy." The threat was plain; the ANC had declared 1986 the Year of Umkhonto we Sizwe—a test of its military capability.

At the end of the year, the verdict was mixed. During 1986, police said there were 231 guerrilla attacks, virtually all of them by the ANC. This marked a slight increase from the year before. Despite the state of emergency, widespread detentions and police and military roadblocks, the number of ANC attacks was four to five times the average annual number of attacks for the previous decade. Umkhonto bolstered the ANC's credibility among a black populace growing more sympathetic to militant strategies. According to a high-ranking Umkhonto official, the fully trained ANC guerrillas in the country numbered 400 to 500.

But the police also scored victories, unearthing arms caches and capturing or killing 181 ANC guerrillas in two years. Despite the dreaded necklace killings of suspected collaborators, portions of the informer network were still functioning.

"The ANC has no military capability, not in the conventional sense," said Brigadier Hermann Stadler, the burly chain-smoking police officer who headed the government's side of the battle. He believed there were no more than twenty to fifty ANC guerrillas operating inside the country. He noted that the ANC has no formal brigades, no tanks, and no ability to do frontal battle with the South African Defense Forces. Its major bases are hundreds of miles from South African borders and are vulnerable because they are located in South Africa's weak neighbors.

"They use what I call bomb commuters," Stadler told me. But he conceded that more and more "bomb commuters" were striking at black police officers, border farmers, shopping centers, and electrical power substations.

If the statistics didn't testify to persistent ANC activity, then the contingent of heavily armed police standing guard at Polley's shopping arcade below police headquarters in Pretoria would. Even Stadler and his top-ranking colleague, Colonel Jack Buchner, conceded that they were unlikely to bring ANC attacks to a halt. Buchner put it this way: "When a flea starts biting you, it can bite you whenever and wherever it wants to."

To describe the ANC attacks as the work of "fleas" suggests a randomness that didn't do justice to ANC strategists. Initially, Umkhonto waged a sabotage campaign, striking at railroads and electrical pylons. In the late 1970s and early 1980s, the ANC pursued a selective campaign of daring and carefully coordinated missions, such as a bomb attack on the white military headquarters outside Pretoria. The purpose of the attacks was to impress blacks with the ANC's capabilities. When guerrillas attacked a government plant that converts coal to oil, "We walked very tall," said Nthato Motlana, the respected Soweto physician who belonged to the ANC when it was legal. When bombs damaged a nuclear-power station under construction, Dr. Motlana said, "We walked on air." In a phase that began in 1985, the ANC began to cultivate a "peoples' war," a less sophisticated but broader-scale insurgency.

ANC leaders and their allies in the Congress movement first considered armed resistance in the late 1950s. "I went underground in 1957," recalled Arthur Goldreich, a member of the first Umkhonto command. "It was very clear that within a short time the organizations would be declared illegal." Goldreich said the Treason Trial had compelled anti-apartheid activists to think of "alternatives to Gandhi-style resistance."

Some older ANC leaders, especially ANC president Chief Lutuli, resisted the idea of violence even after the banning of the ANC made peaceful protest impossible. As a result, Umkhonto was technically a separate organization dominated by individuals from the ANC and the South African Communist Party. Since the Communist Party had been outlawed, many of its members were already operating underground. "Lutuli wasn't convinced until later," a top Umkhonto commander recalls.

Umkhonto launched its first attacks on December 16, 1961, to coincide with the commemoration of the 1838 Battle of Blood River, when Afrikaner settlers slaughtered thousands of Zulu warriors.

Nelson Mandela, Umkhonto's first commander-in-chief, had personally overseen bomb tests at a derelict brick factory. Although Mandela went to Algeria for training during the end of the brutal Algerian war with the French, the ANC's attacks under his leadership bore little resemblance to Algerian strategy. Unlike the Algerians who readily struck at civilians, the ANC focused on railways and economic infrastructure. In its first eighteen months, Umkhonto carried out 150 acts of sabotage.

Then in 1963, police raided Umkhonto's headquarters at a farm in Rivonia, a suburb north of Johannesburg. Unaware of the importance of their coup, the police cruised onto the farm in a laundry truck and seized top Umkhonto leaders. Goldreich was among those captured, but he and two others bribed a prison guard and escaped. Eight others were sentenced to life in prison.

The raid on Rivonia devastated the ANC, smashing its underground, wiping out its leadership and crippling its military activities for more than a decade. Those who escaped remained torn by guilt while their comrades languished in jail. In 1987, Goldreich, by then an architect at Hebrew University, sat in a restaurant in Jerusalem, nervously drawing arch upon arch on a napkin and wondering out loud if launching Umkhonto had been premature. "I was in a Prague museum once," he said. "There was a photo of row on row of people who had been killed in the war. A Czech man nearby said to me, 'There's no ideal time to act.' That heartened me. There are no ideal conditions."

Joe Slovo, a white lawyer, later wrote that the headquarters had been widely known to ordinary ANC cadres and that a period of success "had bred a mood of carelessness and bravado which was, in the end, to prove costly." Slovo himself had visited the Rivonia headquarters as often as three times a day, even though he was under police surveillance.

The ANC learned from the disaster. Slovo, later Umkhonto's chief of staff and now head of the South African Communist Party, concluded that Umkhonto had to operate in smaller groups. Now ANC guerrillas operate in cells that contain as few as two people and rarely more than five. The biggest alleged cell ever was tried in 1986 in Durban; it had twelve people, including a pregnant woman and two doctors. "Those who take part in such work should know only what is absolutely necessary for the performance of their tasks," Slovo said. Prominent anti-apartheid leaders inside South Africa rarely play a role in Umkhonto activities, though many of them endorse ANC political objectives.

Umkhonto's command structure was modeled largely on the Irgun Zvai Leumi Jewish underground that operated in Palestine before Israeli independence. It is believed to have between ten and twelve regional commands and a coordinating high command. Each region is subdivided into sectors. About twenty-five people sit on the coordinating command committee, according to one of its members.

The current commander-in-chief of Umkhonto is Joe Modise, who left South Africa for military training in 1962. Earlier he had been a truck driver from Sophiatown. Little else is known about Modise, who makes highly militant speeches on the ANC's Radio Freedom.

The chief of staff, Chris Hani, is one of few in the ANC who has seen pitched combat. In the late 1960s, he and about 100 ANC guerrillas fought alongside Zimbabwean rebels in an offensive that tied down a segment of the Rhodesian army for nearly three weeks. Hani came from an ANC family; and his uncle was a member of the South African Communist Party. Hani joined the ANC in 1957 at the age of fifteen. Later he considered joining the clergy, but joined the ANC military wing instead. He became one of the first guerrillas trained in the Soviet Union. He later fought with both Zapu, the Zimbabwean group, and Frelimo, the former rebel group that now rules Mozambique. From 1974 through 1980, Hani was based in Lesotho and crossed the South African border regularly. One of the most popular figures in the ANC, Hani has been the target of numerous assassination attempts.[4]

Until 1988, most ANC guerrillas trained in four or five camps in central western Angola. The camps held between 4,000 and 9,000 people, including support staff.[5] After the accord between Angola and South Africa that paved the way for Namibian independence, the camps were moved to Zambia and Tanzania. Much of the equipment used is surplus Warsaw Pact material. A limited amount of up-to-date equipment is provided by the Soviet Union. The instructors include exiled South Africans and Cubans, who speak through translators. Trainees learn to use rocket-propelled grenades, Russian machine guns, 82-millimeter mortars, anti-tank guns, small Russian arms, the standard NATO rifle, and a Portuguese rifle.

Trials of captured ANC members suggest that the military training has been good. One lawyer defending an alleged ANC agent relied on the explosives expertise of his client to poke holes in state allegations about sabotage. In another case, South African military experts were unable to strip and reassemble a captured anti-aircraft weapon. The ANC man on trial did it in a few minutes. Defense lawyers say their clients understand the mechanisms of railroad signal crossings, advanced map-making, and radio communications. "They don't handle tanks, but to some extent, ANC training is comparable to that received by troops in the South African Defense Force," said Brigadier Stadler.

Conditions in the camps are mediocre and reports about camp morale vary. Marion Sparg, a twenty-eight-year-old white woman sentenced in 1986 to twenty-five years in prison for limpet-mine attacks on police stations, said that camp morale was high and trainees sang freedom songs with enthusiasm. But police and ANC defectors said that the ANC had to put down a revolt by discontented rank and file in its Angolan camps. A source close to the ANC confirmed the reports and added that Angolan troops helped put down the revolt. The ANC also kept political prisoners; some were suspected of being spies and others were simply dissidents. One Angolan camp had 180 people jailed. Recently, the ANC admitted that it tortured dissidents within its own ranks.

Two ANC defectors complained that food and sanitary conditions were poor. "They gave us Russian beef. When you opened it you found it was green on top," complained Mr. X, who now works for the South African police. ANC spokesman Tom Sebina conceded that the ANC's two farms in

Angola didn't produce enough food for the troops and that the ANC sent food from Zambia to the camps. "There is a great shortage of fresh vegetables. Sometimes there is no fresh meat for days and we have to hire refrigerated planes to send to Angola." Malaria, rare in South Africa, is a risk in Angola and in Tanzania, where young ANC members attend school.

Defense lawyers say the ANC trainees often feel homesick and lonely in the camps. "The problem is to get my parents, then my people, then myself, all satisfied that I am not a lunatic frastrated [sic] somewhere in the bushes of Africa," a young ANC member wrote from one of the camps. He longed to meet his mother "and settle eleven years of nostalgia."

Some trainees have taken further courses in East Germany and the Soviet Union. Another defector, who introduced himself at police headquarters simply as John, said he went to Odessa for further training in the use of mortars and artillery. He says there were seventy ANC recruits at the camp, plus about thirty other people from Zimbabwe, the Palestinian Liberation Organization, and Oman.

Once selected for missions, ANC guerrillas have returned to South Africa through neighboring countries using false passports and identity documents. Others have crossed streams, mountains, and footpaths along South Africa's broad borders. Many villages straddle the borders and ANC agents have mixed with villagers who cross the border every day. One man crossed a footpath after exchanging a new work uniform for old overalls. He carried dead chickens over his shoulder. Another slipped across a stream to a border farm during the workers' lunch break. Some have relied on the cooperation of mountain villagers.

ANC members have been able to volunteer for assignments. Paul, a driver who gave me a ride in Lusaka, said he volunteered to go back to South Africa. He and two others operated in northern Natal for six months and then slipped back out of the country again.

The ANC has given its guerrillas between $150 and $500 in cash and the names of contacts. Through the contacts, the guerrillas gained access to central arms caches buried by other operatives. They have transported weapons; trained people inside the country in the art of elementary sabotage; distributed pamphlets; carried out reconnaissance of potential targets; established new identities and places to stay; and executed military missions.

Tom Lodge, formerly a lecturer in politics at the University of the Witwatersrand, estimated at the end of 1986 that forty to fifty guerrillas were entering the country every month, outpacing the numbers caught by police. A man from a homeland who claimed that his home was used as a safehouse by ANC guerrillas in transit gave me a comparable number. In his sector alone, he estimated that four men per month were infiltrating the country.

Many guerrillas have been caught immediately in scenes worthy of the Keystone cops. Once, a car full of ANC guerrillas was caught in a speed trap. Another guerrilla transporting grenades was mugged by a group of gangsters. In self-defense, he tossed one of the grenades. It shattered the windows of a nearby house, whose residents chased the hapless guerrilla down the street. He tossed another grenade to scare off the swelling mob and was later caught by police.

Others have walked into traps. Peter Ngwenya, an IBM technician, was recruited in Botswana and instructed to meet a woman and help her transport arms. He dropped her at a hotel in Johannesburg, drove to Soweto and placed the arms in a coal box at the house of a relative. Police were waiting as he left the house. The woman vanished.

Informers have been a problem in general. An Umkhonto source told me that the ANC discovered that one of the members of its Eastern Cape command was an informer. He was summoned to Lusaka for "consultations." He never returned. Still, he damaged operations in the province for months.

Some guerrillas, returning from years of exile, visited their families and often found police waiting for them. Colonel Buchner said police kept track of close to 3,000 suspected ANC guerrillas and watch their families.

On the other hand, many guerrillas have displayed independence and discipline, working against formidable obstacles. Joseph Maja, a guerrilla tried in 1985, was unable to find a safe place to stay. So for months he slept in drainage pipes, discotheques, and unused homes. One group of guerrillas built an elaborate underground hiding place underneath a house in Soweto.

The ANC has signed the Geneva convention on the humanitarian conduct of war, the first liberation movement to do so. Tambo said the group was "notoriously restrained" in attacks until the mid 1980s. The ANC didn't blow up crowded restaurants or nightclubs the way Algerian independence fighters did. When a bomb blew up in downtown Pretoria on May 20, 1983, killing nineteen and injuring more than 200 others, including blacks, Mandela issued a statement from prison that criticized the lack of concern for innocent civilians.

In 1985 tactics changed. While not aiming directly at "soft targets," the ANC decided that it would hit at targets even if it meant civilian casualties.

> We can no longer allow our armed activities to be determined solely by the risk of civilian casualties. The time has come when those who stand in solid support of the race tyranny and who are its direct or indirect instruments, must themselves begin to feel the agony of our counter-blows. It is becoming more necessary than ever for whites to make it clear on which side of the battle lines they stand.[6]

In part, the shift reflected the practical difficulty of striking increasingly well-guarded economic and police installations. And in part, the shift reflected a hardening in attitudes within the ANC. "We must educate the regime about what civilians are," Tambo said in a press conference.

> The children and women they slaughter every day are civilians. To them, they're just blacks. . . . When white people are killed, even a few compared to scores on our side, there is such a row that you'd think something has happened which is unprecedented in South African history. It encourages the view

> by some that to kill whites because they are whites would draw attention to the problem of South Africa.

But Tambo stopped short of endorsing that view, saying the ANC has "No policy of attacking people simply because they are of a certain color. We must fight this struggle with clean hands."

After that, however, several bombs exploded in central white cities. The car bomb, previously the franchise of Lebanon, made its debut into South Africa. In Durban, a car bomb exploded outside a popular bar. Outside the magistrate's court in Johannesburg, a small explosion went off and later, when police were gathered around the area, a second car bomb was detonated by remote control, killing several police officers. Outside a rugby game in Ellis Park stadium in Johannesburg, a car bomb went off injuring scores of people after the game.

Within South Africa as well as in exile, civilian targets became the subject of hot debate. A Soweto resident said that sympathizers of the ANC feared getting caught in a bomb blast along with whites when they were at work. Some blacks believed that only white casualties would awaken whites, who had spent these turbulent years carrying on business as usual, sipping drinks by the pool, stroking tennis balls, and cooking sausages in their gardens. In discussing the attacks, ANC leaders neither took credit for them nor disavowed them. Instead they vaguely suggested that their cadres lacked discipline, an answer unlikely to satisfy anyone.

The story of Andrew Sibusiso Zondo, who was hanged in September 1986, is typical of many ANC guerrillas. Born six years after the banning of the ANC, Zondo drifted into politics during the 1980 school boycotts in KwaMashu township outside Durban. On the way home from a 1981 demonstration, Zondo met a man in his twenties and compared notes about the day's events. In later meetings, the older man gave Zondo a copy of the Freedom Charter and other ANC literature. After four months, he revealed that he was an ANC member and asked Zondo to set up a cell in KwaMashu. Zondo's cell distributed pamphlets and spray-painted walls with ANC slogans.

Zondo briefly went to Swaziland, ostensibly to further his education. In 1983 he was in Mozambique when the South African government retaliated for a Pretoria bomb blast with an attack on a Maputo suburb. Zondo later recalled that South African forces hit a clinic, a daycare center, and a factory.

"It was that day I decided to join Umkhonto. It seemed as if there would be no chance to change the lives of blacks except through violence," he said at his trial. So Zondo gave up his education for military training and spent the next two years in the Angolan camps. "It was the best experience I have had in my life," he recalled later. "I began to feel like a human being. I wasn't a native or a kaffir."[7]

In late 1985, Zondo returned to the Durban townships and was put in command of three cells. He also ran training sessions while remaining undercover. Commands came from an agent who traveled back and forth between South Africa and Swaziland.

On December 20, 1985, South African soldiers assassinated ANC agents and their relatives (including women and children) in a raid in the kingdom of Lesotho. The same day, Zondo's contact in Swaziland—who worked under the name of Tallman—told Zondo to retaliate within four days against a suitable target.

At his trial, Zondo said that Tallman didn't specify the target, but that the ANC gave all cadres explicit instructions to avoid civilian casualties. The Umkhonto explosives pamphlet discovered (and used as police evidence) in a different case starts with the following instructions:

> The target must always be carefully selected. . . . The target must symbolize the people's hatred for the government and its system. . . . The action can be directed against government personnel, police and soldiers, spies, agents, stooges and informers; but not against innocent bystanders of any description.

But Zondo ignored those instructions. Instead he placed a limpet mine in a rubbish bin in a crowded shopping center at the beach resort town of Amanzimtoti. Two days before Christmas, the shopping center was busy with people. Zondo attached a small red fuse, and walked slowly with an accomplice out of the shopping center. He intended to phone a warning to a store, but all the pay phones he tried were busy or broken. The mine exploded half an hour later, shattering the glass in the Christmas displays, killing five whites and injuring forty-eight others.[8]

When he was sentenced to death, Zondo refused to ask President P. W. Botha for clemency. He said he had disregarded ANC guidelines for avoiding innocent civilians and took full blame. The ANC's Hani said "Zondo was highly disciplined, one of our best. But he was deeply affected by the raid in Lesotho and we can't blame him for what he did." Slovo, then Umkhonto chief-of-staff, said "No underground military organization can control every response of every unit on the ground. You're going to get responses from individuals. I don't believe [Amanzimtoti] is a legitimate target, but I'm not prepared to condemn the man who did it. It was a gut reaction and it's human."

The ANC used to insist on two years' training for guerrillas. But in 1982, the group began sending people on two-week crash courses or weekend training programs. With the expansion of such programs, came breaches in security and uncontrolled incidents. Several youths in Duduza lost their hands when police infiltrated their unit and provided them with booby-trapped grenades. Loose groups of comrades in the black townships also appeared to have access to weapons such as AK-47s, and gun battles broke out in chance clashes between youths and army patrols.

A young man from the Western Cape told me he received military training on an isolated farm and was a member of a four or five-person unit that assassinated two black police officers. In one spectacular incident, two ANC guerrillas "kidnapped" a captured ANC suspect from a guarded hospital bed; Hani later boasted that the two who performed the rescue were people trained inside the country.

In 1983, a man from Pietermaritzburg with a full-time job trained in Swaziland on weekends. For eight months, he worked alone. He received coded instructions in telegrams from Swaziland telling him where to pick up limpet mines. He traveled by taxi and planted mines at night. One white taxi driver joked about not trusting black passengers. "You could be carrying a bomb or something," he said. He was right. The ANC agent finally was apprehended outside the Durban city hall with a bomb on the night President Botha was speaking there.

One of the ANC's handicaps has been the absence of safe havens in countries adjacent to South Africa. That problem worsened after Mozambique signed the Nkomati accord in March 1984. Though seemingly a disaster, in retrospect the Nkomati accord moved the front line of combat inside the country. Mac Maharaj said that Nkomati "did us a favor. We had to develop bases inside the country. Trained men from outside had to become an officer corps, not a combat corps, then go back to the country and train people and guide them."

"The ANC will never have the capacity to knock out the state," notes political scientist Tom Lodge. But its strategy of violence remains a key part—along with boycotts, strikes, and sanctions—of an assault on the stability of the government. What Umkhonto can do, Lodge notes, is make black townships unsafe for troops and, most importantly, rally support among blacks. he adds that the ANC "must generate through military activity a wider amount of popular resistance."

The story of two ANC guerrillas who set up a base in late 1984 in the remote region called Ingwavuma provides a fascinating look at the practical problems of mobilizing wider resistance. The mission is documented in a secret diary kept by one of the guerrillas, with the names of contacts coded. It was later presented as evidence in court.[9]

The first breach of security took place even before the pair of guerrillas slipped into South Africa. Their contact had blurted their impending arrival to a friend, who wanted the ANC guerrillas to bump off a local chief over a non-political dispute. "I stressed to him that we were not roaming bands, hired assassins, but rather our objectives are national. It was our duty to weld people together," the guerrilla noted in the diary.

Things settled down for a time. The pair established hiding places for arms and recruited people for training. They crossed into Mozambique and Swaziland for supplies and functioned freely for three months.

Some problems persisted, which ultimately led to their capture. Many people thought they were gangsters. One guerrilla breached security by flirting with a local woman and making contact with a guerrilla from another sector; and recruits often failed to show up for training sessions. Moreover, it was difficult to keep a small rural community from buzzing about two strangers in its midst.

Though receptive, the local people had doubts about Umkhonto's capability. In his diary, one of the guerrillas wrote, "One of our women said we'll start the war and retreat to Swaziland leaving them at the mercy of the police and the army."

The guerrilla recognized the relationship between the ANC's military prowess and its political credibility. He wrote:

> People have no confidence about our capability to strike at the enemy and win. They have accepted us because we talk the truth about oppression and we are their children and brothers. Now it is to us to demonstrate our capability to fight . . . and win the the war. We must not leave them. If need be they must see our dead bodies, they must bury them. So that they say, 'They never left us. They died defending us, teaching us how to fight the enemy.'

The First Family

No one understood the power of martyrdom better than Umkhonto's first commander, Nelson Mandela. In April 1964, he stated at his own trial

> I have cherished the ideal of a democratic and free society in which all persons live together in harmony and with equal opportunities. It is an ideal which I hope to live for and to achieve. But if needs be, it is an ideal for which I am prepared to die.

Sentenced to life in prison, Mandela was fulfilling his pledge hour by hour.

As his days slipped away, his stature rose. After a quarter century, Mandela dominated the political scene from behind bars. Because a majority of black South Africans regarded Mandela as their leader, he possessed something akin to veto power over government reforms. Without his participation, no reform could be considered truly representative. The government was as much a prisoner of his wishes as he was of theirs. He was as potent as any weapon the ANC possessed.

The son of a tribal chief from Umtata, Mandela fled an arranged marriage, worked as a mine security guard, then became a lawyer and practiced with Tambo in Johannesburg. Through the law practice and his ANC activities, his reputation spread.

Though close colleagues, Mandela and Tambo were a study in contrasts, recalled Godfrey Pitje, who worked as their apprentice from 1955 through 1958. Tambo was small and unassuming. He grew up in a backward rural area, and his face bore the scars of ritual cuts he received as a child. "Once Tambo went to Baragwanath Hospital and talked to a nurse, who lost her temper and blew up at him. The supervisor came and the nurse said she couldn't understand this foolish chap. The supervisor looked and said, "Don't you know who that *is?*" But there would be no mistaking Mandela.

Pitje recalled, "Mandela was tall and well-built. He was brought up to be a prince of the Thembus, and his appearance was princely. If he walked into a courtroom, the magistrate took note and the gallery would sit up and expect fireworks."

Cassim Saloojee, a member of the UDF's Transvaal executive committee, was a teenage "stamp licker" for the ANC in the 1950s. Saloojee recalled, "If Nelson greeted us it was a great day." Mandela normally wore suits during the week and on weekends a houndstooth-checked sports jacket. "Once he showed up in a wind breaker, dressed like a teenager, and he still looked so tremendously impressive. He had a special kind of presence."

He had a special kind of absence, too. On Robben Island, he and Sisulu ran courses and debates on politics and economics for other political prisoners and smuggled notes and books. He led delegations demanding improved conditions for prisoners until the government transferred him and Sisulu to Pollsmoor Prison in Cape Town, where, visitors said, Mandela played chess with the warden.

Even from jail, Mandela showed a tremendous ability to gauge the political moment. His writings in the 1950s were lawyerly, methodically building up a case against apartheid. They had few rhetorical flourishes; even the title of his book, *No Easy Walk to Freedom*, was a phrase borrowed from Nehru. Yet in 1976, he sensed the militancy of black youths. In a widely circulated message smuggled out of prison, Mandela said "Between the anvil of united mass action and the hammer of the armed struggle we shall crush apartheid and white minority racist rule." In early 1985, in the midst of the uprising, he refused to renounce violence in return for President Botha's offer of release, and did so in a way that enhanced his reputation as a pillar of strength and reason. In a message read at a rally by his daughter Zinzi, Mandela said,

> I am in prison as the representative of the people and of your organization, the African National Congress, which was banned. What freedom am I being offered while the organization of the people remains banned? . . . What freedom am I being offered when my very South African citizenship is not respected?
>
> Only free men can negotiate. Prisoners cannot enter into contracts. . . . I cannot and will not give any undertaking at a time when I and you, the people, are not free. Your freedom and mine cannot be separated. I will return.

As Mandela approached seventy, occasional visitors said he remained mentally sharp and physically fit through a regimen of reading and exercise. "Nelson was the most disciplined person I ever encountered," recalled Arthur Goldreich, who had rented the Rivonia farm and lived there with Mandela for months. "Time was apportioned. He woke up early and exercised and read. He had a regimen for learning, not for pleasure. He never wasted his time."

In jail he kept up the discipline. Britain's Lord Nicholas Bethell was allowed to visit Mandela and reported that Mandela rose at 3:30 A.M., exercised for two hours, then spent the day reading and tending a vegetable garden. Bethell said Mandela quoted Oscar Wilde, joked gently about Bethell's weight, and demonstrated a keen grasp of current events and an unbowed spirit.

President Botha claimed Mandela was a communist. In reality, Mandela was a moderate in the spectrum of black politics. At his trial, he suggested that some form of socialism is needed "to overcome the legacy of extreme poverty." But he said he differed with Marxists because they "regard the parliamentary system of the West as undemocratic and reactionary. But, on the contrary, I am an admirer of such a system."

Something of an apocalyptic air surrounded the possibility of his release. Blacks awaited it with excitement. Whites worried about what might happen if he were freed—and about an uncontrollable fury among blacks if he died in prison. Some officials believed by releasing Mandela, they would demythologize him. They believed a free Mandela would become embroiled in black political squabbles and lose his stature. More probably, however, Mandela would be the only person able to unify blacks. Through three nonpolitical letters he was permitted to send every month, Mandela kept lines open to a broad range of black political figures. He sent a Christmas card to *The Sowetan* editors, who were sympathetic to the ANC's rivals, the PAC. The editors couldn't have been more surprised. "Best wishes," the card read. "Keep up the good work." Aggrey Klaaste, assistant editor, said, "I have absolute respect for him as a man who has spent almost his whole life in jail. He's no pushover." Mandela also sent a polite note to his nephew Chief Kaiser Matanzima, the Transkei homeland leader vilified by the ANC. Mandela avoided any endorsement of Matanzima, but thanked him for assistance in some family matters. He also sent a diplomatic note to Chief Buthelezi, who craved Mandela's endorsement in a fight with the UDF and ANC. Mandela rebuffed Buthelezi's request for an audience at Pollsmoor, but did so in a way that allowed both Buthelezi and Buthelezi's enemies to claim Mandela's support. Mandela profusely thanked Buthelezi for demanding the release of political prisoners, but said the timing for a visit was inopportune and urged him to meet with the ANC.

Said the ANC's Mac Maharaj, Mandela "is like tempered steel. He gives a little on either side, but in the end he stands straight up."

Mandela had also left behind his telegenic young second wife, Winnie. Her seeming vulnerability and open defiance made her a magnetic popular symbol—in the Western media as well as to her own people. Though a pioneer as the first black social worker at a Soweto hospital, Winnie had never belonged to any political organization. But her marriage catapulted her into the company of South Africa's leading black politicians.

Throughout the late 1960s and early 1970s, Winnie Mandela remained in Soweto as a solitary symbol of resistance. She suffered both restrictions and imprisonment, including a total of 491 days in solitary confinement in 1970 and 1971. In contrast to her husband—who appeared remote and forbidding (even his wife sometimes referred to him as "Mandela")—she was approachable. Her finest moment came in the mid-1970s. While the ANC in exile was wary and fearful of the Black Consciousness movement, Mrs. Mandela "was one of the very few people of standing prepared to give us any support," said Barney Pityana, Biko's ex-colleague. On June 16, 1976, when fighting broke out between police and students, Mrs. Mandela ferried injured students to the hospital in her Volkswagen Beetle. "She was very much of a mother to us," recalled Seth Mazibuko, then a student.

Not long afterward, Winnie Mandela was banished to Brandfort, a small township on South Africa's great plains. She stayed until late August 1985, when her home was firebombed, most likely by police or right-wing whites. With black unrest spreading, Mandela packed up and moved back to her own home in Soweto, unilaterally ending her internal exile. It was an act of public defiance, but the government took no action.

She returned to glory and publicity. By this time, the name Mandela, once only whispered out of fear of arrest, was being shouted in the streets of the townships and scrawled across walls and buildings. Black youths, inspired by her defiance, surged forward to try to touch her when she appeared at political funerals. She looked great on television and excited crowds with her blunt rhetoric. She appeared on the U. S. television news show, "Nightline." A charmed *Newsweek* reporter gushed about her scarf, her beads, her big eyes. When she walked, he wrote, with "her white robes fluttering in the winter wind . . . she held her head high and her chin erect, as if certain that she, and her brothers and sisters, would win."

Only later would most people discover how ill-suited she was to the role history and her marriage had thrust upon her.

"It Is here."

In early 1986, limpet mines exploded on farms along South Africa's northern border. The blasts killed several whites, a few black farmhands, and a dog. A group of reporters visited the site of one of the bombs and talked to a white farmer. The ANC was making a mistake in attacking the farms, he said. Not only had the ANC angered whites, he said, but it had lost support among black farm workers who feared getting hurt, too.

After the farmer made his point, a Reuters photographer lingered, snapping shots inside a barn. Finding herself alone with one of the black farmhands, she asked him what he thought. With his white employer not more than ten yards away, the farmhand said, "We are all ANC here."

It became harder and harder to say who belonged to the ANC and who simply supported it. The organization's support was so widespread, and ANC objectives so closely linked with those of ordinary blacks, that sometimes the distinction was irrelevant. The ANC is not just in Lusaka, noted the white opposition leader Frederik van Zyl Slabbert in his resignation speech from Parliament. He said, "Supporters and members of the ANC work in our gardens, our kitchens, our factories." When asked by a journalist where the ANC was, the widow of an old ANC leader from Cradock tapped her breast. "It is here," she said.[10]

The ANC also discouraged young blacks from fleeing into exile during the uprising of the mid-1980s. The ANC estimates that only half as many blacks left the country to join the ANC during 1984 through 1986 as left after students revolted in Soweto. One young black told me that he went to a training camp in Botswana (which officially didn't have any camps) and after a few days a message arrived from Lusaka instructing him to return to South Africa at once and continue his work as a political activist.

"The fundamental mistake some people make is seeing the ANC as an organization in exile," Thabo Mbeki told me as he sipped a beer in his house in Lusaka.

> The ANC exists in two parts: in South Africa and outside South Africa. No major decision on strategy or important tactics can be reached without consultation with the other part.
>
> When Oliver Tambo broadcasts from Radio Freedom asking people to make the country ungovernable, he is not just hoping and praying that this signal will be so strong from Lusaka. The organized structures of the ANC have to act to make sure that happens. The ANC is active in the youth movement, trade unions, the UDF, the church. We don't have a situation of the ANC finding it is out of touch. The ANC has been talking to people all the time.

Steve Tshwete was one of those people from the moment he walked out of jail in March 1979, sixteen years after he was arrested for being part of the East London high command of Umkhonto. He had gone to prison in his mid-twenties and emerged as a man in his early forties, with a plodding walk, a heavy beard and thick glasses. He had gone to jail before most of the young comrades of the 1980s were born, but Tshwete still burned with the activism of a young person. "They have imprisoned you for sixteen years and you must inflict pain on them," he said in his raspy voice.

That would be difficult for Tshwete. After his release, he was immediately banned and restricted to a township on the outskirts of King William's Town in the Ciskei. Nonetheless, Tshwete became active in community organizations. When the UDF formed a regional executive committee along the border region of the Ciskei and Transkei homelands, Tshwete was elected president.

Tshwete also secretly joined an ANC cell inside the country. Although he didn't take part in any military activities, sources say he became one of a number of people who served loosely as members of the ANC national executive committee. Whether this role was formal or not remained murky, but the ANC consulted them regularly on matters of policy.

"The police quizzed me about ANC connections," Tshwete recalled, "but they had nothing to go on. They used to say, 'You are slowly but surely paving your way back to Robben Island.' But I knew they knew nothing."

Somehow, Tshwete managed to communicate with the ANC in exile about once a week. Word traveled back and forth via written reports, coded radio messages, and couriers. Betrayed in 1963 by a fellow member of the ANC underground, Tshwete was cautious about traps and unreliable colleagues.

> If somebody came to me and said "When do you think the ANC will take power," I said nothing. Then you knew this one is trapping you. A dedicated cadre who is underground would never ask such questions. I would never give the impression that I was hostile to the ANC, but you must distinguish between agents and innocents who want to know. At times you turn away prospective cadres. To those who were obviously police informers, I would tell them directly that the ANC will take power and that informers were like ticks on a cow. We will carry them with us to power.

After the killing of Goniwe, however, Tshwete feared for his life. "They were out to kill me." he said later. The police came for him one night at his home. They told him to get some warm clothes because he would be going back to prison for a long time. While Tshwete was gathering his belongings in the bedroom, a drunken friend came in and began to argue with the police in the living room. The drunken friend offered himself instead of Tshwete. Tshwete came out and appeared to be intervening on behalf of the police to calm his agitated friend. But the police wanted to beat the drunkard. While they were preoccupied with the friend, Tshwete dashed out the front door and ran 200 yards to the railroad station and escaped to friends in the Ciskei homeland.

Tshwete wanted to skip the country, but first he attended a political funeral in Duncan Village, outside East London. He put on jeans and tennis shoes, in case he had to run for his life. Friends drove him past army trucks in a van with dark windows. By the time police realized Tshwete had addressed the funeral, Tshwete was on his way to the Lesotho border. He shaved his heavy beard and his head, tucked his glasses under the seat of the car, and fixed a new photo to a forged passport. Border officials held him for an hour while they examined his passport. They asked Tshwete if he had any other names. "It was tense," Tshwete said. Eventually they let him go. When he later opened his suitcase, Tshwete realized how lucky he had been. A friend had packed his suitcase and included a jacket with a UDF brochure in the breast pocket. If the border officials had found the brochure, it would have tipped them off that the inarticulate bald "migrant" was more than he seemed.

One of the UDF supporters later suspected of driving Tshwete into Duncan Village was less fortunate. Police arrested him and beat him senseless for information about Tshwete. It took the young man months to recover from the injury to his back.

Once in exile, Tshwete rose rapidly through the ranks. He surfaced at the ANC's seventy-fifth anniversary celebration in Lusaka and read the "fraternal greetings" from around the world. He became the number-three man in Umkhonto, before being removed after he contradicted ANC policy by advocating attacks on white civilians. Eager to placate Tshwete's supporters in the Border region, the ANC announced his election to the national executive committee, though the post was probably one Tshwete had held for some time.

Trekkers

Not all of the ANC's contacts in South Africa were clandestine. Many people went publicly to seek the views of leaders in exile. On September 13, 1985, seven white South Africans—including the chair of South Africa's largest mining and industrial conglomerate—and six members of the ANC sat down in the shade of a tree at the private game lodge of the president of Zambia, Kenneth Kaunda. The whites sat on one side of a picnic table and the ANC members on the other.

Protocol came first, more like a multilateral summit than a meeting of compatriots. Anglo American Corporation's chair Gavin Relly said that the ANC was coming face to face with capitalism while the businessmen were coming face to face with the ANC. An engineer by training and cautious by temperament, Relly was no politician. But he had refused to let President Botha bully him into canceling the meeting. He said it was important that the following generation inherit a viable and dynamic economy; no one wished to see a valuable inheritance devastated by strife. Tambo, though strident on public platforms, was modest in person. He stated that "Skin color should not be used to determine a person's worth; people should see the man, not the color of his skin." He joked that the seating arrangement was itself divisive, and the two groups got up and mixed on either side of the table.[11]

Afterwards, the group thrashed out their differing ideas. The business leaders argued that violence would only harden the resolve of the Pretoria regime. The ANC replied that it represented the moderates of black South Africa. Mac Maharaj said even the ANC found it frightening to see young children prepared to die. But the ANC members emphasized that the 1960s crackdown had left them no choice.

The businessmen tried to persuade the ANC leaders to reconsider the nationalization of industry that the Freedom Charter stipulates. But the ANC's Thabo Mbeki said, "The boards of directors of three companies can not take decisions for the whole nation." He added ominously, "Any new government must have the economic power to transform the lives of the people by spreading the wealth." Maharaj urged businessmen to prove their concern for blacks' rights by pressing the government for change and by negotiating in good faith with black trade unions.

They broke for lunch, mingling amiably. At 2:15 they resumed discussion, then posed for photographs together. The ANC representatives joked that they had no fears about posing because the South African Police undoubtedly had their photographs on file already.

President Botha portrayed the meeting as an act of disloyalty by the businessmen, but Lusaka also had the ear of the nation. "It is ridiculous to pretend that the ANC has no standing in the affairs of South Africa," said Relly, although he left the meeting with a negative view of the group. To ignore the ANC had become bad business, counter to the long-term interests of a company that intended to outlive President Botha and white rule.

As the ANC's stature among blacks grew, more South Africans made the pilgrimage to seek its opinions or blessings. The KaNgwane homeland's chief minister Enos Mabuza was granted an audience. Black business people, including the chair of Africa Bank and of the National African Chambers of Commerce, also trekked to Lusaka to pay their respects. White students went. So did Slabbert, when he set up a group to promote contacts across the racial divide. Even the white rugby board consulted the ANC about mixed sports and a way to end the international sports boycott.

The ANC also met people in chance or casual encounters. Both ANC and UDF leaders attended the funeral of Mozambican president Samora Machel. ANC members in exile also had family ties to people with South African passports. Two brothers in exile received a visit from a South African-based brother in the import-export business. International conferences on apartheid often brought people together. At a conference in Botswana, a black trade-union leader huddled with an ANC leader. At the same conference, Thabo Mbeki had breakfast with Dr. Motlana. On his way to conferences in the U. S., Motlana, who for years served as the Mandela family doctor, sometimes stopped in London and dined with Oliver Tambo, an acquaintance from the 1950s.

The ANC sometimes invited groups that were not considered its allies. It courted a delegation of Zulu chiefs from an area where ANC rival Chief Mangosuthu Gatsha Buthelezi draws support and where the UDF had battled Buthelezi supporters. The Zulu chiefs enjoyed several evenings of talk and drinks with ANC leaders. The ANC also invited the National Council of Trade Unions (NACTU), a federation half the size of COSATU that was more closely allied to PAC and Black Consciousness philosophies. Afterwards, NACTU and the ANC agreed to avoid conflict and work toward the unification of the two big union federations. To put an end to factional fighting in the Crossroads squatter camp outside Cape Town, the ANC met in Lusaka with representatives of the Crossroads comrades and their rivals, the Witdoekes. They held four days of meetings in an effort to avoid a repetition of the bloody fighting that devastated the camp in 1986.

Internal organizations asked the ANC to weigh in on specific issues to bolster a faction in a debate. Thus the ANC served as a sort of court of appeals for domestic factions. When some UDF strategists wanted to call off a rent boycott before it fell apart, they called on the ANC to take sides against hard-liners who wanted to continue the boycott.

Eager to please a wide variety of supporters, the ANC was cautious about this role. In the case of the rent boycott, the ANC printed an article in its monthly magazine, *Sechaba*, that said in general terms that campaigns must be called off before they become divisive. The rent boycott continued.

Equals

Not all South African visitors to Lusaka came as petitioners. "The ANC has done a lot of ambassadorial tasks we could not have done. But we unbanned the ANC at home," said a UDF leader, rejecting the notion that the uprising was the work of people in exile. The UDF leader expected ANC leaders to show him the same deference and respect he gave them. "I've never been out of the country without the president himself calling," meaning ANC President Tambo, not Botha. On one overseas visit, his efforts to arrange a meeting were frustrated by ANC bureaucratic bumbling. Irritated, he hung up a phone and said the ANC would have to get hold of him from then on. "They are not my bosses. I'm carrying my baggage. I'm an equal in the struggle, if not more." The next day, the ANC contacted him and fixed a meeting.

At times, both the government and the ANC overstated the influence of the congress, the former to shift blame for the black uprising to an unrepresentative foreign cabal and the latter to claim credit and enhance its stature. In reality, the uprising had its own internally generated dynamic. The ANC took as many cues from blacks inside the country as insiders took from the ANC. Often the ANC had to struggle to keep pace with the internal resistance leaders, who were often more adept and pragmatic than ANC apparatchiks schooled in exile rhetoric and protocol.

The ANC ignored internal black opinion at its own peril, as Thabo Mbeki learned when he did not gauge the views of black trade unions on disinvestment by foreign companies.

At an international conference in Botswana, Mbeki, chief of the ANC information section, was as smooth as any ambassador. He was the consummate diplomat, never raising his voice, calling reporters, foundation officials, and foreign secretaries by their first names in a gentle English accent he had acquired in university. Fingering his pipe, he was commander of the winning smile, master of the elusive reply.

During an interview, Mbeki opined that American companies should pull out of South Africa, close their factories, and help bring the South African government to its knees.

I pointed out to Mbeki afterwards that the black trade unions held a different view: that U. S. companies should turn over their factories to black workers. But Mbeki demurred. "Companies should close down altogether. To give the factories to the workers turns workers into sanction busters if, for example, workers take over Johnson and Johnson and it exports goods. Besides, to keep operations going, whoever the owner, doesn't do what sanctions are supposed to do. The idea is to interrupt the functioning of the economy."

Mbeki flashed a smile, radiating confidence. He told me he heard that a lot of trade-union leaders were "embarrassed" about their earlier position, and predicted that the black trade unions would fall into line with the ANC stance in six months, when COSATU would hold its next national congress.

Six months later after fierce debate the black trade unions didn't budge. "We say that foreign companies should leave their assets to the workers," said COSATU first vice president Chris Dlamini. "They should be handed over as a sign of good will from management who claim they are here because they want to help us."

Some trade-union officials were openly annoyed. Never mind weakening the economy, said an official of the mineworkers union. Didn't Mbeki care about weakening black trade unions? The union official, who viewed black trade unions as the most potent agents of change in South Africa, was also upset by the scant mention made of black trade unions in Oliver Tambo's annual address on the seventy-fifth anniversary of the ANC. In a lengthy speech, Tambo had only devoted two paragraphs to the black trade unions.

In the long run, what mattered more than the union position on sanctions was the way black trade-union leaders saw their relationship with the ANC.

Black trade unions recognized the influence and popularity of the ANC. COSATU president Barayi was an unabashed ANC sympathizer and former member. COSATU general secretary Jay Naidoo visited Lusaka immediately after the launch of COSATU. "The ANC is a progressive organization fighting for liberation," said an official of a major union. "It is losing lives for the liberation of black people. If not the ANC, who will you go for? Where are your interests?" Moreover, the popularity of the ANC and the presence of ANC loyalists within the union movement created pressure to conform to the ANC position.

But neither would the unions simply bow to the will of the ANC. Such internal organizations have minds and wills of their own, even while they acknowledge that the ANC is the leading symbol of the liberation movement. "One should make links [with ANC] before independence. But [unions] still will be there after independence to protect their members. They will stand on their own," a union leader said.

At times, the independence of the unions made it difficult to identify a single black point of view. To American companies and trade unions trying to figure out whether to back disinvestment, it could be frustrating. But it augured well for a democratic future after apartheid.

More than most organizations, the unions looked ahead to a South Africa beyond apartheid. Because of their international links with foreign trade unions, many black union leaders were well traveled and well versed in the dangers that lay ahead for unions after liberation. Thus they jealously guarded their independence, anxious to avert the precedent set in the rest of Africa, where trade unions subsumed their own interests and views to the policies of political parties that came to power at independence.

Both the influence of the ANC and its limits were apparent at the July 1987 COSATU conference that endorsed the Freedom Charter. The National Union of Mineworkers introduced a resolution endorsing the charter, an important statement of the loyalties of the union federation. But some union leaders felt that the Freedom Charter didn't go far enough in asserting that workers would control a post-liberation economy—or in guaranteeing the right to strike. They wanted a workers' charter that would be openly socialist.

Heavy politicking took place at the meeting. Guest political leaders who spoke at the COSATU conference berated advocates of the workers' charter for "being derailed by university intellectuals and influenced by the political 'hobos' expelled by the ANC," according to one delegate. Another guest political figure asserted that the South African Communist Party, not the unions, must be the vanguard of socialism. He said socialism would have to be put on the "back burner," a position the conference endorsed, despite the threat of a walkout by the metalworkers' union.

More than most black activists, union organizers were suspicious of ANC intentions. One delegate at the conference fretted that unions "might be the price we pay for liberation" and said that the ANC "demonstrating [its] political sway over the unions is both a threat and concession to the bosses who are more threatened by the unions' economic policy aspirations than they are by anyone else."

In the end, the unions were persuaded to endorse the Freedom Charter as a "minimum program" for a majority-ruled country.

I met Tseliso Hlalele, the national education chairman of the National Unions of Mineworkers, outside a run-down hotel in Maseru, the capital of Lesotho. His hair was going white and he wore a T-shirt and dusty pants. He walked deliberately. He had been a mineworker, like his father, starting at age eighteen and working for twenty-one years. We sat in his car. A straw hat lay on the back seat and a Holy Cross choir cassette was in the tape player. He was in Lesotho tending to the needs of NUM members fired during the strike in 1987. "I tell them not to lose hope," he said. But he conceded that "starvation causes people to be impatient."

As a key union official, Hlalele had traveled not only to the rural homes of migrant mineworkers, but also to Britain, India, Zimbabwe, and Zambia.

1. A UDF poster.

2. *Albertina Sisulu, co-president of the United Democratic Front, speaking at a political funeral.* (Photo by Gill de Vlieg)

3. *Patrick "Terror" Lekota, publicity secretary of the UDF, at a rally in Shoshunguve township north of Pretoria.* (Photo by Paul Weinberg)

4. *Victim of a "necklace" in Lamontville township outside Durban.* (Photo by Billy Paddox)

5. Bishop Desmond Tutu appeals for black restraint in KwaThema township outside Springs the week after a state of emergency was declared in July 1985. *(Photo by Gill de Vlieg)*

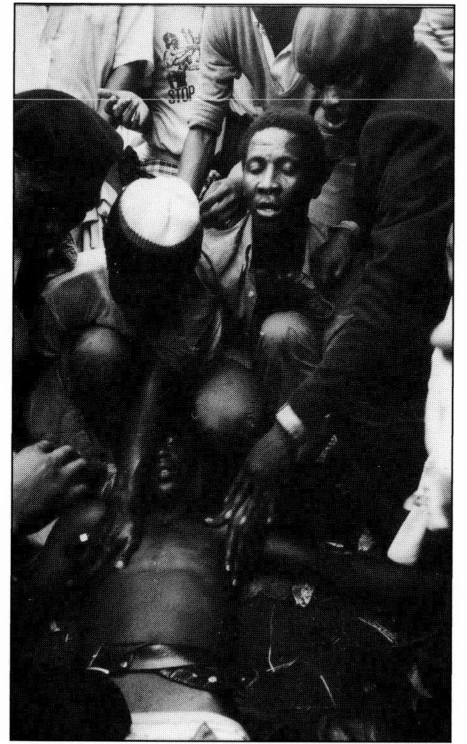

6. Death of a comrade that resulted from fighting with police during a political funeral in New Brighton township outside Port Elizabeth. *(Photo by Steve Hilton-Barber)*

7. "War" in Alexandra township. Residents constructed barricades from damaged cars to block police and army vehicles. (Photo by Anna Zieminski)

8. Comrade winces after police fire tear gas during a political funeral in Crossroads outside Cape Town. (Photo by Guy Tillim)

9. *Mineworkers underground.*
(Photo by Paul Weinberg)

10. *The shower at Jabulani workers' hostel in Soweto.* *(Photo by Santu Mofokeng)*

11. Thabo Mbeki, a leading member of the ANC national executive committee. *(Photo by Steve Hilton-Barber)*

12. Joe Slovo, first white member of the ANC national executive committee and head of the South African Communist Party. *(Photo by Steve Hilton-Barber)*

13. Alfred Qabula, worker-poet, reciting at the Congress of South African Trade Unions cultural day. *(Photo by Rafs Mayet)*

14. The "Berlin Wall." Barbed wire divided the Port Elizabeth townships after a new state of emergency was declared in June 1986. *(Photo by Chris Qwazi)*

15. KwaNdebele chief minister Simon Skosana holds his head in his hands as the KwaNdebele legislative assembly rejects "independence." To his right is Piet Ntuli, an unpopular minister in his government. (Photo by Steve Hilton-Barber)

16. Chief Mangosuthu Gatsha Buthelezi at an Inkatha rally. (Photo by Paul Weinberg)

17. Former President P. W. Botha visits Sebokeng and Sharpeville in June 1987 and receives the "freedom of the townships" from the local black councillors allied to the government. One activist in hiding remarked, "they took my freedom and gave it to Botha." (Photo by Eric Miller)

18. Despite the state of emergency, youths dance at a Johannesburg cultural day held to mark the fourth anniversary of the UDF in August 1987. (Photo by Paul Weinberg)

19. Below a government billboard, a bus station outside Durban is nearly deserted during a general strike in June 1988. (Photo by Eric Miller)

In India, he noted, trade unions are tied to political parties. "When their party is in power, they have influence in making laws," he said. But when their party is out of office, the unions are powerless.

Other countries reinforced Hlalele's conviction that trade unions should be independent. "When I was in Zimbabwe, there was a strike in a gold mine. The minister issued an ultimatum that they [miners] should go back to work or be dismissed," he said in horror. "In Zambia and Zimbabwe, strike action is prohibited. You must apply for permission for a demonstration."

"It is a mistake for the department of manpower to absorb the entire power of the trade union movement. For us, it's committing suicide."

In the 1950s, the South African Congress of Trade Unions (SACTU) was a union federation closely allied to the ANC union. Some leaders sat on the executive committees of both organizations. When the ANC was crushed in the early 1960s, so was SACTU. In the 1980s, black trade union leaders viewed that alliance as a mistake. "SACTU was too close to the party. That's why it was easy for the regime to smash it. The trade union movement must maintain its autonomy," NUM president James Motlatsi told me. At home, COSATU maintained an arms-length relationship with the UDF, often looking down on the UDF as having inferior organization and a less sophisticated understanding of power. When SACTU offered to represent COSATU abroad, COSATU leaders asserted that they would represent themselves.

The dance between the unions and the ANC is instructive. To some extent, being for the ANC within black politics has become like being in favor of Mom and apple pie. But within that loyalty, people argue vigorously over strategy and principle. Since many ANC sympathizers possess their own organizational bases, a post-liberation government in South Africa will have to contend with powerful competing forces.

"Even after liberation, we must keep fighting for liberation," Motlatsi told me. "As long as I'm president of the union I'll fight for the workers' right to strike. Even with an ANC government or nationalized mines, the workers' right to strike cannot be restricted."

The tension between the black trade unions and the ANC reflected a deeper tension within black politics. On one hand, blacks viewed control of the state as the central means to effect sweeping changes. On the other hand, during the struggle to seize state power, the ANC and others looked to centers of power *outside* government: individuals, communities, churches, newspapers, universities, and unions. The people within those organizations believed they wielded some power and could make a difference.

The contradiction emerged at a meeting in the United States about the South African press, where a group of progressive South African journalists debated the problems facing the press under apartheid. At the end, an ANC representative roused himself from a nap and said "The whole discussion was besides the point." He said it was "playing with words" to talk about a free press before the country was free. The South African journalists were stunned and angered.

The Charter

The popularity of the ANC is divorced from a specific post-liberation platform. ANC members range from communists to capitalists, Christians to atheists.

On the more conservative wing of the organization and its sympathizers stand people like Tambo, who in the late 1940s led a move to expel communists from the ANC. "It is not possible to say that the fight is for a capitalistic state or a communistic state—the fight is simply to be free," Tambo told the white businesspeople who came to Zambia. In an interview printed illegally in *The Cape Times*, Tambo said he foresaw "a mixed economy, and certainly nationalization would take into account the realities of the situation." Dr. Motlana, who says he supports the ANC, once suggested at an international conference that Malawi's system of private farming provided a good model for South African peasants. Motlana also said that the principle of nationalizing the gold mines—set out in the Freedom Charter—should be reconsidered. "We would not want to kill the goose that lays the golden egg," he said.

At the other extreme stand people eager to reshape South African society along socialist lines. Many whites fear that blacks will only duplicate the central control, infringement of individual liberties, and bureaucracy imposed by white Afrikaner nationalists.

The ANC's only major post-apartheid policy statement until 1988 was the Freedom Charter. Adopted in 1955, the charter declares that "South Africa belongs to all who live in it, black and white." The charter favors the transfer of the mines, banks, and monopoly industry "to the people" and advocates an end to restrictions on labor, equal opportunities in commerce, free compulsory education, land redistribution, a minimum wage, and a forty-hour week.

"The Freedom Charter has a unique authority because of the mode of its creation," two left-wing academics, Jeremy Cronin and Raymond Suttner, wrote in 1986 in a book commemorating the document. In 1955, the charter was adopted at a meeting in Kliptown, just outside Johannesburg, by 2,884 delegates who had spent several months canvassing the country. "The Congress of the People was not a single event, but a series of campaigns held in huge rallies, small houses, flats, street and factory meetings, gatherings in kraals and on farms," wrote Suttner and Cronin. "South Africa has never had any other similar process of democratic discussion and participation."[12]

In the early 1980s, former ANC members inside the country kept the memory of the Congress of the People fresh. They held seminars on the charter. Even though the ANC itself was illegal, the charter was a legal document. Many UDF leaders had been Freedom Volunteers at the Congress of the People. Christmas Tinto (born Christmas Day, 1925), a member of the UDF's Western Cape executive committee, had collected demands from factory workers in 1955 as volunteer-in-chief from the township of Langa, outside Cape Town. Edgar Ngoyi, president of the UDF's Eastern Cape region, was a volunteer sent from Port Elizabeth townships to collect demands from the rural areas. Martin Mafefo Ramokgadi, who was active in the Soweto Civic Association, still had his old Freedom Volunteer uniform.

Unlike the U. S. Constitution, which has been amended and interpreted, the Freedom Charter has remained frozen in time. The ANC has been unable to debate the charter openly with the South African people, must less implement it. To amend the charter with equal authority would require another convocation of the South African people, something impossible in the 1980s.

In any case, the ANC has been reluctant to change the charter, because to do so would undermine its own claim to being a representative organization. "The Charter must be kept preeminent because it keeps the framers of the charter preeminent," said a disgruntled delegate to the COSATU congress, where the trade-union federation adopted the charter. The Congress of the People had acquired the stature of a foundation myth, comparable to the American Constitutional Convention at Philadelphia or to the covenant God allegedly made with Afrikaner pioneers in 1838. To question the charter was not merely to question policy; to do so was to impugn one's loyalty to the liberation movement.

The ANC's reluctance to update the charter became galling in the 1980s, when for a time the ANC seemed close enough to power for people to take the charter seriously as a political platform. A white agriculture expert went to Lusaka to discuss ANC agriculture and land-redistribution policy, but found no one at ANC headquarters who had given the subject any thought. A foreign diplomat stopped to inquire about the ANC's views on the jury system, but four of the ANC's constitutional experts said they had not given the question any thought. "A journalist from South Africa called the other day and asked what our tax policy was," said Tom Sebina, ANC spokesman in Lusaka. "Luckily she knew as little about taxes as we do."

The ANC was content to leave much of this vague. To clarify its positions would only invite criticism from people it hoped to win over. Black trade-union leaders felt the charter didn't go far enough in articulating a socialist agenda. White businesspeople felt it went too far. "We pin our faith in the Freedom Charter being thirty years old," said Anglo executive Zach de Beer. "The world has turned against the doctrinaire brand of socialism that was popular then." If the ANC remained vague, each group could nurture its separate hopes.

However, conversations with leading members of the ANC and its sympathizers suggest a South Africa ruled by its majority would call itself socialist by name and would address the gross discrepancy in wealth between whites and blacks. Failure to do so would be virtually impossible; by definition a truly democratic government will have to respond to the demands of its constituency, which will be overwhelmingly black and poor.

Large central government, a hallmark of white rule, would probably continue. "We are all statists, from the South African Communist Party to the government," Jakes Gerwel said, with regret. His comment reflected concern among people in black institutions outside government, even though he is the chancellor of the predominantly colored University of the Western Cape, which aspires to be the "university of the left."

According to political scientist Tom Lodge, "Nelson Mandela, writing in 1956 about the charter, saw it as providing the conditions for the development of a non-European bourgeoisie which 'would have the right to own mills and factories.' In the climate of non-racial competitive capitalism, Mandela suggested, 'private enterprise would flourish and boom as never before.'" But Lodge notes that the charter today is interpreted differently. Most of its adherents believe that it guarantees the rights of petty traders, but they see it as a socialist platform.[13]

Nationalization of major sectors of the economy appears likely in post-apartheid South Africa. ANC national executive committee member Pallo Jordan says,

> One is not being dogmatic about nationalizing that, that and that. But we are talking about the state having the capacity to determine how productive capacity is disposed of. That might mean taking controlling interest and leaving the rest in private hands, or it might mean taking over completely. It is the sort of bridge you cross when you get to it. Ways and means can be worked out.

As an afterthought, Jordan adds with a belly laugh, "We could tax companies so hard that they want to give their businesses away."

It remains unclear whether the ANC possesses a tolerant view towards political dissent or whether it will duplicate the authoritarian attitudes of the white government. Unable to reconcile ideological differences with an ultra-left faction within its ranks, it expelled the group, known as the Marxist Workers Tendency. References to the group are steeped in vitriol: an ANC document called for the expulsion of all the group's sympathizers "involved in counter-revolutionary activities which are calculated to confuse our workers, discredit our movement, and derail our revolution."

More disturbing than the ANC's internal battles are some of its informal statements about policy in a post-liberation society. While ANC President Tambo told the *Cape Times* that freedom of speech and the press would exist, Thabo Mbeki told businesspeople in Zambia that the press would have to be nationalized. A member of the group studying constitutional guidelines, Nat Masemola, told a group of academics in the United States that free speech would not be absolute. "There is no absolute freedom at anytime. Especially during the transition period [after majority rule begins], we will not allow unlicensed press freedom. We cannot allow an irresponsible fourth estate. If the world chooses to condemn us, so be it; they have never supported us anyhow." Masemola called the obsequious state-dominated Zambian press a model.

Even during the struggle for freedom, signs of intolerance in the name of a greater good have emerged. The ANC created a cultural committee to influence the selection of theater and music that traveled abroad. Part of the purpose of the committee was to make it easier for South African artists to show their work to international audiences without getting bogged down in the cultural boycott promoted by the ANC.

But the committee had ideological tests. Exiled South African poet Wally Serote explained this to me at the ANC's north London offices. "I don't believe that art is neutral," Serote said. He demanded that artists from South Africa and those visiting South Africa consult the ANC first. Serote would then consult people "at home" about whether to give the ANC's approval.

> If they say the work is not promoting our interests, we'll say no. If they say yes, we'll say okay. If they say yes, and we disagree then we'll still intervene. For example, if the art is saying that all that MK activists have done is for nothing, then something is absolutely wrong. It isn't true. It can't be. It's completely inconceivable.

Serote was quick to add that not every work of art need be political. "It's true musicians sing about love and love makers, but they don't do that from a vacuum. I'm not saying you must sing about Mandela or MK. I'm asking where you belong in national culture."

Many artists resented having pass the test of an ANC committee. They cringed at culture being labeled "progressive" or "reactionary." "For thirty years I've had to live with the threat of being shut, of being silenced, of being closed down, of being censored," said Athol Fugard, South Africa's leading playwright. Fugard had written political plays, but he also wrote others having little to do with apartheid.

> With the cultural boycott comes a demand that all art, to be labelled significant at this moment in time, must be a play, a poem, a painting, whatever, that directs itself to that little bit of human psyche that the political speech directs itself to. I don't buy that. That is to take from art its singular force, its strength and its mystery.
>
> There is a tragic and telling poem by Mayakovsky, the great Russian poet, in which he talks about how he subordinated his writing to the cause and wrote the poems that were needed by the revolution and by post-revolutionary Russian society as it started building itself up. And there are two lines which I remember, because I find them chilling and very frightening: 'I put my heel down on the throat of my own song and died of silence.' He committed suicide, I think four or five weeks after writing that.[14]

In 1988, the ANC issued constitutional guidelines, its first statement of post-liberation policy since the Kliptown conference. Drawn up by a committee of twelve lawyers, the guidelines lacked the authority of the Freedom Charter. Yet they clarified points about individual liberties and stated in a positive way what the ANC stands for, rather than what it is against.

The guidelines promised a bill of rights and a multiparty democracy, subject to prohibitions on "racism, fascism, and nazism." The ANC promised a workers' charter that would protect collective bargaining and the right to strike. The ANC guidelines also endorsed equal rights for women, cultural diversity, and a mixed economy, albeit with heavy state involvement. The most important aspect of the guidelines was their reasonable tone. For example, no call was made for nationalization or land redistribution. Instead the guidelines stressed "corrective action" through state intervention.

The constitutional guidelines were a response, in part, to the growing demand for a bill of rights by whites, who hoped it would protect them from infringements of personal liberty and guard them against what de Tocqueville called the "tyranny of the majority" that can characterize democracy. Albie Sachs, an ANC lawyer who helped write the constitutional guidelines, noted in an ANC discussion paper that concern about correcting past injustice was *not* "to argue that the past humiliation of the oppressed can only be assuaged by the future humiliation of the oppressors." He spelled out that blacks and whites would possess freedom of worship, movement, and assembly.

Blacks, however, viewed this bill of rights with suspicion because the initiative had come from white liberals. Ironically, this suspicion was articulated by Sachs, a white.

> The most curious feature about the demand for a Bill of Rights in South Africa is that it comes not from the ranks of the oppressed but from a certain stratum in the ranks of the oppressors. This has the effect of turning the debate on a Bill of Rights inside out. Instead of a Bill of Rights being associated with democratic advance, it is seen as a brake on it; instead of being welcomed by the mass of the population as an instrument of liberation, it is viewed by the majority with almost total suspicion.[15]

The Sachs discussion paper also spoke to black concerns. Sachs wrote that people in a post-apartheid South Africa would enjoy freedom of speech, "but will lose the right to propagate division and hatred on grounds of race," a phrase vague enough to worry some whites and blacks. Sachs also wrote that white businesspeople "will be subjected to the principles of public interest and affirmative action." A bill of rights, he added, "would have to address itself directly to the question of equal access to resources."

> If [the businessman] and his class prefer to fight to the death, if they threaten to destroy and massacre the workers as a protest against the installation of a democratic government, then they should not be surprised if appropriate counter-measures, including confiscation of land and goods, are taken.[16]

If businesspeople were cooperative, Sachs said, land redistribution could have "a less drastic character."

Some South Africans may have been reassured by the ANC's constitutional guidelines, but other remained uneasy. "The guidelines represent a welcome move away from ideological rhetoric," wrote an Anglo American Corporation official. "It remains to be seen whether this constitutes a change of heart or merely of tactics."

Card Carriers

Whatever uncertainty surrounds the ANC, its members are considered freedom fighters and patriots by the majority of black South Africans because of the ANC's long record of resistance and the willingness of its members to lay down their lives.

To counter that view, the South African government tried to portray the ANC as a cabal of malefactors, controlled by Moscow, foreign to South Africa, and at war with the population. According to President Botha, the ANC was "a terrorist organization controlled by the Communist Party . . . murdering innocent people, not only white people but black people."

"Tambo is the man who appears in a blue suit doing the selling to the West. But the image of the ANC isn't the real ANC," I was told by Jan du Plessis, a consultant for South Africa's Foreign Affairs Ministry. Du Plessis reeled off names of ANC people with alleged communist affiliations and claimed that nineteen of the thirty ANC executive committee members at that time were communist. He spread out a variety of illegal ANC and SACP publications before me on the desk in his office in the Union Buildings in Pretoria. He made special note of an issue of the *African Communist* that quoted Tambo as saying that the ANC and the SACP were the "twin pillars of the struggle." Though all the publications were illegal for ordinary readers, du Plessis possessed special privileges. Apparently he was immune to whatever contaminated ideas the publications possessed. He must have thought that I was too, for I was allowed to take them with me.

ANC leaders acknowledge they have a close relationship with the SACP. "Relations go back sixty years," Thabo Mbeki told me. Mbeki's father Govan, who served twenty-four years of a life sentence on Robben Island before being released in 1987, is a member of the party, but Mbeki the younger claims that he is not. But the ANC leaders don't see any reason to change that close relationship when both groups share the goal of defeating apartheid. Mac Maharaj asks, "What does breaking with the SACP at this stage mean? It means we shouldn't be concentrating our blows against the regime, but turning inwards. Whose interest would that serve except to ensure the formula where white supremacy would survive?"

ANC leaders also insist that the ANC remains distinct from the South African Communist Party. "There has been an overlapping of membership all along the line." Tambo told the *Cape Times*.

> But ANC members who are also members of the SACP make a very clear distinction between these two independent bodies. We cooperate a lot but the ANC is accepted by the SACP as leading the struggle. It is often suggested that the ANC is controlled by the communist party. . . . Well, I have been long enough in the ANC to know that that has never been true.[17]

Such declarations left Pretoria unmoved. They noted that ANC relied heavily on the Soviet Union for funding. According to ANC sources, the ANC had a budget of $30 million to $40 million, the largest single donor being Sweden. Every year, the Soviet Union supplied the ANC with arms worth about the same amount as the organization's cash budget. Du Plessis told me, "When the top echelon is controlled by the South Africa Communist Party, when funding comes from the East bloc, when arms supply and training comes from the East bloc, can you still speak of an independent organization? I don't think so."

Pointing fingers at the SACP, which includes whites, fit into the government's view that behind every black foe there lay a white brain.

Uncle Joe

In official South African demonology, Joe Slovo was the Great Satan. The South African government viewed him as a colonel in the Soviet KGB, as a white communist manipulating earnest black nationalists as part of a "vicious and callous onslaught" to bring Communist dictatorship to southern Africa.

Slovo earned this reputation by dint of his dual role as general secretary of the pro-Moscow South African Communist Party and as one of the architects of the military wing of the African National Congress. The former position, according to Botha, made Slovo and the ANC "pawns of the Soviets." The latter position, in the eyes of white South Africans, placed Slovo at the seat of the ANC's campaign of terrorism.

To the angry youths in South Africa's black townships, however, the government's vilification of Slovo made the Jewish lawyer born in 1926 into a sort of violent messiah—one of the ANC's most potent symbols. Even though Slovo couldn't be quoted in the South African press or on the radio, and had been in exile for a quarter century, in songs and chants young blacks beckoned to him for deliverance. As the tenth anniversary of the Soweto student uprising approached in 1986, pupils in Soweto rechristened a government-run school "Joe Slovo High School." In Alexandra, residents renamed one of the streets after Slovo. In 1985 the ANC made him the first-ever white member of its national executive committee. "Slovo is truly colorless," said one black student activist. "He's just Slovo."

In person, Slovo appears an unlikely candidate for the role of satan or savior. He is a soft-spoken raconteur with a hearty handshake and wavy white hair where his horns or halo should be. His glasses sit cockeyed on the bridge of his nose and he tilts his head back to look at you.

Slovo has indeed played a pivotal role for the liberation movement over four decades. He has been a leading proponent of violence, pushing in the 1950s to transform the ANC from a disorganized group of amateurs into a militant resistance movement. Nelson Mandela gave the ANC its most potent symbol by languishing in jail for twenty-five years, but Slovo has been a symbol of action, not martyrdom; he helped build the ANC organization and provide it with guns.

In the early 1960s, at the outset of the ANC military campaign, Slovo and a handful of colleagues sat in a Johannesburg apartment with mortar and pestle grinding up potash permanganate and mixing it with aluminum powder to make crude incendiary devices that could be ignited with dabs of acid. By the time Slovo stepped down as chief of staff in April 1987, the Soviet-backed ANC military wing had graduated to AK-47s, hand grenades, and car bombs. His connections helped to ensure that the ANC received a steady supply of Soviet weapons.

Slovo had exchanged a successful career as a Johannesburg barrister for a shadowy life of exile. He shuttled between London, Lusaka, and the ANC camps, and rarely slept more than two nights in one place.

Slovo's role in the ANC worried the U. S. Congress, which stuck a clause in the 1986 sanctions bill requiring the State Department to report regularly on communist influence in South Africa. The first such report said the ANC was "deeply beholden" to the Party. The report estimated that half of the thirty members of the ANC executive are "known or suspected SACP members." Of all those, Slovo was the key link between the two bodies.

Slovo straddles several worlds: a white Communist in the company of black nationalists, a son of a working-class family who has lived out the revolutionary fantasies of leftist intellectuals, and a Jewish refugee and grandfather who has touched a responsive chord with alienated black South African youths.

Ridden with lice, Slovo arrived in South Africa with his mother in 1936 from a small town in Lithuania. They joined Slovo's father, who was a struggling fruit vendor. The younger Slovo spoke only Yiddish and had studied only in a synagogue. Soon he was packed off to an English-speaking school where other students prophetically called the newcomer "Bolshie."

Like many Jews in Johannesburg's tight-knit corner of the Diaspora, Slovo saw the Soviet Union as delivering Russian Jews from Nazism and the czar's pogroms. He joined the Communist Party—then legal—at age sixteen. "This was the time of the Red Army advance. To be a leftist and a Communist at that time was relatively popular," he recalls.

With his father periodically confined to debtors' prison, Slovo dropped out of school after eight grade and worked for a pharmaceutical wholesaler. "It was the big wholesale drug house called Syd Brothers and Kinovsky," Slovo recalls. "You don't know Yiddish, do you? We used to call them Syphilis Brothers and Gonivum. Gonovim are thieves." He became a union shop steward and led his first strike at age seventeen. The company settled after four days, and his salary went from four pounds sterling to fourteen.

One thing about the strike disturbed him, though. Black workers weren't allowed to join unions then, so they lost four days' pay and didn't receive any increase.

In 1944 Slovo lied about his age and joined the army at eighteen. (Enlistment age was twenty-one.) He served in Egypt and Italy, but saw little action. While waiting to be repatriated after the fighting ended, Slovo was stationed in Italy near a Catholic school with a library, where he read every single work of Trotsky, the only books in the leftist book section. On his return to South Africa, he was admitted to the University of the Witwatersrand, although he had never attended high school. "I still don't know what an adverb is," he says. The liberal Helen Suzman taught his economics course. He graduated in law with top honors and became a leading political advocate in Johannesburg.

The party Slovo joined had struggled with its attitudes toward race and nationalism since its formation in 1921. Initially the South African Communist Party appealed to white workers. In 1922, white mineworkers who supported the party marched under the banner "Workers of the World, Fight and Unite for a White South Africa." Soon, however, the Party started conducting night schools and organizing trade unions for blacks. By 1928 only 150 of the Party's 1,750 members were white. But the Communist Party still had trouble forging links with black groups. In 1926 the Industrial and Commercial Workers' Union, then the biggest black organization, expelled Communist Party members. In 1930 conservative elements took over the ANC and purged Communists and their allies. Later, other black groups attacked the Communist Party from the left, criticizing its willingness to participate in the all-white Parliament instead of boycotting it.

In the 1930s, a rift in the party opened over the question of a Native Republic, a separate nation of Africans. Moses Kotane and three white members of the party went to Moscow in the early 1930s to have the Comintern settle the question. Only Kotane returned. The others died in Stalin's labor camps in the late 1930s.

Slovo became a staunch defender of Stalin when he came back from the war. "I was a blind defender. I'm deeply ashamed of it now." He asserts, "Stalin and Mao set back the cause of socialism seventy-five years," but adds that responsibility for Stalinism went beyond Stalin. "You can't have a cult without worshipers, and I was a worshiper." Now Slovo declares himself an admirer of Mikhail Gorbachev's "exhilarating" reform drive—with the possible exception of Gorbachev's campaign against alcohol, he says glancing at his third glass of whiskey. (Before the Russian revolution, he jokes, people kept bottles of vodka on the table and documents hidden underneath. Now in the Soviet Union, people keep documents on top of the table and bottles hidden underneath.)

Many of Slovo's critics doubt whether he or the SACP will ever stray far from Moscow's line, whatever it is. The South African Communist Party has backed Moscow over the years on every issue, including the invasions of Czechoslovakia and Afghanistan. Slovo hedges about what he thinks of Poland's Solidarity, saying that certain reactionaries tried to take advantage of it for their own ends.

Slovo insists that his Party isn't controlled by Moscow and says accusations that he is a KGB member are absurd. "If I have been a colonel in the Soviet KGB all these years, I must be doing my job pretty poorly not to be promoted." But he says it "isn't up to us to place every Soviet decision under a microscope." Asked if he can recall any issue on which South African Communists publicly deviated from the Soviet line, he pauses, then says, "I don't think so."

But the Moscow line toward South Africa has mellowed a bit, partly because prolonged conflict is costly to Angola, Moscow's principle ally in the region, and partly because Moscow has changed its view of Third-World liberation movements. The Soviets also doubt the ANC's ability to win a military victory. While the ANC hammers at western countries for not imposing sanctions, Moscow's African experts caution against ruining the South African economy. Vladimir Tikhomirov, a respected young Soviet expert on Soviet Africa, says "Economic depression leads to more repression. In response, the reaction by the opposition becomes more violent." The Soviet Union has begun to seek compromise. At a conference in Europe in 1986, a Soviet expert on southern Africa suggested that a negotiated settlement might include a chamber of Parliament with seats allotted by race, similar to the Soviet chamber of nationalities, or that a post-apartheid South Africa could set aside special parliamentary seats for whites in a fashion similar to the Lancaster House accord for Zimbabwe. The Soviet Union also warned the ANC against pushing too hard for nationalization of industry and socialism. Tikhomirov said at a meeting,

> A number of organizations in South Africa profess to be socialist, but are not really socialist organizations. We are worried about the development of such organizations. If they were to come to power, we could not rule out another Kampuchea. I'm not precluding a socialist future for South Africa, but we're not promoting it.

"We don't want to see the destruction of the South African economy. We too have been taught something by experience," said Appollon Davidson, a Soviet historian of southern Africa. "Many in Africa and around the world have been disillusioned by the socialist path." As a result of the change in climate in Moscow, the Communist Party could even have a moderating influence on uncompromising black nationalists.

In 1950 the Communist Party was declared illegal. At the time it had about 2,000 dues-paying members (including 150 whites and 250 Indians). The Party dissolved and reorganized itself underground in 1953. Throughout the fifties, communists advanced to leadership roles in the ANC and exchanged views with the ANC's non-communist leaders. "Members of the party played a tremendous role in transforming the ANC from a cap-in-hand organization to a national liberation organization," Slovo boasts.

Personal contact bound the Party and the ANC together, too. Slovo has cemented an alliance with black nationalists built on common tactical goals and personal friendships with Oliver Tambo and Nelson Mandela. Acquaintances say Mandela was a regular at raucous parties thrown by Slovo and his wife, Ruth First, during the 1950s. First was a communist party leader and journalist. The couple was at the center of the social and political leftist scene. Slovo and First also helped draft the Freedom Charter. (First later edited a collection of Mandela's speeches and writings—conveniently omitting a passage in which Mandela speaks of the need to bolster the black bourgeoisie.) In 1961 the Communist Party cemented its relations with the future leaders of the ANC by helping them start Umkhonto we Sizwe.

The effect of Slovo's friendship on the nation's two leading black nationalists was dramatic. In the late 1940s Tambo and Mandela tried to bar Communists from the ANC. Fifteen years later, Mandela defended in court the ANC's close ties with the Communist Party. "Communists are the only political group who were prepared to eat with us, talk with us, live with us, and work with us," he said.

Slovo was overseas at the time of the Rivonia raid, and he remained there. The ANC movement was so decimated that for a while Slovo considered taking an academic post in England.

Instead he devoted himself to rebuilding Umkhonto. When other activists were giving up, it took a relentless optimist to think the ANC could build a guerrilla force. "It looked pretty bleak then," he remembers. "The movement was destroyed. You needed the optimism of the will to dominate the pessimism of the intellect." In 1975, before the exodus of black students, he wrote an essay called "No Middle Road" that emphasized the ability of the ANC to win a prolonged guerrilla war and stimulate a revolutionary uprising within the country.

In 1987, Slovo still believed in the importance of Umkhonto. "To step up armed activity is absolutely vital," Slovo said during Umkhonto's most active year since the early sixties. "Even peripheral reforms and the mere mention of the word 'dialogue' from some hard-line racists is a response to what has been done in this field."

Like other ANC leaders, Slovo said the ANC tries to avoid civilian casualties, but he acknowledged that civilians can get caught in the cross fire. He said while he doesn't believe in attacking civilians, ANC cannot control every agent inside South Africa. "It is the measure of a pre-revolutionary situation when actions take place beyond the call of the organized movements. No revolutionary movement can guide and control every street action." Though guerrilla attacks rose sharply during the ANC's Year of

Umkhonto (1986), Slovo said the military wing didn't match expectations and had to choose targets that carried greater symbolic meaning.

But Slovo's ideas had evolved since he wrote "No Middle Road." Slovo became skeptical about the ANC's ability to win a military victory, and said that trade unions might be a more powerful lever for changing South Africa. He said he believed that the ANC should be prepared to negotiate. He didn't see violence as a catharsis, as did Frantz Fanon. "There isn't a single struggle in the postwar period in the colonies which hasn't ended at the negotiating table. If there were a way of settling this thing peacefully tomorrow, we [Communists] would be the first to say, 'Let's do it.' " The preconditions for such talks, he said, would be to unban the ANC, release Mandela, and withdraw troops from the black townships.

Slovo claimed to be flexible beyond those conditions. "The rest can be tossed about: the mixed economy, cultural rights, and the kind of political system. What can't be tossed about is the issue of majority rule."

In "No Middle Road," Slovo stressed that "true liberation" lay in the domination of proletarian workers and peasants over the petite bourgeoisie and the "speedy progression from formal liberation [majority rule] to lasting emancipation [a socialist state]." Twelve years later, Slovo was suggesting a more cautious approach to South Africa's economy under majority rule, saying the ANC wouldn't repeat the mistakes of other African socialists. "I foresee a mixed economy for a long time to come in South Africa, even though it may not be what I prefer," Slovo told me. "Socialist man isn't produced by the issuing of an edict or the raising of a flag. In the transition period, you must bake bread, not just slogans," he added, coining a new slogan.

The time for negotiations about the transition to majority rule and the nature of a post-apartheid economy was still far off, Slovo cautioned. When the National Party won the 1948 elections on a platform of expanding and institutionalizing apartheid, someone asked Slovo how long the government would last. He estimated five years. Three decades later he still said five years. "Someday I'll be right," he said ruefully.

Slovo's position within the ANC military hierarchy and his endorsement of violence placed him in personal danger, about which he at first appeared—traveling alone in Lusaka—unconcerned. But when he tripped on a stair, a gun fell out of a concealed ankle holster. "Oops," he said. "I didn't mean to show that to you."

The former ANC chief of staff seems deeply affected by the 1982 letter bomb that killed his wife in Maputo, the Mozambican capital. Slovo believes the bomb was sent by South African police. When two newspapers, one French and one South African, suggested that Slovo himself had killed First, he sued for libel and won. He couldn't enforce the judgment against the South African paper, but he urged it to set up a scholarship fund in First's name.

Slovo told me that the South African government has sent people to try to kill him. Some of these people, he said, "have been dealt with." That chilling pronouncement is a reminder that although Slovo seems like an amiable guy, running an insurgency isn't a friendly business. The South African government alleged in 1986 that twenty-one people were executed in ANC camps, some of them probably South African government spies. The ANC later produced a few of those alleged victims, alive and well, and allowed them to give interviews with journalists. Those not produced may have met less fortunate ends.

It's a business that appears out of character for a man who still is able to sound almost naively idealistic at times. "Since I believe that man and woman are essentially good, I believe that socialist man and woman can be created in time. Except it is obviously going to take longer than we imagined when we were all starry-eyed utopians in the early days."

In the twenty-fifth anniversary issue of *Dawn*, the magazine of the ANC military wing, while other ANC leaders told heroic stories, Slovo recounted a comic tale of near disaster. At the outset of the first sabotage campaign in late 1961, Slovo went to set fire to the Johannesburg Drill Hall. He and some colleagues had spent days making homemade explosives. They planned to ignite bottles of the concoction by rigging up a fuse made of paper through which acid would drip onto a mixture when turned upside down.

But Slovo inadvertently picked the day the military authorities were having their monthly cleaning. About fifty black cleaners were stacking the wooden chairs and polishing the wooden floor that Slovo hoped to burn. Slovo then went to place the explosive mixture in an administrative office. He had just turned the bottle upside down in a bag when a clipped military voice behind him asked if he needed any help. The startled Slovo made up a story about looking into an army exemption for his brother who had to take some examinations. (Slovo has no brother.) Still holding the bag with the bomb inside, Slovo waited anxiously while the soldier made an inquiry. When told to return another day, Slovo gave the officer a sweaty handshake and briskly walked away. As soon as possible, he reached inside the bag and snatched the bottle to stop the explosion. "Those were the longest three minutes of my life," Slovo said.

Old war stories from a war that seemed far from over.

CHAPTER TEN

The Best and the Brightest

CECIL NGWANE GREW UP far from the front line of the war, on the cloistered grounds of a mission hospital in the Ngutu district, a rural area of the KwaZulu homeland. His mother, a nurse, raised Cecil and three other children in a small, sparsely furnished house in back of the hospital. From their front steps, they looked out on simple huts and the single paved road that stretched to the north. As we drove there across the rolling hills, Cecil drew in his breath. "God I love this country," he said.

The 500-bed hospital was overflowing with people, many of them poor migrants and malnourished children. But to Cecil, the grounds of the Charles Johnson Memorial Hospital fostered an air of camaraderie among the doctors, nurses, and their families. "To call it a multiracial set-up suggests that one was conscious of different colors. In fact, we were not. It was uniracial. People dealt with each other as equals." Cecil even avoided the unpleasantries of Bantu education by attending a Catholic boarding school near Pinetown, about 130 miles from the hospital.

Then Cecil was suddenly lifted out of the Nqutu district and introduced to the realities of South Africa.

In 1979, the Anglo American Corporation dispatched educators to scour South Africa for the best and brightest young blacks and to bestow upon these chosen few the country's richest scholarship packages. The twelve young men and women selected—"the Anglo cadets"—were supposed to be a vanguard of black talent, trained to be engineers, managers, and future leaders. "We talked about creating a pool of talent to create a more just society," said Donald Ncube, Anglo American's most senior black executive, who helped choose candidates.

The gifted youths would first go through a pre-university tutoring program, then attend the prestigious, predominantly white University of the Witwatersrand in Johannesburg. Not only would they get an education, but they would be paid as if they were employees. During vacations they would work on Anglo's gold or diamond mines in a management-training program, supervised by white "mentors" drawn from Anglo management. By graduation, South Africa's best and brightest could be shining examples of what blacks could achieve, ready to shinny up the corporate ladder or excel in society.

In early 1986, the twelve members of the class of '79 should have finished their university degrees and been working for the company. Instead, only two had finished the program and gone to work for Anglo. Two others were still struggling through university. Most had dropped out, disillusioned with the company and torn by conflicting loyalties. One moved to the United States; one was working for International Business Machines Corporation. Cecil Ngwane was a clerk. Another student was working and studying to retake exams he failed; one went to an all-black homeland university; one worked for a trade union. One worked for a community group and became publicity secretary of the UDF in the "border" region near East London; in 1986 he went to prison for nearly three years. One vanished, presumed by his classmates to have skipped the country and joined the African National Congress.

Their personal odysseys told the story of the '80s in black South Africa, a time of political awakening and maturation, upheaval, striving, failure, and achievement. Anglo had tried to shelter them, but it could not. The cadets' experiences as the golden prodigies of the country's largest corporation pointed to the difficulty of dividing blacks across class lines. Blacks, especially the best and brightest, felt a responsibility toward their fellow citizens.

Cecil Ngwane—A Pocketful of Dreams

The five-hour trip from Nqutu to Johannesburg, a city with fifteen times as many people as the entire Nqutu district, was made often by people seeking fortune. Men from Nqutu worked as migrants in Egoli (as they called it in Zulu, the city of gold), and sent money to KwaZulu where their families had to stay behind. When the migrants returned for the holidays, they were worldly. When Cecil and I visited Nqutu on a Good Friday, a crowd had gathered on a barren hill to view the returning laborers bedecked in suits they had bought in Johannesburg. The migrant laborers tried to imitate city slickers they had seen by walking with their chests thrust out, lifting their knees and chins, turning in leaden pirouettes. They were showing off their "sophisticated" outfits from the big city: leisure suits of sky-blue and bright orange, a red shirt with white ruffles, and a white umbrella.

Cecil didn't return from Johannesburg with finery, but he had never been a migrant laborer in search of fortune. He went to Johannesburg full of ideals and hope. Donald Ncube remembers an articulate young Cecil who "knew Keats and D. H. Lawrence. We were wondering what this guy was doing in a commerce program."

"Promise," Cecil said, recalling what the scholarship meant to him. "Lots of promise." For the first time, he could earn and send money home to his family. More importantly, he felt part of an enlightened experiment. "The greatest thing was the dream," Cecil said. "The reason why I wanted to pull myself up was not really personal ambition. We talked about how change must come. We recited it like a litany, every day."

Within a couple of years, however, Cecil was wondering why he had joined the Anglo program. Johannesburg was a "people jungle, a concrete jungle" to Cecil, who felt "too small in a big world." The university also felt alien. "I did not belong to that place. It belonged to the white guys," Cecil said. "When you asked a question in class everybody looked at you like they were thinking 'Where do you come from?' The only times I laughed were before I left Soweto and after I came back to Soweto." Other Anglo trainees shared Cecil's alienation. Two of them shunned the student cafeteria and ate with black university maintenance workers. Anglo, sensing that black students weren't talking to whites, asked each of its protégés to interview and write about a white person on campus. Cecil made one up.

The course work was tough too. Accounting stumped him. (Some black students said the university's accounting faculty intentionally flunked black students.) After he failed accounting a second time, Anglo dropped his scholarship.

The company suggested he take some time off, work at one of the gold mines, study accounting, then return. Cecil went back to Nqutu. He lined up with more than 100 other migrant laborers, waiting two-and-a-half hours at the labor recruiting office, obtaining a contract to work on the mines, then waiting three days for the necessary documents to come through.

He became a clerk in a gold mine. He went through a physical examination as did all the black workers, parading naked in front of white health inspectors who felt them, stared at their private parts and leisurely filled in forms. Cecil lived in a men's hostel on the mine grounds. Twelve-foot walls topped with barbed wire surrounded the compound, and security guards monitored people. Cecil shared a room with three other men in a double-story concrete block that had 69 rooms. Some rooms, no larger than a middle-level managers's office at Anglo headquarters, housed as many as eleven men. "It was similar to boarding school," Cecil said later, "but there were old people there living like schoolchildren. In boarding school, at least everyone knows he will be moving on into the real world and make something of his life. But at the hostels, everyone knows he is down there forever." The privacy and peacefulness of Nqutu was remote. Once, Cecil was sleeping at 7 A.M. on a Saturday and a supervisor rudely woke him up and ordered him to clean up his room.

Cecil despaired. "You come to regard the white man as superior. I was going to ask for a raise, but I was reduced to the point where I thought it was a favor. I almost—almost—said *baas* to my supervisor. You can see yourself losing human dignity," he said bitterly.

Cecil lasted one year and twenty-four days on the mine, finally convincing Anglo to give him a job as a clerk in Johannesburg. That's where I found Cecil, much changed from the idealistic youngster who had left Nqutu six years earlier. In retrospect, Cecil "should have been writing poetry" said David Adler, the educator who advised Anglo on its gifted pupils. "Of all the people who hate Anglo, I think Cecil hates it the most." Cecil was still planning to finish his university degree, more out of love of learning rather than any hope to change the world. He was cynical now. "I've lost all incentive to dream," he said. "I take things as they come."

Jacob Maroga—Standing Out

Anglo must have spent well over $100,000 in scholarships and salaries to groom Jacob Maroga, one of the two who finished the Anglo training program.

Maroga was the second black engineer ever to work at a South African gold mine, and the company was taking care to protect its investment; when I met Maroga, a company official insisted on listening.

South African gold mines are among the most racist places in the country. For years, white mineworkers' union blocked the abolition of the last piece of racial job reservation. The former head of white mineworkers' union won a seat in Parliament on the Conservative Party ticket, drawing heavily on white working-class voters who feared black economic advances. One Anglo cadet said that during his summer holidays working at the gold mines white workers refused to provide him with information he needed to service equipment. Mining supervisors assigned him to the sewage plant. When he reported that the plant was working fine, they told him to sit there and watch the shit being mixed.

For Maroga, once he finished his academic work, more challenges lay ahead. "I have to make the guys look at me as an engineer, not as a black," he told me. Ironically, Maroga benefitted from the conservative white workers' class consciousness. In the status-conscious world of the mines, Maroga stood out. He was the only engineer at Western Deep Levels Mine who completed a university degree instead of an apprenticeship, and thus he commanded grudging respect.

Maroga expected to be treated with appropriate deference. He was enraged when he was thrown in for a physical exam with hundreds of black laborers, and he demanded to be treated like the white engineers. The mine manager quickly rectified the mistake. Though Maroga lived in a hostel, it was an unusually comfortable arrangement. The suite he shared with half-a-dozen semi-skilled blacks looked like a college dormitory room: a stereo sat in one corner, and the walls were decorated with posters of a beach, a waterfall, and the American space shuttle. Maroga started working in January 1986 at a salary of about R1700 a month, far more than his father, an ordinary laborer, had ever earned in his life.

Like the other cadets, however, Maroga's ambition wasn't purely a selfish one. "There's going to be a need for engineers. There are no black engineers now because there are no role models. I must set an example for the guys who come after me," he said.

For all his success, Maroga still faced a problem of identification. Anglo had encouraged him to think of himself as management, but he was still black. "Identification is the central problem," said David Adler. "Whose side are they on in a strike? They are not trusted by either side." I asked Maroga if he ever worried about winding up on the management side of a dispute with black workers and being forced to choose between his position and his skin color. "I think about it," he said noncommittally, glancing at his supervisor.

Theo Qabaka—Fitting In

Perhaps the best-adjusted of Anglo's protégés was Theo Qabaka. He came from KwaZakhele township outside Port Elizabeth. He was the second of five children. His father was an ordinary laborer in a plate-glass factory and his mother worked in the Pick 'n Pay supermarket chain. In 1978–79 Theo had been an exchange student in Alaska on an American Field Service program, and that was where he became interested in mining and engineering.

I met him at a De Beers diamond mine north of Pretoria. He had just been dropped from the cadet program, but he was working while studying to retake three exams for a degree in metallurgy. "Most black people don't know what metallurgy is," Theo said. His own parents, he said, "have given up trying to understand what I do."

Theo Qabaka didn't have any problem with his own identity, precisely because so many people had trouble identifying him. "It's not like being a doctor or a lawyer. This job has no prestige. I like that. You just get lost in the crowd. I get dirty from my work and many guys think I'm just a common laborer. Management is supposed to wear white hard hats, but I have yellow and green ones."

His easy-going manner obviously helped him fit in, even with the right-wing white Afrikaans engineer who shared his office. Theo said, "If he doesn't like your face, he just says it. But once he decides you're buddies, it's okay. We go to have lunch together. He is the first white I'm friendly with." Despite his new friend, Theo knew where he stood. "What happens in the country affects me. If the UDF calls for a stayaway on a certain day, I won't go to work, whatever management says."

Thomas Mdhluli—Success

North past the factories of Pretoria, past the barren scrubland, through the squatter camp of Winterveld and past where the tarred road ends, is a plaster house. This is where Thomas Mdhluli, the oldest of the Anglo cadets, grew up.

The oldest of ten children, Thomas didn't start school until he was nine. He got plenty of encouragement from his parents, but could expect little assistance. His father earned R95 a week working in Pretoria in a factory that makes louvered doors. He was rarely home. To get to work on time, Thomas's father left at 5 A.M. to take a bus to the train; he got home at 7:30 P.M. His mother, a vegetable hawker, was illiterate.

Because of the appalling state of the schools in Winterveld, Thomas' parents sent him to school in Tzaneen, a small town in the northern Transvaal, where he stayed with relatives. He saw his parents twice a year. He received top honors in his matriculation exams, but didn't have the money to go to university. Then he read an advertisement about Anglo's scholarship program. "I knew I would be picked," he said.

Later, he recognized his overconfidence. "If in your village you are a chief, you might refuse to believe there are chiefs elsewhere." The program at the University of the Witwatersrand humbled him. He flunked first-year accounting and realized that "Before you can make it you have to sweat and sweat very hard."

Anglo dropped Thomas after he failed accounting his first year. He repeated the course at his own expense. Anglo resumed his scholarship for his second year of university, but he had failed again. When I met him he was studying at the less prestigious University of South Africa and working at a branch of Standard Bank. He expected to finish a bachelors' degree later that year.

Some of Thomas' problems at Wits, as the university is called, had little to do with course work. At the dormitory in Soweto, other students viewed the Anglo cadets as privileged. "They were rejecting us, totally rejecting us. They would say 'Away with those middle class guys, away with those bourgeois guys.' Others said 'Give me money, just buy me lunch' and if you refused it was a big problem."

Rather than alienate Thomas from his fellow blacks, the problems in the dorm propelled him to political activity. While Anglo wanted the best and brightest to concentrate on engineering and accounting, student organizations were coming back to life. Thomas attended the founding meeting of the Congress of South African Students in 1979. Later the Azanian Students Organization (Azaso), originally part of the Black Consciousness camp, was taken over by young blacks in the non-racial Freedom Charter tradition. Those young blacks included several Anglo cadets like Thomas, who became Azaso's vice president.

One of Azaso's first protests took place in 1981 on Republic Day, a holiday when whites commemorated Verwoerd's 1960 decision to break with the British Commonwealth. At the black student protest at Wits, right-wing white students gathered and waved little South African flags. The black students grabbed the flags and burned them. Police raided the dormitory and arrested Thomas. "Anglo rubbish," they called him during an interrogation.

Black trade unions also were making a comeback. Thomas did some organizing for the General and Allied Workers Union (GAWU), one of the unions later affiliated to the UDF. He also negotiated a recognition agreement between the union and a unit of Premier Milling in a town in the northern Cape.

Was Thomas a success? Not by Anglo's standards; he hadn't finished his degree, nor was he working for the company. Yet Thomas had his own definition of achievement. "The success of the program shouldn't be measured by whether you finished the degree. It should be measured by how many of us came out of the program assertive enough to make it in life."

Mafa Goci—Home Again

One of the first things Mafa Goci experienced in the Anglo training program was being welcomed by Anglo American tycoon Harry Oppenheimer—on video. On the screen, Oppenheimer looked and sounded remote: the titan of South African industry had aging white skin, stringy white hair, a dark business suit and an upper-crust accent.

The strange greeting did little to ease the anxiety Mafa felt upon his arrival in Johannesburg. He came from Duncan Village, a small township spread across a couple of hills within view of the ocean and the small city of East London. Before he started the Anglo program, Mafa had never been to Johannesburg. "I was intimidated by the magnitude of the place," he recalled.

The more he got to know the company, the more his discomfort grew. Anglo took its prize students on tours of the company's coal, diamond, and gold mines. At a gold mine, they went down the shafts. "Underground, there was a sense of imminent danger. The noise and mud and water. There were places where the roof was so low that you had to go on your stomach," Mafa recalled later. "The miners asked us who we were. We said we were students. They wanted to know what kind of work we were doing. We said, studying." It was an awkward moment. "It didn't seem fair that we were being paid for doing nothing." The students were taken to the executive suites for lunch with the mine managers. When they stayed overnight, they were kept separate from the workers, usually at a hotel with "international" status that could accept blacks.

As the pre-university year progressed, Mafa grew increasingly suspicious of the Anglo program. On one hand, Anglo was "all generosity," Mafa said. But on the other hand, he felt like a guinea pig. In a study-skills course, the cadets were taught to speak into a telephone the "correct" way, to perfect their diction and English pronunciation. Video cameras were popular tools. The cadets were filmed while at work, stripping a car, drawing its engine components. They read reports to the videotape, ostensibly to hone their presentation skills. Mafa remembered a report one cadet did on Johannesburg, "the indomitable city." Mafa couldn't remember the subject of his own report, though he remembered the manner of his presentation. "Purportedly I had been making faces at the camera. I was feeling like a monkey, so I was doing my best to show I had not learned anything."

The communications skills teacher was sympathetic. "She tried to interest me in other things: poetry and music. I grew to like classical music and I still like Mendelssohn, Tchiakovsky, and a bit of Bach."

At the end of the first year, *Time* magazine did a story about the cadets. Mafa and another youth, Tiishang, refused to pose for a photo of the group. The *Time* reporter asked whether they weren't grateful to Anglo. "We said no," Mafa recalled later. "We said that the money being used for us was money that rightfully belonged to our fathers who were working at the mines and who weren't paid the money due to them." An Anglo official called Mafa and asked if he believed what he said; Mafa said yes. The official said there would be no problem, but Mafa sensed the company was annoyed. "There are words and then there are words," he said later. "But I already didn't care."

Company educators sensed Mafa's loss of interest and offered to switch him out of engineering to any other course he wanted. For a while he studied occupational therapy and worked at the Ernest Oppenheimer clinic.

Mafa had joined the Black Student Society, which organized protest demonstrations on Republic Day. Later Mafa was elected to the national executive of the Azanian Students Organization. Mafa then dropped out of the Anglo program and transferred to Fort Hare University to study law. He did well on his first set of exams, but after that he was detained for three weeks for stoning the limousine of the Ciskei president, Lennox Sebe. Although students raised money to pay R400 fines for Mafa and twenty-one others, campus turmoil continued to disrupt his studies. During the second semester, students boycotted classes and held mass meetings on campus. Ciskei police broke up the rallies with tear gas, loaded the students onto trucks, dumped them at the train station, and told them never to return to the university premises.

So Mafa came full circle, back to the pocked streets of Duncan Village, far from the University of the Witwatersrand and gold and diamond fields. He became a teacher with Masazane, a community-education program whose name means "Let's help one another." He also joined the Duncan Village Residents Association, lobbying for better living conditions and fighting a government plan to forcibly remove the population of the township to make way for a highway.

Mafa sat in on negotiations over a black consumer boycott of white-owned stores in East London. "The chamber says it is up to individual shop owners to push for government reforms, but if the individual shop owner just sits in his shop and says 'Why me? I like blacks' then that's just childish and doesn't address the real problem."

A white who sat across the table from Mafa in negotiations to end the black consumer boycott found him aloof and tough-minded. He doesn't smile or nod, said Donald Card, a former white security police officer who became a liberal city councillor. "It's as though he's telling some of the guys to stop talking already." Card said that when Mafa spoke, no one on the committee disputed him. The young man's poise and self-assurance puzzled Card. "He is very, very deep. I don't trust him 100 percent. He worries me."

In early 1986, Mafa was elected regional publicity secretary of the UDF at a meeting of 250 delegates. That made him a carefully watched man, and, as he drove a friend's beat-up car through Duncan Village, he pointed out a series of unmarked police cars to me. "Cop," he said quietly as we pulled up to a sandwich shop. In the rear view mirror he had noticed a small white car just jutting out from behind a truck across the street. "Cop," he said, hardly glancing at a car parked along another street.

Looking at the tottering houses of Duncan Village and at the army roadblocks that cordoned off the township, Mafa said that this, not Anglo American was the proper place for him. "My capabilities are an asset for the community. I can pinpoint issues and explain them in laymen's terms."

He said this ability was especially important in combatting the government's threat to demolish Duncan Village to create a major highway. Under the plan, the population would be forced to move far away from the white city of East London, to a township called Mdantsane in the Ciskei homeland. In the eyes of the South African government, this would make the residents citizens of another country, the banana republic of Ciskei.

Mafa and the residents' association were exploring alternate routes for the highway. "This is where one's knowledge comes in. One can explain that it is *not* inevitable that people must make way for a road, that there are ways and means to make a road without disrupting community life," said Mafa.

"It's not just Pythagoras and engineering concepts, but social consciousness that's important," he said. "I'm not knocking the intelligent guys who make it after university, but I wish that their acquired knowledge would be useful to the community. You don't go to university to amass a large check balance and the latest BMW."

Tiishang Makgabo—Disappeared

The most mysterious fate of the dozen was that of Tiishang Makgabo, the youngest. Adler said that the boy disappeared without a trace. "Even his parents have no idea what became of him. He might have been mugged and left dead in ditch for all we know."

When a white child vanishes in South Africa, national television runs photographs of the missing child and urges viewers to call an emergency number with information. The disappearance of a young black receives no public attention.

Tiishang's fellow students were convinced he crossed the border and joined the ANC. The ANC refused to comment on whether he was with them or not. Yet how Tiishang was remembered by his former classmates said much about him—and about them.

Tiishang was only sixteen when he started the program. He had been to Waterford, an elite private school in Swaziland where many wealthy blacks send their children. He was one of the most outgoing of the group. To Thomas Mdhluli, Tiishang "was my best friend." He loved to debate big issues. "He would argue about Martin Luther King. He would say King was just a preacher. He never liked the whole idea of worshipping." Thomas, by contrast, was very religious and an admirer of the Soweto cleric Frank Chikane. "Tiishang would come back to the dorm at night and say, 'Do you still believe in God?' " Thomas recalled later. "He would come wake me at 2 A.M. on a Friday night and say let's continue the argument. I developed big respect for him."

Tiishang would argue with Cecil about how to change society. Cecil recalled that "Tiishang wanted change, but he gave up doing it our way. He said it wouldn't work out." Cecil thought real change lay in the economy, and that as long as blacks didn't have a foothold in the economy there wouldn't be change. Tiishang, however, "said we had to have political power."

"He told me he was going to take a major decision with his life," implying that he was going to skip the country, Mafa remembered. "There was nothing I could say. It is a very involved decision. You leave your parents, friends and go to a place you know nothing about. Even the route is questionable. Whether you will make it is questionable."

Tiishang's decision and the uncertainty of his fate hung over the rest of the group. "I don't know if what I'm doing is of any use ultimately," Mafa said in a moment of doubt. "We are just dealing with bread-and-butter issues, with what kind of houses and street lights. Maybe I'm just dealing with the peripherals. I'm not going down to the nitty gritty, which is the handing over of power to the recognized leaders."

"Tiishang was not emotional or violent. He was very much aware of what he was doing," Cecil reflected. "Probably he was right. I respect his judgment. Maybe that little guy was closer to reality than us. I suppose one could think he is some kind of hero. I think so."

CHAPTER ELEVEN

A Lot of Talk

ON A CRISP DAY in April 1986, Carl Coetzer zipped past miles of brush in his car until he came to the small conservative town of Kirkwood. Mr. Coetzer, the fifty-four-year old manager of a bus company in the Eastern Cape province, pulled off under a tree about a mile from the edge of town, where three of his top supervisors were waiting for him. The four men glanced at their watches, looked up the deserted road, and waited.

The top brass of the bus company had assembled in this unlikely setting to negotiate safe passage for their bus service to Kirkwood's black township Bontrug, whose name literally means 'speckled back.' In a few months of unrest, stonings and petrol bomb attacks had disrupted bus service to the township. The toll: one bus completely destroyed, eleven windows smashed, four seats ripped out, and five other attacks costing a total of $90,000.

Eventually the other negotiating partners—nine black teenagers from a youth congress affiliated with the United Democratic Front—appeared in one of the company's buses. The bus pulled up under the tree and the company managers climbed on board. The youths had insisted on the unconventional venue because of police harassment. Mr. Coetzer said he was concerned about the safety of his buses and about the failure of people to pay fares. He also assured the blacks that his company was non-racial and had many white drivers working under black inspectors. Seventeen-year-old Monde Ngonyama, a tenth-grade student who was spokesperson for the township, said they wanted the gutted dirt roads in the township fixed, a bus shelter built, and free transportation for defendants in political cases who need to travel distances to court. Coetzer said he wasn't in the business of fixing roads, but would get the municipality to do something. A bus shelter could be arranged and free transportation was fine for political, but not criminal cases. Ngonyama said he could supply a list of eight people. Coetzer agreed. The two sides shook hands and the deal was done.

Ideally this would be how the arc of black rebellion ended: with a decision by whites and blacks to accommodate each other, treat each other with respect, address socio-economic grievances, and bury political differences.

During South Africa's black uprising, more than two dozen sets of negotiations like this one took place across the racial and ideological divide at local and regional levels. A pattern repeated itself: blacks rebelled, whites reconciled themselves to talking to popular black leadership, blacks put aside mistrust of the white establishment, and UDF affiliates and whites from business and local government met to seek common ground.

There simply wasn't any other way to resolve the conflict. Black organizations like the UDF and the ANC were politically strong; even with belated political reforms, the National Party government couldn't command the loyalty of black South Africans. At the same time, black organizations were militarily weak; they couldn't dislodge the Pretoria government by force alone. Despite twenty-five years of armed struggle and two years of insurrection, the country's infrastructure was essentially intact; an army of 100,000 soldiers, 80,000 police officers, and 200,000 army reservists still stood between the ANC's ramshackle headquarters in Lusaka and the grandiose Union Buildings in Pretoria.

The ANC understood this. Thabo Mbeki told me that he didn't envision himself riding into Pretoria on top of a Russian tank or at the front of an ANC column. Nor did he envision a South African version of the storming of the Bastille or the takeover of the Czar's Winter Palace. Instead, Mbeki believed that chaos—a combination of violence, insurrection, international sanctions, economic decay, the collapse of local government, strikes, and the ANC's mere survival—would bring the government to the negotiating table. "You shoot and shoot and shoot and people keep coming at you," Mbeki told me. "What perspective can Botha have? The more force he uses the more there's trouble. He is obliged to find a solution."

The series of local negotiations provided substance for Mbeki's hopes. Though limited in scope, local talks gave a tantalizing glimpse of a process that could succeed, and of a way that two sides with wildly different images of one another could begin to reconcile their concerns and aspirations.

In many instances, pragmatism and understanding prevailed. Despite revolutionary rhetoric, black leaders showed surprising flexibility and a reluctance to push people past their tolerance for upheaval. White businesspeople and municipal councils showed a willingness to deal with black people whom the state had classified as "revolutionary elements," sometimes discovering with surprise a common sense of patriotism and humanity.

Unfortunately, the lessons of local negotiations weren't entirely encouraging. Only violence—whether in the form of rock throwing, bus vandalism, or bombings—or boycotts persuaded whites to negotiate. Whites wanted stability, and they frankly conceded that talks stemmed from economic pressure and a fear of widening chaos, punctuated by violence.

Moreover, in its attitude toward local negotiations, the central government seemed distant from taking part in the same process at a national level. Pretoria insisted on dealing with negotiating partners who already agreed with the government, labeling others subversive, revolutionary or communist. While paying lip service to "local options" and regional autonomy, the government would not allow local officials to violate three key pieces of apartheid legislation: the Land Act that restricts black freehold, the Group Areas Act that restricts black residency, and the Population Registration Act that classifies every child at birth by race. Those laws—constricted the space available for meaningful compromise. Police and security officials appeared to override civilian leaders trying to negotiate. Other times, talks failed because local government and business leaders failed to deliver on promises. Black negotiators concluded that where the central government sanctioned local negotiations, it did so in bad faith. This fanned mistrust among blacks about whites' true intentions in negotiations.

Violence: Bringing Whites to the Table

In September 1985, the Cape Flats erupted. Home to hundreds of thousands of coloreds, the Cape Flats lie just outside Cape Town, and whites often have to drive past its colored and black townships. Attacks on motorists prompted one police officer to recommend that airport travelers wear crash helmets in their cars to defend against stones thrown from the road. On the flats, youths set up barricades of burning tires and petrol-bombed government buildings. Students boycotted classes and confronted police and troops. Even on the campus of the predominantly white University of Cape Town, police beat and arrested demonstrating students.

From the Shell office tower in downtown Cape Town, Peter Hugo, newly elected president of the Cape town Chamber of Commerce, could see the smoke billowing up from the sandy flats. Rumors floated that the black consumer boycott that gripped Port Elizabeth might spread to Cape Town. Meanwhile in the civic center, City Councillor Clive Keegan was also worried about the violence. A former student political activist, Keegan now drove a bright red sports car. Still, he was eager to redeem the white City Council in the eyes of the broader Cape Town community and to dampen unrest. "It was particularly disturbing in a city that prided itself on a liberal tradition," Keegan said.

So Keegan and the thirty-four-member City Council put out feelers to the UDF about the possibility of forging a non-racial city government that would include representatives from white, colored, Indian, and black segments of the greater metropolitan area. Although apartheid forced the segregation of neighborhoods, ward lines would be redrawn to ensure balanced representation. A common voters' roll would be established and whites would become a minority on the council.

The council encountered deep suspicion among UDF activists about its motives. Most UDF leaders refused to come to the civic center for fear that to be seen walking into the building would be regarded as an act of collaboration. So Keegan went to visit UDF leaders one by one at homes on the Cape Flats. In the six months from March to September 1986, his visits to twenty regional leaders of the front gradually whittled away UDF mistrust. But a new government crackdown got in the way. At least five of the twenty leaders Keegan met were detained. Even before that, UDF leaders appeared worried about maintaining their public stance of refusing to cooperate with any arm of the government. The strong boycott tradition in the Western Cape, fostered by the Unity Movement, made any leader vulnerable to criticism for talking to the "the system." Where participating began and collaborating ended wasn't clear.

At the same time, Peter Hugo of the Chamber of Commerce held a series of meetings with UDF leaders about how to avert a consumer boycott. At the meetings, the white business leaders and UDF leaders swapped stories about personal experiences. UDF regional president Christmas Tinto told the Shell executive anecdotes about torture in detention and about the appalling conditions in black schools. The process of talking, apart from the substance of the bargaining, eased tensions. A boycott never materialized. After hearing the government label the UDF a dangerous, subversive organization, whites were surprised to find the community leaders to be reasonable people with ordinary concerns. "It sounds silly to say they have hopes and aspirations the same as we do," said Hugo.

Without violence on the flats, most blacks believe the City Council and the Chamber of Commerce never would have reached out to black community leaders, despite white Capetonians' protestations about their city's liberal tradition. In the fifteen years since the Nationalist government had kicked all coloreds off the voters' roll, no white official had advanced the idea of a non-racial municipality. "The violence caused us to think again," Keegan conceded later. Hugo agreed, "It was a strange feeling. Cape Town, where I lived, was normal. But five miles away the place was seething. Sometimes I could hear the sounds of blasts. It was over there, but you knew."

The strategic argument against using violence to change South Africa holds that violence only drives whites further into a *laager,* a circle of ox wagons that was used as a defense by Afrikaner pioneers in the 1800s and which still symbolizes the encirclement many whites feel today. The former leader of the Progressive Federalist Party, Frederik Van Zyl Slabbert, argues that violence only scares whites away from dealing with their black opponents. "If you're trying to persuade people that they can survive life with the ANC and the next day they turn on Radio Freedom and they're told they'll get poison in their coffee, what message are you really conveying?"

In interview after interview, however, white businesspeople and officials cited the double-barreled threat of violence and consumer boycotts as the reasons for talking to blacks. "Things got to the stage of almost armed confrontation," the white-haired Port Elizabeth mayor Ivan Krige later told me in the colonial-style sitting room of the St. George's Club. "We thought it was essential to find out what they wanted. It was the only thing left to do."

The effect on Port Elizabeth's white establishment was dramatic. Unrest in Port Elizabeth's four biggest black townships first forced officials to roll back a rent increase. After more than half the black community councillors resigned and black police fled the townships, Krige met with the Port Elizabeth Black Civic Organization (PEBCO) leaders and called for a non-racial municipality.

By that time, the city was besieged by consumer boycotts. In 1986, a quarter of the members of the city's Chamber of Commerce closed their doors after a second consumer boycott. As a result, the Chamber of Commerce began acting like a UDF affiliate. It protested to cabinet ministers, fed the families of detainees, provided free transportation for political funerals, and supported calls for a wildcat general strike to celebrate the unrecognized holiday of May Day. In later talks, the chamber and PEBCO drew up a plan to buy land and set up a self-sustaining, non-racial residential area in open violation of apartheid laws. The Midland Chamber of Industries proposed that a non-racial municipality incorporate the white city of Port Elizabeth and its colored and black townships. The plan said that a combined budget should be allotted to blacks and whites on an equal, per capita basis. This proposal was revolutionary in a society built on white privilege; it would force government to slash spending on white roads, services, and education.

The threats to physical and financial security unsettled whites in dozens of other towns. In Port Alfred, the two-week consumer boycott in 1985 prompted whites to invite black leaders to white town-council meetings. The white town also petitioned the minister of constitutional planning to permit a non-racial municipality. (No answer was ever received.)

In Oudtshoorn, a small arid town known mainly for ostrich farming, the white town council invited members of the local civic organization (a UDF affiliate) to discuss their grievances after a community councillor was killed, cars stoned, and a consumer and bus boycott imposed.

Bringing Blacks to the Table

Violence and boycotts might bring whites to the table, but why should blacks agree to talk and compromise? Black South Africans have every reason to be wary about negotiations with whites. Talks usually have preceded betrayal. The most searing memory dates from 1960, when a twenty-three year-old wearing shorts led a crowd of more than 15,000 people on a march from a black township through downtown Cape Town to within a couple of blocks of Parliament. A police commander later said he prayed at the sight of the crowd. Beleaguered officials promised young Philip Kgosana, a Pan Africanist Congress member, that he could meet with the minister of justice if he asked the crowd to disperse. Kgosana agreed and the crowd dutifully complied. But later that day when he arrived for his meeting, he was arrested. The lesson for most blacks is that Kgosana should have pressed the crowd forward, and that by failing to do so, he squandered a rare opportunity.

Despite revolutionary rhetoric and the suspicion that the government would use talks to identify leaders to arrest, rather than grievances to redress, black community leaders have remained ready to meet with white leaders. Unrest takes its toll in black communities, and consumer boycotts impose inconveniences on township residents as well. Eager to deliver concrete gains to blacks, black community leaders have mixed confrontation with negotiation.

Mark Swilling attributed this stance to the swelling membership in community organizations.

> Like trade unions, once community organizations have created a mass base, this base needs to be sustained over time by winning, through struggle, short-term gains that improve aspects of daily living, i.e., real material concessions are required to demonstrate the benefits of collective action."[1]

Sometimes the best-laid plans went awry. On July 15, 1985, the day that the consumer boycott started in Port Elizabeth, boycott committee spokesperson Mkhuseli Jack telephoned Chamber of Commerce official Tony Gilson to assure him that they could begin negotiations in about a week, after blacks had flexed their buying power. Before the end of the week, however, President Botha had declared the state of emergency; the detention of Jack and other Port Elizabeth leaders prevented the talks from taking place.

(In November, Jack used a ruse to spur the Chamber of Commerce to action. Jack was mistakenly released after being acquitted on a minor offense in magistrate's court. Realizing that he would be redetained within hours under the emergency regulations, he went straight to see Gilson. He pledged to negotiate an end to the now-four-month-old consumer boycott. Gilson was thrilled. Then Jack asked Gilson to take him to the prison to collect his clothes, knowing that he would be redetained. At the prison, Jack informed a warden in Xhosa that he had come to hand himself over after his mistaken release. Jack and Gilson then stood there waiting with opposite expectations. Jack's expectations were fulfilled. When police redetained him, Gilson was outraged and, as Jack hoped, galvanized the chamber of commerce into action.)

The following year, after the end of the emergency, Jack was free and still pursuing a strategy of negotiation. He visited an area committee meeting at the height of another consumer boycott. Negotiations must take place, he told them. If blacks refused to talk, he said, whites would unite against them. Privately he said national negotiations must take place, too, and that he envisioned a compromise similar to that in Zimbabwe, where whites retained special privileges and protections for a limited period of time.

Port Elizabeth's black leaders kept up contact with the local Chamber of Commerce even while police were trying to round up activists. Sometimes intricate arrangements were made to maintain contact. Gilson was instructed to go to a factory gate, where a car passed by twice. On its third pass the driver motioned to Gilson to follow in his car. At a point inside the township they all piled into a third car and took a circuitous route to a house where members of PEBCO waited.

Though the Port Elizabeth leadership acted in unison, other black township leaders were torn about whether to negotiate with whites. In Oudtshoorn, residents of the black township Bhongolethu (which means "blessings") asked their representatives to negotiate a list of grievances. But some local activists disapproved. "I objected to meeting," said Reggie Oliphant, a colored community leader. "I withdrew my support from my comrades. I feared the municipality was coming to lure our people with beautiful promises. I know they aren't sincere and that they are not ready for fundamental changes."

Nevertheless popular opinion in Bhongolethu wanted a committee of ten (two youths, two ministers, two teachers, two parents, and two members of the women's organization) to speak with the town council. At a meeting, the Bhongolethu committee presented a list of complaints. The town council gave the committee a proposed constitution for Bhongolethu, which the blacks rejected because they believed it was a trick to get them to ratify government structures. Instead the tiny township adopted its own constitution, which read like an American independence manifesto: "We the residents of Bhongolethu, believe that each and every individual has a democratic right to live wherever he or she likes. We are also conscious that true consultations will take place when all people are represented at all levels of government."

After talks broke off, the white town council rectified many of blacks' material grievances. It built new houses, a new school and a new clinic for the black township. It installed a sewer system. But the political goal of recognition for the democratically elected civic association wasn't met. Moreover, many community leaders were detained.

As a result, the merit of negotiations remained in question despite the projects undertaken. "There is no clear thinking on this," said Sterra Stone, one of the Bhongolethu committee members. "Some people think consultations led to the improvements. Activists think it was a waste of time." Fellow committee member Mzukisi Skosana said "Even without meetings there would have been upgrading. People in Oudtshoorn were worried about unrest." Reggie Oliphant remained as adamant as ever. "The upgrading of the township was a response to resistance, not to negotiations," he said. "These meetings where the state makes offers are part of a strategy to destroy the unity we have tried to form among the people for so many years. I'm completely opposed to negotiating before certain conditions are met."

Still, popular sentiment for peaceful negotiations runs strong in the black townships. Conflict takes its heaviest toll among blacks. Of the more than 2,500 people killed in political unrest during South Africa's worst fighting years, only a handful were whites. Stone and Skosana said that if the township residents again asked them to consult with white authorities, they would do so.

Black leaders in other communities said the same. Representatives of Duncan Village spent months negotiating with the East London City Council and the city's National Party member of Parliament about plans that would upgrade Duncan Village. Just when talks appeared to be making progress, the government tried to resuscitate the discredited community councillors, who had fled the township. Negotiations fell apart. Months later I met Matron Andromeda Mbalu, a nurse who was the last free member of the Duncan Village Residents Association; all the others had been detained. Nevertheless, Mbalu said

> The people must be party to negotiations. Even the central committee [of the residents' association] shouldn't dictate to the people. And the people can't just be like a child and reject everything. We hate to be told what is good for us and we have a right to air our aspirations. It was worthwhile to talk. We told them what the black community wants.

In 1987, long after open political activity ended, Rev. Mcebisi Xundu of Port Elizabeth told me that he was still talking to government officials from the Department of Education and Training. Xundu himself wasn't optimistic about the talks, which so far had only produced an increased supply of stationery. Complaints about teachers, curricula, student representative councils, segregation, books, fees, and facilities went unheeded. "The government has its own solution and it thinks it is the only solution. Black leadership is considered to be moderate if it is subservient." But Xundu said he continued to talk "so our people know that everything humanly possible is being done. It is important for mobilizing people for them to realize that the government is being intransigent. Some thought that insufficient effort was made before last year's school boycott."

Back to School

The negotiations to end black school boycotts show how skilled black leaders can be at marshaling black opinion, a key element if national negotiations are ever to succeed. School boycotts had broken out intermittently since 1976. The boycotts spread in December 1983 and January 1984 after the dismissal of Matthew Goniwe as Cradock school principal. They escalated after the Vaal Uprising. As political unrest intensified, students tacked political demands onto their already lengthy list of educational demands. Violence hit school facilities: of the twenty-two higher-primary and eleven high schools in Port Elizabeth's townships, four were destroyed and 40 percent damaged by fire.

Black adults, who treasured whatever education their children could obtain, didn't like the boycotts. Legions of unschooled children would undermine long-term black economic advancement. Even if the boycotts ended, "It would be difficult for students to regain their motivation for learning," said Vusi Khanyile, an accountant and Soweto parent. "You don't just switch that on and off. It's a process, sometimes over generations."

But parents found it difficult to argue with the students. Donald Ncube, the highest-ranking black at Anglo American Corporation, could see why his children might not want to attend school. "It becomes difficult to say that they shouldn't be the way they are," he told me. "We parents say, 'Look at the alternatives,' and they say, 'Look at you. You have the education and you still don't sit on the board of Ango American.' And they're right."

In September 1985, the Soweto Civic Association called an open meeting at St. Margaret's church in the Diepkloof section of Soweto to discuss the black school boycotts that had disrupted two consecutive years of education. Though the boycotts had been spotty in Soweto, since the July declaration of a state of emergency and the banning of COSAS, all schooling had come to a standstill. At one point the police locked up the entire student body of one school, numbering more than 500. Panicked parents, many of them never before involved in politics, hurried to the police station to demand the pupils' release.

The St. Margaret's church meeting was advertized by word of mouth and by an ad in *The Sowetan* newspaper. Nearly 2,000 people crowded into the church pews. Dr. Nthato Motlana, chair of the Soweto Civic Association, rose to address the meeting. Standing before the altar, he bluntly warned that school boycotts were becoming self-defeating. Motlana warned that "Unlearned children cannot rule." He reminded them that the architects of apartheid had wanted blacks to be uneducated so they could be nothing but hewers of wood and carriers of water. Promoters of school boycotts had valid complaints about second-rate education, he said, but no education at all was worse. It would fulfill the wishes of apartheid's founders, such as Hendrik Verwoerd, who once asked Parliament, "What is the use of teaching a Bantu child mathematics when it cannot use it in practice?"

The audience murmured when he sat down. Themba Phiri, a reedy youth sitting quietly next to me edged past me, and walked up to the front of the church. Phiri said that the government had failed to meet students' educational demands, which included recognition of student representative councils, the abolition of corporal punishment, a unified education department for all races and better-qualified teachers. According to the government's statistics, 80 percent of teachers in black schools were underqualified. In some cases, teachers with tenth-grade educations were teaching eleventh or twelfth grade mathematics. And the government conceded that the average black primary-school class contained forty-five pupils, compared to twenty in the average white classroom.

Moreover, the government hadn't met the students' political conditions: the release of detained students, the unbanning of the Congress of South African Students, lower food prices, freedom for Nelson Mandela, and the withdrawal of police and troops from the townships. After each stanza of grievances, murmurs of outrage grew louder. How could students go back to school when white soldiers were patrolling the schools, he asked rhetorically. Students were not safe while troops were occupying the township. As if for extra emphasis, an armored car full of white soldiers drove by the church while he spoke, and people nervously glanced over their shoulders. Phiri said, "When I'm on the street in my shoes, I've got no protection. When I'm in school, I've got no protection. When I'm in my mother's yard, I've got no protection. Where should we go? We are not going to write [exams] until we get our demands." He finished to thunderous applause.

Others followed suit. Speeches grew angrier. One youth charged that soldiers were raping students. Another said children were being "trampled by the iron feet of apartheid." Yet another said, "If we give the schoolchildren shit, they will give us shit. I say, if they want shit, they must go to Tambo's men; he will give them shit." Someone walked through the church shouting "Viva, ANC, Viva" and the crowd roared "Viva."

In defense of the school boycotts, youths said that parents' passivity had left the burden of the liberation struggle on students. Parents, feeling guilty, concurred. "We must fight with our children. They must shoot us, the parents, first," said a man in a suit and bright red tie. "We must move together as one!"

Ethel Mokoena, a stout woman wearing a black beret, said education for blacks had been second rate for too long. "If you can ask a black doctor a question, he won't be able to answer it," she said in a backhanded slap at Motlana. It was a measure of the increasing militance of black politics that Motlana, whose views had changed little since the height of his prominence in the late 1970s, had become an object to derision among many Sowetans.

Then civic association leaders took charge of the meeting, reminding the people "that we may never be able to meet again as we are today." As an army vehicle circled behind the church, the leaders hurriedly decided that parents would march in support of students and resolved that parents and students would form an education committee so they could speak "with one mouth."

The committee that emerged from the meeting took the name Soweto Parents Crisis Committee (SPCC). Its formation was the first of a series of deft political maneuvers by blacks, who felt the school boycott had outlasted its usefulness. Within months, hundreds of thousands of black schoolchildren went back to school, marking an uneasy truce in the battle over the black education.

By hammering parents for inactivity, the students unwittingly set themselves up for parents to take charge of the school issue. Adults on the Diepkloof branch of the civic association had insisted that no more than fifty students attend the St. Margaret's meeting. "We said we didn't want them to bulldoze the parents," said Vusi Khanyile, a member of the SPCC. Students also were in the minority on the twelve-person SPCC, which included two students, two teachers, and several parents.

As soon as the committee was formed, it set about to convince the students to go back to school. Motlana was dispatched to the East Rand, his home region, to talk to students. In a big hall in Katlehong township, Motlana told youths that the crisis committee would negotiate with the government and then insist that the youths go back to school. "Boy, was I in trouble. These kids, just fourteen or fifteen years old, looked at me like I was a piece of dirt," Motlana said later. The students coined the slogan, "No education before liberation," saying that the second-rate education for blacks was worthless.

To take exams, a nineteen-year-old student leader told me, "would make a mockery of everything we've been fighting for." The government hadn't given in to any of the students' demands, and the Congress of South African Students was still banned.

But the SPCC pressed on. "If I wanted to make them really mad, I would tell them that their heroes, Biko and [Aubrey] Mokoena went through Bantu Education," Motlana said.

Other townships formed committees of parents, teachers, and students in an effort to break the schools deadlock. In December, 160 local committees formed the National Education Crisis Committee and scheduled a meeting in Johannesburg at the University of the Witwatersrand.

Even the new national body, whose stature among black youths was higher than Motlana's, couldn't hope to sway the sentiment of black schoolkids on its own. Black students, in Motlana's words, "were under the impression that the organization out there [i.e., the ANC] was in favor of the school boycott."

Indeed, many ANC leaders sided with the students. One black leader was taken by car in London to a secret location where three members of the ANC national executive committee—Joe Slovo, Aziz Pahad, and Alfred Nzo—said they thought that without the school boycotts, the country's revolutionary fervor would die down. But the black leader from South Africa said that by the time liberation came, the ANC would be faced with a whole generation of illiterates at home. Already, black results on matriculation exams needed to go on to university were scandalously low. Advances in the workplace toward semi-skilled and managerial jobs would slow down as a result. "I was in meetings with student leaders from Fort Hare University," one black leader said, referring to the university where Mandela, Tambo and Zimbabwean Prime Minister Robert Mugabe went, "and the guys can't even speak English."

The ANC had another reason to worry about calling for an end to school boycotts. When asked by an American businessman why the ANC didn't tell the schoolchildren to return to class, Tambo said, "What if they don't go back?" The ANC was popular, but its authority largely untested. If masses of black youths failed to heed the ANC's call, it would be a terrible blow to the ANC's prestige.

Eventually the ANC gave in. On Christmas Day, three days before the Wits conference meeting, NECC leaders Vusi Khanyile, Eric Molobi, and H. H. Dlamlenze, the general secretary of the largest teachers' association, went to Lusaka to get the ANC's blessing for its efforts. Four members of the ANC—Chris Hani, Pallo Jordan, Mac Maharaj, and Thomas Nkobi—gave them a written response on behalf of the organization endorsing the NECC's efforts to end the boycotts in consultation with students.

"We used that thing," Motlana recalled. The NECC changed the students' slogan from "Liberation now, education later" to "People's education for people's power." The NECC issued eight demands to the government, but it also decided that blacks would return to school on January 28, 1986. Another meeting was scheduled for the end of March, where Zwelakhe Sisulu was to deliver his historic speech about people's power.

The NECC persuaded children to return to school for tactical reasons. "Workers cannot develop working-class consciousness or power if they are not in the factories to organize together. [Similarly] pupils can only organize and become a force for change . . . if they are at school. Student structures were increasingly weakened by almost two years of stayaway and a general breakdown in discipline," said Ihron Rensburg, national secretary of the NECC.[2] Vusi Khanyile added, "By being an educated activist you'll be a better activist."

Reluctantly, most black schoolchildren went back to class while the NECC started talks with the government. It extracted some concessions from the Department of Education and Training. But while the NECC was able to marshal black opinion, the Department of Education and Training proved less adept at marshalling white opinion. Cabinet members overruled members of the department and reneged on agreements. Moreover, the leaders of the NECC were arrested. To some blacks, it was another lesson in betrayal.

Who Negotiates?

Just as the South African government refused to recognize the ANC as representative of black South Africans, local officials often tried to circumvent the civic associations that represent black townships. Just as the South

African government accused the ANC of being controlled by Moscow, white town clerks often accused civic associations of being instigated by people from other parts of the country.

In the squalid township of Lawaaikamp outside the white city of George, a civic association formed when the municipality threatened to bulldoze the shacks of Lawaaikamp and move people a couple of miles further away from town. In the meantime, the municipality wanted to double rents. George did not plan to pay any compensation for Lawaaikamp homes, where some people had lived for years. One house I visited, though ramshackle on the outside, had tile floors, plaster walls, glass windows, doors, and a carefully laid wooden ceiling.

In theory, something had to be done about Lawaaikamp. Four water taps served more than 5,000 people; the municipality removed excrement only once a week; and there was no electricity. Officially the land was zoned for coloreds, but blacks had settled there slowly over forty years because there was no area designated for blacks in George. The entire region had been a "colored labor preference" area and blacks weren't supposed to move there.

As in other areas, the search for negotiating partners began only after violence erupted. All black municipal workers went on strike one day in February 1986 and were promptly dismissed. Stonings and petrol bombings followed and police killed five people later that month. On March 1, Rev. Allan Boesak spoke at a church service and had to plunge into a crowd to save a suspected informer from being necklaced. Afterwards, 250 people ran through Lawaaikamp shouting slogans, led by a man in combat fatigues and another waving an imitation AK-47. Shortly afterwards, calls for negotiations came from provincial officials and from the National Party Member of Parliament for George. On April 10, the municipal council granted a temporary reprieve to Lawaaikamp.

The municipality initially insisted on speaking to a group it had appointed called the Liaison Committee. The Liaison Committee was made up of eight people, five of them pensioners, and only one of whom could read or write. After the first meeting in which the Liaison Committee informed Lawaaikamp residents of the plans for removal, the committee didn't dare set foot in the shantytown again.

The new civic association had a different complexion. Among its thirteen members were a floor manager at a food-marketing firm, an articulate clerk from a hotel-reservations desk, the owner of a general dealer's store, a teacher, a union shop steward and machine operator at a frozen vegetable plant, a law student, a truck driver, a switchboard operator, and a saleswoman at a furniture store.

The white town clerk, however, refused to recognize the civic association. He believed white liberals were behind the group. He called the association "politically inspired." Instead he threatened the residents. He issued eviction notices, ordered the bulldozing of 150 households, and sent officials to shout warnings and appeals through a loudspeaker. He convened an open community meeting to elect new leaders, but residents insisted that the civic association had to be consulted.

As the outcry grew over the forced removal of the community, the town clerk buckled under to pressure from the residents, the National Party Member of Parliament and the provincial executive. The clerk, Carel du Plessis, conceded that "Certain principles need to be discussed with the whole community" and an official with the provincial executive said "We recognize the civic as the representative body of the Lawaaikamp people." Both still insisted that Lawaaikamp be moved in order to enforce the policy of racially separate communities. But at least they were listening. The civic commissioned a plan for upgrading the community which the town clerk said he wouldn't dismiss out of hand.

Until whites dealt with true black leaders, no progress could be made toward a peaceful settlement of conflict. The government had to accept the political profile of the black townships. In big cities, the civics usually included old-time ANC activists. Half the Port Elizabeth Black Civic Organization's executive was made up of people who had served in Umkhonto we Sizwe in the early 1960s and had been released after long prison sentences. "I don't have to go to Lusaka to talk to the ANC," joked Tony Gilson of the Port Elizabeth Chamber of Commerce, "I can talk to them here." The leadership also sprang from the working class, the unemployed (who number up to half of the people in urban areas) and youths like those from Kirkwood.

Such youthfulness needn't be an obstacle, as the negotiations between the bus company and teenagers from Kirkwood showed. "We appreciate their [the company's] presence. Others didn't come and talk to us," said the teenage Ngonyama after the bus conference. "We burned their buses, but this is like a treaty of peace. They are saying that they are part and parcel of these whites who want negotiations with black leaders." On his way home, the bus company manager, Coetzer, reflected that Ngonyama "is only seventeen, but he seems articulate and he wouldn't have been there if he didn't have support of the people in the township. The biggest thing I can give them is to recognize them as leaders of their community." He said he didn't doubt that the youths could deliver on their promise of safe passage for the buses. After December 1985, although unrest increased, PE Tramways lost only two buses. Coetzer himself had attended a township funeral, at one point charging across the road to an armored car to yell at police who had started firing tear gas and rubber bullets at the crowd.

The *indaba* (Zulu for "meeting") in Natal was the most overt attempt to stage talks as a model for a national settlement. KwaZulu homeland Chief Minister Mangosuthu Gatsha Buthelezi longed to show that his conciliatory approach to whites could yield dividends. Natal's whites hoped the talks would pose an alternative to rebellion and repression. Instead, the *indaba* showed that who talks is as important as what people talk about.

The delegates to the conference included big business interests (especially the province's sugar barons), the government of the KwaZulu homeland (headed by Buthelezi), and provincial officials from the New Republic Party and the Progressive Federalist Party. They sought to merge the white provincial government of Natal and the black homeland government of KwaZulu. It was, as one of its promoters called it admiringly, "a cartel of interests." Unlike the Eastern Cape meetings which took place in secret, the *indaba* was held in the open amid much ceremony, with the consent, if not participation, of the central government.

In substance, the proposals that emerged from the *indaba* were plausible. After more than a year of wrangling, the participants designed a non-racial lower parliamentary house based on one person, one vote, and an upper house divided according to race. The prime minister of the region would come from the majority party of the lower house. Ethnic and racial groups would have certain entrenched "cultural" rights.

Unfortunately, neither the ANC nor the UDF nor the National Party took part in the talks. The ANC (for practical as well as principled reasons) turned down an invitation to attend. The UDF also declined, suspecting that Buthelezi and the white provincial establishment would cut a deal to entrench their own interests. National Party representatives only attended as observers. After encouraging the *indaba* exercise, the government simply shelved the proposals.

The *indaba* showed that in order to negotiate a lasting settlement, bargaining would have to include representative blacks, including the ANC, and the National Party. Because of their popularity and power, they can forge or wreck any agreement. Whatever the merits of the *indaba* proposals, they have gone nowhere.

Suspension of Disbelief

Those two most crucial and stubborn parties to any political agreement in South Africa remained far apart. The ANC laid down certain preconditions for talks: an end to the state of emergency, the removal of troops from the townships, the release of Nelson Mandela and other political prisoners, the unbanning of the ANC, and an acknowledgment that talks would lead to majority rule.

The government refused to meet those conditions. It said the ANC had to renounce violence, its only bargaining chip. "I don't think you speak to terrorists," President Botha said in an interview in his office in October 1985.

The ANC's strategy for changing the government's position rested on duplicating nationwide the conditions that UDF affiliates created locally. It used the combined threats of economic decay and violence, while asserting its openness to whites and its eagerness to pursue peaceful avenues. Bombs and economic sanctions articulated the threatening part of that posture. Diplomatic overtures to white South Africans outside government expressed the more flexible posture.

In the early 1980s, the ANC's Harare representative Joe Gqabi met with groups of Afrikaans students, including the grandson and namesake of apartheid's architect Hendrik Verwoerd. Gqabi was assassinated shortly afterwards, but the younger Verwoerd later voiced doubts about apartheid.

The ANC also made contact with whites at higher levels. In New York, Mbeki dined with the chairman of the Broederbond, the secret society of white South Africa's power elite. Mbeki had invited the Broederbond chair Pieter de Lange to lunch after a heated exchange between de Lange and another ANC man who took part in the same panel discussion. The ANC man had threatened someday to kill people like de Lange. Mbeki's lunch invitation smoothed things over. De Lange went away impressed: "He is cosmopolitan, sophisticated, and quite a likeable fellow."

White households, chosen at random, were sent letters from the ANC. Postmarked from Zimbabwe, the outside of each envelope had drawings of a giraffe and a lion. The letter inside appealed to whites through their pocketbooks. "The standard of living of most South Africans is dropping daily," the letter said, citing the deteriorating economy, the falling rand, high interest rates, and heavy taxes. Warning of further bloodshed, the letter added, "Do not delude yourself that the war will simply go away. It won't."

The ANC believed whites were shaken by both ANC appeals and domestic revolt. Although insulated from unrest in the townships, whites seemed to lack the zeal that once bolstered them. Mbeki noted the high rate of white emigration, capital flight, and absenteeism from military reserve duty as evidence of a white crisis of confidence. Indeed a white South African who had me to dinner told me a joke about a friend who said his son was learning the Zulu alphabet. "Really," my host said he answered. "Yes," the proud father answered, "it starts with A, N, and C."

For a few weeks in early 1986, it looked as though the government might bend and talk to the ANC. In order to forestall sanctions in late 1985, the British government persuaded the Commonwealth to form a delegation to mediate between the government and the ANC, a seemingly hopeless task. The delegation, known as the Eminent Persons Group (EPG), was a distinguished collection of individuals. It included the conservative Lord Barber of Wentbridge, chair of the Standard Chartered Bank, which at the time had a big subsidiary in South Africa. The co-chairpeople of the group were Malcolm Fraser, former prime minister of Australia, and General Olusegun Obasanjo, former military head of state in Nigeria, one of Africa's few leaders to step down from office voluntarily.

Though the South African government vowed that it would never yield to outside pressure, it made the EPG welcome. The EPG's presence was something of a curiosity, given South Africa's diplomatic isolation. Some cabinet ministers even believed they had found a sympathetic ear in Obasanjo, with his knowledge of Nigerian tribal tensions and his sobering experience during Nigeria's bloody civil war.

On April 24, with the Commonweath's six-month deadline approaching, South African foreign minister R. F. "Pik" Botha wrote to the EPG to say the group "could serve a useful purpose" and to encourage the EPG to pursue "the modalities of achieving a suspension of violence and facilitating discussions."

Botha's letter appeared to be a minor breakthrough. The government's insistence that the ANC renounce violence before entering talks had been the major stumbling block. The Commonwealth group had urged a more modest cease-fire. "It was neither possible nor reasonable to have people forswear the only power available to them should the government walk away from the negotiating table," the group asserted. The letter from Pik Botha used the phrase "suspension of violence" twice, suggesting that a cease-fire would be acceptable. The foreign minister also referred to the possibility of lifting the ban on the ANC and PAC.[3]

The EPG rushed forward with a draft proposal for talks. It met with Tambo in Lusaka and Mandela at Pollsmoor Prison. The ANC consented to a suspension of violence. It was good politics to appear flexible and stake out the moral high ground.

Within three weeks, however, things fell apart. On May 15, President Botha gave a nationwide address on television complaining of foreign interference. The EPG sustained some hope, however, because the president also lay down certain "reform" principles that could be interpreted as encouraging. Such hopes soon vanished. On May 16, the group again met with Mandela, who expressed enthusiasm. But later the next day, the group met with Pik Botha, who backtracked from his April 24 letter. He returned to the government's former position, demanding that the ANC lay down arms permanently. He denounced outside pressure and questioned whether the ANC was an appropriate negotiating partner.

On May 19, the South African Defense Force carried out raids against alleged ANC targets in Botswana, Zambia, and Zimbabwe—all Commonwealth members—making the EPG's mission impossible. Some government analysts believe that the doves in the foreign ministry lost a power struggle to the hawks of the defense establishment. But whatever the reason for the attacks, the Commonwealth group felt betrayed. "It was all too plain that, while talking to the group about negotiations and peaceful solutions, the government had been planning these armed attacks," the group wrote later.[4]

A last letter from Pik Botha, dated May 29, sealed the mission's failure. The foreign minister equivocated about the government's need to guarantee freedom of assembly and discussion when security was at stake. He rejected a mere suspension of violence. "To use violence or the threat of violence as a bargaining counter is unacceptable," he wrote. And Botha affirmed that the government would go at its own pace. It would not discuss a "transfer of power." The government would promote "power sharing" through legislation handed out as part of "a new constitutional dispensation."

The EPG concluded that the government's reservations about the ANC concealed a "deeper truth": the "government believes that it can contain the situation indefinitely by the use of force. We were repeatedly told by ministers that the government had deployed only a fraction of the power at its disposal."[5] If the South African government couldn't talk to black leaders like Tambo and Mandela, men who, despite years of exile and imprisonment, display statecraft and a surprising lack of rancor, then, the group concluded, the outlook for negotiations was "bleak indeed."

Some time later, a cabinet minister went to dinner at the home of an Afrikaans business leader. The cabinet minister boasted that the government was still strong. The business leader replied that if that were true, the government should negotiate while it was in a position of strength. Time, he said, would only weaken the government as sanctions gathered strength and the size of the black population grew. The cabinet minister replied that the government would talk only when it had to.

Dispensations

Negotiations at local and regional levels, as well as the EPG talks, left mixed feelings among black South Africans. On the one hand, such talks gave a feel for what might have been and might still be. "If in these small measures, people get together, it can be instructive for the future," observed Jakes Gerwel, the rector of the University of the Western Cape. "They are microexperiments in South Africans living and working together and negotiating together."

But local and regional exercises in negotiation were in the end nothing more than exercises. Every one of the local and regional negotiations failed because of the lack of commitment of the central government, which controls purse strings and the extensive security apparatus. No local or regional accord could survive long while national issues remained unresolved.

As a result, while Gerwel called local negotiations "instructive," many blacks believed the lesson of negotiations with whites was that negotiations were a waste of time. The government treated local negotiations as a tactic of procrastination, or a forum for blacks to concede to the government's views, or, still worse, as a way to identify its most prominent opponents before arresting them. Gerwel noted that blacks viewed limited talks "largely as attempts to circumvent the central process, which is a revolutionary one."

In February, 1986, Bishop Tutu intervened with Alexandra residents to end three days of clashes with police. Tutu calmed militant residents by promising he would personally take their complaints to President Botha. To

Tutu, no issue could seem more important to the nation. At least nineteen people had died in three days of fighting in the township. At one point, a black sniper shot a police officer and held an entire contingent of police at bay by shooting at those who went to help the fatally wounded officer. But when Tutu got to Cape Town, President Botha refused to grant Tutu an audience. Instead the Anglican bishop was shunted aside to Adriaan Vlok, a right-wing lifetime bureaucrat who was then Deputy Minister of Law and Order. Vlok gave Tutu no assurances about the issues that upset Alexandra residents and Tutu went back to Alexandra empty handed. When Tutu reported on his meeting at the Alexandra stadium, a crowd of about 45,000 people booed. For a while, angry youths obstructed the exit from the stadium and menaced Tutu. "Those of us who still believe in negotiations only show that talking doesn't work," said Rev. Frank Chikane later. "Bishop Tutu's exercise is proof. People say 'Now we'll use our methods. Your methods don't work.' "

A young friend of mine from Athlone put it more succinctly. "The problem with 'power sharing' is that whites will never give away things. They'd have to be cuckoo. You'll have to stand there with a gun in your hands."

In certain towns and cities, crisis forced people to negotiate. But on a national level, the sense of crisis wasn't sharp enough. Only 10,000 to 15,000 troops had been deployed at any one time, according to Defence Minister General Magnus Malan.

Moreover a commencement of national negotiations required a leap of imagination that the National Party government hadn't made yet. The increase in spending on facilities in black townships, the abolition of the pass laws restricting black movements, and the loosening of restrictions of black business ventures and careers changed the face of apartheid—all part of what the government called the "new dispensation." But the extent and outcome of these measures were controlled by the government. This style was called "authoritarian reform" or "reform from above." Blacks were expected simply to receive them like morsels from a banquet. Indeed, the word "dispensation" was a telling one, for the act of dispensing—to give out or distribute in portions—is very different from the act of negotiating.

PART 3

The Government Strikes Back

CHAPTER TWELVE

Crackdown and Breakdown

And I ask you
I ask you
I ask you so nice
Why are those dogs barking at the gates of Paradise.
—David Kramer, Afrikaans songwriter

ONE DAY NEAR THE MIDDLE OF 1986, Mrs. Mashinini tapped the wooden table in her living room, as though it could give her dream timber. In her dream, she said, liberation arrives and her three exiled sons come back to South Africa from Liberia, Angola, and Tanzania. They walk in the front door of the Mashinini house in central Soweto and sit down for lunch at the wooden table, a lunch as ordinary and spectacular as waking up.

As the tenth anniversary of the 1976 Soweto student rebellion approached, more and more black South Africans dared to dream such dreams. Fezi Tshabalala, the youth who on June 16, 1976, passed the day playing pinball at the bus station near Baragwanath Hospital, assured me that "We're going to be free very, very soon. It won't take long, I'm sure of that."

Who could stave off a tremendous sense of anticipation by the middle of 1986? The government seemed to be retreating in the face of international and domestic uproar. In March, the government had lifted the year-old state of emergency, apparently eager to ease the gathering pressure for the Commonwealth nations to pass economic sanctions against South Africa. In April, the government had abolished the pass laws, preempting a deadline set by the black trade-union federation, COSATU, whose president threatened to call on members to burn their passes. On May 1, blacks made a show of force as unprecedented numbers stayed home from work to celebrate May Day. Even the state-owned coal-to-oil Sasol plant had recognized the workers' strength by agreeing to let its employees leave at noon to attend May Day rallies. Later that month, residents of Soweto launched a boycott of rent and service charges paid to the government. With the approach of Halley's Comet, even the heavens seemed to be sending a sign.

But hopes for liberation were mixed with nagging fears that the countdown to the June 16 anniversary would end in a showdown between black anti-apartheid groups and the government. Amidst blacks' gains, there were signs of stiffening attitudes among whites. In Warmbaths, a sleepy resort town known for its hot springs, blacks called a two-day general strike on March 3 to protest police brutality, rent increases, and corporal punishment in a local primary school.

Such protests were common. But this time, Warmbaths boiled over. Whites circulated a pamphlet that asked "Isn't Warmbaths beautiful all white?" and urged employers to fire any blacks who stayed home. White boys not more than nine or ten years old substituted for black workers at filling stations, wrestling with gasoline hoses that were too heavy for them and wearing work shirts that hung down around their knees. A woman in a sandwich shop said, "Some customers say they enjoy the food more when it's been made with white hands."

Blacks responded by staying home another ten days.

Warmbaths showed how bitter the escalating conflict could become. Every day, nationwide, three to four people—almost all of them black—were being killed in politically related violence. The government, like the whites of Warmbaths, had shown its stubborn streak by breaking off talks with the Commonwealth's Eminent Persons Group and bombing alleged ANC bases on May 19.

Tensions were rising. Schoolchildren, unhappy over the government's failure to live up to the agreement made with the National Education Crisis Committee, were threatening to go back on strike. There were rumors about a possible ANC guerilla offensive timed to coincide with the tenth anniversary. All over Johannesburg and Soweto, posters were appearing with the slogan "Ten Fighting Years" and the famous photograph of a boy carrying the body of Hector Petersen, the first victim in 1976, with his sister running and crying alongside. A national student newspaper printed the same photo with the date June 16 in red ink running down the page like blood. Behind the three figures were dozens of names of people who were killed in the 1976 rebellion. One headline described June 16 as "the day that never ended" and the cover declared that "the spirit lives on."

"Things are so tense here in Soweto," a township resident said, "it is as though someone poured petrol all over the floor and we're just waiting for someone to throw the first match."

Emergency—Again

In early-morning raids on June 12, heavily armed police seized documents from community organizations and trade-union offices and arrested union leaders, clergy, and activists. More than 2,000 people were arrested in a few hours. Later that day, President Botha declared a state of emergency, an announcement delayed so as not to tip off activists, who might go into hiding. Unlike the 1985 emergency, the new clamps applied to the entire nation, not just selected districts.

There was a recklessness to the government's emergency declaration, given the certainty that Europe and the United States would answer with economic sanctions. The government seemed resigned to any international repercussions. "The government is aware that stricter security measures will bring criticism and punitive measures from the outside world. But South Africa will not crawl before anyone to prevent it," said a defiant P. W. Botha on national television.

The government became stupid with power.

Under the new regulations, the government barred the taking of photographs of any disturbance, boycott, strike or police action without permission. One clause enabled the government to prosecute anyone who made, printed, or recorded a "subversive" statement, which included any remark "weakening or undermining the confidence of the public." The government also curtailed the already limited access of detainees to counsel, and extended the broad powers of police to search buildings and people.

At a meeting with half a dozen South African newspaper editors, information deputy minister Louis Nel answered questions aimed at clarifying the sweeping terms of the emergency. According to one editor's notes of the meeting, Nel was asked if a headline in that day's *Pretoria News* saying, "Isolation looms" would be subversive.

"It could be," Nel replied.

Would it be a violation of the regulations to suggest that the emergency, like Rhodesia's, could last for twenty-one years and eventually be used by the ANC as Rhodesia's are used by Zimbabwean Prime Minister Mugabe? another editor queried.

"It would be," Nel said.

Would it be a violation of the emergency regulations to quote Lord Acton's adage that "Power tends to corrupt and absolute power corrupts absolutely?"

"It could be subversive," Nel said.

Ken Owen, the editor of *Business Day,* later reflected on the government's rules in an editorial. Noting the government's complaints about foreign journalists calling it a "regime" instead of a government, and its emergency "draconian," Owen asked, "Is our government a regime or our regime a government? Are the emergency regulations totalitarian, draconian or just stupid?"

Black activists took precautions. That winter, it seemed everybody wore hats. Amos Masondo wore a worker's hat and Seth Mazibuko wore a woolen hat. Murphy Morobe pulled his cap with the snap in front down further over his face.

Mpho Mashinini and his girlfriend Hloyi headed straight to the nearest church, where a minister from the African Methodist Episcopal church married them. The new state of emergency clinched Mpho's decision to wed his girlfriend of eight years. That way, if either one of them were detained, the other would be entitled to spouse's visiting rights.

Hundreds of activists went into hiding. In downtown Johannesburg, the corner of Bree and von Wielligh streets boasted a number of "escort agencies" peddling attractive female escorts. "Charmant," said the hot pink sign of one. Le Paradis was the name of another. Across the street was E'loise with rust-colored chairs and platinum-blond-haired women. Next door to E'loise there was a black cutting salon with a sign advertising the latest styles. Blacks in town for the day could stop in for a "Hollywood," a "super curl" or "magic curl," a "blow out," or a "special feeling." Upstairs was a drab apartment building, with cream-colored plaster walls, a rickety elevator, and a dark slippery staircase. In apartment 28 on the seventh floor, Seth Mazibuko took refuge during the days after the emergency was declared. The apartment was equipped with a couch and a television. Amos Masondo came to stay, dressed in work overalls.

For a while, it seemed that all of Soweto's black leadership had moved to downtown Johannesburg. Certain neighborhoods had become almost entirely black as whites had abandoned old apartment buildings for the suburbs. So activists could circulate inconspicuously while most of the police were keeping watch over Soweto.

Restrictions on the press made it difficult to keep up with the extent of the damage. Reporting the names of detainees was technically illegal. Even if it were legal, it would have been difficult to tell who had gone underground and who had gone to jail. "My cousin hasn't been home in three or four days and we don't know what happened to him," said one Soweto resident.

Several youths were threatened by vigilantes or police. Sometimes it was hard to tell the difference. In Soweto, a vigilante group named Inkatha (without any connection to Chief Buthelezi's group) killed several comrades. One was shot dead in his yard. Several Soweto residents reported seeing an unmarked white Ford Sierra with police marksmen assassinating youth leaders. The *New Nation* editor Zwelakhe Sisulu was abducted from his home one night by gun-toting men wearing masks. Only after urgent protests by prominent whites and the American embassy did the government bend its rules on identifying detainees to assure people that Sisulu had been arrested by police and was "safe" in jail.

The emergency fell especially heavy on the small, tight-knit townships of the Eastern Cape. In the Lawaaikamp squatter camp, police detained 150 people. In Bongolethu, the tiny Oudtshoorn township with fewer than 5,000 families, more than a hundred people were scooped up, including the entire executive committee of the Bongolethu civic association. In Duncan

Village, two hundred people were detained as police rooted out not just civic leaders but ordinary street committee members. When that roundup failed to cripple the Duncan Village Residents Association, police detained a hundred more people.

Even those not active in political organizations were suspect. Vincent Maphai, then a political philosophy lecturer at the University of the Witwatersrand, was sleeping at his home in the Diepkloof section of Soweto when police pounded on the door at 2:30 one morning. Realizing the futility of trying to keep them out, Maphai invited them in and asked them to sit down while he got dressed. After he was dressed, the two white policemen and two black policemen spent forty-five minutes searching the house. One of the black policemen found a copy of a book about Mandela in Maphai's bedroom and triumphantly presented it to one of the white policemen.

"Are you interested in politics?" the white policeman asked Maphai.

Weariness got the better of Maphai. "I think you'd have to be an idiot to live in South Africa and not be interested in politics," he answered. The policemen apologized for disturbing Maphai and took their leave.

The first four days of the emergency ended with nineteen dead. So it seemed appropriate to go back to the Vaal Triangle, where the cycle of violence began with the rent revolt of Bloody Monday, September 3, 1984. Now, twenty-two months later, armored vehicles rolled along the paved road between the townships of Sebokeng and Evaton, like cars in a funeral procession.

At the edge of Evaton in the poorest section of the township, Desmond Tutu marked Sunday, June 15, with an outdoor service. There amidst the dust, the dirt roads, and the decaying houses, stood the famous Anglican bishop in full regalia: white-and-red robes and conical hat, gripping the shiny cross and silver chalice.

"We worship a wonderful God, who rules in glory inaccessible," Tutu said to about 500 people. Notwithstanding the pomp of the service, on the fourth day of the new state of emergency God seemed more inaccessible than wonderful. Tutu reminded the congregation that when God came to earth, "He came as an ordinary human. The people He chose were not high and mighty, not important people, not the wealthy. No! God chose a simple, humble village carpenter and an equally humble village girl. And the place He chose was not the prestigious palace of kings and princes."

Praying for black students killed by police ten years earlier, Tutu repeated the words he uttered at a funeral a year earlier during the first state of emergency: "I know we will be free because our cause is just."

The neatly dressed audience looked blankly at the bishop. A bright yellow police paddywagon had parked nearby and soldiers in helmets had surrounded the churchyard, clicking the safety catches on their rifles. "Why do you act like you are doubting?" the Nobel-Peace-Prize winner asked, hardly glancing at the soldiers. The people laughed softly. "Do you doubt that you're going to be free?" he pressed. "No," they replied.

People took communion, and Tutu, focused entirely on those who came to listen to him, waved the incense burner, the smell mingling with the odors of the worshipers, the dust of the township, and the choking smoke of home fires.

Tutu took off his white robes, and saw that even though the service was over, people were hesitant to leave the churchyard because the police were waiting at the gates. So Tutu and his wife Leah, hand in hand, walked to the gate, stopped, and motioned for the people to follow. The people followed, pausing one by one to shake Tutu's hand and Leah's hand, then went their separate ways as the police stood by the empty paddywagon.

It seemed as though Tutu had parted the Red Sea so the blacks of Evaton could pass through, back into their own wilderness where their faith would be tested again.

Soweto, June 16, 1986

"The place looked like a ghost town," said one resident of Soweto on the tenth anniversary of the Soweto student revolt. "The trains were moving, but nobody was inside. There were no buses moving at all." People didn't go to work; they didn't go to the store. In the afternoon, some black youngsters congregated in the streets near the railroad stations, making sure no one had gone to work and apprehending those who had. But there were few people to intercept.

The army came out in force. Thousands of troops patrolled the nation's black townships. Near Regina Mundi, the big Anglican church on the south end of Soweto, soldiers stopped and searched every vehicle, and body-searched every pedestrian. Bishop Tutu was stopped at three roadblocks that morning. The police searched him and his car at two of the roadblocks. "It doesn't matter if you're Bishop of one of the most important dioceses in this province, it doesn't matter if you're a Nobel Peace Prize winner in this country. What matters is that you're black," he said bitterly. As an afterthought, he added "That is good for Tutu to remember."

The government cut off telephone service to the black townships and ordered Winnie Mandela to stay at home and not talk to journalists. Soldiers guarded the entrances to the township. Avoiding the main highway, I drove to the edge of the township by traveling the back road through the colored township of Newclare. But as I came up the last incline, just past the billboard advertising the government's propaganda song, "Together We'll Build a Better Future," I came upon several cars of soldiers blocking the road. The soldiers stopped me, searched the car, and found an article I had filed earlier and had carelessly left in the glove compartment. They read the entire article to an officer over the radio. Then they waited, until they received permission to let me go back to Johannesburg.

Just about the only word that came out of the township all day came from Tutu. "The government has used the iron fist before with pitiful results," Bishop Tutu said in a church service attended mostly by white liberals and reporters in downtown Johannesburg. "The government seems to be unaware of the law of diminishing returns. It uses greater and greater repression with smaller and smaller results."

Through arrangements I had made earlier with acquaintances in different parts of the township, I received word of incidents that took place during the day. Not everyone had been silenced. A train track was damaged slightly by a limpet mine. Police were riding the trains. A bus belonging to the state-subsidized transportation company was stoned. Soldiers had pitched tents near the stadium in Orlando and by an open soccer field. More members of the Soweto Civic Association were caught at a roadblock, bringing to seven the number of executive committee members detained; only two were at large, one of whom was at an overseas conference. In Meadowlands, youths built barricades of burning tires and cars. Two youths were shot by police riding in an white unmarked Ford Sierra; one of the victims was a four-year-old girl. The other was a boy who borrowed a woman's dress as a disguise, then went for medical help.

Church services were poorly attended or disrupted. More than a dozen army vehicles parked outside the Twelve Apostles Church in Meadowlands Zone 9 and gave the congregation three minutes to disperse. In Meadowlands Zone 4, about 500 blacks met secretly in a Dutch Reformed church. Youths directed people driving cars to park at some distance. People walked in small groups to be less conspicuous. Youth congress leader Dan Montsitsi, who had witnessed the shooting of Hector Petersen a decade earlier and who spent five years on Robben Island, spoke to the group. Seth Mazibuko spoke briefly. The crowd sang freedom songs and chanted ANC slogans, believing it had outfoxed the police.

Beneath the surface, chaos reigned. Street committees were foundering in the absence of community leaders. Youths were taking over meetings. "These boys actually want to rule the street committees, while most members of the civic are in hiding. This is causing a lot of chaos," Seth Mazibuko said.

One day about three weeks later, Mazibuko returned to the apartment over E'Loise escort agency. He reached for the door handle and a policeman greeted him. "Come in, Seth," he said. Later in the police cells, an interrogator showed Mazibuko photos of him during the weeks of "hiding." Walking out of Khotso House, hopping on buses, talking to reporters like me. An informer had given the police a tape of the "secret" church rally in Soweto on the sixteenth.

A "Moment of Truth"

The force of the government assault on the United Democratic Front was a perverse tribute to what had been accomplished in the front's first three years. The UDF had been founded to oppose President Botha's new constitution providing for a tricameral Parliament. The front forged a coalition of local organizations devoted to local issues such as housing, transportation, and education. In the course of opposing the new constitution, the UDF put the demands of these disparate organizations into a national context.

"Suddenly the UDF became the symbol of resistance and was seen as an alternative to the status quo," said Abdullah Omar, a lawyer and UDF leader from Cape Town. "When we talk today about the limitations of the UDF, we are talking about the UDF's limitations as it strives and competes for power." The original objective of the UDF was far narrower—to resist power, not to wield it.

But political power quickly became the objective in the eyes of thousands of enthusiastic UDF supporters, from the black townships that ring South Africa's cities to the homelands.

In April 1986, Mkuseli Jack had declared to a cheering throng at a political funeral that "This is the moment of truth in our struggle." By the end of 1986, the moment of truth appeared distant in Port Elizabeth. If the period from mid-1984 to mid-1986 had been South Africa's Prague Spring, then the state of emergency had ushered in a Russian winter that threatened to kill off the brief flowering of political activity in the townships. Though the emergency seemed a temporary setback at first, as weeks and months passed activists realized that it would be long lasting. The high-profile, anti-apartheid politics of the mid-1980s had become impossible.

The government was mounting a full-scale assault on the UDF and its 700 affiliates, and in many ways it was winning. New Brighton, once called a "liberated zone," was sealed off with rings of razor-sharp barbed wire. Police roadblocks monitored people entering and leaving the township. Some of the checkpoints of this "Berlin Wall," as it had been nicknamed, were manned by some of the same young comrades who once hailed Jack. Mass funerals of the kind that galvanized the townships every weekend since 1984 had been banned by the government; the black consumer boycott had petered out.

Henry Fazzie, the master of disguise during the first state of emergency, was picked up at the "Berlin Wall." After weeks in hiding, Mkhuseli Jack also was arrested. He was sent to a remote jail. The regional president of the UDF was standing trial for murder in connection with a necklace killing. (He was eventually acquitted, and jailed again under emergency regulations.) Only one regional UDF leader remained at large. The government detained so many political leaders in the Eastern Cape that it was forced to ship common criminals all over the country to make room in the local jails for political prisoners. In the depressed port city, prison construction had become the only growth industry; nine were being built in late 1986.

The street committees designed to keep the UDF going during the anticipated crackdown were operating sporadically. Even then they lacked purpose and direction. Attendance at the Forum, the weekly policy conference once attended by heads of forty UDF affiliates, dwindled to five people, three of them youth representatives.

Some activists called the emergency a time for "consolidation," partly code for organization work, partly code for chaos. A UDF leader in hiding in Uitenhage told me that the organizations were coming up with new strategies that were still secret—perhaps because they didn't yet exist. Other leaders admitted that they were at a loss about what to do next. A leading UDF official said to his cousin that South Africa might be entering a phase like that of the mid-1960s, when government repression stifled black protest for more than a decade. The following week he, too, was detained for a few days.

Nowhere were the setbacks to the UDF more evident than in its one-time stronghold in the Eastern Cape, especially in Langa.

Langa had been the site of the 1985 police massacre of twenty people on their way to a funeral, the bloodiest single shooting incident of the uprising. After the shooting, eighty thousand people attended the funeral in the township. Block by block the UDF had organized street committees that dealt with all issues facing the residents. By early 1986, students were boycotting classes and enforcing a black-consumer boycott of white-owned stores in Uitenhage. The UDF affiliates grew stronger.

The biggest fear of Langa residents was the threatened removal of the entire population of the township to KwaNobuhle, the newer township tucked a few miles past the industrial section of town. The UDF affiliates in Langa took the government to court to stop the removal. "We will fight them legally and if that fails and they try to move us, we'll fight them again," Weza Made, a leader of the effort against removal, told me at the courthouse in Port Elizabeth, where the township's case was heard. Sympathetic architects and city planners came up with ways to upgrade the township, offering a practical alternative to removal. The Midland Chamber of Industries offered to help pay for building materials in a meeting that took place the day before the state of emergency was imposed.

Today Langa doesn't exist. When the emergency was declared, police rounded up Langa's leaders, then drove flatbed and pickup trucks into the township and bundled everyone off to KwaNobuhle. Much of the demolition took place at night. Police threatened people over loudspeakers and tore up slips from Langa's lawyer that quoted the town clerk's assurance that people would not be moved against their will. At KwaNobuhle, thousands of people were put into tents because there weren't enough houses. Their furniture and other belongings were piled outside in the rain. Four people died of carbon monoxide poisoning after making a fire to keep their tent warm. Eurilia Banda recounted all this outside the house at Number 3 Ntungwana Street, where she grew up in Langa. It was the only house left standing. The entire hillside that was Langa stretched out vacant except for four empty churches that the God-fearing white authorities didn't dare bulldoze. Green scrub bushes had already grown over the bits of rubbish.

The leaders of Langa heard about the fate of their home while sitting helplessly in detention. Weza Made managed to smuggle out two notes scribbled in jail. "I've heard of what happened to my township," he wrote, without further comment on the removal. Instead he complained of hunger and isolation. "I have written many times and sent many messages, but I get no reply. I am having a difficult time. For three days I had one meal a day and sometimes I sleep very hungry." He begged a relative for a visit or food parcel. "I suffer greatly from hunger and loneliness. I feel lost, as if no one cares for me any longer.

Why did Langa's residents climb onto the trucks instead of lying down in front of them and fighting to a more bitter end? The answer lies not only in the sheer force of the crackdown, but in the breakdown of UDF affiliates.

Even before the destruction of Langa, the UDF faced serious disaffection among its followers there. It pushed the school boycott too far, upsetting parents who wanted their children in school. The township had only four shops, and the boycott of whites' stores made shopping difficult. The peoples' courts in Langa, run by UDF officials, meted out harsh punishments to suspected informers, people who declined to join the boycott, and common criminals. There were numerous necklace killings; people were hit with *sjamboks* (bullwhips) or given strokes with canes. Reginald Gomono, who headed the peoples'courts, was known in Langa as "Kannemeyer," the name of the Afrikaans Supreme Court justice who conducted the inquiry into the Langa massacre. But John Gomomo, chief shop steward at the Uitenhage VW plant, differed with his brother over the way the courts were run. "The UDF didn't have control over these young guys at all," John Gomomo said.

Chaos in the streets was matched by chaos within black leadership. The Langa Coordinating Committee was "riddled with tensions," said one former resident. Some members of the committee were angry with members of the National Allied and Automobile Workers Union, which represented workers at the local Volkswagon plant. The committee thought the NAAWU leaders could do more to pressure employers to defend Langa.[1] When the emergency was declared, most of the Langa Coordinating Committee was detained. On June 19, the Uitenhage Residents Congress (also representing Langa) then set up an Anti-Removal Committee that included auto workers and clashed with what was left of the Langa Coordinating Committee. In the confusion that reigned, a call by the auto workers' union for a general strike on June 20 was widely ignored.

After the forced removal of Langa residents, a gang of vigilantes in KwaNobuhle turned on the comrades who had eluded police. On the night of January 4, 1987, the vigilantes assembled a mob of 400 people. Wielding spears, iron bars, and clubs, they killed four UDF activists and beat several others. Reginald Gomomo was rescued from a vigilante group by his brother John.

The vigilantes had their own organization, called the African Parents Concerned Committee. It was trying to cultivate followers by handing out food, but most people believed the food was donated by the government. The APCC also had at least the tacit support of the police. Bands of armed men holding captured UDF supporters were waved through police roadblocks.

Surprisingly few tears were shed for the Langa comrades. Many residents were fed up with more than two years of upheaval. Kelman Befile, a store owner from Langa who had given evidence against the police at the Kannemeyer inquiry into the massacre at Langa in 1985, turned to the APCC. When I visited KwaNobuhle, some of Befile's young supporters guided me to a plot of land next to KwaNobuhle. Chickens wandered around the house. Befile sat nervously on a chair and explained why he soured on the UDF. He complained that the comrades extorted "contributions" of R300 a month plus donations of goats, turkeys, and chickens. They reasoned that he was earning extra money because the black consumer boycott of white stores was bringing in extra business. They cited a clause from the ANC's Freedom Charter that says "the people shall share in the country's wealth." A young friend of Befile, Lukhaniso Matschaka, acknowledged that he was among the 400 people who went on a rampage against UDF followers. "I was woken up around 4 A.M. by a number of people carrying sticks who said we must chase the comrades. I went with them. Willingly."

Strains within the UDF's national leadership also emerged as government opponents, previously confident of their own power, looked for someone to blame for the demise of the resistance. To blame the government alone would be to admit the inherent weakness of the anti-apartheid forces. So some UDF leaders began to search for a plot within the movement.

Segments of the UDF, led by Aubrey Mokoena and members of the Release Mandela Campaign, claimed that a "cabal" had taken over the UDF. According to this conspiracy theory, an inner circle of UDF leaders, largely Indians, had made important strategic decisions without consulting the UDF as a whole.

"Supposedly, there is a small coterie of individuals—a cabal—controlling the UDF," Dr. Jerry Coovadia said. "I'm supposed to be one of a group of seven." The group allegedly included leading Natal Indian Congress members like Farouk Meer and Yunus Mohammed, a lawyer. It was also said to have allies among Indians in the Transvaal and among Africans who had fallen under the Indians' influence. Because Archie Gumede shared office space with Mohammed, Gumede was believed to be under the influence of the cabal. It was said that Gumede, a Zulu, was part Indian.

There was a degree of substance to the tensions between the cabal and anti-cabal factions, dating to the birth of the UDF, when the Natal Indian Congress favored participation in the referendum about the new constitution creating the tricameral Parliament. In 1987 the question of participation had become a hot issue again. Because of the new state of emergency, Archie Gumede believed the UDF should reconsider its position. Contesting elections would permit the UDF to operate publicly and to openly express its views, Gumede argued. With the popularity of the UDF, Gumede added, there would be little chance of losing. Then the UDF representatives could refuse to take their seats and hobble the government. Gumede's suggestion provoked an uproar within the UDF, but little real reexamination of strategy. Most UDF leaders still favored boycotting the elections. Moreover with thousands in jail, the emergency that Gumede said necessitated a change in strategy had also precluded one.

But there was also an ugly aspect to the tensions within the UDF, stemming from anti-Indian racism and jealousy about the financial strength of Indians, who helped bankroll the UDF. Mokoena and his closest associates openly mocked people such as Murphy Morobe and Popo Molefe for their alleged connections to the Indian "cabal" and referred to them by Indian surnames "Bubulia" and "Cachalia."

The emergency inflamed sore feelings between the alleged cabal and its foes, because it became more difficult for the full UDF executive committee to meet and hammer out differences. The Release Mandela Campaign, which had relied on other UDF affiliates to further its aims, began to build a national organization that could serve as an anti-cabal power base. Two veteran members of the Natal Indian Congress quit, alleging that the cabal had usurped power.

I witnessed a vehement argument between two old friends. One was furious because he heard that he had been discussed at a meeting of the Johannesburg "cabal" that his friend attended. His friend didn't deny that a meeting had taken place, but he played down its significance. The activist excluded from the meeting shook his head and threatened his old friend, half in jest, but half in earnest.

Perhaps the most consoling aspect of the infighting was that it failed to split the UDF. Most UDF supporters never knew about the bickering going on at the national leadership level. The word "cabal" was derogatory, suggesting a group working against the democratic principles central to the struggle. Even if such a cabal existed, it could never admit its own existence or function openly. Moreover, the ANC stayed out of this fray and urged the factions to reconcile their differences.

Many black political leaders said that tensions within the UDF were exaggerated. Tshwete said that, "In a mass organization like the UDF you must expect that tensions might surface. They are more the result of building tension within the country than any ideological difference." Dr. Coovadia attributed the resignations of the NIC veterans to their personal shortcomings, claiming that despite the veterans' supposed devotion to democratic decision-making, those who had quit had been unwilling to work with new leaders. "They had a sense that leadership figures are owed respect. They think, 'This is my due. I'm in the struggle for twenty years now and no little chap is going to tell me what to do.' They were unwilling to work collectively."

The anti-cabal forces were dealt a setback when Mokoena's associate Jabu Ngwenya called for a black Christmas boycott of white stores in Johannesburg that fell flat. Mokoena eventually met with members of the so-called cabal and resolved their differences.

Even among the most devoted members of the UDF, the government sowed conflict in the soil of the suspicion by detaining some activists and inexplicably leaving others free.

"A prisoner whom we saw for a few minutes told us another leading activist is an informer," a foreign diplomat said.

> Two weeks later, a civil rights lawyer confided to us her view that the prisoner is an informer. . . . The wife of an imprisoned UDF leader from Pretoria is so certain that another Pretoria UDF activist is an informer that the activist is no longer welcome in the prisoner's home. The activist, like many, is suspected because he was released while others were kept in detention.

In Graaff Reinet, the small outpost in the Great Karoo, the police detained Joyce Stuart, a colored secretary at the local primary school, and her husband, Xavier. The Stuarts were once at the center of Graaff Reinet protest. Visiting UDF leaders like Matthew Goniwe and Oscar Mpetha slept on the extra cot in the Stuarts' bedroom. Joyce was the secretary of the Graaff Reinet Residents Association, a UDF affiliate. Their involvement had cost Xavier his job as a carpenter and forced him to sell vegetables. The police offered the couple R1,000 a month each if they would work as informers. Both say they flatly refused.

But while in police custody, Xavier was driven around the town in the back of a police car to make it appear as though he was cooperating. Officers would stop at a cafe and ask for a soda and sandwich. "It's for Xavier," they would say. Using wiretaps of meetings and phone calls, police gave some activists verbatim accounts of conversations that took place in the Stuart's living room and asserted that the Stuarts were informing. By the time the Stuarts got out of detention, suspicion about them was rife. "We are quite isolated now," Joyce Stuart told me. After some hesitation, Joyce went with me to the neighboring black township, where she once went almost daily for meetings. It was her first visit in eight months.

Rev. Hufkie, a white-haired Congregation minister who lived in the colored township a couple of blocks from the Stuarts, was once close to them. At the end of 1986 he said he still had "high regard" for Joyce, but he no longer trusted Xavier. Indeed Hufkie, who spent five months in jail in 1976 and six months in jail in 1985, had abandoned all organized political activity. "I operate entirely on my own. I don't belong to any organization. I don't attend their meetings. I don't really trust any of them."

"Do you know what the really big word is, Helen?" one character asks another in a play by Athol Fugard. "Like most people, I suppose I used to think it was 'love'. But there's an even bigger one. Trust. And more dangerous. Because that's when you drop your defenses, lay yourself wide open, and if you've made a mistake, you're in big, big trouble."[2]

In Graaff Reinet, many people were wondering whether they had made mistakes. The isolation of the town only worsened the effects of mistrust. In Graaff Reinet, and in its small colored township Kroonstad, the cruelty of an evasive stare, a hostile glance, the unreturned greeting cut deeper than elsewhere.

Later, after I had driven out of Graaff Reinet, I found myself thinking about trust, and, like the others, wondering about Xavier. I wondered about the police officer who had come and talked quietly with Xavier in the garage the night I was there. Was Xavier shielding me from an inquisitive cop who noticed my presence in the colored township? Or was it something else? Was the stress Joyce felt due to fatigue and harassment, or due to doubts she could never share with anyone? After all, they had not been together in detention? No, I decided. I must not be like the rest. Xavier had been generous to me. He had shared his home and his time. He had translated the complaints of poor farmworkers I interviewed without minimizing them. Xavier himself had urged me to go see the distrustful Rev. Hufkie. Moreover, Xavier had suffered from apartheid and expressed to me his bitterness toward a government that had expropriated his childhood home and turned it into a whites-only hotel. How could he be an informer?

For months government strategy succeeded. The UDF tottered between crackdown and breakdown. Not only did the UDF bicker over strategy, cabals, and informers, it also failed to take elementary security precautions. Discretion has never been the strong point of the South African opposition, which sometimes seems amateurish. Important breaches of security took place over the telephone; valuable documents were left in vulnerable offices and apartments. One veteran activist left banned ANC literature lying in his apartment after he had assumed the high-profile job of publicity secretary of the Release Mandela Campaign. When the government investigated the funding of newspaper adds that advocated the unbanning of the ANC, it used knowledge of sensitive financial dealings that it had collected from telephone taps of prominent activists like Rev. Boesak, who should have assumed that their phones were tapped.

CHAPTER THIRTEEN

WHAM!

Our kingdoms lay in each man's mind. A province would be won when we had taught the civilians in it to die for our ideal of freedom.
—T. E. Lawrence

IN 1890, A REACTIONARY RUSSIAN THINKER named Konstantin Leontyev suggested that the czar could put himself at the head of the socialist movement the same way that Constantine the Great had taken charge of organized Christianity. Leontyev believed that by seizing the ideas of his opponents, the czar could rout the Russian radicals and stay seated on the Russian throne during a period of social change.

In South Africa, the equivalent of such a plan would make it possible for President P. W. Botha to take up calls for the abolition of apartheid and emerge as the leader of black South Africans, firmly ensconced in the Union Buildings in Pretoria and in Parliament in Cape Town. He could change his title from President Botha to Chief Botha.

As far-fetched as that sounds, the South African government attempted to do just that after declaring the 1986 state of emergency. While cracking down on black political leaders, the government also tried to seize the initiative in the black townships. It took up the socio-economic grievances of black South Africans, hoping to pull the rug from under the feet of black political activists.

Central to this effort was the belief that blacks' economic demands were more important than their political ones. "I think that for the masses in South Africa democracy is not a relevant factor." said Defense Minister Magnus Malan in an interview in an Afrikaans magazine. "For them, it is about satisfying their material needs: housing, education, employment opportunities, clothing, bread and butter."[1]

As a result of that view, a public-works offensive was launched amidst the 1986 crackdown on dissent. In a black shantytown called Lindelani outside Durban, white contractors graded a bed for the community's first paved road. A chunk of one of the hillsides was leveled to create a soccer field and two tennis courts. (The settlement still had no schools, however.) The size of Bongolethu township outside Oudtshoorn was doubled; the new section of the township had a health clinic, new houses, and paved streets.

The government even brought its economic offensive to the troublesome township of Alexandra. The government built a couple of dozen new houses in the worst neighborhood of the township near 22nd street. Workers erected three new primary schools, several prefabricated apartment blocks, and a children's recreation area across the creek, where the only previous structure was an old leprosy clinic. A couple of streets were paved and a new sewer was laid. Some black adults were employed in these construction projects. Schoolchildren were taught cricket to keep them out of trouble and kids ran around with team T-shirts and bats.

In early 1987, soldiers were handing out a comic strip explaining the government's efforts. On the cover of the comic, a smiling black boy with the name "Alex" on his shirt was depicted with a smiling dog, a smiling bumblebee, and a smiling bird. "Alex and Friends" was the title of the comic. On the reverse side, the bird cooed, "I wonder what is going on in Rooseveld [sic] street. Maybe Alex knows." Alex explained in the next panel that "They are busy putting in a new sewerage system." Then, a scrawny creature who wore a shirt labeled "comrade rat" chimed in: "Hmff!!! I bet it's going to take *years!!*" Alex responded that "I've got a surprise for you comrade rat. . . . " He explained that construction would continue through the holidays and that the sewer eventually would provide a third of the houses in Alexandra with flush toilets. Without promising when the project would be finished, Alex said another two sewerage systems were planned for the future.

Lifting the living standards of the black masses was as important a part of the South African government's counter revolution as the crackdown under the state of emergency. Nor did the government see any contradiction between the two. President Botha believed "revolutionaries" had "exploited" legitimate grievances to undermine the "legitimate" government, as though the origin of those grievances had nothing to do with his government. A cabinet minister explained to an acquaintance in private that it was a two-handed approach, with one hand cloaked in a velvet glove, and the other clenched into an iron fist.

A System without Faces

To wage the counterrevolution, the State Security Council set up a shadow government, circumventing Parliament and elected local officials. For every major white town and its satellite black townships, a "joint management committee" was formed by the State Security Council. The identities of the committee members were kept secret and members served by invitation only. They included journalists, business leaders, military officers, civil servants, and local officials—all sympathetic to the government. These committees (JMCs) plotted strategy in a military style, keeping rooms of maps with "enemy" areas marked off and planning offensives that combined repression, upgrading projects, and propaganda. Unlike elected officials, JMC members could work swiftly, cutting out slothful and corrupt bureaucrats. Because their identities were secret, the JMC members did not risk becoming targets of popular outrage. It was, an observer noted, "a system without faces."

The size of this shadow government was substantial. According to one minister, there were ten provincial JMCs, sixty regional committees or sub-JMCs, and 260 local committees, or mini-JMCs.[2]

Accountable to neither white nor black public opinion, the JMCs could be ruthless. The JMC office responsible for the Khayelitsha and Crossroads squatter camps outside Cape Town fomented and sanctioned a small civil war in the squatter camps between comrades and the Witdoekes, a group of older, conservative camp residents who were armed and aided by police. While the fighting took place, white soldiers stood by and watched as the Witdoekes routed the comrades. Huge sections of Crossroads, which the government had tried to remove with bulldozers for years, were burned down once and for all.[3] Afterwards the JMC launched a reconstruction program. Thousands of refugees from the fighting poured out of the area and were resettled further from Cape Town.

Later a visitor to South Africa was taken on a tour of the JMC office for Khayelitsha and Crossroads. He noted that

> the place was a normal, University-type of meeting room, with simple furniture and a conference table to sit about twenty to thirty people. In this room, I was told, the JMC members meet once or twice a week.
>
> The room was fitted with all the cliches and romanticism of counterinsurgency and anti-revolutionary warfare. The walls were plastered with large maps of the townships. Areas under control of the witdoekes or of the comrades (more correctly once under the control of the comrades), areas for upgrading or reconstruction, for people to be moved, etc., were indicated with different colors and arrows. More amazing, however, all over the place you found hanging maplike papers with excerpts of the writings of famous revolutionaries, like Mao, Giap, Che Guevarra, or of counterinsurgency experts and strategic thinkers, like Liddle Hart and the old Chinese military thinker Wuntzu.
>
> Then I was led to a paper in especially large writing and was told that this is from a book on which everything is based: *The Art of Counterinsurgency War,* by John J. McCuen.[4]

Written in 1966 by an American army colonel, *The Art of Counterinsurgency War* was distributed by the State Security Council to leading politicians, military officials, and civil servants. It became a Bible for those planning a strategy to both "defeat the revolutionaries" and "winning hearts and minds" of blacks—an approach some officials dubbed WHAM.

The manual advised that "a governing power can defeat any revolutionary movement if it adapts the revolutionary strategy and principles and applies them in reverse." Doing so had both a destructive and a more positive side. On the one hand, McCuen advised that the government could not spare any tactic in wiping out the organization of its opposition. However mismatched the opposition might seem against the state, it posed a threat to the survival of the government; the government should react accordingly. McCuen, who didn't write specifically about South Africa, made no distinction between legal peaceful opposition and violent guerrilla groups. To him, they were intertwined in an assault on the government. "The main objective in the strategy of counter-terrorism is the annihilation/neutralization of the enemy political organization amongst the local population."

Mark Swilling, a University of Witwatersrand politics lecturer who was close to UDF leaders, tried to hammer home the implications of this for the UDF. "WHAM is significantly different from earlier security strategies," he said. The ex-police chief General Johan Coetzee had "argued that the United Democratic Front, low-level protest action, trade unions and other township organizations should be allowed to exist but controlled through infiltration, selective bannings and detentions."

McCuen wanted to destroy, not monitor the opposition. He recommended the formation of loyal militias and the exploitation of factional differences among the people. "Government forces can form counter-guerrilla gangs by sending in military teams to get minority or dissident groups together, to arm and train them and even to assume command over them." The purpose would be to "annihilate revolutionary guerrillas and take control over the population."

In waging this war, the government should not treat all people as enemies, the booklet cautioned. "Who are you? You are not only the fighting forces, but also your bases and the population; with the emphasis on the population," the manual advised. "McCuen warns that this is the most violated principle of counter-revolutionary warfare." That's why the government had to formulate a positive program, the pamphlet said, "in close cooperation with the population so that it will be in accordance with their aspirations."

To implement that program, the manual said the government must have its own counter-organization. Quoting Mao, the counterinsurgency pamphlet advised the government to copy the techniques of the Chinese revolutionary. "The government must win the favor of every possible person by getting him involved through persuasion. A well considered attempt must be launched to activate the masses to establish societies, clubs and organizations at all levels. There must be visible proof that he benefits by this."

Before long, government officials of all stripes were quoting faithfully from the works of Chairman Mao. "In my study, I have the Red Book of Mao. Go read it." General Malan told an Afrikaans magazine. "The radicals were winning the war [from 1984–1986] because we weren't catering to people's basic needs," said Victor Milne of the Transvaal Provincial Administration. "It's easy to mobilize communities with genuine grievances. That's what Mao Tse-tung did."[5]

The size of the government's economic counter-offensive was immense. During the 1987/88 fiscal year, the South African government spent R3.2 billion upgrading thirty-four of the most volatile black townships in the country, places it sought to make showcases of its strategy. McCuen called this the "oilspot" approach, taking on the "enemy" in its most secure areas.

The enormity of the program stretched the government's resources. President Botha declared that he would sell state-owned industries and utilities and that the R16 billion in proceeds would go to the directorate of urbanization in the Department of Constitutional Development and Planning for upgrading another 200 townships. But economists doubted that the government windfall from the privatization of state-owned enterprises would match Botha's expectations. And plowing all those proceeds into black townships would doubtless cause a revolt by whites, who would demand their share.

As big as the spending program was, after four decades or more or woeful neglect, the job of providing decent living conditions in the townships demanded an even larger effort. In order to meet its stated goal of housing everyone by the year 2000, the government would have to build 210,000 low-income dwellings a year. Yet the South African Housing Trust Ltd. and the Urban Foundation, the biggest providers of inexpensive housing, said they would build only about 35,000 homes over the three years starting 1989.[6]

The government's own propaganda revealed the shortcomings of the economic offensive. The cartoon distributed in Alexandra bragged about the new sewer system, but that system would deliver flush toilets to only one-third of the people in the township. That fraction was based on an estimate of the current Alex population that was probably low. And every day, squatters were slouching into town, tacking together more sheets of cardboard and corrugated metal.

Similar pressures existed elsewhere. Prior to its destruction, the township of Langa was growing at the rate of about ten shacks a day as people flocked there from drought-stricken rural areas in search of work and lodging. After the destruction of Langa, people migrated to Kwanobuhle. The government distributed shiny $450 prefabricated tin shacks, but it couldn't keep pace with basic needs. The tent town where Langa residents were dumped on a "temporary" basis in 1986 still existed two years later. It had no running water or sewerage. People drank out of large black open-topped rubber vats that collected rainwater, disease, and dirt. A tank truck occasionally refilled the vats.

One morning at four, my telephone rang. "The shacks are going up," a friend told me, "I'll come get you now." Forty minutes later we stood in the dark at the edge of a field in Tembisa, the township between Johannesburg and Pretoria, looking at thirteen shining shacks of corrugated metal. Six others were still being built. A bleary-eyed Joe Mhlapo, wakened by the banging of hammers, looked at the shacks from his house across the street. "Well, if people have no place to go, what can you do?"

A white activist looked at the shacks with pride. Planact, an organization of mostly white architects and urban planners, had worked with the Tembisa residents' association and purchased three tons of metal and drawn plans for shacks that would cost only R248 each. Squatters, tired of waiting for better housing, decided to buy the materials and make their own homes.

"I had to get away from my folks," one young homesteader said as we walked along the dirt field. Another woman, aged forty-three, said she had eight children and three grandchildren and was still living in her mother's house. She wanted to have a house of her own. Official figures probably underestimated the number of people living in Tembisa. But even those figures told the story. About 220,000 people were living in Tembisa, but there were only homes for 180,000.

Three hours after we arrived, the police arrived too. They ran at us, swearing in Afrikaans. "Who are you?" one of them screamed at me. "An American journalist," I said. "For what magazine? *Sechaba*?" he sneered, suggesting that I was working for the ANC monthly publication. My friend and I were bundled into our car with an army escort and taken to the township police and army headquarters. A skull and crossbones was tacked on the wall near the photographs of three blacks. A large map of the township covered the wall. We waited and listened over the army radio on the table nearby to what was happening with the shacks. The army was sealing off the township to journalists and the police were trying to decide whether to knock down the shacks. After about an hour, an officer ordered us to leave the township without passing by the shacks or talking to anyone.

We later heard that the would-be homesteaders employed a clever stalling tactic. They asked to see the black mayor, and the police were eager to do anything to bolster the stature of the mayor, whom most Tembisa residents regarded as a collaborator. What the police didn't know, however, was that the mayor, fearing for his life, had fled to the homeland of Boputhatswana and it would take a couple of days to bring him back to Tembisa. After a couple of days, however, police destroyed the shacks. The government wanted controlled housing expansion, not urban homesteading by poor blacks.

Despite its limitations, the government's economic-based counteroffensive threw the black opposition off balance. How should the opposition handle the change in government strategy? Some organizations allied with the UDF scrambled to take advantage of the money the government was pouring into black areas. Planact came up with plans to upgrade living conditions in squatter camps in the Pretoria-Johannesburg area.

But the Kagiso Trust, a foundation close to the UDF, criticized Planact for making apartheid livable. Similarly, some activists criticized Operation Hunger, a famine relief organization, for feeding hundreds of thousands of starving people in rural homelands. They said Operation Hunger was reinforcing the homeland system.

Both Planact and Operation Hunger disagreed. A Planact member said,

> You can't tell people that they can only get decent housing after the end of apartheid. Because then the state can come and give people decent housing and they'll think, "Well we didn't need the end of apartheid." We must shape changes.
>
> If we say that by giving people housing the government is trying to buy people off, we make good housing seem like a bad thing. It must be seen as a good thing, and it must be interpreted as a concession. That means we must call for better housing, because if we never call for better housing, progressive organizations can't claim credit when the government provides better housing. There must be a strategy for concessions.

Planact also argued that the premise of the government's counteroffensive was wrong. You don't necessarily make people less radical by improving their living conditions.

Statistics backed up Planact's claim. According to Bobby Godsell, Anglo American Corporation's head of industrial relations, black income had increased substantially in the decade before the turbulent eighties. In 1970, blacks received about 30 percent of the country's aggregate earned income and whites received about 70 percent. In 1980, blacks' share of the country's aggregate earned income was about 45 percent and whites' 55 percent. On the gold mines, the shift was more pronounced. The share of wages taken home by whites was 60 percent of the total in 1970, versus 40 percent for blacks. The share of wages taken home by whites slipped to just 40 percent of total in 1980, versus 60 percent for blacks.

"A ten-year shift of this dimension is not anything you'll see in the U.S. in any decade," Godsell argued, attributing the shift to unionization and the movement of black workers into semi-skilled jobs. And yet, the unprecedented redistribution of income and job skills had not quenched black aspirations. Indeed it preceded the country's greatest period of political unrest.

In part, this was because even if white aggregate income rose at a slower rate, the gap between blacks and whites widened. Moreover, modest improvements raised expectations; blacks wanted equality with whites. Shifts in aggregate income still left whites—fifteen percent of the population—with a commanding economic advantage.

United Democratic Front spokesman Murphy Morobe rejected the notion that massive public works projects would pacify the black population. Morobe said,

> Whites, after suppressing our people for 100 or 150 years, say here's all the manna you need and we have to say "Lord, Lord" to them. No. They take our people for granted and think they know what's right. They think better roads will lead to an element of conservatism. But not here where the basic issue of political power isn't addressed. Peoples' thoughts have gone beyond better roads and better houses. The main question is who rules and how whoever rules does the governing.

Dividing the Masses

Government measures to uplift the black masses marked a departure from a decade-old effort to divide the black masses.

In the wake of the 1976 student uprising, government and business took steps to create a black middle class that would have better education, better housing, and easier access to urban residency than blacks in the homelands and remote townships. By giving middle class blacks a stake in the status quo, the government and business community hoped to create a depoliticized buffer against black radicals.

This goal could not be achieved through public-works projects. Instead, it required reforms to provide opportunities for black entrepreneurs and professionals, people with disposable income and initiative. Talk of free enterprise became fashionable in a government that previously tried to control every aspect of the lives of black people.

Although the government portrayed itself to Western nations as a bastion of free enterprise resisting an onslaught by communist radicals, before the 1980s free enterprise had been an abstract idea for blacks. Not only did the government restrict blacks' right to sell their labor where they wanted, it owned all black township housing and owned or controlled monopoly licenses for virtually every business in the townships, from cinemas to beer halls to bus service. As a result, blacks were "totally unbankable," according to one black business leader. They had no collateral. "Banks were okay when it came to taking deposits, but when it came to lending money it was like getting gold from Fort Knox," said a black banker. Blacks' savings only served to stimulate investment and economic growth in white areas.

Blacks who needed loans joined *stokvels,* which worked on trust. A group of people would get together for a dinner party once a month. Everyone contributed to a kitty, which went to the host. Over the next eleven months the host paid back that amount in eleven installments as the dinner party moved from house to house of other people in the group. In effect, the host received an eleven month, no-interest loan from friends. I once attended a smoky high-priced *stokvel* in Soweto where the host, a shebeen owner, was showing off a room he had built with the previous year's kitty. It had paid for itself many times over.

Even if blacks could obtain loans, they couldn't do much with them until the early 1980s. Until 1975, blacks were allowed to enter only twenty-six types of trades or businesses. Until 1978, no black was allowed to own more than one business, to take in a partner, or to share profits without the approval of a white township bureaucrat. Black entrepreneurs had to go for monthly health checkups, and every month they had to have their identity documents, or reference books, signed by the township superintendent. High education requirements for artisan apprenticeships effectively disqualified the blacks most likely to seek that type of work.

In the late 1970s and early 1980s, the government loosened economic shackles on blacks. In Soweto, the government built luxury neighborhoods, banks opened branches, and big business founded a special school. But the government failed to win allies among the growing black middle class, in part because of its own half-hearted implementation of reforms.

Even when blacks were entitled to run businesses, the sheer weight of government bureaucracy—usually staffed by right-wing whites—smothered initiative. In many cases, licensing discretion was left to bureaucrats and local authorities. When Black Chain, the largest black-owned supermarket chain, wanted to open a new branch, local authorities said the chain didn't have enough capital. When the supermarket chain exhibited ample financial backing, authorities said the chain's owners had enough money and didn't need another store. "You speak of free enterprise. I don't know what that means," said H. S. Majola, managing director of Black Chain. "There's no free enterprise for us."

Henry Fihla waited ten years to obtain a site for his grocery store in Soweto. Empty plots were given out at the whim of the township administrators or black community councillors. "You have to go to the township councillor and grease him to get a site. There isn't any open bidding," said Fihla, who took over an elderly man's store.

Doing business in the white city also remained difficult. After the first Botha reforms, blacks couldn't own more than 49 percent of a business in a white area. To circumvent that law, blacks needed white figureheads many of whom exacted fees in return for their signatures. Later reforms permitted blacks to own all of a business in white areas, but only with the approval of white municipal councils.

The most sweeping economic reform was the introduction of freehold and ninety-nine-year leaseholds in the townships. This reform had far-reaching implications for the relationship between black individuals and the state. Through that simple stroke, blacks would no longer be tenants of the government. Rent boycotts would become meaningless. Blacks with savings would have some of those savings in their homes, making them concerned about stability and violence. Workers with homes might be more reluctant to go on strike, because a loss of income could mean the loss of a home.

By letting blacks buy their own houses, the government was removing a point of friction between the government and blacks, simply by eliminating a point of contact. The government would have nothing to do with privately owned homes. A private company, employer, bank, or building society would hold the mortgage and be responsible for collecting payment or evicting defaulters.

To many blacks, however, economic reforms were designed to entrap blacks, not free them. City Ketlhoiloe was a biology teacher in the black townships outside Bloemfontein. In 1987, he was earning R1350 a month and he just had bought a house for R51,000. He did not put down a deposit and he had to pay off the house over twenty years. That meant he owed R762 a month to the bank, well beyond his means. But he only paid R249 a month. His employer, the state Department of Education and Training, was paying R513 a month, a benefit that could not be exchanged for cash payments if he wanted to live more modestly. Before buying the house, Ketlhoiloe paid R31 a month in rent for a small, four-room house. The new house was sprawling; except for a stereo and a couple of pieces of furniture in the spacious bedroom, it was empty. Once whetted, however, Ketlhoiloe's appetite for luxury seemed to grow. He complained that the new house wasn't good enough. He wanted a second oven—probably so he could run a shebeen out of the house—and fencing around the yard.

The consequences of his purchase were immense. Locked into his house payments, Ketlhoiloe could not afford to join a teachers' boycott of schools. He would have to think twice before joining a general strike. Switching jobs would be tricky, too. "This way you've got to stay in teaching whether you like it or not," Ketlhoiloe conceded. It also became pointless to withhold payments that would only penalize the bank and the bank might repossess the house.

Where blacks weren't eager to undertake such financial obligations, the government pushed them. In 1979 when journalist Gabu Tugwana applied for a house to rent, he was told that he was number 20,193 on the waiting list. "I was told that my chances were very, very slim," he said. Instead the government urged him to buy a house for R27,200 in Dobsonville, a middle-class area of Soweto. He had worked eight years and his employers gave him a loan against his pension. "Enforced middle-class housing," Tugwana called it. When the rent boycotts hit Soweto in mid-1986, Tugwana boycotted payments of water and electricity to the state-owned utilities, but he kept paying the bank that holds the deed to his house. If the utilities were privatized, boycotts of service payments also would become meaningless gestures.

During the first half of the century, the black elite was made up of teachers, chiefs, clergy, independent proprietors, and a smattering of professionals. Originally they were drawn disproportionately from the Xhosas in the Eastern Cape, who had been exposed to British colonists and missionary education. While they retained strong links to traditional rural areas, they were mostly Anglicans and Methodists, distinguished by their Western ways and literacy.

These blacks saw themselves as people of influence, as intermediaries between two worlds preserving the best of their African past while adopting the style, values, and Christianity of the modern world. In the 1930s, T. D. Mweli Skota sold 12,000 copies of his *African Yearly Register,* a who's who of black elite with more than 370 sketches of "progressive" Africans. The book was a self-conscious attempt to define the nature and role of the "civilized" black elite.[7]

After the National Party came to power in 1948, the black elite was pushed down among the black masses. Apartheid in the 1950s hit hard at the class of people who aspired to the same rights and standards as whites. Once-respected teachers were forced to teach Bantu education, the second-rate curriculum and school system forced on blacks since the 1950s. African nurses lost the equal rights they had only recently won. Homeowners in places like Sophiatown were dispossessed. Regardless of their stature within the black community, black people were forced to carry passes. No longer able to straddle two worlds, their stature among blacks as well as whites plunged.

State control of schools, property, hospitals, and licenses turned most of the black elite into employees of the state or clients of state patronage. Even "independent" African traders depended on the state for licenses and the allocation of business sites. When the ANC was banned in 1960 and the black elite was no longer able to vent its frustration, many of its members left. Between 1960 and 1970, the number of Africans with university degrees *fell,* despite the production of hundreds of new graduates. "The cream of African society was driven out of its jobs and in many cases out of the country," wrote one observer.[8] Skota, who had tried to define the members and nature of the black elite, died destitute in Soweto in June 1976, the month the Soweto student rebellion began.

No amount of government reform could resurrect Skota's elite. Fifty years after the publication of Skota's *African Yearly Register,* the black middle class was markedly different in size and standing. Literacy alone was no longer a distinction. There had been an explosion in the number of blacks who were literate and who worked in white-collar jobs. Between 1946 and 1980, the number of African technicians and professionals increased more than eightfold, from 24,411 to 190,089. In 1980, there were 86,951 Africans working as supervisors in different sectors of the economy. Despite competition from whites and licensing difficulties, black independent commercial proprietors increased in number from 761 in 1946 to almost 15,000 in 1980. There were also 1,575 African restaurant and hotel owners within "white" South Africa.[9]

Members of the new black middle class did not see themselves as an elite.

Within the professions, they were usually consigned to subservient positions. Africans outnumbered whites among health professionals, but numbered only 4 percent of the doctors. Africans made up 47 percent of the country's teachers (versus 35 percent for whites) but they constituted only 33 percent of the country's school inspectors. Even in manufacturing, where blacks advanced to minor supervisory positions, real responsibility lay in the hands of whites further up the corporate ladder.[10]

Once notables, the educated and successful black no longer commanded respect. A person of wealth and education who drove a good car was more likely to be a target to black youths than to be shown deference.

A large part of the contemporary black middle class was made up by the government's own black bureaucracy, bloated by homeland civil servants and township administrators. In the Transkei, 7,000 salaried black civil servants formed the backbone of urban society in the homeland's capital, Umtata. Obedience and loyalty, not education or competence, were the qualifications for these jobs.

If this was the black middle class the government wanted to create, it was a self-defeating exercise. It was not a source of political stability. "There is a myth that as soon as blacks get some material things, they will drop political demands," said Donald Ncube of the Anglo American Corporation. "It's a myth. It is precisely those people—educated people—who are politicized quicker. It is the black middle class that is most radical in terms of analysis." Ncube said he was an example of the failure of a strategy to divide blacks by class. "I don't feel part of the privileged class, not until I can vote and own land," he said. Ncube warned that "Hungry people cannot fight revolutions. It is the people who are rich who fight revolutions."

Even members of the black middle class who were not fighting revolution professed little love for the government. They felt they had succeeded despite the system, not because of it. Eric Mafuna spoke with an accent difficult to place because it was so proper. His suits were tailored perfectly. A former director of the advertizing firm J. Walter Thompson, Mafuna was an executive with his own marketing consulting company in downtown Johannesburg.

Despite his material success, Mafuna was troubled. Because the Group Areas Act prohibited blacks from living in white areas, Mafuna often found himself socializing with business colleagues in one world, then returning to another.

> You go to a Sunday lunch in Bryanston [a well-to-do white suburb of Johannesburg] and you taste the good life you know your money entitles you to. Then come three or four and you have to drive back to Soweto. The difference is stark and jolting. Past a certain point you know you're out of the city. There are no lights, everything is third world. You're now in Africa, and you just came from California where you spent three or four hours. You can't ignore these things. They eat away at the very fabric of life you're chasing.

Nor was Mafuna happy about his new ability to buy his township home. "What good is freehold when my freehold is the size of a postage stamp.

My business colleagues live in places seven times the size. My place is the size of his tennis court."

As a marketing and advertising consultant, Mafuna was paid to know what blacks were thinking. Fundamental to what blacks thought, he said, was something that went beyond the ghetto feeling of Soweto, and that something explained why blacks weren't impressed by half-hearted political and economic reforms or by the new public works projects. "We're not talking about the price of bread," he said. "We're talking about human dignity. That's why people say the changes so far are cosmetic, they are issues that deal with the quality of life. It's not the quality of life. It's the maintenance of human dignity, the thing that quality of life flows out of."[11]

CHAPTER FOURTEEN

The Black Face of Apartheid

IN 1960, PRIME MINISTER HENDRIK VERWOERD, the architect of grand apartheid, outlined his plan to create eight (later ten) separate "bantustans" for different African tribes, reserving the major cities, ports, mines, and beaches for "white" South Africa. To justify this scheme of resettlement, Verwoerd said that every race and tribe was entitled to "separate development" and that each bantustan (now known as homelands or self-governing territories) would rule itself, with its own black ministers, police and civil servants.

Verwoerd's plan seemed absurd. On November 24, 1960, the *Cape Times* ran a cartoon depicting Verwoerd in blackface, smiling from ear to ear and singing an amended version of the Al Jolson song, "How I love ya! How I love ya! My dear old Bantustan . . ."

Today white ministers no longer need to don blackface. Thousands of blacks work for the various arms of the South African grand apartheid government, as chief ministers of tribal homelands, members of segregated houses of parliaments or community councils, as police, even as foreign ambassadors.

"Fools, crooks, and eunuchs," is how Terror Lekota once dismissed the blacks who work within the structures of apartheid. Nonetheless, these blacks cannot be dismissed so easily. Together they form an army of civil servants and make up roughly half the total police force, outnumbering the blacks in exile with the ANC. With the UDF in disarray, black officialdom and black police became more prominent again.

Some black officials lived up to their reputations for avarice, but others argued that working within the system was the only way to bring about change. "Our participation doesn't mean acceptance" of the system, an Indian member of the tricameral Parliament said. "We view participation as a strategy, not a principle. The fear of cooptation is always there, but it behooves all of us to use the only platforms we have." The emergency only bolstered this view. Chief Buthelezi declared that UDF members had "tried the impossible and failed." He said the way the UDF leaders had attacked the government was like "bashing their heads against a solid brick wall . . . and their noses are now bloodied and it is their fault." Such "tactics and strategies have failed us in the past."[1]

KwaNdebele

Where the power of apartheid's black faces began and ended was difficult to discern, especially in the never-never lands of separate development like KwaNdebele.

There aren't any border posts at the boundaries of KwaNdebele. A sprawling shantytown of corrugated metal and mud huts marks the end of "white" South Africa. A sign by the side of the road says "KwaNdebele housing; we will build your dream house."

Like other homelands, KwaNdebele is a strange combination of fact and fiction. In the terms Verwoerd used to justify grand apartheid, it is a piece of fiction. Though the homeland was ostensibly designed to restore the Ndebele tribe's cultural, political, and social traditions, those traditions are irretrievable. The Ndebeles long ago broke away from the Zulu kingdom and plundered the northern Transvaal province. In the 1800s, Afrikaner settlers drove most of the Ndebeles into what is now Zimbabwe. The rest were scattered, largely as farm workers employed by whites.

The Ndebeles never put down roots where KwaNdebele is located. The government created this Ndebele "traditional homeland" by purchasing land from nineteen white farmers about eighty miles northeast of Pretoria. Over two decades, the government forcibly resettled the Ndebeles from white farms and urban areas. Yet for all the government's efforts, half of South Africa's Ndebeles still live outside the homeland, and about a quarter of the residents in the homeland aren't Ndebele. That includes the 120,000 people of Moutse, an old, predominantly Sotho settlement.

Economically, there is nothing independent about this homeland. Surrounded on all sides by "white" South Africa, it lacks any significant industry of its own. Most residents make a several-hour commute by bus to jobs in Pretoria. In 1982 only 12 percent of the per capita wages of KwaNdebele residents' was earned inside the homeland.[2] Though the population was 32,000 in 1970, it exploded to about 350,000 by the end of 1985. Still the "nation" possessed not one hospital.

Despite these absurdities, many people treated the KwaNdebele homeland as fact, not fiction, as Moutse resident Alfred Cheare discovered.

On New Year's Day 1986, Cheare was awakened by seven armed men—also black, with white crosses painted on their foreheads—pounding on his front door. The men barged in, hit Cheare on the back of the head with an ax and announced, "Today, Moutse is under KwaNdebele."

Cheare recovered, but it was a rude awakening to the news that the Pretoria regime had let KwaNdebele annex Moutse to satisfy the imperial ambitions of KwaNdebele's chief minister Simon Skosana, a former truck driver. The South African government had appointed Skosana and the other members of the KwaNdebele Assembly. Skosana, who had failed to finish the eighth grade, was the second-best educated member of the cabinet. The sacrifice of Moutse was the price paid to win Skosana's cooperation.

Instead of enhancing South Africa's stability, the homeland system created archipelagoes of instability. By allowing Skosana to annex Moutse, that instability spread.

Before fighting broke out that day, Moutse had been peaceful, with no unrest or school boycotts. Moutse's people weren't particularly radical. The conservative Zion Christian Church had a strong following there. And the traditional chief had sent representatives to the Lebowa homeland assembly.

But Moutse resented the growth of KwaNdebele. Moutse's people had lived in the area for more than a century, before the Republic of South Africa existed. They had freehold title to farms bought before the 1913 Land Act. The only Ndebeles in the area before 1960 lived there because a Moutse chief had given them sanctuary in 1925. Now Moutse felt the Ndebeles had taken advantage of its hospitality. Moreover, Moutse's people didn't like the laws of KwaNdebele, where criminals were flogged in public and women couldn't vote.

Moutse's people also believed the South African government was contradicting its own policies by redistricting Moutse into KwaNdebele. Instead of upholding its oft-stated devotion to the principle of "non-interference in a group's own affairs," Pretoria disregarded the wishes of Moutse's Chief Mathebe. As soon as KwaNdebele became formally independent, all residents of Moutse would lose their citizenship in "white" South Africa and be considered aliens in cities as near as Pretoria. "What the State President is doing now in Moutse is contradictory to speeches of reform he's giving," said Godfrey Mathebe, the chief's brother and Moutse's representative in the Lebowa homeland assembly.[3]

President Botha never showed his face in Moutse to explain himself. Only Simon Skosana did. He wasted little time making his rule felt in his new dominion. Led by the KwaNdebele minister of the interior, thugs from a vigilante gang called the Mbhokoto (literally, "grinding stone") attacked Moutse. Four of the Mbhokoto were killed in what was believed to be an attempt to kidnap Chief Mathebe. About 400 of Moutse's people were abducted and taken to a large hall in KwaNdebele, where Skosana and his interior minister, Piet Ntuli, celebrated the new year by whipping Moutse residents such as Alfred Cheare. According to one of the prisoners, Ntuli "taunted us the whole time, calling us dogs and many more vulgar things." Outside people shouted "Kill the dogs." Skosana spoke briefly. KwaNdebele vigilantes then flooded the hall with water and detergent and forced the prisoners to strip to their underwear and lie on the floor. KwaNdebele vigilantes and police kicked the people, who would then slide across the floor into one another.[4]

The black face of KwaNdebele barely masked the role played by Pretoria. Because the homeland had not yet gone through the formalities of receiving "independence," a white civil servant named Gerrie van der Merwe was acting as commissioner general of the territory.

The accusations of the Moutse people were unfair, he assured me when I visited the KwaNdebele capital shortly after the Mbhokoto attack. Nor would Moutse's dissent deter Pretoria from granting "independence" to KwaNdebele later that year. He calmly explained that the South African government couldn't refuse the demands of the "fiercely independent Ndebele people." Pretoria, he said, measured this Ndebele devotion to independence by consulting Skosana and his cabinet. "Skosana is the real leader of his people," van der Merwe said.

I never met Skosana that day. Van der Merwe insisted that the chief minister was busy and didn't speak English very well.

By August 1986, resistance to KwaNdebele "independence" had grown not only in Moutse but within KwaNdebele itself. Leading members of the Ndebele royal family declared their opposition to the plan. Skosana's own sons barely spoke to him any longer. Though the new state of emergency chased the country's black leadership into hiding, widespread fighting in a "war of independence" forced police to seal the borders of the homeland. From the distance, all that could be seen was the smoke of burning tires.

Part of the reason for the rising resistance was that even though homelands were part of a plan called separate development, they did not develop separately when it came to politics. Because most of the people in KwaNdebele and other homelands were migrant workers, news and political ideas of the big cities had traveled to rural areas. In one of Skosana's last public appearances, the KwaNdebele legislature voted against independence.

The next time I visited KwaNdebele was to attend Skosana's funeral. Skosana had died of uncertain causes, either from diabetes or poisoning.

Earlier Skosana's Interior Minister Piet Ntuli had been killed by a car bomb. The ANC had claimed responsibility and people had celebrated by slaughtering animals for traditional feasts. It was like a harvest festival. A well-placed white civil servant confided to me that he suspected the South African Police had done away with Ntuli because he had been an embarrassment. Only police had access to Ntuli's parking lot, the civil servant whispered, and a police explosives expert had been sent to a nearby base just before the assassination and transferred away just afterwards. With the deaths of the two ministers, it appeared that dreams of an "independent" KwaNdebele were dead, too.

Skosana's funeral resembled a scene from *The Godfather*. While traditional Ndebele women with metal rings fastened around their ankles and necks prepared food for the funeral feast at the Skosana household, the veil of mourning barely concealed political intrigue. Black-suited white cabinet ministers from Pretoria attended the funeral, and an all-white South African police marching band played as the casket was carried to the cemetery. Representatives of the Mahlangu royal family, the rightful traditional leaders of the Ndebeles, came, too. One of the pallbearers was Prince Cornelius Mahlangu, a KwaNdebele cabinet minister, whose brother James was in detention on the suspicion that he was in league with the comrades.

The homeland's warring factions unofficially declared a one-day truce. Skosana's son Peter, a comrade who opposed his father and who had been in hiding for two weeks, appeared at the funeral within view of a high-ranking white police officer responsible for law and order in the homeland. Throughout the funeral, people whispered speculation about who would succeed Skosana. As a member of both the dissident royal family and the cabinet, Prince Cornelius was seen as the leading candidate.

During the funeral, I was sorry I hadn't insisted on interviewing Skosana before he died. But later, it seemed appropriate that I never met him. In the end, he really didn't matter. Neither did Prince Cornelius nor any of the other scheming pallbearers. The will of Pretoria seemed paramount when the victor of the power struggle emerged. He was an obscure KwaNdebele legislator named George Mahlangu (a cousin of the royal family) who had been a member of the Mbhokoto vigilante gang. Though George Mahlangu proclaimed his intention to make KwaNdebele "independent," Pretoria shelved the issue indefinitely after realizing that an independent homeland might be more unstable than a dependent one.

Like KwaNdebele, other homelands were in turmoil. The president of Boputhatswana only survived a coup attempt because South African Defense Force units came to his rescue. A major general in the Transkei army overthrew the government of Kaiser Matanzima and uncovered evidence of massive corruption involving Matanzima, Transkei bureaucrats, and white businessleaders. The leader of Lebowa died and his successor modeled himself on the KaNgwane leader who had visited the ANC.

Accused Number 39

It would be easy to understand South Africa if blacks and whites fit neatly on opposite sides of politics. It wouldn't even be too difficult to comprehend South Africa if blacks could be sorted out into supporters of the liberation movement and government collaborators. But in which category does John Mavuso belong?

In the great Treason Trial of the 1950s, John Mavuso was Accused Number 39. His picture is right there in the history books with Nelson Mandela and Walter Sisulu.

To Africans, he was a patriot then. According to the government, Mavuso was a traitor. The government charged that he and 155 others, allegedly in league with the Communist Party, had conspired to overthrow the South African state by violence. Even after his acquittal, as a one-time stalwart of the ANC, Mavuso was banned off and on until 1979; his picture still appears side-by-side with the communist Ruth First in a book of photos sold by ANC supporters in London.[5]

By 1988, views of John Mavuso had reversed. Africans suspected he was a traitor to their cause, while the government trumpeted him as a patriot. Mavuso had become one of the most powerful blacks in the South African state apparatus. He sat on the Transvaal executive committee, which controls the allocation of certain funds to different municipalities (similar to state governments in the United States). It was the first time that a black man had anything to say about spending money in white areas. Moreover, he freely consulted with National Party leaders, and it was rumored that he might join the cabinet. If so, he would become the first African ever to serve as a minister in the national government.

In 1988, when most of his former comrades were exiled, dead, or guests of the South African prison service, John Mavuso was the guest of the South African government in a posh mid-town Manhattan hotel on a tour of the United States. In the lobby there, I met him and David Madhiba, the mayor of Kagiso township. It soon became clear that Mavuso was, as one pro-UDF theorist said, "not your average sellout." Mavuso himself argued that he was no crook, no fool, and no eunuch.

"I cut my political teeth in Alexandra in 1946," Mavuso said. At that time, blacks had freehold rights in Alexandra. Because of overcrowding in the township, people decided to stake new claims to empty land north of Alexandra.

"I was one of the young scribes," Mavuso said. "We measured off sites and people paid fifty cents to stake claims and join a squatters' association." In subsequent negotiations with the government, the squatters agreed to move back inside Alexandra. In return the government let them use vacant land in the middle of the township.

During the 1950s, Mavuso rose through the ranks of the ANC. In 1951 he was elected secretary of the ANC's powerful Alexandra branch. Alexandra waged three bus boycotts, with thousands of residents participating. Mavuso became head of a seven-person regional ANC committee. Alfred Nzo, later the second-highest-ranking official of the ANC in exile, was secretary of the committee. In 1955, when many major figures were restricted, Mavuso was elected to the ANC national executive under Chief Lutuli. That position guaranteed him a place in the treason trial.

Even after the ANC was banned, Mavuso kept in touch with its exiled leaders. Nzo often sent his regards to Mavuso through people who visited ANC offices in London and Lusaka. Mavuso's brother Mike, known also by his code name Mfundisi, was a founding member of MK, the ANC military wing. In April 1979, while working for MK's intelligence department, Mike Mavuso died in an air crash shuttling arms from Luanda to the Zimbabwe guerrilla group, Zapu. John Mavuso heard the bad news straight from ANC president Tambo. "Oliver phoned and spoke to me. For the December 1980 unveiling of my brother's tombstone, Oliver told me to collect an air ticket at a certain office in Johannesburg. The ANC paid for the ticket. I flew to Lusaka and went with my late brother's wife to Luanda, where Joe Modise [commander of MK] drove me around."

Mavuso maintained that accepting a government post was "a logical evolution" from his stance as an ANC member. In the 1950s, "we were guided by the principle that we wanted a voice in running the country," Mavuso told me. "As long as [government] structures remained advisory, it was inappropriate to participate." He endorsed the ANC's decision to have its delegates resign from the Native Representative Council in the late 1940s. "Their representations to the government were not being heeded," Mavuso conceded.

However, the government was listening now, Mavuso said. He believed that his advice speeded the release of the Soweto Committee of Ten from prison in the mid-1970s and expanded the government's plan to loosen the restrictions against blacks owning homes. A boycott of government structures was an outdated strategy, Mavuso insisted. He blamed a "Trotskyite" faction of the ANC for pushing the boycott strategy. "The government has concluded that the participation of blacks in central government is inevitable and the question is how," Mavuso said. "President Botha is waiting at the table."

"Life goes on with or without the ANC's stand on non-participation," Mavuso said.

And as life went on, a certain amount of power accrued to the blacks who took part in the apartheid system. Mavuso said: "The government has become more and more dependent on black government that is grappling with day-to-day concerns of our people." In the black townships, "blacks don't go to an office now and see a person of another color saying whether they can get a house. They see their own people."

Black radicals ignored that participation at their own peril. Mavuso believed even his black opponents would be forced to recognize his authority. His colleague, Kagiso's Mayor Madhiba, gave an example. The head of the UDF affiliate called the Kagiso Residents' Association had no choice but to apply to Madhiba when he wanted a house for his family. "If that's not recognition of authority, I don't know what is," said Madhiba.

"The ANC in Lusaka, they too have a problem," said Mavuso. "They have to come to terms with us. We are in a pivotal situation."

In Rhodesia, Bishop Abel Muzorewa once believed that he, too, possessed real power. Whites were willing to deal with him, and for a time he became prime minister of his country. Though his power was limited, he believed he could parlay it into something greater after a transition period. To Muzorewa's surprise, however, white power brokers negotiated over his head with black guerrilla groups. Free elections soon followed and the guerrilla leader Robert Mugabe trounced Muzorewa.

Today in black politics, Muzorewa's name is synonymous with failure. He was a man of fleeting consequence, viewed by whites as malleable and treated by blacks as a "useful idiot"—but useful only for a short time.

Madhiba raised Muzorewa's name. "We shall be wary of allowing ourselves to be used as Muzorewas, as stepping stones." To prevent that, Madhiba and Mavuso said they would not forsake fellow blacks. "We are not in competition with the ANC. What is different is the strategy. Our goal is the same," Mavuso insisted. "This is why I insist on a black forum that must by *seen* to be negotiating for the release of political prisoners and the unbanning of organizations [like the ANC and PAC]," Madhiba added. Whether that forum really deserves credit for those concessions won't matter as long as it is *seen* to have obtained them. That way Madhiba and Mavuso hoped to parlay their seeming influence into positions at a national conference table, and not be abandoned in a liberated country.

In the mid-1970s, when the conservative white politician Connie Mulder was at the height of his power as the crown prince of the National Party, he went to chat with John Mavuso, then merely an old black political hand who had faded from prominence.

"I need your help," Mavuso remembered Mulder saying. Mulder was troubled by the blacks then serving the government. Through its own intolerance of opposition, the government had reduced these black officials to flunkies. As a result, when Mulder really did want advice from black officials, he couldn't get it.

Mulder explained the dilemma by taking a matchbox from his pocket. He could put a matchbox flat on the table and ask a black official if it were best to put the box of matches that way or, Mulder said, standing the matchbox on one end, he could ask whether the box would be better upright. The black official would stare at the upright box of matches and say "This way is alright." Then the black official would finger the matchbox and lay it down flat and say "This way it is also alright."

Connie Mulder had instinctively come to a conclusion similar to one reached by Lenin in another context. Lenin recognized that the Russian revolution could exploit so-called moderates, people Lenin dubbed "useful idiots." Conversely, Connie Mulder had realized that in trying to hang onto power, idiots were not useful at all. Indeed they could be dangerous.

What made a person like Mavuso useful to the government was that he was not a mere idiot. Thus he could be credible to international observers, helpful as an analyst of black opinion, and creative as a strategist against more radical blacks. Conscious of black political pressures, Mavuso insisted that 70 percent of the units in new housing schemes be designed for lower income blacks. Squatters too destitute for those homes should receive subsidies from a national housing commission, Mavuso said. His unrealized goal was that by 1990 all homes in black townships would be privately owned. "Hopefully the whole [housing] stock will be disposed of," Madhiba said.

Private home ownership by blacks would have immense effects on blacks and black politics. It would be a step forward for blacks. As for the nettlesome rent boycott, "We will bury it," Madhiba laughed. "We want to see how you boycott your own houses."

"That effect is just coincidental," Mavuso observed.

A "Clever Stooge"

Mayor Tom was trying to convince me that he was no Uncle Tom. Clearly this was a matter of some debate. Because Tom Boya had run for mayor in government-sponsored elections in the black township of Daveyton, many blacks considered him a quisling. His house was stoned. His car was attacked. In self-defense, his office windows were swathed in wire grating.

"People say to me, 'Boya, why do you agree to serve?' I don't think there is anything wrong with working within the system," he said, sitting in a leather swivel chair in his dimly lit office. "Working within the system you can actually achieve something you can point to. People want achievers, not just someone who pays lip service to helping them."

It was difficult to know what to make of the noble words of Tom Boya. On one hand, Mayor Boya didn't seem to be very modest. Like Mavuso, he too claimed credit for persuading the government to extend limited freehold rights to blacks. "Through my negotiations and leadership, land is being transferred to local authorities," he proclaimed. He had covered his office wall with newspaper clippings about himself and hung his portrait. At one point he picked up the phone and said "I'm thirsty," like a spoiled child. A secretary dutifully brought him a glass of water.

On the other hand, whatever self-aggrandizing motives had driven Boya to run for mayor in 1979 at the age of twenty-eight, he was at least, as a friend of mine called him, "a clever stooge." When the Daveyton UDF wanted to use the community hall, Boya obliged. He supported the general strike that marked the tenth anniversary of the 1976 student uprising. He demanded the release of detained children and helped the elderly. And when the government tried to entice him onto a national statutory council for blacks, he said he would only join if Mandela were released from prison.

He talked a good game; he wasn't blind to what blacks wanted. Boya said his goals were the same as those of the African National Congress: better living conditions for blacks and majority rule. "The most important thing is to break through, to remove the hurdles to government at the national level," he said. He said that by serving within the government's apartheid system, he was acting as a caretaker for blacks while the struggle continued. "Representation at the highest levels? Yes! But what do we do right now? We must not forget that people should eat, get better housing and be educated while we keep fighting."

Yet by running for office—and accepting perquisites like a fancy car and good salary—he had flaunted the boycott policy of the anti-apartheid movement and put himself in a tenuous position. Scores of municipal councillors had been attacked and several had died since the Vaal uprising. Indeed part of the key to Boya's electoral success—nine consecutive one-year terms dating to 1979—was that he usually ran unopposed.

Boya was clever enough to know that he was risking his life and the lives of his five children. After Boya's house was attacked in 1985, some of Daveyton's UDF leaders went by his house to express their sympathy. They said they were not against Boya as an individual, but against the position he was holding. They said they needed a leader like Boya because of his experience with local government and they invited the mayor to quit and join the UDF executive. Boy declined. "I stand for what I stand for," he said.

The mayor grabbed a piece of paper and drew five circles on it. He pointed to the one furthest to the left and said it represented the "left radicals." The next one represented "frustrated blacks who don't see what people in the center are doing or feel that they are not going anywhere." The far right circle represented "white radicals who will take up arms against blacks." The second circle from the right represented "insecure whites." In the center, he declared, were people like Tom Boya. But, he warned, "the center is going to collapse."

"Tom Boya has got to start producing results," he acknowledged. If the government didn't accelerate reform, violence between the extremes would escalate, he said. And then, "Whoever wins in South Africa will rule over tombs."

The Chief

On May 1, 1986, Chief Mangosuthu Gatsha Buthelezi stood in a stadium packed with 70,000 supporters and declared that his political organization, Inkatha, "has kept its hand of brotherhood stretched out to all who wish to hold it."

Below the speaker's platform, some of his followers were menacing a black reporter who had written articles critical of the chief. They ordered him to leave. A Buthelezi supporter reassured the reporter's concerned colleagues: "Don't worry. If we were really angry, he'd already be dead."

The scene in the stadium showed the two faces of the most prominent black working within the apartheid system. Advocating black unity and peaceful change, Chief Buthelezi presents himself to the world as the moderate alternative to black radicals. Yet his followers, thousands of whom came to the stadium armed with clubs, shields and spears, have waged a bloody fight against the chief's black political rivals. Hundreds have died at their hands.

Chief Buthelezi has been the whites' favorite black.

Though he proclaims himself a foe of apartheid, he has accepted his place in the architecture of apartheid by serving as chief minister of the KwaZulu homeland, an archipelago of land fragments scattered across the white province of Natal.

Though he wraps himself in the colors of the liberation movement, the chief says blacks cannot topple apartheid through violence because the government is too strong.

> The struggle of violence is futile. The white regime hasn't even shown one quarter of its power. It hasn't bared its claws because it hasn't had to. When President Botha says, "Don't push us too far," I know exactly what that means: Don't push him to a situation where whites scorch the earth.

The chief opposes economic sanctions. "It frightens me that anyone should be trying to destroy the foundations of this country," he says. "Then political emancipation will be meaningless."

In small gatherings, he is gracious, displaying old world manners and a playful smile. He punctuates his conversation by exclaiming "quite so." He once gave a white politician in Natal a black cowhide shield, and wryly apologized that black was such an "unprepossessing color." According to one admirer, the white political scientist Lawrence Schlemmer, the chief is "a lover of classical music and a lifelong student of history."

Most whites who can imagine a black president of South Africa can do so because they long imagined he would be Chief Buthelezi. This could be viewed as an achievement or an indictment, depending on whether you think Buthelezi has changed white opinion or molded himself to it. Buthelezi already strides the international stage like a diplomat. He has posed with President Reagan in the Oval Office, sipped tea with Prime Minister Margaret Thatcher, and met with other Western heads of state, who deem him a "moderate" black who could lead a democratic South Africa.

"Chief Buthelezi is a social democrat," said Schlemmer. In an article called "Towards Orchestrated Liberation" written for the *Financial Mail*, Schlemmer praised Buthelezi for his "strategic adaptation to reality" marked by a recognition that "the black political struggle will for a long while yet lose a head-on confrontation with the South African state." Schlemmer said Buthelezi occupies "the middle ground" and would "assure white interests without perpetuating the material and symbolic injuries which black people endure."

The *Financial Mail* declared Buthelezi "man of the year" at the end of 1985, a year of upheaval in which Buthelezi had played virtually no role at all. The magazine hailed Buthelezi as an "unabashed free marketeer" who recognized that "a solution to the country's problems has to be found in a political compromise."[6]

But the battles the chief fights on his native ground undermine the notion that Chief Buthelezi is a man of compromise. Among blacks, Chief Buthelezi is a divisive figure. Members of his political organization, Inkatha, have been implicated in firebombings, beatings, and assassinations aimed at his black rivals, particularly members of the UDF. In May 1986, a court issued a restraining order against an Inkatha central committee member accused of arson and assault. Another Inkatha leader, cradling a gun in his lap, told an interviewer: "With this I will leave hundreds dead on the battlefield."[7]

Ian Mkhize, a former Inkatha member who defected to the UDF, said "Inkatha is fast shedding its political image and is becoming a military structure." He alleged that police stood by and watched while Inkatha members with flame throwers attacked a township that didn't want to be incorporated into Chief Buthelezi's territory.

Chief Buthelezi began his career as a loyal ally of the liberation movement. When he was a student at Fort Hare University, he was expelled for boycotting a visit by the governor general. "He was a terrific revolutionary: willing, able, and committed to change," said Dr. Motlana, a classmate.

Buthelezi took a position in the Natives Affairs administration. Later he assumed the chieftainship of the Buthelezi clan after receiving the approval of then-ANC president Chief Albert John Lutuli. Like many ANC leaders, Lutuli believed the ANC could use such posts even though they required government approval. The late Johnstone "Johnny" Makatini, then the ANC's rural organizer, said he could always rely on Buthelezi for a safe place to stay.

In 1970, Buthelezi agreed to serve as chief minister of the KwaZulu homeland. In 1975, he founded Inkatha ye Nkululeko ye Sizwe, borrowing the name from a Zulu cultural society founded in 1922 by the Zulu King Solomon Dinizulu to counter growing support for the left-wing Industrial and Commercial Workers Union. *Inkatha* means traditional headband. Though Inkatha is open to all blacks and aspires to being a national liberation movement, its membership is almost exclusively Zulu and its constitution stipulates that the president of the organization must be a Zulu. This clause violates the spirit of the ANC, which strives to transcend tribalism.

Nevertheless, the ANC in exile gave its quiet blessings to both moves. Buthelezi threw a monkey wrench into government plans in the 1970s by rejecting so-called independence for KwaZulu, a stance he maintained despite government pressure and financial enticements.

Inkatha adopted the colors of the ANC. Its youth brigade used uniforms identical to those of the old ANC Youth League. And in KwaZulu schools, children learned about the ANC in Inkatha textbooks. At a women's brigade meeting, Chief Buthelezi's press team handed out thick packets of verbatim transcripts of the ANC's Radio Freedom, whose broadcasts were jammed and banned.

In the demoralized years between 1963 and 1976, the ANC thirsted for such exposure. "You must remember that no one dared talk politics at that time," explained Makatini, who was a member of the ANC national executive committee. "We thought Inkatha would give us an above-ground presence. At first it seemed to go beyond our wildest expectations. It adopted ANC colors and uniforms, our anthem and slogan. 'Amandla!' It was great!"

Inside South Africa, however, some blacks didn't think it was so great. Steve Biko, then at the height of his influence, called the homelands "the greatest single fraud ever invented by white politicians." Biko said that blacks who said homelands could be exploited to wring concessions from whites "have already sold their souls to the white man," since the homelands would only confuse the black masses.

Biko granted that Transkei president Kaiser Matanzima and Buthelezi

> are perhaps more than anybody else acutely aware of the limitations surrounding them. It may also be true that they are extremely dedicated to the upliftment of black people and perhaps to their liberation. Many times they have manifested a fighting spirit characterising true courage and determination.

But Biko condemned them anyway. In an article written under his pseudonym Frank Talk, Biko said, "If you want to fight your enemy you do not accept from him the unloaded of his two guns and then challenge him to a duel."[8] Biko said whites were using Buthelezi, not the other way around. The more Buthelezi shouted his devotion to liberation the more he suited whites' purposes.

> For white South Africa, a man like Buthelezi . . . solves so many conscience problems. . . . The combination of Buthelezi and the white press [also] make up the finest ambassadors that South Africa has ever had. . . . When you use bantustan platforms to attack what you do not like you epitomize the kind of militant black leader who in South Africa is freely allowed to speak and oppose the system. You exonerate the country from the blame that it is a police state.[9]

An increasing number of Biko's supporters agreed. In 1978, at the burial of PAC leader Robert Sobukwe in Graaff Reinet, Buthelezi was jeered and stoned at the funeral by young Black Consciousness followers. Tutu advised the chief to leave. In the haste to usher the humiliated chief to safety, one of the chief's bodyguards shot and wounded three of the mourners.

The incident presaged a split between Buthelezi and the ANC. In 1979, exiled ANC leaders met the chief in London as they had many times earlier.

Buthelezi wanted to make the meeting public. But the ANC, eager not to alienate the young Black Consciousness followers it was recruiting, wanted to keep the meeting secret. According to the ANC's Mbeki, who was present, the participants finally promised to keep the meeting confidential. Two days later, the chief revealed the meeting to a Sunday newspaper. "That was the beginning of the problem with Gatsha," said Mbeki later. "Everyone said, 'No, this man has his own agenda.'" Buthelezi defended his action, saying he "can't negotiate behind the backs of my people."

Buthelezi fell further afoul of his former allies in the Congress movement after clashes between Inkatha supporters and black students. Secondary-school students boycotting classes in KwaZulu in May 1980 were attacked by a mob armed with spears and *assegais,* hardwood spears. Buthelezi himself said "I know that the people do not seek to march behind a string of scrawny, scaggly, tattered cockerels dancing to the tune of an international band orchestrated by no-good clerics and long-haired intellectuals." [10]

At the University of Zululand at Ngoye, the national student organization, Azaso, was banned from the campus, not by Pretoria but by the KwaZulu homeland government.

In October 1983, students denounced an impending visit to the campus by Buthelezi. As a result, Inkatha *impis*—warriors wielding spears and clubs—were bused in from all over the province. Students entering the campus were searched for weapons, but the impis were permitted to pass through the checkpoints with their weapons.

> Students claim the morning mist had hardly lifted when Zulu warriors armed with the traditional weapons of war, spears, cowhide shields, *kieries* [sticks] and battle-axes slipped on to the campus. Unaware of the impending terror, students said they were eating leisurely Saturday breakfasts when the still mist was shattered by the pounding of sticks and shields and war cries as the Impis swept through the campus. Dazed and startled students stumbled from their hostels to be confronted by the attacking impis. Some in western dress or Khaki uniform with khaki colours, but most wearing leopard-skinned battle dress. Terrified students fled screaming "It's the Amabutho." [11]

The students fled to their dormitories and barricaded themselves in their rooms. But the impis broke down the doors and attacked the students. Four students were killed and more than 100 others stabbed. One student was singled out for disrupting an earlier speech by Oscar Dhlomo, a KwaZulu cabinet minister. The student was dragged out of the dorm, hung upside down from a tree and beaten until he was dead.

Buthelezi later said the Inkatha followers were provoked and said they "did no more than defend my honor and the honor of His Majesty the King." [12]

The gulf between Buthelezi and other black leaders isn't always appreciated by outsiders. The Reverend Jesse Jackson once tried to patch up a quarrel by inviting Desmond Tutu and the respected Soweto physician Nthato

Motlana to dinner at a Johannesburg hotel with Chief Buthelezi. But the dinner was marred when one of the chief's aides nearly came to blows with Dr. Motlana. Motlana said later, "You can't, over a meal, resolve irreconcilable differences about change."

Throughout the black uprising of the mid-'80s, the rift between Buthelezi and the ANC grew while the ANC's popularity soared. He felt his contributions in the 1970s were not appreciated. "When others whispered about the ANC, I stood there in broad daylight boldly reading the words of Nelson Mandela. . . . Instead of giving me credit . . . you sneer at me!" he wrote in a letter.

Buthelezi disavowed two of the ANC's four pillars of struggle—violence and sanctions—and raised nettlesome questions about their effectiveness. "There is not a single bridge that is not standing, there is not a single factory that is not operating because of the ANC's war effort," he noted. "Every railway line is intact, every pipeline is intact and the very worst that the ANC can do takes the South African government only an hour or two to make normal again."

Moreover, Chief Buthelezi opposed virtually every campaign waged by groups sympathetic to the ANC, like COSATU and the UDF. Chief Buthelezi condemned school and consumer boycotts and worker strikes. "How the hell does he think we're going to change things?" asked the ANC's Mbeki.

Chief Buthelezi presented himself as the rightful heir of ANC tradition, carrier of the true mantle of black resistance, suggesting that the "mission in exile" had gone astray. "Now we have to deal with this Frankenstein we created," Makatini said.

Protected by his status as representative of the official homeland government, Buthelezi has used the space given him to build Inkatha into an imposing political machine in the country, claiming 1.2 million members in 1986. Though an Inkatha organizer told me that only a quarter of them were paid up, that still made Inkatha larger than the ANC was before it was banned in 1960.

In rural KwaZulu, youngsters knew nothing but Buthelezi. At a fifth-grade classroom at the Blood River primary school, most of the forty-four students thought Buthelezi was king of the Zulus. (In fact, the king is named Goodwill Zwelethini.) Only three children said they knew who President Botha was. One called him "chief of the whites." When asked whether Botha was the ruler of South Africa, only eight of the children guessed yes.

Chief Buthelezi has built a thriving bureaucracy in KwaZulu. Ulundi, the capital, is perched amid rolling hills with scores of government buildings constructed in concentric circles similar to the pattern of the traditional royal Zulu camps. There Buthelezi, with his salary and the budget of the homeland underwritten by Pretoria, dispenses patronage to his allies.

And it is an odd collection of allies: Natal whites on one hand, Zulu tribal chiefs on the other. Both groups share a natural conservatism. The

Zulu chiefs are threatened by the UDF and reformers who would loosen tribal control of rural areas and give more land to private farmers or collectives. "As long as Inkatha is closely linked with chiefs, there is no chance of serious agricultural reform," said one of Buthelezi's former lawyers. "To organize land on a more shared basis, you must smash chiefs' ownership and organization. This is a revolutionary proposal that Inkatha would never touch."

Buthelezi also has cemented ties with local leaders like Thomas Mandla Shabalala, who controls the rapidly growing Lindelani shack settlement outside Durban. Shabalala is a tall man whose face is scarred from ritual childhood cuts his parents made on his face. Little happened in Lindelani without Shabalala's approval; he was the Godfather of the slum, caring for his followers and dealing ruthlessly with his enemies. As the population of Lindelani soared, Shabalala became more important. In 1985 he was placed on the Inkatha central committee. Little changed in Lindelani, except that Shabalala hung a large portrait of Buthelezi in his living room and made loyalty to him synonymous with loyalty to Inkatha. His house was surrounded by cement walls. Bodyguards kept watch and did his bidding. He dispensed food supplied by the South African Red Cross, whose director was a white liberal woman who backed Buthelezi.

Follow the paved road toward Ulundi. Just before the KwaZulu capital you come to a bridge over a creek. Turn onto a dirt road before the bridge and in a couple of miles you will find an Inkatha youth camp, where 200 blacks are trained to become the future Inkatha elite.

The youths keep a rigorous schedule. At 4:30 A.M. they rise and undergo physical training until 6 A.M. After washing, eating breakfast, and saying prayers, they attend classes from eight until ten in the morning. The classes are in agriculture, home economics (for women only), building (for men only), community development, leadership, and health education. They break for tea, then classes continue until 11:30. Another hour of physical training precedes lunch. Classes and hands-on projects take up the afternoon. The camp grows its own food. There are a variety of evening activities. On Mondays they hold meetings. Tuesday evenings are for studying. Wednesdays are for movies. Thursdays and Fridays are for studying, Saturdays for films, and Sundays for indoor games and dances.

I visited the camp one Sunday, and after church the clean-cut students assembled in a large hall that resembled an airplane hanger. The leader of the group explained how to set up an Inkatha branch and urged everyone to join. A woman instructor said that all the teachers at the camp were Inkatha members. They read from the Inkatha constitution. Afterwards, the group rose and shouted "Amandla"; they began to clap in unison and sang "Shenge is ours/Through him we will conquer." Shenge is a name for Buthelezi, whom my young guide at the camp kept calling "His Excellency."

"Opinions in the group must be the same," one of the campers, Audrey

Mnguni said to me. If not, "You must try to influence the people who disagree," added Peaceful Mavuso, another camper.

"People of the UDF are against us," said Busisiwe Mbhense, whose mother taught in a KwaZulu primary school and whose father worked for the KwaZulu government as a driver. "They say they will liberate this country by blood and by fire and by tires. It's nonsense," said Zakhele Mthembu.

Inkatha, by contrast, "motivates people to help themselves. We must do it on our own," said Peter Kunene. The camp would train them to fight ignorance, disease, and poverty, Mavuso said.

This camp was for the elite Inkatha youth. But other youths went to general training camps. "We take school dropouts and train them as mechanics," said Ntwe Mafole, national organizer of the Inkatha youth brigade. Mafole said, "We run the camps along paramilitary lines with an established hierarchy: platoon leaders, commanding instructors, etc. At least we can instill discipline, a kind of military discipline among young people."

Mafole was a leading figure in the Inkatha organization. When I met him in early 1986 he was twenty-eight years old. He wore a name bracelet and was dressed in spotless white pants and a printed patterned shirt.

Mafole had been a member of the Evaton student representative council during the peak of the Black Consciousness influence in the black secondary schools. But he said he was drawn to Inkatha because it was bold by the standards of the 1970s. "For the first time I heard a man [Buthelezi] stand on a public platform and demand the release of Nelson Mandela. Many people before had been just whispering it." The first Inkatha rally he attended drew 45,000 people, more than Mafole had ever seen at a political rally.

After Black Consciousness groups were quashed, Mafole concluded that students' efforts had yielded little. "Nineteen-seventy-six carried a lot of defeats for black people. It emphasized a lesson for me: we should not risk challenging the government with armed struggle at this stage." So Mafole joined Inkatha and became a full-time paid organizer in 1980.

While Mafole claimed that only "peaceful means" could bring the liberation of blacks, one had to wonder about the sincerity of this slick young man. Just a couple of days before I met him, police had stopped his van in a nearby township and arrested him and nine other Inkatha Youth Brigade members on charges of arson and attempted murder. The charges stemmed from an incident in which Mafole and other Inkatha members allegedly burned the home of a UDF activist and fired shots into the house as its residents tried to escape. The morning of the day we met, he had been released on R1,000 bail, itself a tribute to Inkatha's influence. A UDF man arraigned on similar charges would never be granted bail. Mafole told me he was innocent. "The shots fired into the house came from a shotgun, whereas we only had a 746 Beretta," he explained.[13]

I saw him again from time to time at Inkatha rallies, in front of regiments of Youth Brigade members dressed in their khaki uniforms and black berets.

At the rally in Jabulani stadium in Soweto, Mafole—one of the few Tswanas in Inkatha—translated for the chief, whom he called even in casual conversation "His Excellency, the president of the movement." He looked a little like a college football cheerleader; he led the faithful in chants and songs.

On May 1, 1986, Chief Buthelezi launched an avowedly capitalist trade union to rival South Africa's largest black trade union federation, COSATU.

Inkatha bused supporters—thousands armed with shields, clubs and spears—to a stadium in Durban for an inaugural rally for the union, called the United Workers Union of South Africa, or UWUSA. As 70,000 people watched, an Inkatha leader conducted a mock funeral for the rival COSATU, then trampled a black coffin with the names of COSATU's two top officials written on it.

Two miles away, the well-established COSATU held a smaller rally. Extra police and army troop carriers patrolled the streets of downtown Durban to prevent tensions from getting out of hand.

Buthelezi had decided to launch his own trade union after Elijah Barayi, president of COSATU, attacked homeland leaders in his maiden speech in December 1985. Insulted, Buthelezi charged COSATU leaders with "piracy" in turning the union federation to political objectives. He said COSATU's support of foreign investment sanctions would rob blacks of needed jobs. A poster held by one follower criticized Archbishop Tutu, who backs foreign disinvestment. "Bishop Tutu deserves execution," the poster said.

COSATU general secretary Jay Naidoo said Inkatha's May Day rally "makes a mockery of a working class symbol" and blamed Inkatha for more than a dozen attacks on COSATU leaders in the previous four months, including the shooting of a union organizer the week before May Day. Inkatha said the new union would introduce some healthy competition into union organizing.

Labor activists were distraught. They said the rivalry would weaken all unions by making them appendages of political movements. "It is tragic for the labor movement," University of Natal labor specialist Ari Sitas said. "Labor unions elsewhere in Africa subordinated their demands to national liberation movements and in the end became quite toothless." Moreover, the rivalry pitted the country's two most organized black groups against one another.

The images of the two unions differed vastly and said much about the differences between Buthelezi's camp and other black organizations. COSATU was headed by Barayi, a lifetime mineworker whose fiery rhetoric excites the union's militant membership. The top official of the new Inkatha union was Simon Conco, a soft-spoken entrepreneur without any previous union experience. A leading Inkatha member and the whip in the KwaZulu legislature, he ran a general store and was a director of a group of wholesale and retail outlets. He opposed the needless use of strikes, saying, "If you destroy the economy—as you do through strikes—it will be difficult to rebuild it when you are liberated."

Inkatha was trying to appeal to workers worried about job security at a time when black unemployment generally was running between 25 percent and 60 percent depending on the area. UWUSA said COSATU's demands for higher wages and disinvestment threatened jobs. But the pitch didn't work well. While Inkatha claimed more than a million members, many of them were also members of COSATU. COSATU unions had proven their mettle in negotiations over several years. By contrast, UWUSA appeared to be collaborating with the bosses. Inkatha pressured employers in Natal for favors and many employers eagerly obliged, contributing money to UWUSA in order to weaken established black unions. Inkatha's only prior experience with unions had been with sugar workers. That union was started with money from a sugar-growing company and with the help of a company personnel manager.

By throwing the weight of Inkatha behind the new union, Buthelezi alienated many loyal followers by forcing them to choose sides. Even the May Day launch betrayed signs of weakness. Though the stadium was full, many in the audience grew weary and left while Buthelezi, hoarse and barely audible, was still speaking.

The policy and strategy differences between Chief Buthelezi, the ANC, the UDF, and COSATU could wait until after blacks win majority rule—if not for personality clashes. Even in late 1987, after hundreds of people had died in fighting between the UDF and Inkatha in the townships outside Pietermaritzburg, UDF president Archie Gumede wrote to the chief that

> the decisive question is not necessarily that of working within or outside the state structures. . . . In the mid-1970s too there was no problem in supporting the struggle of the Labour Party to destroy the CRC [colored representatives council] from within. Nor has there been any contradiction in the UDF sharing a platform with Enos Mabuza [chief minister] of KaNgwane.[14]

But Buthelezi doesn't take criticism lightly and doesn't want rivals. "He likes you to look him in the knees," says a white politician. Every year he makes a 200-page policy speech before the KwaZulu Legislative Assembly in which he repeats and rebutts every criticism leveled at him.

Buthelezi's thirst for admiration is apparent at his public rallies, where a recitation by his praise poet usually precedes the chief's appearance. The recitations are given by his cousin Ephraim Buthelezi, who was given the name Phakathikwempi, meaning "in the midst of enemies." Ephraim said that his role as praise singer was revealed to him in a dream in 1974. In the dream, men in traditional attire urged him to sing the chief's praises. Three or four years later, he had the same dream. So at a youth rally, he started reciting praises where he was seated. The chief heard him and called him to the front of the crowd.

Carrying a cowhide shield, animal skin and spear, Ephraim began to attend every meeting he could. He said that the urge to sing praises was "like when you're hungry and you haven't eaten."

Unlike the praise poets of the nineteenth century who often criticized their chiefs, Ephraim Buthelezi, who cleans and prepares tea for a company that makes artificial limbs, only flattered the chief. He called Buthelezi a "big mountain," admired his "fearsome fleet of cars," and recited a litany of honors bestowed on Buthelezi ranging from the AFL-CIO in the United States to a Rotary club in Natal.

> You went to Lesotho.
> They gave you a hat and when you put it on, it was for you.
> You are beautiful Shenge.
> They gave you a skin blanket.
> When you put it on, it was for you.
> You are beautiful Shenge.
> They then gave you a stick,
> When you had it in your hands, it was for you.
> You are beautiful Shenge.
> Then Masupa gave you a horse.
> The horse was meant for you.
> You are beautiful Shenge.

Though Inkatha is an impressive political machine, the way Buthelezi runs KwaZulu belies any notion that he is, as Schlemmer once said, "a social democrat." Chief Buthelezi runs KwaZulu as a one-party state under his personal stewardship. Any distinction between the Inkatha organization and the KwaZulu homeland apparatus has faded. Those who won't pledge fealty to the chief, Inkatha, and the KwaZulu cabinet ministers risk losing their pensions or jobs.

Alois Mngadi lost a KwaZulu scholarship to medical school when he wouldn't sign a pledge never to criticize Inkatha, the KwaZulu government, or any member of the KwaZulu cabinet. Mngadi had once served on his student representative council, but the ultimatum came at a time when he was no longer active politically. Disillusioned with political organizations, he had turned to the Catholic church. "It wasn't that I was against Inkatha. I just took them as one of many organizations that I wasn't a member of," Mngadi said. The idea of signing away his already limited freedom of speech rubbed him the wrong way. After finishing medical school on borrowed money, he received a job offer from a desperately understaffed rural hospital in KwaZulu. Few black doctors opted for rural hospitals; most preferred to stay in big townships where they could make more money. Mngadi, by contrast, loved rural KwaZulu. But the KwaZulu health ministry blocked the appointment because Dr. Mngadi hadn't signed the pledge.

"It is painful to me," said Dr. Mngadi, whom I roused one morning at a hospital operated directly from Pretoria. Ironically, the white regime had no illusions about such pledges; it couldn't expect them and didn't ask for them. But Dr. Mngadi knew his skills were in greater need in rural KwaZulu.

> I ponder almost daily: maybe I should sign for the sake of that hospital that needs a doctor. But I feel I would lose my principles by signing the pledge for the sake of getting a job, and once you've lost your dignity and principles, you've lost them. They are hard to regain.

The chief's followers in Inkatha haven't hesitated to express, as the chief delicately puts it, "the anger of the people," which means they beat the daylights out of anyone who disagrees with the chief.

Peter Mann, a political journalist formerly based in Durban, says he got along well with Buthelezi until he quoted someone criticizing the chief. After that, all interview requests were turned down. But in 1979 after Mann wrote a feature about a white man who had a dog named Gatsha, Chief Buthelezi's private secretary summoned Mann to Ulundi. Mann said the article wasn't meant to be flattering toward the dog owner. Apparently the chief didn't take it that way. When Mann arrived at the chief's office in Ulundi, he was met by angry protestors who denounced his coverage of KwaZulu. Upstairs, Mann was sequestered in a room while the mob surged into the building, banged on the door, and threatened him. From there, he heard the chief arrive, receive cheers from the crowd, and walk to another part of the building. Then Buthelezi's personal secretary took Mann from the waiting room and led him through a fifty-foot corridor lined with Inkatha members who struck him and tore his clothes. At the end of the corridor Mann was pushed by the secretary—for safety, he thought—into a room. Because of the jostling in the corridor, Mann says, he "shot through the door like a champagne cork." When he got up off the floor he saw the entire KwaZulu cabinet seated at a table. Chief Buthelezi looked at Mann and said, "Yes? You wanted to see me?"

After discussing Mann's reporting, Buthelezi ordered his secretary to check Mann's car. A tire was slashed. Buthelezi was angry and said, "I told them not to do anything to the car." He ordered the tire changed, then got up to leave. When he opened the door, a group of men with sticks were standing outside. The chief said, "These people are all very angry with you and you owe them an apology." Mann said later "I didn't feel I had anything to apologize for, but it was a question of whether I'd get out of there or not." He apologized.

Black journalists also came under pressure. Inkatha bought the only Zulu language newspaper in the area and sacked the journalists who had criticized the chief.

Parliamentary opponents haven't fared any better. In 1976, the KwaZulu legislature passed a resolution that said, "We are still in bondage and we therefore see no need for the formation of [political] parties." When a rival chief Mhlabunzima Maphumulo tried to start another party, Inala, with the support of members of the Zulu royal family, he was arrested and charged with "misconduct" and plotting "the unconstitutional overthrow of the [KwaZulu] government." Though acquitted, Maphumulo was later assaulted outside the offices of the KwaZulu legislature.

Supporters of the UDF often fared worse. "The practice of democracy requires that at least four pre-conditions are met," Archie Gumede wrote in a letter to Buthelezi. "Unfortunately, in Natal-KwaZulu such pre-conditions do not exist for the UDF . . . elements of Inkatha and the KwaZulu government play an active role in ensuring that members of the UDF are not allowed to freely associate, speak, move, organise, and, indeed, live."[14]

Residents of KwaMashu township were coerced into contributing money to Shabalala and Inkatha. A Methodist minister from KwaMashu said, "I was made to walk down the road in broad daylight [by Inkatha supporters]. Many of the men were armed. I was forced to wave my fist in the air and chant, 'The UDF is a dog.' . . . I no longer live in KwaMashu as I fear for my life."[15]

In late 1987 and early 1988 heavy fighting erupted in the Pietermaritzburg townships, and more than a thousand people died. Inkatha and UDF forces attacked each other in gangs, often armed with bricks, sticks, rifles, or AK-47s. Content to let black rivals destroy one another, white South African troops stood by and watched the bloodshed.

The fighting weighed heavily on the thin-skinned chief, who still saw himself in opposition to the government. He blamed Inkatha-UDF clashes on "bands of comrades" that he said would "ever increasingly become embarrassments to the ANC because they are totally out of control." Responding to criticism, however, he expelled Shabalala from the Inkatha central committee.

None of these incidents disturbed the chief's white supporters. In every phase of conquest and rule, whites have exploited divisions among Africans to maintain and expand white domination. In the Eastern Cape in the early nineteenth century, British colonists exploited endemic rivalries between Xhosa chiefdoms. These rivalries were compounded in 1835 when the colonial government made allies of 17,000 Mfengu, who arrived in the area as refugees from the bellicose Zulu king, Shaka. The Cape government settled the Mfengu on land the colony had seized from the Xhosa. Subsequently, the Mfengu fought the Xhosas, who were trying to regain their land.[16]

Afrikaner settlers also relied on African allies. In 1835, the voortrekkers were assisted by a Tswana chief when they drove the Ndebele chief Mzilikazi north of the Limpopo river. Settlers in the Orange Free State used Baroleng allies in wars against the southern Sotho.[17]

The Pretoria government in the 1980s also worked on the theory that the enemy of its enemy must be its friend. So it has appeared to have at least a tacit alliance with the chief against more radical black groups. After emergency regulations were reimposed in June 1986, Chief Buthelezi was one of the few black leaders allowed to operate freely and openly. Four days after the emergency was declared and all UDF meetings were banned, Chief Buthelezi received permission to hold a rally at Jabulani stadium to commemorate the Soweto uprising.

Inside the stadium, an electric band played, while outside thousands of *impis* converged from three directions, and took part in mock fights. KwaZulu police in riot gear surrounded the stadium, but South African government troops were virtually absent.

Buthelezi arrived by helicopter, sending dust flying around the stadium. He wore a blue safari suit and a yellow scarf he had bought at Harrod's in London. Behind him on the stage, plainclothes white security agents hovered with walkie talkies. The KwaZulu Minister of Pensions and Welfare sat with pistol protruding from his pants.

Nor were Natal's whites shaken from their faith in Buthelezi by the repression he exercised in KwaZulu. One diplomat opined that "Gatsha is liked by the white person who thinks blacks are savages who have to be kept under control and you need a strong man to do it."

I thought that a harsh assessment until I met Frank Martin, one-time leader of Natal's white provincial government. "As an ex-military man I like dealing with disciplined people because then I know what to expect," Martin said. "They know what standards to expect from me and I know what standards to expect from them." Asked whether reports of repression inside KwaZulu worried him, Martin said that was none of his affair.

> One can never judge that from outside. You can only judge that from inside as a Zulu. They have their customs; they have their traditions. The rest of tribe will accept punishment meted out by custom or *induna*. We can't begin to understand, just as I can't judge what would be done to an Arab if he's caught drinking. No one questions Saudi Arabia. That's their business.

What some whites called "liberalizing" South Africa had nothing to do with "democratizing" South Africa. "I want to uphold certain standards no matter what. It doesn't have to be based on race, it has to be based on standards," Martin had said. "The tragedy of South Africa is that it has never recognized the members of the elite unless they've been white. If you can join elites no matter what group you belong to, then the mass of poor will sort out themselves."

Martin's reformist view of South Africa was at heart not a revolutionary one. Like him, many white people praised Chief Buthelezi because they feared everything else in black politics since 1976. They feared the commoner more than they feared any power on earth, because the commoner would bring a populist agenda and a liberation that could not be "orchestrated," to borrow the word Schlemmer used in his *Financial Mail* article.

"Whites Are Not Blacks"

"Whites are not blacks," goes a saying among blacks, one that roughly translates to "Blood is thicker than water."

Mpho Mashinini told me about his first detention in 1977. A white police officer came to talk to Mashinini. The officer came with two black police officers and engaged Mashinini in a discussion about the reasons for blacks' discontent. The white police officer tried to convince Mashinini that whites were open-minded and prepared to treat blacks as equals. He nodded to his two black colleagues and said that he worked with them all the time; they trusted him and he trusted them. Mashinini replied, work with them yes, but never trust them. Because they are black.

The white cop looked at the two black cops, but they turned away, staring at the walls and the floor. The discussion ended abruptly. The white officer left the room. The two black police officers looked at Mashinini and said nothing.

No matter how closely blacks worked with the Pretoria government, a tension ran through their relationship. Black officials still felt they did not receive fair treatment from whites, especially given that they were reviled by other blacks for being collaborators. On the other hand, whites didn't entirely trust black officials. They worried that black "moderates" or "collaborators" were still, when the name-calling was over, black.

Indeed, even blacks working within the system were touched by the rebellious spirit of the times. In March 1986, 500 black police officers in Soweto went on strike for a 50 percent wage increase. They were earning R265 to R370 a month, but they were unhappy about poor overtime pay, long working hours, and discrimination within the force. The blacks refused to resume duties—including guarding council property and councillors' homes—until their demands were met. The government fired the police officers but reinstated them after court proceedings were initiated by their union.

The next year black municipal police officers in the township of Sebokeng mutinied because they were dissatisfied with their slow rate of promotion and angry about the treatment they were receiving from a white officer. White reinforcements were brought in and a shootout took place between black and white police. Many armed cops fled and took refuge among the people who usually regarded them with suspicion. Most of the black mutineers were eventually brought back onto the police force, but a handful of comrades made contact with some of them. At least one black municipal police officer was giving the youths lessons in how to fire rifles.

Tensions showed at the highest levels of government as well. The colored

Labor Party leader Allan Hendrickse, who took part in the tricameral Parliament and accepted a seat in the white cabinet, was angered when the government refused to allow coloreds to swim at the same beaches as whites. Hendrickse defied the government and went for a well publicized dip. The president rebuked Hendrickse in a twenty-five-minute television address. When Parliament met again, Hendrickse's wife refused to attend the opening ceremony. A humiliated Hendrickse apologized.

Later Hendrickse spoke about the Land Act and the Group Areas Act in a speech before the white assembly. No African or colored man had ever spoken in that room before. But Hendrickse, whose father was thrown out of his home under the laws, was ruled out of order for calling an act of Parliament an "act of theft."

The final insult for blacks working within the apartheid system was that they could expect little gratitude from whites for placing themselves on the front-line of the government's battle for control of black politics. Nor could they expect to be treated as equals. Their reception among whites could be as unfriendly as their reception among blacks.

On one occasion Tom Boya, Mayor of Daveyton, and his wife were invited by his counterpart in the white town of Benoni to a formal dinner for mayors. Because most black mayors had resigned or were avoiding public appearances, the Boyas were the only blacks who could attend. Arriving early, the Boyas took their seats at the second of three tables. As the white guests arrived, some went to the first table, others to the third. "Some even preferred to eat in the halls," Boya said later in amazement. But none sat down with the Boyas.

"We are called black mayors, yet we can't even sit down at the same table! All those mayors are elected leaders. If they can discriminate against a counter-part of theirs, what about a garden boy? Even with reforms, the most important attitudes of South Africans haven't changed."

As a result, black government officials often threatened to walk away from their posts. "The government should not expect us to be puppets. We are there to see that our people get a good deal, not just to listen to a raw deal." Boya said.

"We are not their puppets," Kagiso Mayor Madhiba said. Mavuso agreed. "If they have those notions, it will be foolhardy of them. They'll be facing the shock of their lives."

Almost every time Chief Buthelezi met with State President Botha the two traded barbs. Once President Botha wagged his finger at the chief and said, "I can be very nasty." To the chagrin of Botha aides, the chief answered: "That is nothing new because the white man has been nasty to me my whole life."

CHAPTER FIFTEEN

A Half-Extinguished Fire

Sometimes this war will seem to end; but these people will not hate you any the less; it will be a half-extinguished fire that will smolder under the ash and which, at the first opportunity, will burst into a vast conflagration.
—BARON LACUÉE ON ALGERIA, 1831

NIGHT SETTLED OVER SOWETO, but the township was already dark from thick coal dust from winter fires. It was late April 1987 and a dry chill had set in the high southern African plans. Trudging home from work, people stared with bloodshot eyes and greeted each other in low raspy voices.

Far into the township, in a section known as Deep Soweto, one of South Africa's most-wanted activists, Murphy Morobe, slipped out of the night and, without knocking, stepped into a detached room in the backyard of one of the township's 79,000 matchbox houses. The stocky Morobe, dressed in a heavy woolen sweater and a tweed cap, came to solicit a favor, and motioned a friend back out to the street. There he pointed to a pickup truck with a covered rear portion and asked the friend to drive the truck from Soweto into one of the white neighborhoods of Johannesburg. Morobe needed to transport pamphlets to a meeting. The friend stared; it was the eve of a major work "stayaway"—a one-day general strike—to protest evictions, and it was a good night to remain indoors, away from the police.

"Now?" the friend asked. Morobe nodded. Morobe, a United Democratic Front leader who had been in hiding for nearly a year, didn't want to drive the pickup himself because police were more likely to stop and check a pickup truck than the passenger car he was driving. His friend didn't find this reassuring. "We need this bakkie [pickup truck] tomorrow," Morobe said. The friend peeked suspiciously underneath the canvas covering the rear of the truck. "Is it clean?" he asked, meaning that all subversive pamphlets and posters had been taken out of the back. Morobe smiled and nodded. "Bring along your girlfriend and you won't look so suspicious," he said.

So they drove separately and met in "town," as they called the smaller white part of the Johannesburg metropolitan area. The friend handed over the keys to the pickup and hitched a ride back to Soweto.

Morobe functioned underground for more than a year, the longest period of underground activity by a high-profile political leader in two decades. Even under the state of emergency, with more than 25,000 people in jail, Morobe was able to rely on a network of safe houses and sympathizers. Morobe was arrested in July 1987, but a year later he and two others escaped while under guard at a Johannesburg hospital, and took refuge in the American consulate. After negotiations between the American and South African governments, the three went free.

Morobe's comings and goings showed that while the emergency had dealt a heavy blow to the UDF, black opponents of the white Pretoria government were learning to cope with a permanent state of emergency, carrying on the business of resistance with more circumspection. Clandestine street committees continued to meet intermittently in many parts of the country. In Soweto, a key area-committee strategy meeting regularly drew leaders from most of the major community and union groups in the Johannesburg area. Other black South Africans met monthly to discuss political issues and books. When it became impossible to hold mass meetings in Soweto, union and community organizers worked on the commuter trains from Soweto into Johannesburg. "We are gearing ourselves for a much longer haul ahead," Morobe said two months before he was picked up by police. "The challenge is to withstand whatever repressive onslaught the state may embark upon."

The perseverance of black political groups distinguished the aftermath of the 1984–1986 uprising from revolts that took place in South Africa in the early 1960s and the mid-1970s. After the mid-'80s uprising, Pretoria was unable to completely defuse the atmosphere of crisis within the country. Though blacks weren't able to topple the government, they still resisted government initiatives. The leaders of the uprising still commanded respect among blacks. The crackdown didn't secure much rest for the South African police and armed forces. Some government ministers boasted of a lull in black political activity, but it was a turbulent lull. From September 1986 through February 1987, 187 people were killed in political violence—an average of one a day. In early 1987, there were still about 8,000 white troops on patrol in the black townships. And in late 1988, more than two years after the emergency was imposed, about 2,000 people were still held in detention without charges. As South African Defense Force Chief Jan Geldenhuys once said, "We have controlled unrest action, but not unrest thinking."

Evidence that a spirit of resistance still lived could be found even during the harshest days of the crackdown. In the small seaside town of Port Alfred, I wandered into the back room of a grocery store and waited while a black attendant heated a chicken pie for me in a microwave. It had been months since I visited the town and the ramshackle black township up the hill. A year earlier the township had been highly organized with a network of street committees and a spirit of resistance unparalleled in the country. By early 1987, the government had tracked down and detained the leading township figure. And the township itself was cut off to visitors by an encampment of soldiers and municipal police in tents at the only entrance.

I made some small talk with the attendant, mentioned that I had passed through before and vaguely asked how things were in the township. He shrugged, suggesting that things could be better and that he was open for another question. I dropped the name of Nkwinti, the detained leader, and said that the township had seemed pretty organized a year earlier. Was it all gone? I wondered aloud. The attendant said no. Glancing through the door where he could see the white manager busy at the cash register, he said quietly that some people were still meeting secretly. He gave me the name of a woman who could give me details. Then he gave me my chicken pie.

Later on my way out of town, I picked up a hitchhiker. The unemployed young man didn't seem attuned to political events. I gave up trying to ask him about street committees (he said they were all finished) and we talked about rugby. He was a great enthusiast. I asked how many rugby teams the black township had. Fourteen, he replied. After I moment I asked, "How many street committees did the township have before the emergency?" He laughed knowingly and answered, "Fourteen."

In Soweto, the second state of emergency had the same galvanizing effect as the first emergency had had on the Eastern Cape.

In May 1986 a rent boycott had started in the Orlando West and Moroka branches of the Soweto Civic Association. Though black leaders thought the township wasn't prepared to sustain a rent boycott, the emergency prevented further branch meetings and the boycott spread by word of mouth. By the end of June, 80 percent of Soweto residents had stopped paying rent.

The revenue lost by the government was substantial, but not of vital significance. A modest increase in the price of gold exports (and gold tax receipts) offset any money lost from black township rent boycotts nationwide. In fact, the rent boycott had a beneficial effect; it had served as a tax cut. Many stores, long ailing from recession and widespread unemployment, said business grew brisk when the rent boycott started.

Nonetheless the boycott was an affront to the authority of the state, and the government tried to break it. The government urged people to pay secretly by mail. When that didn't work, it shut off the electricity of boycotters. That didn't work either; workers in the municipal union, an affiliate of COSATU, would come and turn the electricity back on. The military would return a month later and turn off the electricity again, and boycott sympathizers within the union would turn it on again. At one house, soldiers removed the box controlling the electricity, but workers building new houses had extra ones, and they reinstalled the boxes and switched the electricity back on. "I'm not involved," the resident said innocently. "I'm not an electrician."

Then the government started evicting people. In White City, the Soweto neighborhood where Murphy Morobe lived, five residents were threatened with eviction in September. The next day, street committees in White City met to discuss the threats. Eighty to ninety people crowded into the backyards of houses to attend the meetings. Some youths in the street saw police coming and blew whistles to alert the others. Fearful that the evictions had begun, White City residents ran into the street where police opened fire, killing twenty-seven and wounding 120. One eyewitness said a township resident returned fire with an AK-47. Outrage over that incident sustained the boycott in later months. "People said, 'What business do we have giving [the government] money to buy guns?'" a White City leader said.

The evictions continued. The government picked as examples twenty-five residents from each section of the sprawling township. In one area of Deep Soweto, soldiers ransacked the house of a man who had lived there for thirty years, dumping his belongings into the street and impounding his only valuable possession, a television set. The man complained that his street committee just stood around and watched. "They didn't do anything," he said.

In response, blacks active in street and block committees decided to call a three-day stayaway. The issue was settled at a series of clandestine committee meetings over a two-week period. The few remaining prominent leaders in Soweto were skeptical about the idea. Opposition groups already were planning stayaways on May Day and again on May 5 and 6 to protest the all-white parliamentary elections. The leadership worried about pushing people too far and endangering peoples' jobs. The debate over the rent protest raged for the weekend, but the street and block committee leaders wouldn't back down.

Two days later, Tuesday April 21, the committee activists—mostly in their early twenties—printed up leaflets announcing the stayaway.

> To stop evictions, the freedom loving people of Soweto are called upon to stage a three day stayaway protest from Wednesday to Friday. When the people of Soweto took the life and death decision not to pay rent it was for legitimate and valid reasons. These reasons still exist and are not resolved up to now.

The leaflets called for negotiations and for the state to hand over the deeds to houses in Soweto, reasoning that over thirty years people had paid off the cost of the houses. The leaflets also urged youths to exert restraint in enforcing the boycott.

Black adults at work didn't have any inkling of the call that would reach them that evening. The stayaway debate and its leaders were completely unknown to most Sowetans. Nonetheless hundreds of thousands of Soweto residents heeded the stayaway call. In early stayaways, young comrades enforced general strikes by whipping adults who tried to go to work. The brutality and disrespect for elders angered many residents. The April stayaway organizers were more sophisticated. They enlisted the backing of the taxi association and watched train stations to impede transportation into city offices and factories. On the first day of the stayaway, a couple of thousand people marched on the chambers of the official community councillors. Police dispersed the crowd with tear gas. By the third day, the stayaway crumbled, but it was regarded as a success by most activists. The rent boycott continued and evictions ceased for a time.

Two weeks later, people in Soweto and across the country stayed home again to protest the all-white elections.

On Thursday night August 2, 1987, rumors again swept through White City that evictions would take place the next day in an effort to break Soweto's seventeen-month-old rent boycott. The rumor probably came from a black worker in the Soweto Council offices.

Even with Morobe in detention, street committees arranged a work "stayaway" for White City residents overnight. The following morning a large group of residents—mainly women—marched on the council offices. Police intercepted the group and arranged talks between representatives of the crowd and the town clerk for Soweto, Nico Malan. Malan met with the representatives that Monday, August 6, and a detailed written report of the meeting was circulated to all the street committees for comment.

Negotiations broke down, but the incident showed that blacks could still organize under the harshest repression. Activists later worried that a government offer to sell Soweto matchbox houses for R400 each would weaken the rent boycott. Even that offer represented a victory of sorts for the community groups. The figure was half of what four years earlier the government said it would sell the houses for. As it turned out, however, about seventy percent of Sowetans kept boycotting rent.

The government employed tactics different from those used in the crackdowns on the African National Congress and the Black Consciousness movement. Many government ministers felt that the ANC acquired a mystique precisely because it was removed from the day-to-day practicalities of functioning within black communities. Moreover the ANC leaders serving life prison sentences, such as Mandela, and Black Consciousness leaders who died in detention, like Biko, had become martyrs.

Thus instead of banning the UDF, the government disrupted the UDF by selectively arresting its most prominent leaders, sweeping up virtually all middle-level leaders, banning UDF rallies and meetings, and cutting off outside funding. (The UDF had been receiving increasing amounts of money from sympathetic Western governments, foundations, and unions.) "The government has tried to turn the UDF into a turtle on its back," said one foreign diplomat.

But even on its back, the UDF did more than wave its arms. One regional leader said that he was contacted every three days by a confidential briefer from another province and that messages were passed to the black community via street committees. Despite the restrictions under the emergency, in 1987 the UDF's affiliates managed to hold a meeting of one hundred top leaders, many of them fugitives, to debate strategy. The meeting was guarded by other activists equipped with walkie-talkies that could be used to warn if the police were coming. The UDF also launched a new national affiliate, the South African Youth Congress (Sayco), at a congress at a secret venue. Blacks continued to respond to calls for mass stayaways and rent boycotts in the major black townships continued despite threats of eviction.

In addition, street and block committees still met in some areas. The venues became more secret. Often committee members wouldn't even know the place until they were picked up by another organizer. In Duncan Village, police detained more than 200 people and later an additional hundred people in an effort to break the street committees. Even so, when I visited the township later, committee meetings were continuing quietly.

Operating in secret tested the democratic commitment of the opposition. Guarding against discovery didn't lend itself to open debate. The UDF became less democratic after June 1986 because of necessities dictated by the state of emergency. Its members couldn't talk easily with each other. In 1987, it would take three days for the closest colleagues of Eric Molobi, a top official on the National Education Crisis Committee, simply to get in touch with him.

An activist from one province turned up in another region, where he was in hiding. He was using a different name. Unaware that I knew his true identity, he would stop by my apartment to go jogging and talk politics. Once I hinted that I knew who he was by saying that I met someone from his home province who knew him, but he never broke his facade or used his real name. He never gave me a phone number.

"You do without routines," said Morobe. "Rather than phoning, you just arrive."

Working that way put a strain on individuals as well. Before his detention, Morobe came by my apartment for an interview. As we chatted in the living room, there was a noise in the corridor. Morobe stopped talking. "What was that noise?" he asked. It took me a moment to realize what noise he was talking about. Then I told him it was the cleaning man putting down his metal bucket. "Are you sure? It sounded like a police radio crackling," he said. I said I was sure and asked if he would like me to go into the corridor and look. No, he replied. If I recognized the noise then it was okay, and he resumed the interview. Later he confided how difficult it was to be in hiding. "Here we are twelve months into the emergency and I'm still jumpy about some things. You are so much on the lookout for danger that every little sound has a meaning and unless it has a meaning it becomes suspect."

Did he think he could stay in hiding indefinitely? "I don't know," Morobe said. "A slight mistake and overconfidence can let you down. Staying safe isn't an individual matter but a collective matter. Whatever mistakes I do make will have the consequence of putting more people in danger."

The success of the Soweto rent stayaway suggested that the black opponents of the South African government would sustain themselves even if people like Morobe made mistakes. "It's not 1964," said the ANC's Thabo Mbeki in Lusaka.

> Certain things, like mass meetings, aren't possible anymore, but organized structures reach quite deep into black communities. We have to learn to cope with a permanent state of emergency. People underground must understand that they aren't underground for just three months but for a much longer period of time. We have got to learn to work like that.

Catching a glimpse of a newspaper photograph of Morobe, Mbeki said, "Is that guy still running around? We hear they (the police) might be closing in on him." Two months later he turned out to be right. But even with Morobe in prison, there was no hint that the roots of another black rebellion had been pulled up. In February 1988, the government slapped more restrictions on the UDF and seventeen of its most important affiliates. Seventeen UDF leaders were barred from talking to the press and were confined to their homes between 6 P.M. and 5 A.M. The measures were a concession that the emergency hadn't succeeded in silencing the government's black critics. UDF leaders responded by broadening their contacts even further, establishing relations with white politicians, lawyers, and academics. Statements and calls went out in the name of the "mass democratic movement" instead of the front.

The government put the "mass democratic movement" to the test by calling local elections for October 1988. The elections were designed to cap the government's counteroffensive by promoting fresh legions of black officials who would take over some of the day-to-day management of black communities—even if the faceless joint management committees continued to pull strings behind the scenes.

It seemed incredible that the government would once again hold black elections, almost inviting blacks to demonstrate their rejection of the government again. It had been only four years since elections for the tricameral Parliament sparked the formation of the UDF and the entire uprising. The intervening years of upheaval had done little to win the government new admirers, notwithstanding the recent public works projects.

The government was wary about a repeat of the 1983 and 1984 elections, so this time it banned any talk of an election boycott. At a candidate's rally in the black township outside Stellenbosch, a young woman protestor was shot and she bled to death while the mayoral candidate continued speaking. "There is nothing more difficult than giving a speech in South Africa. The election boycott is the issue at the moment and it is against the law to address it. People organize meetings and there's nothing to talk about," one activist said.

Meanwhile the government launched a multimedia advertizing blitz to urge blacks to vote. "The People will decide on October 26," one pamphlet said, imitating the lingo of the UDF. "The most important people on election day are we, the voters, because we have to choose the people to whom we will give the authority and responsibility to manage our town or city."

The government also aired television commercials, though it puzzled for a while over how to produce them. The government wanted two people in the ads to discuss the elections, but since whites and blacks would be voting, it couldn't decide whether to make the two white or black. It decided to use animals, but an anthropologist told government propagandists that blacks associated certain animals with whites. Finally the media managers chose two squirrels, animals found only in a small part of the Western Cape of South Africa, to discuss the merits of voting. (The voices were done by whites.)

The real issue in the elections in the segregated black localities wasn't whom blacks would vote for, but whether blacks would vote at all. The government tried to do everything to make voting easy. Polls were open for a week before the official election day. People could vote without identification if they brought any person who would vouch for who they were. People could vote in other townships where they would not be known or seen by their neighbors. Police would hand-deliver ballots to people's houses. Black candidates were given funds and vehicles to bus people to the polls, and the candidates promised to shower voters with houses, lower rents, and other favors.

Archbishop Tutu defied the government and publicly called for a boycott of the elections. Murphy Morobe and two other activists escaped from detention and took refuge in the American consulate, where they called on people to vote their consciences, a thinly veiled call for a boycott. Because meetings were illegal, activists boarded the trains to the black townships and urged commuters to spread the word. Pamphlets were distributed secretly door to door. An unsigned photocopied pamphlet read

> Do not vote for apartheid. The apartheid Botha regime is once more trying to bribe us into its long rejected apartheid policy by calling on us to vote for oppression. . . . This we must regard as an insult to us as we long called for the resignation of councillors and lowering of rent . . . instead our people were cold-bloodedly massacred in townships. . . . The State has resorted [sic] to rule us at gunpoint in protection of the undemocratic and unrepresentative Town councils.

The ANC smuggled pamphlets into the townships, too. "The African National Congress says to all our Black Compatriots: Boycott the ghetto elections! Advance to people's power!" The ANC referred to the government's WHAM campaign.

> The regime is issuing blood money to buy off a section of the people through so-called "upgrading schemes," to recruit informers and puppet candidates and for its propaganda against the people and their organizations.
>
> Promises are being made by the killers and oppressors about new toy telephones such as the National Council and honorary places in the so-called Electoral College—all of which amount to an attempt to find black collaborators to decorate seats in the machineries of oppression . . .
>
> LET BOTHA'S FOOLISH SCHEME COLLAPSE!
> BOYCOTT THE DUMMY ELECTIONS!
> ADVANCE TO PEOPLE'S POWER![1]

On election day, millions of blacks stayed home. The government claimed 25.1 percent turned out, but a crude estimate of the voting-age black population suggests that only 5 percent or less voted, most of them pensioners bused in by black officials. It was hardly the mandate the government was seeking. In key areas, turnouts were appalling. In Tembisa, only 3.6 percent voted. In Soweto, 11 percent voted, about the same as the number who voted five years earlier. Only this time the government could not blame "intimidators" because emergency regulations were so tight. "The state of emergency and the security forces saw to it that we could take this stand in an intimidation-free environment," wrote black journalist Mandla Tyala. "No revolutionary elements could tell us this time not to vote. Intimidation has been blamed for low polls in the past. But what do we blame for this year's [polls]?"[2]

In most areas, rejection of the government was so great that there were fewer candidates than seats. In Cradock's township, no one stood for election. In the Cape Town townships of Guguletlu, Langa, and Nyanga, eight candidates stood for twenty positions. Nationwide, only one third of the seats were contested.

Despite expectations of voter fraud, it seemed the government ran a clean election. As a result, many prominent black officials went down in defeat. Steve Kgame, mayor of Dobsonville, lost to his own illiterate chauffeur. Kgame, who the night before told a British Broadcasting Corporation interviewer "I am not a puppet," had been president of the Urban Councils Association of South Africa and the only elected black official who had agreed to serve on the government's national statutory council.

Tom Boya, who had headed a rival group, the United Municipalities of South Africa, won a Daveyton council seat, but his fellow councillors rejected his bid to serve another term as mayor. In Soweto, Mayor Nelson Botile was ousted after winning only 526 votes.

In Alexandra, nine nominations were received for nine seats on the new community council. But the council crumbled soon after its inauguration when one member was disqualified and four others resigned. One of the councillors who resigned, seventy-eight-year-old Simon Sebotha, told the newspaper *Business Day* that his children were against his participation because "They felt there would be a day when the community would explode and attack me." Sebotha concluded that "it would be against the wishes of the community to claim to represent them within a government-created structure."[3]

A postscript to the elections came four days after the polls closed. The white television actor Don Lamprecht, who had been the voice of the squirrel urging people to vote, was arrested and charged for sodomy, the possession of tapes depicting the sexual abuse of children and the possession of printed pieces of child pornography.

Black candidates who were elected refused to do the government's bidding. In December 1988, the new Soweto community councillors met a six-person delegation that included Rev. Frank Chikane, Archbishop Tutu, the mineworkers' union president Cyril Ramaphosa, and UDF co-president Albertina Sisulu to negotiate a pact to end to the rent boycott. The "mass democratic movement's" decision to deal with black community councillors represented a departure from past strategy. The newly elected mayor, however, was a street committee number and his party, the Sofasonke Party, had campaigned on a populist platform that promised that no one would pay more than fifteen rand a month in rent. Sisulu had still been reluctant to talk to the councillors, but Chikane reminded her that in the 1940s the Sofasonke Party had fought to allow blacks, including the Sisulus, to remain in Soweto rather than be deported to the homelands.

In the accord, the council agreed to write off two-and-a-half years of rent arrears, to end evictions, to compensate tenants who had been evicted earlier, and to give away houses to Soweto residents who paid rent. Provincial administrators demanded that the mayor repudiate the agreement, but he refused.

The "mass democratic movement." went through a more severe test in handling the downfall of the heroine Winnie Mandela. Since returning to Soweto, Winnie squandered the admiration that had grown for her during her internal exile. Her defiance toward Pretoria turned out to be part of a general, and ultimately dangerous, belief that she could do as she pleased. Whereas Albertina Sisulu had worked within community and women's organizations, Winnie Mandela refused to join them, an offense to disenfranchised blacks, who put a premium on democratic process and "consultation." And the vulnerability that won her sympathy turned out to be all too real. She was vulnerable to depression, to loneliness, to the flattery of admirers and informers alike, and to the intoxicating effects of power and privilege. "She could withstand prison and the burning of her house, but she could not withstand fame," an ANC member said. Before long, rumors spread of indiscretion in her personal life, of extravagance and arrogance.

Her mercurial nature and dubious judgment had done more to harm her reputation than the security police could ever do. Not only did she endorse necklaces when black leaders were trying to stop them, but she also subordinated political causes to personal ones. Mandela threatened to ruin Operation Hunger after the relief organization fired three of her followers for stealing sacks of food and dropping them at her house. Then after Nelson had forbidden her from knocking down their existing home, which he said should be preserved for historical reasons, she acquired a new lot and built a California-style mansion on a prominent knoll, flaunting wealth in a township of two and four-room houses. "That's not a house; that's a whole village," Albertina Sisulu muttered.

Winnie Mandela's downfall was hastened by the Mandela Football Club, a group of wayward youngsters she took in. Soccer, however, was never the club's principal activity. They were admirers, bodyguards, and a roving "peoples' court" as well.

For one "case" that came to Mrs. Mandela's attention, a van full of the soccer players drove Mrs. Mandela to a humble house where they listened to a teenage mother describe a dispute she had with an elderly man who had adopted and raised her. Mrs. Mandela sat as prosecutor, judge, and jury. The elderly man apologized and said he had been under the influence of alcohol. A member of the soccer team asked him if he was in the habit of saying nasty things when drunk. The elderly man stared at the floor, shook his head, and said to the girl, "I find this very hurtful that I have lived with you for so many years and treated you like my own child and when today we have a difference, you call a gang for me." Mrs. Mandela reproached him. "You must never call these children a gang," she said. "We will not tolerate that type of language in our homes." The soccer team collected the young girl's belongings and moved her out of the house. As the group drove off, a disapproving onlooker said, "Where will all this end?"

It didn't end. Two youths later testified in court that the Mandela soccer team seized them and accused them of being "sellouts." They alleged that members of the soccer club used a knife to carve the words "Viva ANC" and the letter "M" on their chests and thighs. Mrs. Mandela allegedly served tea and cake to the youths after her soccer team poured acid on the wounds. After allegations that team members raped a young girl, a group burned down the home that Nelson Mandela wanted preserved. Neighbors, angry at the "reign of terror" of the soccer team, watched without making any move to put out the flames.

When the house burned down, a committee of Soweto community leaders launched an elaborate backstage effort to save Mandela from herself. The committee included her long-time friend Aubrey Mokoena, Cyril Ramaphosa, Frank Chikane, and Sister Bernard Ncube, a community worker. The ANC urged her to "cool it."

But Mandela refused to disband the team. In December 1988 the team kidnapped and beat four youth leaders, allegedly killing a fourteen-year-old named Stompie Moeketsi who had been the leader of a small army of youths under the age of fourteen in the Orange Free State. Two of the kidnapped youths escaped and said that Mrs. Mandela administered some beatings herself. The only outsider to see the youths while they were at the Mandela home was the respected Indian physician Abu-Baker Asvat. Soweto sources said Dr. Asvat urged Mandela to take the fourteen-year old boy, then ailing but alive, to the hospital. But Asvat himself was mysteriously gunned down in his office just after his visit to the Mandela home. Mrs. Mandela said Asvat was the only person who could substantiate her story that her bodyguards had saved the four youths from being sexually molested at a Soweto Methodist church.

Many commentators said "the Winnie affair" damaged the anti-apartheid movement. But if anything, the response of anti-apartheid groups revealed the strength of the South African opposition. Unlike African countries that have clung to corrupt and power-crazed leaders, unlike Western countries that have covered up improprieties of their leaders, the "mass democratic movement" made a clear declaration of its principles by exposing and disavowing Mandela's actions.

After Winnie spurned a last-minute attempt by the Johannesburg council of shop stewards to see her, leaders of the mass democratic movement issued a statement. While paying tribute to Mrs. Mandela's own suffering, it said,

> The democratic movement has uncompromisingly fought against violations of human rights from whatever quarters. We are not prepared to remain silent when those who are violating human rights claim to be doing so in the name of the struggle against apartheid. . . . We are of the view that Mrs. Mandela has abused the trust and confidence which she has enjoyed over the years. . . . Often her practices have violated the spirit and ethos of the democratic movement.

There was wide consensus inside South African black politics over this statement. It was written after consultation with the past and current heads of the South African Council of Churches, the spokesperson and co-president of the United Democratic Front, the head of the Release Mandela Campaign, officials of the country's biggest black trade-union federation, the general secretary of the mineworkers' union, and others—black leaders from every walk of life, every generation of protest, every province.

The difficulty of casting out Mrs. Mandela should not go unappreciated. Because of Nelson's absence, many blacks felt that protecting Winnie was part of their responsibility to him. But Nelson Mandela made things easier by placing political considerations above personal ones. Despite his dependence upon Winnie as his main link with the outside world, Nelson Mandela had ordered construction of the Soweto mansion halted. When Winnie Mandela tried to profit from the Mandela name by giving marketing rights to a black American entrepreneur of dubious repute, Nelson repudiated the deal. No one could own the Mandela name, he said. Similarly, he sided with the "mass democratic movement," endorsing its censure of his wife and urging her to disband her soccer team.

What went wrong with Winnie Mandela? "Power," said a young black who used to stay at Mrs. Mandela's house in Brandfort during her banishment. "She misused the Mandela name. She thought she was beyond organizations' disciplinary codes. She thought she could take the law into her own hands."

"She wanted to have her little kingdom," said Seth Mazibuko, formerly one of Mrs. Mandela's most ardent admirers. "And now that little kingdom is exploding."

The October 1988 vote of no confidence in the government, the Soweto rent boycott, and the handling of "the Winnie affair" showed that even though the most public protests were snuffed out by the June 1986 emergency, the government had not defeated black South Africans. The legacy of South Africa's fighting years was a continuous black resistance.

The black opposition survived the crackdown for six reasons. First, the 1984–1986 uprising involved a larger number of people than earlier revolts. The sheer scale of protest dwarfed anything that came before. A broad cross section of the black population had grown impatient with the pace of government reform and the presence of troops in the townships. Even with 2,000 black leaders in jail, campaigns against the government continued.

Second, the structure of the United Democratic Front differed from that of the protest groups of earlier generations. The UDF was a loose coalition of more than 600 organizations, each with its own leadership. To crush all UDF affiliates required a much more extensive effort from the government than ever before. When the government chopped off the head of the UDF by detaining its executive committee members, the UDF body politic grew another head. Furthermore the UDF was rooted in local bread-and-butter issues that remained compelling even when the goal of liberation from apartheid looked remote. After June 1986, the UDF fell back on the grassroots organizations formed between 1979 and 1983 and waited for space for national protest to open again. Unlike the early 1960s, when black resistance was crushed, black protest came out of the 1980s substantially intact both in spirit and organization.

Third, blacks opposed to apartheid had become entrenched in legal institutions in society, which could not be brushed aside easily. The most potent symbol of these institutional changes was the selection of Desmond Tutu as

Archbishop of the Anglican Church. The church became a sanctuary for political activity. Tutu seemed to possess almost diplomatic immunity to speak his mind. In addition, Tutu's elevation made a deep impression on white Anglicans who had to confront the integration of a "white" institution. Tutu relished this role, indeed, frolicked in it. Sweeping aside suggestions that he live in a black township outside Cape Town, he settled into the luxurious official residence of the archbishop and opened up the swimming pool for lessons for blacks from the townships.

Institutional advances placed substantial financial and organizational resources at the disposal of blacks. The letters that Steve Biko used to write pleading with a white church official for a couple of hundred rand are things of the past. Through the church, Tutu directed money and services. When the UDF held a fund-raising concert, it sold tickets through the South African equivalent of Ticketron. Hundreds of UDF organizers held fulltime paid posts in the front or in sympathetic groups such as rural action groups. Politically conscious blacks held key positions in the $9-million-a-year relief program of Operation Hunger. They ran classes through the South African Council for Higher Education (SACHED), which receives hundreds of thousands of dollars from foreign governments and foundations. The colored academic Jakes Gerwel ran the University of Western Cape, where he was once a protestor. Gerwel had transformed the university from a "Bantu college" into the "university of the left." UDF supporters also controlled the Kagiso Trust, a multimillion-rand foundation. They ran a newspaper, the *New Nation*, which could count on the Catholic Bishops' Conference for funds.

Fourth, labor unions sustained black opposition to the government. The government had tried to funnel black labor unrest into a formal labor-relations process. It succeeded, to some extent. Most strikes were short and ended in negotiated settlements. But in abiding by labor registration and mediation rules, trade unions had acquired a measure of protection against the crackdown. The legalized black trade unions then filled the vacuum the UDF left in some areas. With public political meetings banned, union meetings became forums for political speeches. The political agendas of the UDF and the unions grew increasingly similar. The Congress of South African Trade Unions began to push a Living Wage Campaign that included issues not directly tied to the workplace. Moreover, trade-union leaders believed they wouldn't fully realize their goals for improved wages and living conditions for workers until apartheid ended. Because workers saw each other in factories as well as at union halls, there was little the government could do to close the space for union activity without shutting down industry.

Fifth, the existence of the ANC was a major difference between the turbulent lull of 1987 and the quiet periods that followed earlier crackdowns. More than a symbol of the survival of resistance, the ANC carried out attacks every week. And it drew from a reservoir of exiled youths to send people back to help organize and recruit new members.

Sixth, demographics are eroding the government's power. The burgeoning townships have become spaces unto themselves, stretching the capacity of police surveillance. After dark, police often withdraw from the townships because they are unsafe, thus allowing political organizing work to continue.

Soweto best illustrates how black society has become an independent center of gravity in South Africa. There is something facile about the stock description of Soweto as a huge township of matchbox houses. It suggests an orderliness and homogeneity that doesn't really exist. To whites, Soweto might represent a monotonous labor barracks. But to blacks, it is the Big City. It has its wealthy neighborhoods—like Diepkloof and the Beverley Hills section of Orlando, with houses comparable to those in white suburbs—and its poor squatter settlements. In between there are the matchbox houses with yards full of subtenants.

Indeed the word "township" is a misnomer. Soweto is a metropolis, with doctors, lawyers, business people, clerks, bums, gangsters, ditchdiggers, day laborers, garbage collectors, clerics and religious fanatics, schemers and political activists. People can get lost in Soweto. Now more than ever it is a place of night lights and smoky shebeens, of crime and opportunity, of danger and freedom.

From Soweto and other black cities and compounds, a host of new faces is emerging, keeping up a struggle for democracy. To some, as de Tocqueville wrote in another context, the democratic tendency "appears to be novel but accidental, and, as such, they hope it may still be checked; to others it seems irresistible, because it is the most uniform, the most ancient and the most permanent tendency that is to be found in history."

Black South Africans believed history was on their side. In December 1988, a South African court convicted Terror Lekota and Popo Molefe of high treason for their role as the original full-time officials of the UDF. A judge sentenced them to twelve and ten years, respectively, in jail, blaming them for the September 1984 Vaal Uprising and the upheaval that followed. As they began their sentences, the UDF leaders smuggled a joint statement out of prison.

> Somewhere in the future lies a date when black and white South Africans will take a second look at these moments in our history. They will evaluate afresh the events now in contention and our role in them. And since the privilege will belong to them, they will pass final judgement. We are convinced that theirs will be contrary to the present one. They will vindicate us.

Undoubtedly the "final judgement" of history will go even further and say that South Africa's fighting years reshaped the way an entire generation of blacks think about authority, resistance, and the future of their country.

Since the early 1970s when most blacks viewed resistance as futile, debate among blacks has shifted from *whether* liberation will come to *when* it will come. "I think we will celebrate the eightieth anniversary of the ANC inside the country," Steve Tshwete said at the group's seventy-fifth anniversary in Lusaka in January 1987. Others are less confident of an early victory, but no less sure of ultimate victory. "There is a strong possibility that I may never be able to share in the good things in life, that we'll be in a constant revolutionary process and I will never see the pot bursting and overflowing," a colored teenager from Athlone said when he was feeling low. "But my children will, or their children." In Cradock's black township, the late Matthew Goniwe wrote in his private notes, "Whether it should take a thousand years, the South African government realizes that the writing is on the wall."

This millenarian view of resistance has three sources. One is the religious faith that God in divine justice will deliver blacks from the hands of tyrants. As Bishop Tutu says, "Our cause is just, and therefore victory is certain." The second is the economic determinist view that economic forces, like forces of nature, will wear down apartheid and "empower" blacks as they become indispensable to industry. The third is faith that revolution will sweep away the apartheid order.

In May 1856, an earlier bout of millenarianism seized black South Africans. A sixteen-year-old Xhosa girl named Nongqause said that spirits—"eternal enemies of the white man"—told her that if the Xhosas killed all their cattle and left their fields fallow, then on a certain day a million fat cattle would spring up along with fields of corn. On the same day, the sky would fall, crushing the white people and all non-believers. Over the next few months the Xhosas slaughtered all their cattle, only to discover the falsehood of the prophecy in February 1857 as the appointed day passed without event. Tens of thousands starved to death while others threw themselves on the mercy of the English colonists.

The millenarianism of the 1980s was palpably different from the great cattle killing. Though optimistic, black South Africans saw victory coming from their own efforts, not from some miracle or prophecy. "Our people have learned through bitter experience that freedom and democracy do not simply descend from the sky—they have to be struggled for and won," wrote Archie Gumede in a letter to Chief Buthelezi.

Concessions made by the government over a decade of upheaval—ranging from the legalization of black trade unions to constitutional reform, from public works projects in the townships to the partial abolition of pass laws—convinced blacks that they *can* be vehicles for change. "We are instruments of change, agents of change," Goniwe wrote in his private notes. "Change will NOT come if we DON'T stand up. Change will NOT come if we expect other people to bring it—each and every one of us has a contribution to make."

The belief in revolt generated by blacks themselves found expression in

South Africa's culture of revolt. When the township poet Mzwakhe transformed the "winds of change"—a metaphor first used by British Prime Minister Harold Macmillan—into the "drum beats of change," he made an important statement about how apartheid would end. Change, Mzwakhe was saying, will not breeze into Pretoria from Britain or anywhere else; change is coming from Africans. Hence when Mzwakhe recited his poem, he practically shouted the phrase "I am" to show where change will come from.

> I am the drum beats of change in Africa
> Deafening the ears like the winds of change
> Get it from me.

The sense of black South Africans that they hold their future in their own hands makes continued resistance certain. If at times it looks as though black opposition to white rule has weakened, appearances could be deceiving. As Thole "Boy" Majodina, a black lawyer who handled political cases in Port Elizabeth, said during the worst of the crackdown, "The townships are so quiet. There will be a lull for some time. There is a feeling in the townships that these things [the incidents of unrest] have gone on too long. People want things to return to normality," he said, laughing on the word "normality." "Township life as we know it," he explained. "But we know it is just temporary. We seem to have been subdued, but history repeats itself. It is a vicious cycle. And what they call peace is not really peace. It is just a mirage."

CHAPTER SIXTEEN

The Funeral

THE FUNERAL FOR RAYMOND MAVUSO took place in Ntumbane, a village in a valley where Raymond's mother lives, near the border of Swaziland. I arrived with some township comrades from the Bethal Youth Congress, all of whom looked awkward in the valley of waist-high grass. Their township street savvy seemed terribly out of place.

The village family was nervous, expecting trouble between Raymond's comrades and Raymond's half brother George, a policeman who stood menacingly in his green overalls, dirty from digging the grave. After some discussion, a deal was struck about the format of the funeral. The family, members of the Nazareth Baptist Church, dressed themselves in white robes and carried Raymond's body for a couple of hundred yards and sang church hymns. Then the comrades, in their city clothes, carried the body and sang freedom songs. Then they alternated again. At the gravesite, the family and comrades also took turns singing and eulogizing Raymond.

The family representative recounted Raymond's life and death in heroic terms that inspired murmurs of admiration and outrage. It seemed that Raymond Mavuso had lived an entire life during the brief time I was in South Africa. The day I arrived in South Africa in 1985 to cover its first state of emergency, unrest broke out in the black township adjoining a white town called Bethal, about 100 miles east of Johannesburg. Police fired tear gas at a meeting of students who were boycotting classes to protest the inferior education given to blacks. The youths counterattacked, and the police fled. One of the youths remembered it as the first time he ever saw the police close the roof of their armored car. But the police returned with reinforcements; they shot and killed two black youths and arrested twenty others.

Mavuso, then a member of a government-sponsored youth group called Zwelitsha (meaning "new world"), had had nothing to do with the political developments since 1976. He was appalled, however, by the shooting, and went through his own rapid political awakening. He worked through the newly formed Bethal Youth Congress to get students back to school and to make future protests more purposeful. As talks dragged on between youths and the government, Raymond grew more and more firmly planted in the opposition. He acquired new friends, a new awareness, and a new sense of purpose.

The month I was expelled from South Africa, Raymond died in a hospital after sustaining two gun shot wounds in the back. The shots are believed to have been fired by vigilantes recruited by Raymond's own half brother George, the police officer.

His fatal encounter with the vigilantes was told in detail while George stood by in silence. After the thugs shot Raymond, the story went, the police came and stood over Raymond. "Finish off what your dogs started," Raymond allegedly told them. Who are the people who shot you?, the police asked. "I'm looking at them," Raymond reportedly replied.

During the eulogy, a white pickup truck with police in it drove back and forth surveying the funeral from a road in the distance. Technically, the funeral constituted an illegal gathering because its size, though modest, violated limits on crowds that the government imposed under a state of emergency.

But what a gathering it was, a cross section of black South Africa. Around the hole in the ground stood three different generations from Ntumbane. There were cousins who were rural cattle herders and brothers in blue overalls from the state electricity-generating company; eighteen young comrades from Bethal, and women wrapped in traditional plaid blankets, carrying Raymond's clothes bundled up in sheets. An ambulance driver who had taken Raymond to the hospital arrived on a motorcycle with his black leather jacket, and a former black community councillor, whom Raymond and the other youths had convinced to resign, watched somberly in his natty brown pin-striped suit. Weeping women fell to the ground and the hardened young radicals allowed themselves a few tears.

After Raymond was lowered into the ground, people took turns throwing dirt in to seal the hole, then marked the spot with a mound of plain stones.

Epilogue: *Mandela Unbound*

TWENTY-SEVEN AND A HALF YEARS after he was captured along a lonely road in Natal, Nelson Mandela walked out of custody before a live international television audience. He appeared fit, but a bit shorter, a bit thinner than some remembered.

While he was in jail, Mandela had reached the stature of a messiah for many black South Africans. Once released, he became a mere mortal. "Forget the saintly Mandela who was going to soar above politics to bind the wounds of South Africa," said the *Economist* magazine. "That was the invisible, jailed Mandela who lived mainly in the imagination of his hagiographers."

But South Africa didn't need a messiah. It had had enough holy war, righteous rhetoric, and crusading. If justice rolled down like a mighty stream, the seas could run red with blood. What South Africa needed was a pragmatic lawyer to search for compromise.

Within days of his release, Mandela the man proved to be infinitely more useful than Mandela the symbol. Before even setting foot outside the prison farm where he was last held, Mandela helped nudge the new South African President F. W. de Klerk into freeing most of the leading political prisoners and unbanning the ANC, PAC, and other groups, the first steps toward normalizing the country's political life. And he forced the ANC to abandon some of its rhetoric and think realistically about negotiations with the government. He also traveled to Natal, where fighting between Inkatha and the UDF had degenerated into turf battles and revenge killings that had little to do with politics. Brushing aside ANC and UDF grudges against Buthelezi, he appealed to the chief to help make peace.

The effects of these efforts were impressive, but something less than miraculous. Fighting in Natal didn't come to an instant halt and many obstacles lay ahead on the road to majority rule. Moreover, the vast majority of South Africans hadn't even begun to consider the difficulties a majority rule administration would face in governing the country.

Nonetheless, while the free Mandela was human, he was clearly an unusual human. His stature was not simply the product of his longevity or the duration of his captivity. He was just as skilled a politician as his guarded letters from prison had suggested.

Mandela grasped the essential elements of leadership. Even during the most demeaning years in prison, he had maintained his dignity through regimens of exercise and learning, and through his bearing among his fellow prisoners and jailers. Gradually even his keepers came to appreciate his stature and show him deference. For a few months prior to his release, Mandela stayed in a house built for a prison warden and his guards slept in servants' quarters.

The ANC leader also understood the importance of compromise, as well as its prerequisites. By refusing to compromise his principles while in jail, Mandela had become uniquely capable of forging a national compromise. By refusing to renounce violence, by refusing to confine himself to the Transkei, Mandela had prolonged his sentence by years. No one could doubt his willingness to give his life for the struggle. Upon his release, he made a point of endorsing the armed struggle and the nationalization of industry to show that he had not made any deal to gain his own release. While that disappointed some people who hoped for a message of national reconciliation, Mandela had to establish his position among black South Africans before bridging the gap between blacks and whites.

A lesser man could be accused of ambition. But Mandela did not ignore the political leaders who had emerged during South Africa's fighting years. Instead he worked with them, holding court at the prison farm with leaders from the UDF, COSATU, and other political groups before his release.

Mandela understood well—maddeningly well for those who longed for a messiah—that a true leader must demonstrate humility and a respect for democratic procedure. He stressed in his first speeches that he was not a prophet, only a mediator. At first, he spurned the mansion his wife had built and returned to the modest home where he lived during the 1950s and which had been rebuilt after the fire. He protested his obedience to the ANC and his lack of elected office to a nation that would choose him by acclamation. Like Cincinnatus, Mandela would only gain more power by renouncing all claims to it. Within three weeks, the ANC national executive committee named him deputy president. Since ANC President Tambo had been incapacitated by a stroke the previous year, that effectively made Mandela the organization's top official.

Even then, Mandela couldn't soar above the political landscape. He had to operate within the context of black politics as they had been formed during South Africa's fighting years. Though the ANC and the government had agreed to negotiate, the talks could last some time. The two sides were still far apart on many issues. Tensions were bound to emerge both between and within the groups that participated in talks. Moreover, if change were to have any lasting value, it could not depend on one person.

Mandela's release and de Klerk's new-found commitment to embrace blacks as fellow citizens appealed to Americans' penchant for great leaders and grand gestures. But the release would never have happened were it not for the process—which elsewhere has been called "refolution"—of grudging reform from above pried loose by a popular rebellion from below.

The dynamics of that popular rebellion will continue to shape South Africa's political future. The different elements of the rebellion—ranging from Robben Island veterans to young comrades, from the UDF affiliates to the ANC in exile—will mesh as the ANC reconstitutes itself as a legal, aboveground organization inside South Africa. The sense of economic injustice in the townships, the influence of the black trade unions, the well-placed members of the South African Communist Party, and the popularity of SACP chief Joe Slovo will influence the debate over socialism and the nationalization of industry. The tolerance of the ANC and its allies toward opposing views will affect the willingness of whites to accept majority rule.

The degree of loyalty of the government's black allies will affect the process of reintegrating apartheid structures (such as homelands) into the country as a whole. To anyone familiar with the black face of apartheid and the divided loyalties of blacks working within the system, it came as little surprise in March 1990 when a coup in the Ciskei homeland ousted Pretoria's man and installed a black military government that proclaimed its loyalty to the ANC, freed political prisoners, and declared Ciskei's decision to renounce "independence" and rejoin the republic.

Of course, many dangers lie ahead: the ire of right-wing whites; the soaring expectations of blacks in a troubled economy; the long-suppressed ambitions of many blacks; the magnitude of social problems of illiteracy, alcoholism, delinquency, and crime that are part of apartheid's legacy; and the resurgence of the long-moribund Pan Africanist Congress, which continues to favor the seizure of power through violence instead of a negotiated settlement.

Yet there remain many reasons to hope that South Africa will not, as so many white South Africans fear, follow the rest of the continent into economic decay and dictatorship. In most African countries, seizing control of the state radio station practically amounted to a successful coup. The extent of political awareness and activity outside the capitals has been relatively slight. South Africans—both black and white—are far more sophisticated, and governing the country, as the National Party has discovered, requires a legitimacy across a broad spectrum of the people.

In addition, many black South African leaders shun the privileges and trappings of power so many others have craved. Upon Walter Sisulu's release from prison, the UDF assigned youths to stand guard outside the ANC leader's house. Sisulu was unaware of this and one day, puzzled, he walked into his driveway and asked a young guard why he was standing there instead of attending school.

Further reasons for hope lie in the nature of the rebellion against apartheid. South Africans have shed the passivity apartheid once relied upon and have become open and assertive about their opinions. Moreover, while violence and economic pressure pushed whites toward accommodation with blacks, even more important was the degree to which the government and its appendages had become irrelevant to society at large. Contrary to what people once feared about repressive regimes in the modern technological era, the state had failed to fill every interstice in society and failed to smother individual thought. Instead, what the Polish theorist Adam Michnik calls "civil society" had emerged in South Africa, where people met and wrote and debated *outside* government and came to be a countervailing, indeed an overwhelming force against government excess. If these civic associations, unions, cultural, youth, and church groups maintain a degree of independence from government under majority rule, then they can become bulwarks of democracy in a truly free South Africa.

Fact Sheet on South Africa

IN 1985, SOUTH AFRICA had a population of 33.7 million, constituted as follows:

25.0 million (74 percent) Africans
4.9 million (15 percent) whites
2.9 million (8 percent) "coloreds" (people of racially mixed ancestry)
0.9 million (3 percent) "Indians" (people of Indian or other Asian ancestry)

Four major languages are spoken. Two out of every five South Africans speak an Nguni dialect (Zulu, Xhosa, Swazi, or Ndebele) while one in four speaks a form of Sotho (North Sotho or Pedi, South Sotho, or Tswana). One in six speaks Afrikaans as a first language. English is the first language of only one in twelve, but it is the closest thing to a lingua franca.

The country is divided into four provinces: the Transvaal in the north, the Orange Free State in the central plains, the Cape in the south, and Natal in the southwest. A barren arid area, the Great Karroo, divides the wheat-growing area of the Orange Free State from the moist coastal parts of the Cape. The Transvaal tends to be dry, like central Texas. Natal is hot and humid. The Cape resembles northern California.

The major white cities are: Johannesburg, the industrial, mining, and commercial center; Pretoria, the administrative capital; Cape Town, the seat of Parliament; Durban, a major port; Port Elizabeth, center of the automobile industry; and Bloemfontein, the biggest city in the Orange Free State.

Under the Native Land Act of 1913 and other legislation, Africans residency rights are severely curtailed. About 40 percent of Africans live in rural reserves set aside for blacks. The government's policy is that these areas will become independent countries, each with a distinct African ethnic, or tribal, base. The rest of Africans live in "black townships." There are nearly 300 such townships set apart from white residential areas. The largest township is the amalgamated South Western Townships (Soweto) outside Johannesburg.

Much of what is known today as apartheid took shape long before the word was invented. Racial conflict dates from the arrival of Dutch settlers in 1652. These Dutch settlers gradually acquired a distinct identity and language known as Afrikaans. English colonists conquered the Cape and Natal; Afrikaner settlers clashed with African chiefdoms and kingdoms as they pushed north. With the discovery of gold in 1886, conflict intensified between British and Afrikaners (over wealth) and between whites and blacks (over labor).

In 1899, war broke out between the British and Afrikaners. The Anglo-Boer War (*boer* is Afrikaans for "farmer"), ended in defeat for the Afrikaners, but was costly for the British. The union of South Africa was formed in 1910. While part of the British empire, the union was essentially autonomous.

The African National Congress, the oldest independence movement in Africa, was founded in 1912 to appeal for rights for Africans. It was the first organization to unite Africans across ethnic lines. It has been through four stages of protest: petitions in 1912, participation in government advisory councils in 1936, civil disobedience in the 1950s, and (after the organization was outlawed in 1960) armed struggle.

The last two stages were a direct result of the victory by the National Party in the 1948 white elections. The National Party campaigned on a platform of racial *apartheid,* Afrikaans for "separateness." In the 1950s, the National Party enacted laws that further segregated an already divided country: the Group Areas Act designating separate white residential areas, the Mixed Marriages Act barring interracial marriage, the Separate Amenities Act, and laws forcing Africans to carry passes that restricted their ability to live and work in urban areas. The National Party still rules.

South Africa became an independent republic in 1960 with a new constitution. In 1983, white South Africans adopted another constitution, the country's third, that created a tricameral Parliament with segregated houses of Parliament for whites, Indians, and coloreds.

Notes

Introduction

1. Aggrey Klaaste, "The Lovely Kids We Turned Into Monsters," *Frontline,* September, 1985.
2. Mosiuoa Patrick Lekota, "From a Pretoria Jail, A Plea to Blacks," *The New York Times,* November 20, 1988, Week in Review section, p. 23.
3. The Matthew Goniwe Papers, Manuscripts and Archives, Yale University Library, New Haven, Connecticut.
4. *New Nation,* January 16, 1986, p. 6.

Fast-Forward

1. Johannes Rantete, *The Third Day of September; an eye-witness account of the Sebokeng Rebellion of 1984* (Johannesburg: Ravan Press, 1984).
2. Ibid.

1. The Day That Never Ended

1. This account is based on interviews with Brigadier Ebenaezer van Niekerk, Andries Treurnicht, Seth Mazibuko, Harry Mashabela, Lekgau Mathabathe, Mono Badela, Lawrence Ntloaka, Fezi Tshabalala, Mohlomola Ntoane, Tshidiso Mogale, Fani, Barney Pityana, Mcebisi Xundu, Frank Chikane, and Mpho Mashinini. Other materials include the late Percy Qoboza's 1976 interview of Tsietsi Mashinini and an American radio interview with Mashinini in 1977 (transcript provided by Thomas Karis of the Ralph Bunch Institute on the United Nations, City University of New York).
2. Interview with Mono Badela, January 1988.
3. The church groups included the Student Christian Movement, Youth Alive, Young Ambassadors, and Teenage Outreach, according to Mazibuko.

4. There are various published spellings of the boy's surname. Zolile Hector Pieterson is how it appears on his tombstone, along with the words: "Time is on the side of the oppressed today. Truth is on the side of the oppressed today. One Azania, One Nation, One People."
5. Harry Mashabela, *A People on the Boil* (Johannesburg: Skotaville Press, 1987), p. 28.
6. Interviews in June 1986 with Fezi Tshabalala, Seth Mazibuko, Brigadier Ebenaezer van Niekerk, Mohlomola Ntoane, Harry Mashabela, Lekgau Mathabathe, and the mother of Tsietsi Mashinini.
7. From *Native Life in South Africa* by Solomon T. Plaatje, 1916. Extract in Thomas Karis and Gwendolen M. Carter eds., *From Protest to Challenge; A Documentary History of African Politics in South Africa 1882–1964,* vol. 1 (Stanford: Hoover Institution Press, 1972), p. 136.
8. Can Themba, *The Will To Die* (Cape Town and Johannesburg: David Philip, 1982), pp. 46–47.
9. David Harrison, *The White Tribe of Africa* (Macmillan, Johannesburg: 1981), pp. 190–191.
10. *A Survey of Race Relations in South Africa 1976* (Johannesburg: South African Institute of Race Relations, 1977), p. 207.
11. Based on separate accounts, one by Chikane in an interview and one in a profile of Chikane by Wessel Ebersohn, "The Kingdom and the Power" in *Leadership South Africa* magazine, vol. 6, No. 5, p. 43.
12. Gail M. Gerhart, *Black Power in South Africa; The Evolution of an Ideology* (Berkeley: University of California Press, 1978), p. 286.
13. Percy Qoboza, Interview with Mashinini, *The World,* August 10, 1976.
14. Transcript of interview produced by Gil Noble on WABC-TV's "Like It Is" on January 9, 1977. From the files of Tom Karis, Ralph Bunche Institute, City University of New York.
15. Steve Biko, *I Write What I Like* (London: Heinemann), pp. 28–29.
16. Gerhart, p. 285.
17. Gerhart, pp. 274–277.
18. Page 13,131 of the testimony of Popo Simon Molefe, co-defendant in The State vs. Patrick Mabuya Baleka and 21 Others, known as the Delmas treason trial, after the white town where the trial began.

2. Take Up the Black Man's Burden

1. Interview with Thozamile Botha, February 8, 1989.
2. Carole Cooper and Linda Ensor, "PEBCO: A Black Mass Movement" (Johannesburg: Institute of Race Relations, 1981).
3. Ibid.
4. Ibid.
5. Interview with Badela, January 1988.
6. Interview with Xundu, April 18, 1988.
7. Interview with Morobe on the tenth anniversary of Soweto student uprising. "The Day That Never Ended," *Saspu National,* vol. 7, no. 3, June 1986, pp. 10–11.
8. Tom Lodge, forthcoming paper for the Ford Foundation's *Update* series.
9. Hannah Arendt, *On Revolution* (New York: Penguin Books, 1963), p. 62.
10. Indeed, the opulence of white society has probably deceived blacks into thinking

that the country is richer than it actually is. A post-liberation government might be hard pressed to fulfill black expectations.

11. Francis Wilson and Mamphela Ramphele, *Uprooting Poverty* (New York: Norton & Co., 1989), pp. 17–18. South Africa's Gini coefficient was 0.66.
12. Source: Mark Swilling, Centre for Policy Studies, University of Witwatersrand.
13. From a confidential report prepared for the Urban Foundation. Erica Emdon and Sue Albertyn, "The Viability of Non-racial Local Government in the Sandton/Alexandra/Marlboro Gardens Complex" by Erica Emdon and Sue Albertyn, unpublished, February 1987.
14. *Weekly Mail,* vol. 4, no. 8, March 4 (to March 10) 1988, pp. 1, 3.
15. Wilson and Ramphele, p. 108.
16. Robert Coles, "Blacks in South Africa Need Outside Medical Help," on the op-ed page of the *New York Times,* January 29, 1985, p. 27.
17. Stephen R. Lewis, Jr., "Economics and Apartheid: The Impact of South Africa's Economic Policies," unpublished manuscript.
18. From *Apartheid: South Africa's Answer to a Major Problem* (Pretoria: State Information Office, 1954). Quoted in *The Anti-Apartheid Reader* edited by David Mermelstein, (New York: Grove Press, 1987), pp. 94–98.
19. Peter Delius, "Abel Erasmus" in *Putting Plough to the Ground; Accumulation and Dispossession in Rural South Africa 1850–1930,* edited by William Beinart, Peter Delius, and Stanley Trapido. (Johannesburg: Ravan Press, 1986), p. 185.
20. Ibid.
21. Solomon T. Plaatje, *Native Life in South Africa* (Johannesburg: Ravan Press, 1982) [first published 1916], p. 21.
22. Ibid., pp. 44, 49, 87.
23. Merle Lipton, *Capitalism and Apartheid* (Aldershot, England: Gower Publishing Co. Ltd, 1985), pp. 23–24.
24. The South African Institute of Race Relations as quoted in the *Johannesburg Weekly Mail,* December 24, 1987, p. 4.
25. Miriam Horn, "Theater as a Weapon" *U.S. News & World Report,* July 4, 1988, p. 53.
26. Pages 13,110–13,130 of the testimony of Popo Simon Molefe, general secretary of the United Democratic Front, in the Delmas Treason Trial. Molefe was arrested in 1984, and in 1988 was sentenced to ten years in jail. He was released in 1989.

3. The Politics of Refusal

1. Transcript presented as evidence in State vs. Mawalal Ramgobin and 15 Others, known as the Pietermaritzburg treason trial, pp. 41–44. Karis-Gerhart Collection.
2. Phrase used by Tiego Moseneke, president of the Azanian Students Organization (Azaso). Quoted in pamphlet issued on day of UDF launch, Karis-Gerhart Collection.
3. *Uprooting Poverty,* Wilson and Ramphele, p. 259.
4. Heribert Adam, *Modernizing Racial Domination* (Berkeley: University of California Press, 1971).
5. Allan Boesak, *Black and Reformed: Apartheid, Liberation and the Calvinist Tradition* (Johannesburg: Skotaville Publishers, 1984), p. 128.

6. Former Robben Island prisoner and long-time political activist Neville Alexander had called for a broad front to oppose the new constitution and had formed the Disorderly Bills Action Committee and the National Forum. Boesak himself was a member of the National Forum, but the United Democratic Front quickly surpassed the National Forum in importance.
7. "Statement by the Commission of the Feasibility of a United Front Against the Constitution Reform Proposals", January 23, 1983; in papers collected by Thomas Karis, of Ralph Bunche Institute on the United Nations, City University of New York, and Gail M. Gerhart, Columbia University.
8. Testimony of Patrick "Terror" Lekota in The State versus Patrick Mabuya Baleka and 21 Others, pp. 15, 472.
9. Ibid.
10. Boesak, p. 16.
11. Ibid., p. 42.
12. The Delmas treason trial, examination of Popo Simon Molefe by Arthur Chaskalson, August 3, 1987, pp. 13,149–13,150.
13. "National Launch, Cape Town; UDF Unites-Apartheid divides!," pamphlet, August 20, 1983, Karis-Gerhart Collection.
14. The Delmas treason trial, examination of Molefe, pp. 13,146–7.
15. *Survey of Race Relations in South Africa 1983* (Johannesburg:South African Institute of Race Relations, 1984), p. 258.
16. Frank Chikane, "Analysis of the 1983 Black Local Authorities Elections," UDF Transvaal Press release, December 12, 1983.
17. Ibid.
18. *Race Relations Survey 1984* (Johannesburg: South African Institute of Race Relations, 1985), pp. 127–128.
19. Ibid.
20. Compiled by the UDF and submitted as exhibit D7 in the Pietermaritzburg treason trial. Quoted in unpublished paper by Mark Swilling, "The United Democratic Front and Township Revolt in South Africa," the University of Witwatersrand.
21 "UDF and the New South African Constitution," unsigned position paper, 1983. Karis-Gerhart Collection.
22. "UDF One-Year Rally: Selbourne Hall, Johannesburg, 19 August 1984," p. 5 of transcript presented by police as evidence in the Pietermaritzburg treason trial.
23. "The role of teachers under the present status quo: the role of progressive teachers," p. 13 of undated notes. The Matthew Goniwe Papers, Manuscripts and Archives, Yale University Library, New Haven, Connecticut.
24. C. P. de Kock, N. Rhoodie, and M. P. Couper, "Black Views on Socio-Political Change in South Africa," a compilation of HSRC surveys in *South Africa: A Plural Society in Transition,* ed. by D. J. Van Vuuren et al. (Durban: Butterworths, 1985).

4. The Forgotten Well

1. Thomas Karis and Gwendolen Carter, eds., *From Protest to Challenge,* vol. 2 (Stanford: Hoover Institution Press, 1973), pp. 426, 494.
2. Gail M. Gerhart, *Black Power in South Africa: The Evolution of an Ideology* (Berkeley: University of California Press, 1978), pp. 195–6.
3. Ibid., pp. 208–10.

4. Edward Roux, *Time Longer Than Rope* (Madison: University of Wisconsin Press, 1963), p. 405.
5. To Steve Tshwete, president of UDF in the Border Region, quoted in Molefe's testimony in the Delmas treason trial, pp. 13,537–13,538.

5. Violence

1. Matthew Chaskalson, Karen Jochelson, and Jeremy Seekings, "Rent Boycotts, the State, and the Transformation of the Urban Political Economy in South Africa" unpublished paper, University of the Witwatersrand, p. 4.
2. Interview with Arthur Chaskalson, lawyer for UDF leaders accused of fomenting unrest in the Vaal Triangle.
3. Albert Lutuli, *Let My People Go* (London: Fontana Books, 1962), p. 114.
4. These and much of the detail of the day of the shooting come from the "Report of the Commission Appointed to Inquire into the Incident Which Occurred on 21 March 1985 at Uitenhage," June 4, 1985 by South African Supreme Court Justice D. D. V. Kannemeyer, the sole member of the commission.
5. President Ronald Reagan immediately accepted Le Grange's version of events. Reagan said, "I think to put it that way, that they [the blacks] were simply killed and [that] the violence was coming totally from the law and order side, ignores the fact that there was a riot going on."
6. Remarks at March 19, 1986 meeting in the Catholic church mission on the edge of Uitenhage, according to the notes of John de St. Jorre, who attended the meeting.
7. Source: Mark Swilling, lecturer in politics at the University of the Witwatersrand.
8. Mandla Mashego, *Caught in the Web of Orderly Urbanisation; Forced Removals in Langa* (Yeoville, Johannesburg: Planact, no date).
9. Kannemeyer report.
10. Interview, January 1988.
11. Affidavit No. 14, from "Memorandum on Police Conduct in the Eastern Cape," issued by the Black Sash, Johannesburg, p. 18.
12. Affidavits filed by Blackburn and other witnesses.
13. As reported in U.S. Embassy cables to State Department, from South African Broadcasting Corp. commentary on the international service in English.
14. Radio Freedom, ANC broadcast in English from Lusaka, March 22, 1985, as reported by Foreign Broadcast Information Service cable to State Department.
15. Speech in Parliament in April 1986, quoted in *1985 Race Relations Survey* (Johannesburg: South African Institute of Race Relations, 1986), p. 533.
16. These details, like most of this account of that day, come from the testimony and evidence in the trial of five alleged members of the mob that killed Kinikini. State vs. Sydwell T. Mpumlo and others, South East Cape division of the Supreme Court of South Africa. Additional material from the unsuccessful appeal against the death sentence heard by the South African Appellate Division in Bloemfontein.
17. Albert Camus, *Caligula and 3 Other Plays* (New York: Vintage Books), pp. 258–260.
18. Lutuli, pp. 113, 115, 197.
19. Ibid., p. 115.
20. Thomas Karis and Gwendolen Carter, *From Protest to Challenge, vol. 3* (Stanford: Hoover Institution Press, 1972), pp. 716–717.

21. Frantz Fanon, *The Wretched of the Earth* (Middlesex, England and New York: Penguin Books Ltd., 1967), p. 74.
22. Transcript provided by confidential source in South Africa.
23. Mark Swilling, "The United Democratic Front and Township Revolt in South Africa," unpublished paper, the University of Witwatersrand.
24. Camus, p. 259.
25. Willem Ebersohn, "Ring of fire," *Leadership,* 1987.
26. Aggrey Klaaste, "The Lovely Kids We Turned Into Monsters," *Frontline,* Johannesburg, September 1985.
27. Jon Qwelane, "A crowd bent on butchery has no mercy for the innocent," *The Star,* July 30, 1985.
28. Ibid.
29. Nelson Mandela, *The Struggle is My Life* (London: International Defence and Aid Fund for Southern Africa, 1978), p. 161.
30. George Orwell, "Reflections on Gandhi," in *The Penguin Essays of George Orwell* (Harmondsworth: Penguin Books, 1984), p. 470.
31. *From South Africa—A Challenge to the Church!* (Closter, N. J.: Theology in Global Context Program, no date), pp. 11–13.

6. Dual Power

1. "Part One; Protest to Challenge; What does the NEC mean when it talks about the UDF moving from 'Protest to Challenge'?," unsigned, May 1985, Karis-Gerhart Collection.
2. Hannah Arendt, *On Revolution* (New York: Penguin Books, 1963), p. 257.
3. Lawrence G. Green, *Karoo* (Cape Town: Howard Timmins), p. 32 ff.
4. Roger Thurow, "The ANC is Banned But It Is in the Hearts of a Nation's Blacks," *The Wall Street Journal,* vol. 211, no. 79, April 22, 1988, p. 1.
5. "Resignations seen in perspective," undated notes, p. 2, Matthew Goniwe Papers, Manuscripts and Archives, Yale University, New Haven, Connecticut.
6. *Weekly Mail,* Johannesburg: January 22–28, 1988, pp. 1–2.
7. The phrase "ringleaders" was used by Law and Order Minister Louis le Grange.
8. *Race Relations Survey 1985* (Johannesburg: South African Institute of Race Relations, 1986), p. 389.
9. Georgina Jaffee, "Beyond the Cannon of Mamelodi," *Work in Progress,* no. 41, April 1986, pp. 4–10.
10. Ibid.
11. Thomas Karis and Gwendolen Carter, eds., *From Protest to Challenge vol. 3* (Stanford: Hoover Institution Press, 1972), pp. 35–40.
12. From evidence produced in the indictment of Moses Mayekiso and four others on charges of treason, subversion, and sedition.
13. Ibid.
14. Arendt, p. 251.
15. Interview November 1985.
16. Robert C. Tucker, *The Lenin Anthology,* (New York: W. W. Norton & Co, Inc., 1975), pp. 301–304.

7. Black Mamba Rising

1. South African Labor Bulletin report on the founding of the Congress of South African Trade Unions, January 1986.

2. Steven Friedman, *Building Tomorrow Today; African workers in trade unions 1970–1984,* (Johannesburg: Ravan Press, 1987), p. 37–38.
3. Friedman, pp. 13–14.
4. Ibid., p. 64.
5. Ibid., pp. 39–40.
6. The National Manpower Commission report as quoted in the *Weekly Mail,* vol. 4, No. 19, May 20–26, 1988, p. 17.
7. Mandlenkosi Makhoba, *The Sun Shall Rise for the Workers or Ilanga Lizophumela Abasebenzi,* Ravan Workers Series. (Johannesburg: Ravan Press, in association with the Federation of South African Trade Unions, 1984).
8. Yunus Carrim, "Working-Class Politics to the Fore," *Work in Progress,* no. 40, Johannesburg, pp. 4–13.
9. *Isizwe, the Nation,* vol. 1. no. 2, March 1986. (Cape Town: United Democratic Front), p. 24.
10. *Isizwe* vol. 1, no. 3, November 1986. (Johannesburg: United Democratic Front)
11. Interview with Philip van Niekerk in *Leadership* vol. 5, no. 1, 1986, pp. 81–82.
12. Reconstruction of the strike based on South African Labour Bulletin account, November 1987. Also, interviews with James Motlatsi, Marcel Golding, two dismissed officials in Lesotho, Bobby Godsell, and three other union organizers who prefer to remain unnamed. Also based on a visit by Motlatsi to a mine hostel in January 1988 and conversations with coal miners there.
13. Coletane Markham and Monyaola Mothibeli, "The 1987 Mineworkers Strike," *South African Labour Bulletin,* vol. 13, no. 1 (Johannesburg, 1987), p. 61.
14. Interview with James Motlatsi.

8. A Culture of Revolt

1. Lekota's testimony in the Delmas treason trial, p. 15, 449.
2. Steve Biko, "We Blacks" in *I Write What I Like,* (London: Heinemann, 1978), p. 29.
3. Landeg White and Tim Couzens, eds., *Literature and Society* (London: Longman Group Ltd., 1984), p. 186.
4. Ibid., p. 49.
5. The only written eyewitness description of Mzilikazi at this reading. The white missionaries weren't fully aware of what was happening.
6. White and Couzens, p. 12.
7. Ibid., p. 30.
8. Interview with Western Kunene, February 1987.
9. Mzwakhe Mbuli, "The Beat," on *Change Is Pain,* Shifty Records, 1986.
10. Michael Parks, "Poet of the Struggle," *Los Angeles Times,* December 1, 1987, Part 5, p. 1.
11. Mzwakhe.
12. "The Play Is the People!" unsigned article, *Grassroots,* April 1984, p. 8.
13. Interview with Fana Kekana, New York City, 1987.
14. Temple Hauptfleisch and Ian Steadman, eds., *South African Theatre* (Pretoria: HAUM Educational Publishers, 1984), p. 150.
15. From the unpublished script of Kente's musical comedy, "Lobola."
16. Based on notes of interview with Makhene by Miriam Horn, reporter for *U.S. News & World Report.*

17. Ibid.
18. Miriam Horn, "Theater as a Weapon," *US News & World Report,* July 4, 1988, p. 51.
19. Ibid., p. 52.
20. Steve Biko, *I Write What I Like* (London: Heinemann, 1978), p. 29.
21. Leonard Thompson, *The Political Mythology of Apartheid,* (New Haven: Yale University Press, 1985), pp. 65–66.
22. Thompson, pp. 64–65.
23. "Slavery—The Facts," *New Nation,* January 16, 1986, p. 11.
24. "Frances the Fighter," first of "a series on the labour leaders who put workers on the map," the *New Nation,* January 30, 1986, p. 13.
25. *What Is History? A New Approach to History for Students, Workers and Communities* (Johannesburg: NECC and Skotaville Press, 1987), p. 1.
26. James T. Campbell, Unpublished thesis on the African Methodist Episcopal church, Stanford University.
27. Quotes from Solomon T. Plaatje, *Native Life in South Africa* (Johannesburg: Ravan Press, 1982. First published in 1916), p. 45. The list of plays Plaatje translated from the introduction by Tim Couzens to *Mhudi,* by Sol T. Plaatje (London, Heinemann: 1978), p. 1.
28. Plaatje, *Mhudi,* p. 187.
29. Plaatje, *Native Life,* p. 137.
30. David Bunn and Jane Taylor, eds., *From South Africa; New Writing, Photographs & Art,* special issue of *TriQuarterly69* (Northwestern University, Evanston, Illinois, Spring/Summer 1987), pp. 276–277.
31. Federation of South African Trade Unions.
32. Recited during interview.
33. Ari Sitas on worker poets in *From South Africa,* p. 278.
34. Campbell.
35. Interview, July 1986, with Hein Kern, general manager of TV2, TV3, and TV4.
36. Miriam Horn, "Theater as a Weapon," *U. S. News & World Report,* July 4, 1988, p. 53.
37. In *The Wretched of the Earth,* Frantz Fanon observed among the French in Algeria a similar concern with the preservation of the indigenous traditions and a disdain for cultural innovation. Fanon compared the French colonial officials to white jazz specialists who disparaged new black jazz styles such as bebop after World War II. "In their eyes jazz should only be the despairing broken down nostalgia of an old negro who is trapped between five glasses of whisky, the curse of his race, and the racial hatred of the white men," Fanon wrote. The black who possessed self-confidence and understanding would play differently, Fanon added. "When he gives birth to hope and forces back the racist universe, it is clear that his trumpet sounds more clearly and his voice less hoarsely."

9. Black, Green, and Gold

1. Interview with Chris Hani by Herve Léonard and Anne Dumas of *Liberation.* 1987.
2. Dikgang Nene, "Richard 'Barney' Molokoane," in *Dawn,* the journal of Umkhonto we Sizwe, twenty-fifth anniversary issue, p. 54.
3. Document from trial.

4. Interview with Hani given by Dumas and Léonard.
5. These estimates vary. They are based on ANC interviews and statistics from the United Nations High Commission on Refugees.
6. "Report, Main Decisions and Recommendations of the Second National Consultative Conference of the African National Congress—Zambia, June 16–23, 1985," distributed by the South African government, December 12, 1986 in an effort to discredit the ANC, p. 10.
7. "Kaffir," Arabic for "non-believer," is the South African equivalent of "nigger."
8. Fatima Meer, *The Trial of Andrew Zondo* (Johannesburg: Skotaville 1897), p. 3.
9. Thanks to advocate Dennis Kuny for a copy of this diary.
10. Roger Thurow, "The ANC is Banned, But It Is in the Hearts of a Nation's Blacks," *The Wall Street Journal,* April 22, 1988, p. 1.
11. Based on "Notes of a meeting at Mfuwe Game Lodge, 13 September 1985," by one of the white South Africans present.
12. Raymond Suttner and Jeremy Cronin, eds., *30 Years of the Freedom Charter* (Johannesburg: Ravan, 1986), pp. 12–13.
13. Tom Lodge, "'Freedom in Our Lifetime': Popular Resistance Politics in the 1950s and the 1980s," in *Reality,* November 1986, p. 9.
14. David Beresford, "When Anger Speaks with Two Voices," *The London Guardian,* January 30, 1988.
15. Albie Sachs, "Towards a Bill of Rights in a Democratic South Africa," draft discussion paper, March 1, 1988, p. 3.
16. Ibid., p. 33.
17. Anthony Heard, "A Conversation with Oliver Tambo of the ANC," *Cape Times,* November 4, 1985, p. 9.

Interviews:

ANC in exile: Joe Slovo, Thabo Mbeki, Frene Ginwale, Steve Tshwete, Aziz Pahad, Tom Sebina, the late Johnstone Makatini, Pallo Jordan, Nat Masemola, Mac Maharaj, Wally Serote, Albie Sachs, Barney Pityana, and various anonymous sources.

Inside South Africa: Nthato Motlana, Dennis Kuny, George Bizos, Chris Waters, Brigadier Hermann Stadler, Colonel Jack Buchner, Jan du Plessis, Aggrey Klaaste, Godfrey Pitje, Cassim Saloojee, Helen Suzman, Frederik Van Zyl Slabbert, Albertina Sisulu, Winnie Mandela, Frank Chikane, Desmond Tutu, Mcebisi Xundu, Gavin Relly, Zach de Beer, Anthony Bloom, Chris Dlamini, James Motlatsi, Tshidiso Hlalele, Jakes Gerwel, and various sources who prefer to remain anonymous.

Also: Appollon Davidson, Tom Lodge, Tom Karis, Arthur Goldreich, Robert Matji, Aracelly Santana.

11. A Lot of Talk

1. Mark Swilling, "Local-Level Negotiations: Case Studies and Implications," Urban Foundation, August 1987, p. 44.
2. Ingrid Obery, "People's Education: Creating a Democratic Future," interview with Ihron Rensburg, *Work in Progress,* no. 42, May 1986, p. 8.
3. *Mission to South Africa; the Commonwealth Report,* the findings of the Commonwealth Eminent Persons Group on southern Africa (Harmondsworth: Penguin Books, 1986), p. 119.

4. Ibid., p. 120.
5. Ibid., p. 135.

12. Crackdown and Breakdown

1. These tensions are well described in a paper by Mandla Mashego, "Caught in the Web of Orderly Urbanisation; Forced Removals in Langa" (Yeoville, Johannesburg: Planact, 19).
2. Athol Fugard, *The Road to Mecca* (New York: Theatre Communications Group, 1985), p. 22.

13. WHAM!

1. Hermann Giliomee, "In gesprek met Genl. Magnus Malan," *Die Suid-Afrikaan,* Winter 1986, Stellenbosch, pp. 12–13.
2. Lynda Schuster, "Pretoria's Bid for 'Hearts and Minds'," *The Christian Science Monitor,* May 11, 1988.
3. For journalists it was the bloodiest battle of the uprising. A South African journalist, George D'Ath, working for foreign television, was killed by vigilantes, and two foreign journalists were wounded by gunfire.
4. Private letter, whose author prefers anonymity.
5. Schuster.
6. Ibid.
7. James T. Campbell, "T. D. Mweli Skota and the Making and Unmaking of a Black Elite," University of the Witwatersrand history workshop, 1987.
8. Craig Charney, "Janus in Blackface? The African Petite Bourgeoisie in South Africa," unpublished paper, Department of Political Science, Yale University, p. 29. Presented at the annual conference of the Association for Sociology in South Africa, Durban, July 1988.
9. Ibid., p. 4.
10. Ibid., pp. 6–7.
11. Mafuna may have been hinting at his own internal torment as he tried to straddle the worlds of blacks and whites. His wife later accused him of trying to kill her with scalding water.

14. The Black Face of Apartheid

1. Speech, March 1988, before the Sixth Session of the Fourth KwaZulu Legislative Assembly, p. 35.
2. Nicholas Haysom, *Mabangalala; The Rise of Right-wing Vigilantes in South Africa,* Occasional Paper no. 10, Centre for Applied Legal Studies, University of Witwatersrand, Johannesburg, pp. 63–64.
3. Because Lebowa was not yet "independent," Moutse residents could carry South African passports.
4. Haysom, p. 76.
5. Book of photos taken by Eli Weinberg and sold by the International Defence and Aid Fund.
6. *Financial Mail,* December 6, 1985, pp. 36–38. Unsigned editorial.
7. *City Press* June 1, 1986, p. 1.
8. Steve Biko, "Let's Talk About the Bantustans," in *I Write What I Like* (London: Heinemann, 1978), p. 85.

9. Ibid., pp. 85–86.
10. Haysom, pp. 83–84.
11. Ibid., p. 85.
12. Ibid., p. 86.
13. Eventually Mafole was convicted of the charges and sentenced to two years in jail. He appealed the decision.
14. Six-page letter from Archie Gumede to M. G. Buthelezi, p. 3.
15. Ibid., p. 4.
16. Philip Curtin, Steven Feierman, Leonard Thompson, and Jan Vansina, *African History* (Boston: Little Brown and Co., 1978), p. 315.
17. Ibid., p. 329.

15. A Half-Extinguished Fire

1. Photocopy of two-page pamphlet, "Issued by the African National Congress: Internal unit RSA," July 1988.
2. Mandla Tyala, "Whites Given Messasge in Black Poll Boycott," *Sunday Times* (Johannesburg), October 30, 1988.
3. Sipho Ngcobo, "Who Is Going to Administer Alexandra?" *Business Day,* November 9, 1988.

Bibliography

Books and Articles

Adam, Heribert. *Modernizing Racial Domination*. Berkeley, University of California Press, 1971.

African National Congress. "Report, Main Decisions and Recommendations of the Second National Consultative Conference of the African National Congress—Zambia, June 16–23, 1985." Reprinted by the South African government, December 12, 1986.

Arendt, Hannah. *On Revolution*. New York: Penguin Books, 1963.

Biko, Steve. *I Write What I Like*. London: Heinemann, 1978.

Boesak, Allan. *Black and Reformed: Apartheid, Liberation and the Calvinist Tradition*. Johannesburg: Skotaville Publishers, 1984.

Bunn, David, and Taylor, Jane. eds. *From South Africa: New Writing, Photographs and Art*. Evanston, Illinois: special issue of *TriQuarterly69*, Northwestern University (Spring/Summer 1987).

Buthelezi, Mangosuthu G. "Policy Speech before the Sixth Session of the Fourth KwaZulu Legislative Assembly." March 1988.

Campbell, James T. "T. D. Mweli Skota and the Making and Unmaking of a Black Elite." Paper published by the University of the Witwatersrand History Workshop 1987.

Camus, Albert. *Caligula and 3 Other Plays*. New York: Vintage Books, 1958.

Charney, Craig. "Janus in Blackface? The African Petite Bourgeoisie in South Africa." Unpublished paper, Department of Political Science, Yale University. Presented at the annual conference of the Association for Sociology in South Africa, Durban, July 1988.

Chaskalson, Matthew; Jochelson, Karen; and Seekings, Jeremy. "Rent Boycotts, the

State, and the Transformation of the Urban Political Economy in South Africa." Unpublished paper, the University of Witwatersrand.

Chikane, Frank. "Analysis of the 1983 Black Local Authorities Elections." UDF Transvaal press release. December 12, 1983.

Cooper, Carole, and Linda Ensor. *Pebco: A Black Mass Movement.* Johannesburg: South African Institute of Race Relations, 1981.

Curtin, Philip, Steven Feierman, Leonard Thompson, and Jan Vansina. *African History.* Boston: Little, Brown and Co., 1978.

Delius, Peter. "Abel Erasmus." In *Putting Plough to the Ground: Accumulation and Dispossession in Rural South Africa 1850–1930.* Edited by William Beinart, Peter Delius, and Stanley Trapido. Johannesburg: Ravan Press, 1986.

Emdon, Erica, and Sue Albertyn. "The Viability of Non-racial Local Government in the Sandton/Alexandra/Marlboro Gardens Complex." Confidential report for the Urban Foundation. Unpublished, February 1987.

Fanon, Frantz. *The Wretched of the Earth.* Middlesex, England and New York: Penguin Books, 1967.

Friedman, Steven. *Building Tomorrow Today: African Workers in Trade Unions 1970–1984.* Johannesburg: Ravan Press, 1987.

Fugard, Athol. *The Road to Mecca.* New York: Theatre Communications Group, 1985.

Gerhart, Gail M. *Black Power in South Africa: The Evolution of an Ideology.* University of California Press, Berkeley, 1978.

Goniwe, Matthew. The Matthew Goniwe Papers, Manuscripts and Archives, Yale University Library, New Haven, Connecticut.

Hauptfleisch, Temple, and Ian Steadman, eds. *South African Theatre.* Pretoria: HAUM Educational Publishers, 1984.

Haysom, Nicholas. *Mabangalala: The Rise of Right-Wing Vigilantes in South Africa.* Johannesburg: Occasional Paper No. 10, Centre for Applied Legal Studies, University of the Witwatersrand.

Horn, Miriam. "Theater as a Weapon." *U.S. News and World Report,* July 4, 1988.

Jaffee, Georgina. "Beyond the Cannon of Mamelodi." *Work in Progress,* no. 41, April 1986.

Kannemeyer, D. D. V. *Report of the Commission Appointed to Inquire into the Incident Which Occurred on 21 March 1985 at Uitenhage.* Completed June 4, 1985.

Karis, Thomas, and Gwendolen M. Carter, eds. *From Protest to Challenge: A Documentary History of African Politics in South Africa 1882–1964.* 4 vols. Stanford: The Hoover Institution of Stanford University, 1972.

Karis-Gerhart Collection. Documents of African Politics in South Africa. New York: Ralph Bunche Institute on the United Nations, City University of New York, and Columbia University.

Lekota, Mosiuoa Patrick. "From a Pretoria Jail, A Plea to Blacks." *New York Times,* November 20, 1988, Week in Review section, p. 23.

Lewis, Stephen R. *The Economics of Apartheid.* New York: Council on Foreign Relations Press, 1990.

Lodge, Tom. *Black Politics in South Africa since 1945.* Johannesburg: Ravan Press, 1983.

———. Unpublished paper for the Ford Foundation *Update* series.

———. "'Freedom in Our Lifetime': Popular Resistance Politics in the 1950s and the 1980s." *Reality,* November 1986.

Lutuli, Albert. *Let My People Go.* London: Fontana Books, 1962.

Makhoba, Mandlenkosi. *The Sun Shall Rise for the Workers; or, Ilanga Lizophumela Abasebenzi.* Johannesburg: Ravan Worker Series, published by Ravan Press Ltd. in association with the Federation of South African Trade Unions, 1984.

Mandela, Nelson. *The Struggle Is My Life.* London: International Defence and Aid Fund for Southern Africa, 1978.

Markham, Coletane, and Monyaola Mothibeli. "The 1987 Mineworkers Strike." In the *South African Labour Bulletin* (Johannesburg), 13. no. 1, November 1987.

Mashabela, Harry. *A People on the Boil.* Johannesburg: Skotaville Press, 1987.

Mashego, Mandla. "Caught in the Web of Orderly Urbanisation; Forced Removals in Langa." Yeoville, Johannesburg: Planact. No date.

Meer, Fatima. *The Trial of Andrew Zondo.* Johannesburg: Skotaville, 1987

Mermelstein, David ed. *The Anti-Apartheid Reader.* New York: Grove Press, 1987

National Education Crisis Committee. *What Is History? A New Approach to History for Students, Workers and Communities.* Johannesburg: NECC and Skotaville Press, 1987.

Orwell, George. *The Penguin Essays of George Orwell.* Harmondsworth, England: Penguin, 1984.

Plaatje, Sol T. *Mhudi.* London: Heinemann, 1978

———. *Native Life in South Africa.* Johannesburg: Ravan Press, 1982. Originally published in 1916.

Rantete, Johannes. *The Third Day of September: An Eye-Witness Account of the Sebokeng Rebellion of 1984.* Johannesburg: Ravan Press, 1984.

Roux, Edward. *Time Longer Than Rope.* Madison: University of Wisconsin Press, 1963.

South African Institute of Race Relations. *A Survey of Race Relations in South Africa.* 1976, 1983–85. Johannesburg: SAIRR, 1977.

Suttner, Raymond, and Jeremy Cronin, eds. *Thirty Years of the Freedom Charter.* Johannesburg: Ravan, 1986.

Swilling, Mark. "The United Democratic Front and Township Revolt in South Africa." Unpublished paper at the University of the Witwatersrand.

Themba, Can. *The Will to Die.* Cape Town and Johannesburg: An Africasouth Paperback published by David Philip, 1982.

Thompson, Leonard. *The Political Mythology of Apartheid.* New Haven: Yale University Press, 1985

Tucker, Robert C., ed. *The Lenin Anthology.* New York: W. W. Norton & Co., 1975.

Walzer, Michael. *Just and Unjust Wars.* New York: Basic Books, 1977.

White, Landeg, and Tim Couzens, eds. *Literature and Society.* London. Longman Group Ltd., 1984.

Wilson, Francis and Mamphela Ramphele. *Uprooting Poverty.* New York: W.W. Norton & Co., 1989.

Court Documents

The State vs. Patrick Mabuya Baleka and Twenty-one Others. Commonly known as the Delmas treason trial.

The State vs. Moses Jongisizwe Mayekiso et. al.
The State vs. Ashwell Mxolisa Zwane and Seven Others.
The State vs. Sydwell T. Mpumlo and Others. Case number CC582/85, heard before Justice T. M. Mullins in the South East Cape local division of the Supreme Court of South Africa.

Newspapers and Magazines

Business Day
The Cape Times
The Christian Science Monitor
City Press
Dawn
Die Suid-Afrikaan
The Financial Mail
Frontline
Grassroots
The Guardian (London)
Isizwe
Leadership
The Los Angeles Times
The New Nation
The New York Times
Saspu National
South African Labour Bulletin
The Star
The Sunday Times
The Wall Street Journal
The Weekly Mail
Work In Progress

Index